Transdisciplinary Perspectives in Educational Research

Volume 2

Series Editor

Dennis Beach, Education, Högskolan i Borås, Borås, Sweden

This book series presents and discusses topical themes of European and international educational research in the 21st century. It provides educational researchers, policy makers and practitioners with up-to-date theories, evidence and insights in European educational research. It captures research findings from different educational contexts and systems and concentrates on the key contemporary interests in educational research, such as 21st century learning, new learning environments, global citizenship and well-being. It approaches these issues from various angles, including empirical, philosophical, political, critical and theoretical perspectives. The series brings together authors from across a range of geographical, socio-political and cultural contexts, and from different academic levels.

The book series works closely with the networks of the European Educational Research Association. It builds on work and insights that are forged there but also goes well beyond the EERA scope to embrace a wider range of topics and themes in an international perspective.

More information about this series at https://link.springer.com/bookseries/16480

Jenna Gillett-Swan • Nina Thelander
Editors

Children's Rights from International Educational Perspectives

Wicked Problems for Children's Education Rights

Springer

Editors
Jenna Gillett-Swan
Faculty of Creative Industries, Education, and Social Justice
Queensland University of Technology
Brisbane, Australia

Nina Thelander
Faculty of Humanities and Social Sciences
Karlstad University
Karlstad, Sweden

ISSN 2662-6691 ISSN 2662-6705 (electronic)
Transdisciplinary Perspectives in Educational Research
ISBN 978-3-030-80860-0 ISBN 978-3-030-80861-7 (eBook)
https://doi.org/10.1007/978-3-030-80861-7

This Springer imprint is published by the registered company Springer Nature Switzerland AG
The registered company address is: Gewerbestrasse 11, 6330 Cham, Switzerland

Preface

The United Nations Convention on the Rights of the Child[1] (UNCRC) is the most widely ratified human rights treaty in the world. In ratifying an international human rights treaty, the State agrees to be bound by its terms, including incorporating the provisions therein into national law. As such, each member State may incorporate the Convention differently based on their national context. The UNCRC consists of 54 articles (rights), which outline the obligations of States parties and their representatives in respecting, protecting, and fulfilling children's rights. This includes rights relating to education. Education rights are broadly considered in terms of Article 28 (right to education) and Article 29 (aims of education) but are also recognised as extending beyond this and intertwined with other articles.

Discussions about the complexities and nuances of children's rights and education within and across different national contexts feature in the annual Network activities of the 'Research on Children's Rights in Education' European Educational Research Association (EERA) Network 25. During these discussions, it was recognised that Article 28 seemed to dominate broader discussions about educational rights within the field. There seemed to be much less attention towards Article 29 – the 'aims of education' and what education should be all about from a rights perspective. It is here that the necessity for this book arose. The discussion continued to evolve during the annual ECER conference over a number of years until the opportunity arose to contribute to EERA's new book series. The decision was made to focus on a topic that many within the Network had been grappling with for a long period of time.

The need to broaden the research focus within the field to include more than *just* the right to education was also picked up by others outside the Network at around the same time. While initially there was not much being said about children's rights *in* and *through* education relative to rights *to* education, there was now increasing attention directed towards this less visible (but equally important) educational rights

[1] The full text for the Convention is available via the United Nations Human Rights Office of the High Commissioner – Convention on the Rights of the Child site https://www.ohchr.org/en/professionalinterest/pages/crc.aspx

focus for children. The resulting discussions within and outside the Network teased out some of the complexities associated with increasingly narrow and reductionist conceptualisations of children's education rights. The increased interest also presented greater opportunities to further interrogate and broaden the ways in which specific articles, rights principles, and the Convention itself are conceptualised, discussed, and understood in educational rights research across different national contexts.

The contributions in the book take an *education* (rather law/legal) perspective on children's education rights. Education perspectives are used to illustrate different ways that Article 29 is or could be afforded, while also problematising multiple tensions that remain. In doing so, the book offers a snapshot of some of the important practical, conceptual, and theoretical issues relating to enacting children's rights to education and the aims *of* education in different national and international contexts. Through investigating factors contributing to (or hindering) the realisation of children's rights in and through education in different contexts, each chapter highlights varying interpretations of the same educational mandate in practice from an educational research perspective.

While Article 29 is the central focus of the edited collection, many chapters also tie their descriptions of education-related rights to other rights such as those relating to participation, inclusion, expression, and non-discrimination. Unless otherwise stated or redefined by authors within their chapters, when using practical examples, the book focuses on education rights in formal schooling contexts, such as in early childhood, primary, and secondary school. However, it is also recognised that education rights can, and do, also extend beyond these contexts.

The diverse international perspectives represented in this volume provide European and global relevance to realising the importance of *how* the wide-ranging contexts for children's rights in and through educational practice exemplify the variability in implementation. The chapters therefore provide scope for those interested in educational enhancement to further consider *how* and *why* focused enactment of the 'aims of education' may serve to ensure educational prerogatives are better suited to children's rights and their holistic development, or *whether* something more is needed.

Given the Network is part of the European Educational Research Association, the volume predominantly includes chapters from EERA member countries in Network 25, including those from England, Finland, Northern Ireland, Poland, Portugal, Scotland, Spain, Sweden, and Switzerland. These perspectives are complemented by those from other international contexts including the USA, Mexico, and Australia. The diversity in our small research network is not only shown through the range of different national perspectives represented, but also through the breadth of chapters from new, emerging, and established scholars in the field. It is our aim that the volume can be used as a starting point for further research, discussion, and provocation, recognising that each chapter can only provide a snapshot of an aspect of Article 29's enactment, towards furthering knowledge in a field that is still in its infancy, despite the Convention being around for more than 30 years. While consideration of rights for children should be at the core of critical discussions about education and its purpose, quite often, rights are rarely thought of beyond an add on to existing practice, if they are considered at all. It may be now that a timely reminder of General Comment[2] 1 on Article 29 (United Nations 2001, §8) is required in reiterating that 'children do not lose their human rights by virtue of passing through the school gates'. Instead, for this volume, it is where the discussion begins.

Brisbane, Australia Jenna Gillett-Swan

Karlstad, Sweden Nina Thelander

[2] General Comments developed and released by the Committee on the Rights of the Child aim to clarify and elaborate on provisions outlined in the respective human rights treaty. The first General Comment released by the Committee on the Rights of the Child was on Article 29 (1) the 'Aims of Education', which is the central focus of this edited collection of work.

Contents

About the Contributors

Fátima Antunes is an Associate Professor in the Department of Social Sciences of Education and a researcher at the Research Centre on Education (CIEd) of the Institute of Education/University of Minho (PT), Portugal. She coordinated project Educating Places: practices, voices and pathways of inclusive education (2016–2019) (PTDC/MHC-CED/3775/2014) and the Research Group on Education Policy, Governance and Administration (2012–2018).

Anna Babicka-Wirkus is an Associate Professor in the Institute of Security and Management at Pomeranian University in Slupsk, Poland. Her main research interests are children's rights, resistance in education and school culture. Recent work includes: *Children's Rights and Human Rights as a Key Condition for the Education of Transformative Teachers* (ed., Verlag Barbara Budrich, 2019).

Elisabetta Biffi is an Associate Professor at the Riccardo Massa Department of Human Sciences and Education, University of Milano-Bicocca (Italy), where she teaches Pedagogical Consultancy as part of the Master's Degree Course in Education. She participates in Italian and European research projects on the topics of: childhood protection and children's rights; educator and teacher professional development; pedagogical documentation; narrative methods; and arts-based methods for educational research.

Lotta Brantefors is a researcher and a former Senior Lecturer in Curriculum Studies (Didaktik) in Uppsala University, Sweden. Her research interests include Didaktik, curriculum theory, pragmatism, and diversity with a special interest in the role of education to support children's growth as holders of rights in on-going practice.

Noelia Ceballos a Lecturer in Early Childhood Education (ECE) at the University of Cantabria, Spain. Her research interests are concerned with the study of children's rights; inclusion/exclusion processes and the pedagogy of democratic participation in ECE. She makes use of qualitative research approaches and participatory research.

Alison Cook-Sather is the Mary Katharine Woodworth Professor of Education at Bryn Mawr College and Director of the Teaching and Learning Institute at Bryn Mawr and Haverford Colleges. She has developed internationally recognised student-teacher pedagogical partnership programs, written over 100 invited and peer-reviewed articles and book chapters, and published eight books.

Heather Curl is Core Faculty at Antioch University, teaching in the following programs: Master of Teaching, Master of Education, Environmental Education, and Doctorate of Educational Leadership. Her primary research interests include social mobility, cultural capital, theories of change and reform and student and teacher voice.

Kate de Bruin is a Senior Lecturer in Inclusive Education at Monash University, Australia. Her research examines inclusive education in policy, systems and schools, focusing on evidence-based practices that ensure equitable schooling for all. Her current projects explore instruction and intervention within Tiers 1 and 2 of multi-tiered systems of support.

Dorota Duda is a doctoral candidate at University of Lower Silesia, Poland, and a primary school teacher. She holds MA in Early Childhood Education and Care. Her research interests include children's rights, early childhood education, children's participation, and social classes.

Katarzyna Gawlicz is an Assistant Professor at the Department of Education at University of Lower Silesia, Poland, where she teaches courses in early childhood education and care. Her research interests include democratic and alternative education, children's rights in education and teacher training, with a focus on transforming teaching practices through action research.

Jenna Gillett-Swan is an Associate Professor in Education at the Queensland University of Technology. She co-leads the 'Voice and Wellbeing' research program within the Centre for Inclusive Education (C4IE) and is current co-convenor of EERA's *Research on Children's Rights in Education* Network (25). Her research seeks to understand and address threats to wellbeing in students' educational experiences through participatory rights-based approaches to educational transformation and school improvement.

Julia Häbig is a Senior Researcher at the Centre for School Improvement of the Zurich University of Teacher Education, Switzerland and holds a PhD in education. Her research interests are student participation and school improvement with the focus on how the students' perspective can be integrated in research and school improvement processes.

Amy Hanna is a high school teacher in Queensland, Australia. She completed her PhD at the Centre for Children's Rights at Queen's University Belfast. Amy's study explored uses and experiences silence as a feature of the right to be heard in school, and how this right is implemented in practice.

Jess Harris is an Associate Professor in the School of Education, the University of Newcastle, Australia. Her research interests include leadership, reform, and issues of equity in schools and higher education. She has a specific interest in qualitative research methods, particularly case study research and conversation analysis.

Pascale Herzig is a Senior Lecturer at the Zurich University of Teacher Education, Switzerland. She holds a PhD in geography. Her main areas of interest include diversity, social in- and exclusion, and migration studies as well as ethnographic research in school contexts.

John I'Anson is currently the Deputy Director of the Centre for Child Wellbeing and Protection at the University of Stirling, Scotland. His writings focus on educational theory, religious and cultural difference, children's rights, and equity. He is currently Principal Investigator for a Scottish Government funded educational project, 'Making a Positive Difference', which investigates teachers' understandings of equity.

Felicia Jaremus is a doctoral researcher in the Teachers and Teaching Research Centre at the University of Newcastle, Australia. She has worked on multiple projects focused on equity, student aspirations and teacher professional development. She has a particular interest in equity in mathematics education and mixed methods research.

Tomi Kiilakoski is a leading Senior Researcher in the Finnish Youth Research Network. His areas of expertise include children's rights, participation, youth work and cultural philosophy. He engages actively in promoting participation and developing youth work and educational policy on the local and state level in Finland.

Joana Lúcio is a Fellow in Science and Technology Management at the Research Centre on Education (CIEd) of the Institute of Education/University of Minho (PT), Portugal. In 2016–2019, she was a Research Fellow in the project Educating Places: Practices, voices and pathways of inclusive education (PTDC/MHC-CED/3775/2014). She holds a PhD in Educational Sciences from the University of Porto (PT) and finished a post-doc in Sociology of Education at the University of Minho.

Gabriela Martinez Sainz is an Ad Astra Fellow and Assistant Professor at the School of Education at University College Dublin, Ireland, researching and teaching on children's rights, global citizenship, and education for sustainable development. She is co-convener of the UCD Rights Education Network (REN) and of the #ChildRightsChat project.

Chiara Carla Montà is a PhD student in 'Education in the Contemporary Society' at the Riccardo Massa Department of Human Sciences for Education of the University of Milano-Bicocca, Italy. Her research interests concern children's rights and education.

Zoe Moody is a Professor at the University of Teacher Education Valais and Senior Research Associate at the Centre for Children's Rights Studies, University of Geneva, Switzerland. Her interdisciplinary research and teaching activities cover children's rights and interculturality in education, socio-cultural diversity and living together in schools, discriminations, and school bullying.

Daniela Müller-Kuhn is a Research Assistant at the Centre for School Improvement of the Zurich University of Teacher Education, Switzerland. Her research focuses on student participation, examining its different forms and concepts.

Reetta Niemi is a Lecturer at Viikki Teacher Training School, Faculty of Education, University of Helsinki, Finland and a Research Associate at the University of Johannesburg, South Africa. She has focused on developing participatory pedagogy and on understanding how children's meaningful experiences can help teachers to develop their practical theories and pedagogical actions in classrooms.

Grace O'Brien is a Lecturer in Education at the Queensland University of Technology, Australia. She has worked in partnership with First Nations communities throughout Queensland, Australia, for many years. Her research addresses the need for urgent educational reform to prevent the exclusion of young First Nations males from school in order to disrupt the school to prison pipeline.

Ángela Saiz-Linares has a PhD in Education. She is currently working as a teacher in the Department of Education at the University of Cantabria. She has participated in several funded research projects. Her research interests include participatory research and student voice, initial teacher training, practicum, reflective practice, and socio-educational inclusion/exclusion.

Nerida Spina is a Senior Lecturer in Education at the Queensland University of Technology, Australia. Her research interests include the datafication of education and literacy. She is particularly interested in teachers', principals' and pre-service teachers' work. She also researches social justice and equity using the sociological method of inquiry, Institutional Ethnography.

Marcin Starnawski is an Assistant Professor at the Department of Education at University of Lower Silesia, Poland, where he teaches courses in sociology and comparative education. His research interests include studies in prejudice and discrimination, cultural identity, political socialization, and applications of world-systems analysis in educational research.

Teresa Susinos is Professor of Education at the University of Cantabria, Spain. Her research interests are concerned with the study of inclusion/exclusion in schools and society and with the pedagogy of democratic participation and the common good. She makes use of qualitative research approaches, such as ethnographic, narrative, and participatory.

Nina Thelander is a Senior Lecturer, Vice Dean and Researcher in Educational Work at Karlstad University, Sweden. Her main research interest concerns children's rights in educational contexts. Her other research foci are on teaching and learning human rights, democracy, and teacher education.

Satine Winter is a Lecturer in Inclusive Education at James Cook University and an Adjunct Research Fellow with the Griffith Institute for Educational Research, Griffith University, Australia. She actively researches in the field of autism, disability and inclusive education and is passionate about translating research into practice.

Michael Wyness is a Reader in the Department of Education at the University of Warwick, England. He is a sociologist with broad interests in childhood studies, including participation, schooling, migration, and human rights. He is currently writing a book for Anthem Press entitled *Kid Power: inequalities and intergenerational relations.*

Enikö Zala-Mezö is a Professor at the Zurich University of Teacher Education and Head of the Centre of School Improvement in Switzerland. She is interested in different forms of research practice partnerships and especially in the role of student participation in school improvement processes.

Chapter 1
Setting the Scene for Children's Rights and Education: Understanding the Aims of Education

Jenna Gillett-Swan, Nina Thelander, and Amy Hanna

Children do not lose their human rights by virtue of passing through the school gates.

United Nations (2001, §8).

Abstract Since it came into force, the Convention on the Rights of the Child has initiated much discussion in various academic fields interested in different aspects of the lives of children and young people. Consisting of 54 articles, the Convention on the Rights of the Child integrates ideas from several historical previous child rights movements and clarifies what human rights involve for children as a distinct group. This chapter provides the background to understanding the aims of education articulated in Article 29 of the UNCRC from an educational and research perspective.

Keywords Child rights · Aims of education · Education rights · Article 29 · Rights education

J. Gillett-Swan (✉)
Faculty of Creative Industries, Education, and Social Justice, Queensland University of Technology, Brisbane, Australia
e-mail: jenna.gillettswan@qut.edu.au

N. Thelander
Faculty of Humanities and Social Sciences, Karlstad University, Karlstad, Sweden
e-mail: nina.thelander@kau.se

A. Hanna
School of Social Sciences, Education and Social Work, Queen's University Belfast, Belfast, Northern Ireland
e-mail: ahanna499@qub.ac.uk

J. Gillett-Swan, N. Thelander (eds.), *Children's Rights from International Educational Perspectives*, Transdisciplinary Perspectives in Educational Research 2, https://doi.org/10.1007/978-3-030-80861-7_1

Introduction

Since it came into force, the Convention on the Rights of the Child (United Nations, 1989) has initiated much discussion in various academic fields interested in different aspects of the lives of children and young people. Consisting of 54 articles, the Convention on the Rights of the Child integrates ideas from several historical previous child rights movements (Reynaert et al., 2009) and clarifies what human rights involve for children as a distinct group. Since its inception, the text of the Convention itself has changed only once, with a change in the number of Committee members. However, while the text of the Convention may be static, its enactment is a dynamic process lived through the different national and international interpretations and translations of the Conventions' provisions (I'Anson et al., 2017; Robinson et al., 2020). Over the past 30 years, emphasis on contemporising the Committee's text has been through General Comments. The first of these General Comments was on the 'aims of education' (United Nations, 2001), which relates directly to Article 29 in the Convention.

Education Rights

Education is not only a right in itself, but also an important means for realising other rights (Lundy et al., 2016; Tomasevski, 2003). Consequently, discussions about international human rights relating to education are more effectively understood as education rights. Although not exclusive to children, education is a long-established element of international human rights law which is enjoyed mainly by children and young people (Lundy et al., 2016). Each international human rights treaty attempts to define the aims of education in some way. Prior to their provision in Article 29 of the United National Convention on the Rights of the Child, education rights featured in the Universal Declaration of Human Rights of 1948 (UDHR), which was later elaborated in the 1966 International Covenant of Economic, Social and Cultural Rights (ICESCR). Article 26(2) of the UDHR specifies that:

> Education shall be directed to the full development of the human personality and to the strengthening of respect for human rights and fundamental freedoms. It shall promote understanding, tolerance and friendship among all nations, racial or religious groups, and shall further the activities of the United Nations for the maintenance of peace.

Of course, the UDHR reflects the socioeconomic and international context of the post-World War Two period, with a view to preserving peace and tolerance among nations. Article 13(1) of the ICESCR included, in almost identical terms, the aims of education laid out in the UDHR, but with the development of *the human personality and the sense of its dignity* and an explicit reference to the role of education in enabling *all persons to participate effectively in a free society*. The role of education in broader society and democracy is thus explicitly recognised. However, these efforts to define the aims of education are not isolated to international human rights law. Perhaps most notably, Dewey's (1916) *Democracy and Education* examines aims in education as part of Dewey's educational philosophy, a concept not divorced from the question of what quality of education States parties are required to provide for their citizens. Dewey's theories and ideas have been further developed by other educational theorists. For example, Biesta (2015) emphasises that, in education, the question of the aims of education are to be found *in* education, which is where the action of education is taking place. The aims of education are therefore also multi-dimensional. Questions related to the aims of education are (and have been) of interest within education often without a specific rights lens. For children in particular, even before the United Nations Convention on the Rights of the Child (the Convention), education has been a widely endorsed right and consequently features in the 1924 Geneva Declaration of the Rights of the Child and the 1959 UN Declaration of the Rights of the Child. Article 7 of the latter states that:

> He [sic] shall be given an education, which will promote his general culture and enable him, on a basis of equal opportunity, to develop his abilities, his individual judgement, and his sense of moral and social responsibility, and to become a useful member of society.

It is against this backdrop that Article 29(1) of the CRC provides the most comprehensive statement of the aims of education. While Article 29 largely mirrors the ICESCR, it also features additional references to respect for cultural identity, language and values, and the natural environment:

1. States Parties agree that the education of the child shall be directed to:
   (a) The development of the child's personality, talents and mental and physical abilities to their fullest potential;
   (b) The development of respect for human rights and fundamental freedoms, and for the principles enshrined in the Charter of the United Nations;
   (c) The development of respect for the child's parents, his or her own cultural identity, language and values, for the national values of the country in which the child is living, the country from which he or she may originate, and for civilizations different from his or her own;
   (d) The preparation of the child for responsible life in a free society, in the spirit of understanding, peace, tolerance, equality of sexes, and friendship among all peoples, ethnic, national and religious groups and persons of indigenous origin;
   (e) The development of respect for the natural environment.
2. No part of the present article or article 28 shall be construed so as to interfere with the liberty of individuals and bodies to establish and direct educational institutions, subject always to the observance of the principle set forth in paragraph 1 of the present article and to the requirements that the education given in such institutions shall conform to such minimum standards as may be laid down by the State. (United Nations, 1989, Article 29).

Article 29 is undoubtedly visionary, not only in terms of describing the right to education as set out in Article 28, but also in terms of incorporating a package of education rights that are applicable to children throughout their schooling. Often overlooked and underestimated, Article 29 *strengthens* all other rights within the Convention by setting out the object and standard of education, its inherent value, and its instrumentalist function (Lundy & Brown, 2020) in a manner that is not only ambitious, but perhaps also idealistic (Lundy & Martinez-Sainz, 2018). Moreover, the general statements in Article 29 are also variably interpreted as they are translated within different contexts and built into educational policies based on national imperatives in focus at the time (Brantefors & Quennerstedt, 2016). It is perhaps its function as a medium for all other rights (Lundy et al., 2016) that may help to understand why Article 29 has acquired little substantive focus in the children's education rights literature; its oversight has been because the children's rights gaze has landed on its *means* of implementation: participation, anti-discrimination, and best interests.

The UN Committee on the Rights of the Child (the Committee) has been explicit in addressing this underestimation of Article 29, however, stating that the wide-ranging and general terms of the article have "led many States parties to assume that it is unnecessary, or even inappropriate, to ensure that the relevant principles are reflected in legislation or in administrative directives" (United Nations, 2001, §17). It directs, instead, that Article 29 is to be implemented with and through all other articles because:

> [I]t emphasizes the indispensable interconnected nature of the Convention's provisions. It draws upon, reinforces, integrates and complements a variety of other provisions and cannot be properly understood in isolation from them. (United Nations, 2001, §6)

It is perhaps this inalienable and interconnected nature of the Convention that captures the reasons for its oversight in the literature; such an ambitious and onerous provision can only be implemented throughout and in tandem with the other provisions of the Convention. These provisions are probably those that take account of the many and varied relationships that broadly define education, particularly those that take place in contemporary school environments. Relationships with children from all cultures and socioeconomic backgrounds and the State are conjoined through formal education and through individual teachers who are state actors; indeed, school is for many children their first engagement with the State. As education is the gateway to all other rights, it requires the implementation of Article 29 through multiple *relational* lenses: discrimination towards disability and culture; participation and student voice; and the best interests of children. The need to educate children and young people as rights holders emphasises knowledge and practice of rights *in* education *through* education as crucial (Quennerstedt et al., 2019). It must be recognised that children have a right to know about their rights and doing so, supports the dual aims of both Articles 29 and 42 (*making the Convention known*) (Todres, 2020).

Despite this gap in education rights research, several typologies of education rights have emerged over the years, the most well-known of which include Tomasevski's (2001) '*4-A*' scheme of availability, accessibility, acceptability and adaptability, Verhellen's (1993) tripartite model of rights *to*, *in*, and *through* education. Rights *through* education in Verhellen's model have been linked with Article

29 and the general aims of education (Lundy, 2006), reflecting the Committee's statements that "'education' goes beyond formal schooling to include all life experiences and learning processes which enable children to develop and participate in society" (United Nations, 2001, §2). The Committee explicitly states that education is not limited to teaching and learning, but also includes "efforts to promote the enjoyment of other rights", which "must not be undermined and should be reinforced, by the values imparted in the educational process" (United Nations, 2001, §8). This includes not only curriculum content, but, importantly, "the educational processes, the pedagogical methods and the environment within which education takes place, whether it be the home, school, or elsewhere" (United Nations, 2001, §8). Jerome (2016) argues that the Committee takes an overtly ideological position by later criticising education which prioritises competition and adopts a narrow understanding of knowledge acquisition (United Nations, 2001, §12).

Rights Articles as a Research Focus

Whilst literature on education rights abounds with discussion from the perspective of student voice and children's participation rights (e.g., through Article 12), research on Article 29 to date largely omits educational relationships that are of considerable significance when considering a child's education. These include peer relationships between children and young people, as well as their individual and collective relationships with adults and the broader community (Lundy & Brown, 2020). While Sargeant (2018) contends that participation rights in education are *implicit* in the 'aims of education' stipulated in Article 29. By actioning these aims through voice-inclusive practice, Article 29 is more likely to succeed. Even so, there is still a distinct absence of empirical research expressly dedicated to the 'aims of education' specifically. This absence is reflected in a dearth of empirical guidance to education practitioners about how these highly aspirational aims are to be implemented, and which clearly relate these obligations to Article 29 in a deeper way. Quennerstedt and Moody (2020) also identify few studies of rights education in classroom practice that attend to processes of rights education, processes that the Committee specifies as crucial in its General Comment on the 'aims of education' (United Nations, 2001).

Through General Comment 1 (United Nations, 2001), the Committee has explicitly stated that the 'aims of education' are to "promote, support and protect the core value of the convention: the human dignity innate in every child and his or her equal and inalienable rights" (§1). In doing so, the General Comment emphasises the need for education to be "child-centred, child-friendly and empowering" (§2). In their argument for a rights-respecting pedagogy, Lundy and Cook-Sather (2016) focused on the human dignity of every child, starting with respect for the worth of the child, which may demand a profound re-evaluation of the status of children in society as a whole, not to mention in education. This focus echoes the Committee's direction in stating that the implementation of Article 29 does not lie in teaching children about rights, but in children's experiences of human rights values and standards (United Nations, 2001). Significantly, Lundy and Brown (2020) argue that a major challenge in the context of education rights does not lie, for the most part, in understanding what needs to be done, but in the *doing* of it. One crucial reason why this may be problematic in education is that teaching and enabling children to challenge breaches of their rights in education is associated with a fear that this would be disruptive to education itself (Lundy & Martinez-Sainz, 2018). It would also involve a fundamental disruption to the very nature of dominant educational structures, as well as the social and structural position of children within child-adult/adult-child and child-child educational power hierarchies. The aims of education codified in Article 29 would require a radical rethink of educational relationships and how education is delivered: practices that would require significant cultural and attitudinal shifts (Gillett-Swan & Sargeant, 2019; Sargeant, 2018) together with critical discussions of *what, why,* and *how* teaching and learning processes take place in educational settings (Quennerstedt et al., 2019).

These kinds of educational shifts may demand a greater recognition that children's education rights, rather than being externally prescribed, are embedded in the social structure of communities such as school (United Nations, 2001). Rights are not isolated from children's relational contexts but exist in the ethical framework prescribed in Article 29; children's education rights are not only about rules, but also about *relationships* and *processes* (Lundy & Brown, 2020; Quennerstedt et al., 2019). According to the Committee, part of the significance of Article 29 lies in recognition of education that reconciles diverse values through dialogue and respect. The successful application of Article 29 therefore requires an examination of the aims of education through lenses of discrimination (including gender, culture, ethnicity, disability, and socio-economic backgrounds), balanced with children's rights to participation and to prioritising their best interests. These lenses are of particular significance given the recent global wave of conservatism and nationalism, and the growing climate emergency. The convergence of these lenses reflect a number of tensions between the aspirational aims alluded to in Article 29 and the many and diverse rights of children from different cultures, socioeconomic backgrounds, and capacities – not to mention the values of adults through which education rights are often accessed. It is some of these issues that contributors to this volume attend.

These tensions are perhaps indicative of a gap in the education rights literature that addresses the relationships and processes of education rights. At this point it is necessary to draw a distinction between a *vertical* orientation of the international treaty, whereby duties are placed on the State to respect the human rights of individuals, and the *horizontal* realisation of a rights culture, which emerges and occurs in human relationships; between private individuals. In formal education, it is the relationships between teachers and students that are significant for the horizontal implementation of the Convention. Indeed, Lundy and Brown (2020) call for the horizontal orientation of rights that is fundamental to realisation of children's education rights, and where it is so vital to educate young people about their rights (Lundy & Martinez-Sainz, 2018; Quennerstedt et al., 2019). Children who not only learn about but also *experience* their rights are those who understand the content and the responsibilities of rights (Lundy & Brown, 2020). Therefore, the implementation of Article 29 should not be achieved exclusively through the teaching of values, but also in the "reflection of human rights values in the daily life and experiences of children" (United Nations, 2001, §15). Consequently, teaching and learning of rights is more than *knowing* what rights are, it is also about practising and *doing* rights in relation with others. For this, we need well-trained teachers with child rights competence including knowledge of children's rights *as well as* child rights skills (Quennerstedt et al., 2019). Hence, having rights educated teachers is also vitally important.

Although research on children's rights *in* education has recently drawn more attention than ever before (Quennerstedt & Moody, 2020), there is little *educationally* focused research that, unlike the more applied articles such as Article 12, seems to engage with Article 29 in any substantive way. When interrogating different aspects of children's educational rights through the lens of Article 29, extensive and highly diverse questions are raised due to the scope and parameters of the article consisting of more than what appears to be on the surface. Together, this provides an opportunity for discussing a variety of critical questions about the breadth of children's education rights, and a chance to engage more thoroughly with Article 29 from an *educational* and research perspective.

'Wicked Problems' and Critical Questions

As with all international human rights, children's rights are interpreted and integrated into national and local communities where various contexts and circumstances are considered. When rights are interpreted into various national educational practices, translation is necessary. Enactment of the Convention should therefore also be recognised as a *process* rather than just an end unto itself (Freeman, 2018). In every step of translation, transformation also takes place. In each transformation, the interpretation becomes further away from how it was originally portrayed and might ultimately depart quite significantly from the original intent (I'Anson et al., 2017). Even though some variations in understanding and implementation might be explained by the different national and local contexts, it is also related to the translation of language and interpretations therein. Sometimes, interpretations as well as misinterpretations even start to live their own lives. For example, "dignity" in the English language version of the Convention is translated in parts of the Swedish version as "value". In English, these words have slightly different meanings, which may also affect implementation. A further example is in conflations between common understandings of particular rights and what is *actually* provided through the rights in the Convention itself (Lundy, 2019). For example, while children's participation rights and "voice" and "input" are increasingly acknowledged, the provision of this right has a tendency to be conflated with the (mis)perception that the right provides children the right to *make* the decision, rather than it being that they have the right to provide *input* and their views given *due weight*.

Through the lens of translation, it becomes clearer how variability and inadequacies in rights affordances may initially go unnoticed by States parties until these issues are officially highlighted by the Committee through its concluding observations to States party reports. Even then, identification of these inadequacies do not always lead to action. This identification does not justify practices and provisions that are inadequate, or ultimately breach an individual's rights outright, but it does provide insight into how variations of rights could occur in different contexts undetected. For example, in national and local curriculum where teaching and learning is accomplished differently in different countries and contexts (Brantefors & Quennerstedt, 2016). What is culturally and contextually suitable in one context may differ vastly from another context. This does not necessarily mean that either (or both) contexts are not pursuing what they ultimately consider to be in the best interests of the children with whom they work. However, being *accepted* practices does not necessarily make them rights-respecting. The question, then, of how the same educational mandate may be interpreted, understood, and applied in different national and international contexts in different ways poses an interesting focus for investigation beyond considering the provision of education (through Article 28) alone. The issue of translation also occurs with the multiple variations of the Convention's text including simplified and child friendly versions that may emphasise different aspects from the original text. This variation can be a positive and a negative thing. While a simplified version may make content more accessible than the full text, a simplified version may also not necessarily reflect the whole content of the actual text of the Convention. This disconnect can lead to multiple interpretations of the simplified interpretation, resulting in framings that are not necessarily accurate. The variability in focus for each Article within simplified versions has been noted in recent years, resulting in a partnership between UNICEF and Child Rights Connect to produce a children's version of the Convention supported by the Committee on the Rights of the Child (UNICEF, 2019). Versions not endorsed by the Committee, therefore, are likely to less accurately reflect the full scope and intent of each Article and should be used with caution, if at all.

The Convention on the Rights of the Child has been a starting point for conceptualising, enacting, and considering children's rights for over 30 years, but the extent to which it is understood and embraced within the discipline of education varies. Using the Convention as the foundation for educational research seems essential as it reflects the difference between viewing education as a fundamental human right – afforded to *all* without discrimination of any kind and core to individual development – and simply viewing rights as an add-on to educational practice. Perhaps this is one of the 'wicked problems' of the discipline. 'Wicked problems' are those that are difficult to solve, difficult to define, and have no clear right or wrong solution (Peters, 2017). The issues that the contributors to this volume explore could arguably also be considered 'wicked problems.'

It is through this lens that the volume is structured to progress through considering the following broad issues plaguing educational rights research in; the issue of translation; inequality and power; participation and inclusion; and rights education and knowledge. Specifically, what does it mean to translate legal texts into particular educational contexts (**I'Anson**) and how is the intent of Article 29 reflected in national contexts that have not ratified the Convention (**Curl and Cook-Sather**)? Critical questions are explored including whether the Convention goes far enough in terms of affordance and provision of education rights for all children (**Winter and de Bruin**), what the role of educational institutions and policy in perpetuating questionable rights practices may be (**Starnawski, Gawlicz and Duda**), and how children's capabilities and social development can be understood with a rights lens (**Biffi and Monta**). Attention is also directed to school contexts, practices and the role of education to foster equality (**Lúcio and Antunes**). Questions such as how education may currently perpetuate discrimination (**O'Brien**), (in) equality (**Spina, Harris and Jaremus**), and exclusion (**Häbig, Zala-Mezö, Herzig and Müller-Kuhn**) for children and young people are also raised.

Within the field of children's rights research there has also been significant focus on children's voices and participation. This seems to be an unsolved riddle for many education rights researchers. How can children's rights be fully afforded when children's participation rights in education are either not recognised (**Wyness**), provided (**Ceballos, Susinos and Saiz-Linares**), or teacher practices lack critical reflexivity in the extent they empower (**Babicka-Wirkus**) and enable children's participation in educational contexts (**Kiilakoski and Niemi**)? What role, then, does teacher training have in the preparation of child-rights ready teachers (**Moody**) and fostering their commitment to children's rights in and through their practice (**Martinez Sainz**)? And, in research, is there a need for the field more broadly to take a more critical perspective when theorising children's rights (**Brantefors and Thelander**)? The volume concludes by questioning how schools can then become more effective 'sites for rights', emphasising the need for greater child rights knowledge and awareness within and beyond educational contexts (**Gillett-Swan and Thelander**).

This volume contends with some of the common and persistent issues within the field of children's rights in education and considers their complexity through the lens of Article 29. The scope of these issues requires continual re-examination as they remain challenging, unresolved issues for the field. This emphasises how these problems that *still* plague the field are, at their core, also fundamentally 'wicked' problems with no clear solutions. At the same time, the contributions in the volume also point to new insights and ideas as well as promising practices, and opportunities for change and development. These contributions acknowledge that, even though change takes time, it also has much to do with attitudes – individual, systemic, cultural, and collective – in various societies throughout the world.

Conclusion

It is recognised that a rights-focused text would be remiss to not acknowledge the interconnectedness, indivisibility, equality, inalienability, and interdependence of *all* rights, and the important role that each right has in supporting and reinforcing each of the other rights. The focus on Article 29 in what is to come is not to be at the exclusion of other rights articles relevant to the discussion for each example provided. Instead, Article 29 is used as a reference point to provide a new way of viewing common questions and education situations, where focus may previously have had a different rights basis. By looking at each of the common examples from diverse national contexts, from multiple vantage points, it provides a re-grounding of the role that education has – not only in terms of provision, but also in terms of its substance, aims, and content.

Using international case study examples to show how children's rights in education might exist in different local and global contexts, this book critically examines contemporary educational practices with a children's rights lens and critiques the implementation of Article 29 and the 'aims of education' across diverse educational contexts from theoretical and practical perspectives. Through investigating the factors that contribute to (or hinder) the realisation of children's rights in education in different contexts, the chapters herein explore various tensions, possibilities and realities of different attempts to interpret and realise children's educational rights in practice. In doing so, the overall message of the book aims to demonstrate how a rights framework for education advances the agenda for achieving international educational priorities and goals and leads to preparing the child for a responsible life in society and preparing society for their responsibility to each child.

References

Biesta, G. (2015). *Good education in an age of measurement: Ethics, politics, democracy*. Routledge.

Brantefors, L., & Quennerstedt, A. (2016). Teaching and learning children's human rights. A research synthesis. *Cogent Education, 3*(1), 1–19.

Dewey, J. (1916). *Democracy and Education*. Free Press.

Freeman, M. (2018). *Children's rights: New issues, new themes, new perspectives*. BRILL.

Gillett-Swan, J. K., & Sargeant, J. (2019). Perils of perspective: Identifying adult confidence in the child's capacity, autonomy, power and agency (CAPA) in readiness for voice-inclusive practice. *Journal of Educational Change, 20*, 399–421.

I'Anson, J., Quennerstedt, A., & Robinson, C. (2017). The international economy of children's rights: Issues in translation. *The International Journal of Children's Rights, 25*(1), 50–67.

Jerome, L. (2016). Interpreting children's rights education: Three perspectives and three roles for teachers. *Citizenship, Social and Economics Education, 15*(2), 143–156.

Lundy, L. (2006). Mainstreaming children's rights in, to and through education in a society emerging from conflict. *The International Journal of Children's Rights, 14*(4), 339–362.

Lundy, L. (2019). A lexicon for research on international children's rights in troubled times. *International Journal of Children's Rights, 27*, 595–601.

Lundy, L., & Brown, A. (2020). Revisiting the three R's in order to realize children's education rights: Relationships, resources and redress. In J. Todres & S. M. King (Eds.), *The Oxford handbook of children's rights law*. Oxford University Press.

Lundy, L., & Cook-Sather, A. (2016). Children's rights and student voice: Their intersections and the implications for curriculum and pedagogy. In D. Wyse, L. Hayward, & J. Pandya (Eds.), *The SAGE handbook of curriculum, pedagogy and assessment* (pp. 263–277). SAGE.

Lundy, L., & Martinez-Sainz, G. (2018). The role of law and legal knowledge for a transformative human rights education: Addressing violations of children's rights in formal education. *Human Rights Education Review, 1*(2), 4–24.

Lundy, L., Orr, K., & Shier, H. (2016). Children's educational rights: Global perspectives. In M. Ruck, M. Badali-Peterson, & M. Freeman (Eds.), *Handbook of children's rights: Global and multidisciplinary perspectives* (pp. 364–380). Routledge.

Peters, B. G. (2017). What is so wicked about wicked problems? A conceptual analysis and a research program. *Policy and Society, 36*(3), 385–396.

Quennerstedt, A., & Moody, Z. (2020). Educational children's rights research 1989-2019: Achievements, gaps and future prospects. *International Journal of Children's Rights, 28*(1), 183–208.

Quennerstedt, A., Tellgren, B., Brantefors, L., & Thelander, N. (2019). Teaching children's human rights in early childhood education and school: Educational aims, content and processes. In *Reports in education 21*. Örebro University.

Reynaert, D., Bouverne-De Bie, M., & Vandevelde, S. (2009). A review of children's rights literature since the adoption of the United Nations Convention on the Rights of the Child. *Childhood, 16*(4), 518–534.

Robinson, C., Quennerstedt, A., & I'Anson, J. (2020). The translation of articles from the United Nations Convention on the Rights of the Child into education legislation: the narrowing of Article 12 as a consequence of translation. *The Curriculum Journal, 31*(3), 517–538.

Sargeant, J. (2018). Towards voice-inclusive practice: Finding the sustainability of participation in realising the child's rights in education. *Children and Society, 32*, 314–324.

Todres, J. (2020). Making children's rights widely known. *Minnesota Journal of International Law, 29*(1), 109–150.

Tomasevski, K. (2001). *Human rights obligations: Making education available, accessible, acceptable and adaptable*. Primer No. 3. The Right to Education Project.

Tomasevski, K. (2003). *Education denied: Costs and remedies*. Zed Books.

UNICEF. (2019). *The United Nations Convention on the Rights of the Child – The children's version*. Available https://www.unicef.org/child-rights-convention/convention-text-childrens-version

United Nations. (1948). *Universal declaration of human rights*. UN General Assembly.

United Nations. (1989). *UN Convention on the Rights of the Child*. United Nations.

United Nations. (2001). *UN Committee on the Rights of the Child, General Comment No. 1 Article 29: The aims of education. CRC/GC/2001/1*. United Nations.

Verhellen, E. (1993). Children's rights and education: A three-track legally binding imperative. *School Psychology International, 14*(3), 199–208.

Chapter 2
Article 29 and Its Translation into Policy and Practice in Scotland: An Impossible Right to Education?

John I'Anson

Abstract This chapter concentrates on the intersection of the right to education through UNCRC Article 29 with traditions of education. It is, therefore, concerned with some of the implications of translating this legal text into the specific educational contexts impacting on the lives of children and young people at the present time. The chapter, therefore, responds to recent work in the field of children's rights that calls for approaches that are both more critical and more theoretically adventurous. This critical and theory-informed approach necessarily extends to thinking about the kinds of education that are both implied and enacted – in the name of the UNCRC – within particular settings. Here, a case study of the translation of children's rights within the context of the Scottish education system will ground the discussion and help surface assumptions that might otherwise remain hidden. The chapter concludes with some observations concerning difficulties faced in constructing a universal appeal to education and, in the light of this, the importance of attending to ways of negotiating difference.

Keywords Article 29 · Education · Governance · Heuristic · International economy of rights · Pedagogy · Translation · Scotland

J. I'Anson (✉)
Faculty of Social Sciences, University of Stirling, Stirling, Scotland
e-mail: john.ianson@stir.ac.uk

J. Gillett-Swan, N. Thelander (eds.), *Children's Rights from International Educational Perspectives*, Transdisciplinary Perspectives in Educational Research 2, https://doi.org/10.1007/978-3-030-80861-7_2

Introduction

This chapter is concerned with the intersection of the right to education through UNCRC Article 29 (United Nations, 1989) with traditions of education and hence with thinking through some of the implications of translating this legal text into the specific educational contexts that impact upon the lives of children and young people at the present time. As such, the direction of travel accords with recent work in the field of children's rights that calls for approaches that are both more critical (Quennerstedt, 2013; Reynaert et al., 2012) and more theoretically adventurous (I'Anson, 2016; I'Anson et al., 2017; Holzscheiter et al., 2019). This critical and theory-informed approach necessarily extends to thinking about the *kinds of education* that are both implied and enacted – in the name of the UNCRC – within particular settings. Here, a case study of the translation of children's rights within the context of the Scottish education system will ground the discussion and help surface assumptions that might otherwise remain hidden. The chapter concludes with some observations concerning difficulties faced in constructing a universal appeal to education, and, in the light of this, the importance of attending to ways of negotiating difference.

Article 29: The Aims of Education

On first reading, Article 29 appears relatively uncontentious: all children are to be accorded a right to an education that promotes:

(i) the holistic development of the full potential of the child (Article 29.1a), including development of respect for human rights (29.1b),
(ii) an enhanced sense of identity and affiliation (29.1c), and
(iii) his or her socialization and interaction with others (29.1d) and
(iv) with the environment (29.1e) (taken from General Comment No. 1: The Aims of Education (Article 29), United Nations (2001))

However, it is not immediately clear to which distinctive tradition of education this makes appeal. In this connection, it is helpful to recall that Biesta (2011; Stoltz & Biesta, 2018) identifies a number of distinct (western) traditions of education, each holding fundamentally different – and incommensurable – assumptions about what "education" consists in. These traditions include the dominant Anglo-American approach in which education is regarded as not being a distinct discipline in itself, but as constituted by, and reliant upon, other disciplines such as psychology, philosophy, history, and sociology. Such an understanding is classically set out in the writings of Hirst (1966). This understanding is so deeply rooted within Anglo-American contexts that the very idea that education might be considered a discipline in its own right, with its own characteristic matters of concern and ways of going on is, for many, quite unthinkable. But for those within continental contexts, where traditions of educational inquiry such as *Bildung* and *Erziehung* have a long history, the idea of education as a discipline in its own right is not without plausibility.

So to which characterisation of education does Article 29 appeal? Whilst the concept of 'Education' appears to be unproblematic, and therefore presuming a shared matter of concern, the subsequent principles that are laid out might nevertheless appear to cut across extant traditions. Thus dimensions (i) and (ii) of Article 29 might, on the face of it, appear to align with the continental tradition of *Bildung*, given their emphasis on self-formation; for, as Hu (2015, p. 17) has observed, this tradition:

> emphasizes a process of holistic growth, self-realization of the individual as an entirety, freedom, and self-understanding as well as a sense of social responsibility, and which puts the development of the individual's unique potential and self at the centre of educational processes.

However, the insistence in (i) upon 'including development of respect for rights' might be considered as an instrumental concern that lies outside the specific resources of *Bildung per se*. Dimension (iii) with its explicit concern with socialisation might fit with an Anglo-American multi-disciplinary approach in which the sociology of education has a foundational role. If the educational provenance of Article 29 remains somewhat unclear within the text of the article itself, its subsequent elaboration within the General Comment issued in 2001 (hereafter, GC), draws out this article's implications far more definitely. It is to a consideration of this that we now turn.

The General Comment (United Nations, 2001) outlines the contours for a rights-inflected account of education that claims to draw its key principles from a reading across the corpus of rights (United Nations, 2001, §6). The text foregrounds a "holistic" (§12) "child-centred" education (§9), that is "balanced" and in which children themselves "bridge" tensions (United Nations, 2001, §4). Such metaphors do considerable rhetorical work in terms of holding together the narrative advanced, but the account presented is clearly ambitious – even quite radical – in scope, claiming its promotion of values, policies and ethos apply "not only within schools and universities but also within the broader community" (United Nations, 2001, §19). Nor does the ensuing narrative only hover at an abstract level of principle; the promotion of a curriculum that is relevant to a child's multiple contexts requires the development of requisite 'tools' that afford the possibility of:

- critical thinking,
- ethical capacities (that enable the taking on of responsibility, resolution of disputes in non-violent ways, and to act sustainably), and
- confidence in making significant life decisions. (United Nations, 2001, §7, §9, §13).

This manifests a concern to ground the values and principles enunciated earlier. In like manner, the meaning of the term 'discrimination', for example, is not left hanging, but is carefully differentiated into a number of specific forms that this can take, such as gender inequality, illness, racism, and hostility to other forms of difference (United Nations, 2001, §10–11). The significance of a practice orientation to children's rights is also drawn out (United Nations, 2001, §15).

The net effect of this elaboration of rights principles and values would appear to be an alignment with, or at least an affinity for, child-centred discourses of progressive education, such as those associated with Pestalozzi and Froebel (Darling, 1994), albeit one legitimised through appear to children's rights principles. The GC recognises that such an account of education represents an explicit challenge to existing grammars of schooling (United Nations, 2001, §18). However, if the UNCRC had previously been characterised as presenting a "peculiar combination of bold intent and potential toothlessness", as Lee (1999, p. 457) once put it, within the GC there are unequivocal steps taken to try and ensure this approach to education has critical and universal traction. Thus a considerable amount of space is given over to elaborating measures through which States parties might instantiate the values, principles and practices outlined, with clear expectations with regard to reporting and accountability, including steps to be taken when things go awry (§20–28). And so, whilst the GC acknowledges that the aims and values of education are set out in "quite general terms and their implications are potentially very wide ranging" (§17) there is, nevertheless, a clear expectation that the translation and formal incorporation into States parties' respective legislative, administrative and education policies will take place "at all levels". Just as the UNCRC might be seen as promoting an understanding of childhood that has itself become constitutive, governing understandings of what are, and are not, deemed to be appropriate ways of being a child (Holzscheiter et al., 2019) so, too, is this the case in regard to education. In a parallel way, in Article 29, as elaborated in the GC, the UNCRC appears to be promoting its own distinctive form of education to which States parties are accountable.

The Issue of Translation

Given that Article 29 presents a distinctive vision of education, along with quite detailed expectations regarding its implementation, how, in practice, do States parties enact these requirements? Here, it is necessary to say a few words about the work of translation, especially given the significance that is attached within the GC of Article 29 to a series of technologies through which this understanding of education is to gain presence within national law, policy and professional guidance. Having outlined a theoretical approach to translation, it then becomes possible to focus more specifically upon how Article 29 is translated within a specific educational context: that of Scotland.

The metaphor of translation is useful in foregrounding the kinds of practices and mediations involved in this work. Translation derives from the Latin *trans-latio*, which means to "lift across, move, transfer" (Readings, 1992, p. 183). In the process of transfer change takes place, and identifying the specific stages involved in this work of bridging make it possible to mark both the different kinds of translations that are performed and the kinds of assumptions that are in play.

Theoretically, such an approach draws upon work associated with socio-material approaches such as Actor Network Theory (ANT) and in particular upon the work of Bruno Latour. In his early work, Latour noticed that scientists' own accounts of their work tends to play down – and to overlook – many of the routine material activities that actually go on in the laboratory as integral to scientific practice. His study with Woolgar, *Laboratory Life*, provided an empirical description of scientists' work that was quite ground-breaking at the time with its focus upon what scientists actually do (Latour & Woolgar, 1979). An especially clear illustration of the value of such an approach can be found in Latour's (1999) subsequent study where he accompanied a variety of scientists investigating the edge of an Amazon rainforest. Here, Latour tracked the ways in which a material substance, such as soil, via various tests and associations, became translated into data, which, in turn, informed the development of concepts that eventually became academic texts. These academic papers were then circulated, engaged with, and taken up by readers considerably removed from the actual circumstances of their initial production. A key insight in this study was that this work necessarily involved a series of translations; at each stage of translation, something was gained in terms of generalisability, but something too was lost in terms of the specificity of location and materiality. Latour also noticed that, as each stage in this process was achieved, the successive translations that were a condition of its possibility, tend to become invisible. Noticing the translations that cumulatively enable a particular achievement is, therefore, quite difficult after the event.

A parallel approach to the socio-material translations noted by Latour, can be helpful in identifying the various translations through which a legal text, such as an article of the UNCRC, must pass if it is to inform actual situations of intergenerational practice. In an earlier paper I'Anson et al. (2017) argued that it is important to acknowledge an international economy of translation in relation to children's rights. Figure 2.1 (below) identifies no fewer than five (5) such points of translation:

Table 2.1 (below) summarises each point of translation, together with a description of the relevant section (§) in the GC (United Nations, 2001):

Just as in the scientific studies recounted above, transformation takes place at each of these points of translation. At each point, once a specific translation has been achieved, the work involved tends to become invisible and forgotten. Consequently, practitioners seeking to enact a particular policy prescription or performance indicator that is the outcome of work by policy makers to mediate a legal text to their situation of practice, will tend to regard their actions as 'simply doing rights' rather than as the outcome of one particular translation that might have been performed differently. In one sense, the international economy of rights enacts translations in a reverse order from that described by Latour in so far as the process here is from a pre-given text to its embodiment within actual situations of practice. This, as we will see, creates certain tensions with regard to negotiating between the

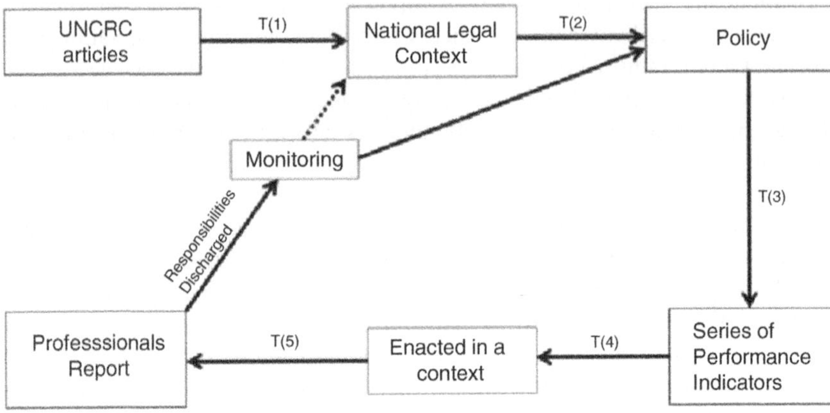

Fig. 2.1 The international economy of rights. (From I'Anson et al., 2017, p. 59)

Table 2.1 Summary of Points of Translation within the International Economy of Rights, with connections to the United Nations Article 29 General Comment

Translation	Description	Relevant GC § (United Nations, 2001)
T(1)	The legal translation of the UNCRC articles into member states' legislative systems.	§17 formal incorporation of principles in legislation at all levels
T(2)	The translation from legal instantiation to policy discourse at multiple levels (state, regional, local levels etc.).	§17 formal incorporation of principles in educational policies §23 Comprehensive national plan of action Obligations not being met
T(3)	The translation of policy into organisational and professional expectations, typically through the construction of a series of performance indicators. In Scotland these are designated as "quality indicators" as they become distributed across multiple forms of professional accountability – e.g., Teacher Professional Standards (GTCS 2013).	§22 measuring change over time; national level monitoring
T(4)	The translation of organisations and professionals in engaging with these indicators in their practice.	§18 Fundamental re-working of curricula, textbooks, materials, teaching methods, etc. Pre-service and in-service training §19 school environment
T(5)	The translation in professionals' reports on the success, or otherwise, of their mobilisation of rights as indicators.	§20 Reporting §25 Review of procedures re. complaints §26 Identification of priorities

demands of Article 29 and diverse cultural contexts.[1] Having outlined an approach to understanding the work of translation, which is necessarily involved in mediating children's rights into practice, we now consider an empirical case study of this translation work within Scotland.

Case Study: Translating Rights Within Educational Contexts in Scotland

Scotland is an interesting case study given its aspiration to have an education system that is thoroughly rights informed. Indeed, according to the Scottish Government's (2019, p. 5) Consultation on Children's Rights:

> We believe that delivering the rights of children and young people as enshrined in the UNCRC is fundamental to making children's rights real and Scotland the best place in the world to grow up.

How, in practice, does this ambition translate into the field of education? In recent years one discourse in particular has been foregrounded within the Scottish education policy context, where the approach taken to children's rights has become inseparable from that taken with respect to children's health and wellbeing.[2] Indeed, this pairing of children's rights with their health and wellbeing is a key feature of the "landmark" legislation passed by the Scottish Parliament in 2014 – the *Children and Young People (Scotland) Act 2014* (CYPA). This effectively puts much of the "Getting it Right for Every Child" (GIRFEC) initiative onto a legal footing. GIRFEC identifies eight indicators of wellbeing, and these are often summarised under the acronym SHANARRI, that stands for – Safe, Healthy, Achieving, Nurtured, Active, Respected, Responsible and Included. An influential publication that provides guidance for practitioners describes GIRFEC as the "bedrock" for all children's services (Scottish Government, 2012, p. 6). A wide range of curricular initiatives draw upon this framing, and it is particularly evident in recent national curriculum policy such as *Building the Ambition: National Practice Guidance on Early Learning and Childcare* (Scottish Government, 2014). One of the reported advantages of the GIRFEC approach to realising the government's obligations has been the possibility of a common language between different professionals working with children and young people, such as teachers and social workers.

Notwithstanding these advantages, Tisdall (2015, p. 807) contends that children's rights and children's wellbeing "differ conceptually, methodologically and politically" and should not, therefore, be regarded as equivalent discourses. Such an

---

[1] The focus on the processes of translation from finished text (UNCRC) to its material instantiations also tends to eclipse from view the process of the text's own construction during the years 1979–1989: see Quennerstedt et al. (2018) on this.

[2] Space does not permit a detailed analysis of the understandings of 'health and wellbeing' that are in play in this discourse: on this, see Spratt (2016, 2017) for a detailed account.

acknowledgement would suggest that rather than simply conflating the different genealogies of wellbeing and rights it is necessary to acknowledge these differences and present them as different – rather than unified – discourses. It might be objected, however, that, despite such differences, the discourse associated with GIRFEC does effectively address what are sometimes referred to as the "3Ps": rights concerned with provision, protection, and participation (Quennerstedt, 2010). The difficulty with this position is that it neglects the ways in which these are realised in practice; it is noteworthy, for example, that the GIRFEC discourse, beyond providing information to children about the SHANARRI indicators, tends to privilege *a professional's judgement* as to whether or not a particular concern might be raised. It is not primarily concerned with educational or pedagogic issues, such as how children might come to acquire the critical and ethical tools identified in GC §7, 9 (United Nations, 2001) discussed above. Moreover, the strong association of children's rights with a health and wellbeing discourse in Scotland also runs the risk that other, specifically educational, imperatives become side-lined (I'Anson, 2018). And so, whilst acknowledging the seriousness with which Scotland has foregrounded children's health and wellbeing in recent legislation and policy, it is necessary to ask critical questions as to the extent to which such measures actually address a children's rights agenda and, more precisely, State parties' specific educational obligations as set out in Article 29, GC. Here, the use of an educational heuristic may be useful in further pinpointing some of the issues at stake.

In this connection, it is worth recalling that education derives from the Latin *ēducēre*, which means, quite literally, "to lead out" (Masschelein, 2006, 2010a, b); from this root, it then becomes possible to trace a number of significant lines along which a distinctively educational approach might be articulated. One such educational heuristic characterises education as consisting in three elements: the critical, experimental and ethical elements, respectively (I'Anson & Jasper, 2017). Each element is characterised in the following terms; firstly, the critical element, aims to situate knowledge within the discursive and material conditions of its production. This problematises particular claims in relation to knowledge where this "restrict[s] or limit possibilities of insight, comparison and considered practice" (I'Anson & Jasper, 2017, p. 145). Secondly, the experimental element opens up inquiry to empirical investigation, so as to explore the socio-material effects that "comprise relations between entities and practices" (I'Anson & Jasper, 2017, p. 143). Finally, the ethical element is concerned with the complex relational implications and responsibilities "in thinking through the implications of educational practice" (I'Anson & Jasper, 2017, p. 143). Although distinct, each of these three elements is, in practice, mutually constitutive and so each is a necessary dimension of education. Within these terms, therefore, a distinctively educational translation of children's rights will seek to develop policies and pedagogies that actively keep in play the critical, experimental and ethical elements. Conversely, a translation that neglects one or more of these elements would, within these terms, be regarded as lacking in these respects. Such a heuristic has affinities with the principles advocated in the GC in so far as this acknowledges the specific tools and pedagogic practices necessary if this "leading out" is to be meaningfully accomplished by children. By the same token, it becomes possible to identify and locate possible barriers to education being realised, where pedagogies are limited in both scope and challenge.

It is here that one might wish to raise a series of critical questions concerning the educational restrictions that a translation of a children's rights agenda within a health and wellbeing framing brings in its train. With such an approach, it might be argued, the ethical element is foregrounded at the expense of the other two educational elements: the capacities for critique and experimentation. Within these terms, we might wish to ask how, for example, a child or young person might acquire critical literacy practices or be afforded opportunities for trying things out empirically so as to learn from such experiences. Important though a health and wellbeing translation is, it is clear that this does not fully encompass the educational requirements of Article 29: whilst the GIRFEC approach addresses the ethical element, an exclusive focus upon health and wellbeing may lead to a forgetfulness of the critical and experimental elements of education. Consequently, such a translation may neglect the kinds of critical and experimental capacities that the intersection between education and children's rights might otherwise engender.

Within the Scottish educational context, therefore, significant steps have been taken as regards the translation of a children's rights agenda within the terms of an ethics of care, but wider questions remain *vis-à-vis* ways in which broader educational principles, values and practices might be realised.

The foregrounding of a dynamic understanding of the three elements of education also opens up questions as to the role that specific subjects might play in relation to a broader rights-informed education, especially given the prominence attached to sustainability in the GC (United Nations, 2001). This is to raise a series of educational questions as to the kinds of knowledges and practices that are implicated in thinking more fully about the requirements of Article 29. A renewed concern with media literacy, for instance, might be considered especially vital at a time of "fake news", when politicians can peddle false statistics on the side of a bus with impunity, and the media reiterates negative and one-sided representations of "Islam" on a daily basis. Likewise, a more extended educational discussion of rights might include within its purview some of the complex ethical issues raised by acts of cultural appropriation (Young & Brunk, 2012).

The implications of engaging the right to education are therefore far-reaching indeed, with ramifications that cut across multiple subject areas, activities and environs. This raises a challenge to many settled areas of practice, for the GC §18 (United Nations, 2001) makes it clear that the simple adaptation of existing approaches is insufficient:

> Approaches which do no more than seek to superimpose the aims and values of the article on the existing system without encouraging any deeper changes are clearly inadequate.

The pedagogical implications of this potentially extend to a questioning of many routine teaching activities – that are so taken for granted that they are all but hidden. John Law (2009) once remarked that, as a rule of thumb, to the extent that something is invisible, it is probably doing quite a lot of work in holding a particular state of affairs in place. A good example of this is the practice of lesson planning – which is as ubiquitous as it is consequential. As Allwright (2003), observes, lesson planning approaches that students on Initial Teacher Education (ITE) programs are inducted into, tend to have a behaviourist genealogy and a teacher-centred orientation. If a children's rights-based approach is subsequently introduced, this is typically grafted upon this already habitual approach to lesson design. The effect of this is that practices to elicit young peoples' feedback can appear somewhat tokenistic and peripheral to the main lesson aims that have already been determined by the teacher. Rather than beginning with rights-informed questions that might foreground consultation and the promotion of children's capacities to meaningfully engage in pedagogical issues, a foundational practice keeps traditional teacher-centric approaches in play. This is just one issue that is illustrative of the kinds of pedagogical re-thinking that the intersection of children's rights and education might provoke.

Of course, the question then emerges as to how a children's rights-based approach is evaluated: at what point is a professional's educational responsibility to children discharged, how is this determined, and by who? At the present time, professional codes of conduct typically resolve such questions in terms of lists of performance indicators that an individual professional is expected to evidence in particular ways.[3] Whether this issues in a more radical educational questioning (in terms of, for example, the three elements of education), and whether this issues in a preparedness to reconceive the purposes of education in the light of Article 29, is an open question.

Decolonising Article 29: Towards a New Ecology?

A critical reading might question the extent to which the discussion of education hitherto is couched primarily in terms of western traditions – derived from minority world contexts – and also note that the direction of policy travel within the existing "international economy of rights" tends to be one way: from a prescribed and authorised text to its translation into multiple contexts of intergenerational practice – in majority world contexts. The acknowledgement that majority world contexts may instantiate different values and relational priorities that are in tension with the promotion of autonomy and agency that tend to characterise western approaches, has potentially far–reaching repercussions in relation to rights (Tisdall & Punch, 2012). In this connection, it is noteworthy that Schweisfurth's (2011) study of 72 projects concerned with instituting learner-centred education in contexts with different

[3] In Scotland, the General Teaching Council Scotland (GTCS), the official body responsible for teacher registration, has various Professional Standards for different roles and stages in a teacher's career, each with multiple indicators (GTCS, 2019). School Inspectors use a text entitled *How Good is our School?* (Education Scotland, 2015), which consists in hundreds of performance indicators (renamed "quality indicators") that are used to assess educational practice. As regards the latter, it is noteworthy that at no point is the "good" in the title actually defined; it is simply resolved into a successful alignment with the aforementioned performance indicators.

cultural logics identified significant and consistent failures in the translation of this approach to education, with "cultural mismatch" being recognised as one of the main factors. A greater sensitivity to power relations, broader expectations and a more nuanced approach to cultural translations are desirable in the light of this (Thomson, 2013). In moving forward, perhaps a different understanding of governance is also necessary in which the critical issue is sustained engagement with educational matters of concern rather than alignment with a pre-given ordering. This is to gesture towards an ecology of rights, in which there is scope for feedback (and forward) from situated and embodied practice within particular locales. In this connection, the identification of "gaps" in understanding is significant as a potential resource for understanding difference: not for these to be "closed" but as a means for creating and sustaining conversation across this divide. Such an approach is well articulated by Jullien (2014) in his work that is specifically concerned with creating dialogue between western and Chinese traditions. Once a gap in understandings has been identified this becomes a site from which another's point of view can be approached. This has the advantage that not only does this promote a hospitality to difference, but such practice can also enable a surfacing of hitherto unknown aspects of one's own culture, since this is approached from another's vantage point. Whilst a detailed consideration of possible ways of re-imaging the kinds of dialogue that a children's rights approach to education might promote lies beyond the scope of this particular chapter, the identification of critical tensions and possibilities is nevertheless opened up from a consideration of the Scottish case study that has been our focus here.

Conclusion

There is an inherent ambiguity in the approach taken to education within the UNCRC. As we have seen, Article 29 is not specifically aligned with any one tradition of education, although the approach described in the GC might appear to have close affinities with certain forms of progressive education. The position taken is to ground these principles, values and practices in a reading drawn from across the articles of the UNCRC itself. Of course, were Article 29 to specify which "education" it was appealing to, it would, perhaps rightly, be charged with a kind of cultural imperialism – an educational colonisation – in so far as a specific disciplinary tradition of education was to be imposed upon areas where other cultural logics and values obtain. On the other hand, the refusal to specify (and to articulate a position from) a specific tradition of education, inevitably results in difficulties in ascertaining the extent to which a given translation addresses specifically educational principles, values and practices. Given that Article 29's grounding is in other-than-educational principles, the approach taken to education is ultimately instrumental and performative, which issues in a centre to periphery approach to governance. As the case study of Scotland's response to Article 29 demonstrates, the translations involved are both complex and educationally demanding. It can be difficult, in practice, to ascertain the extent to which a serious concern with children's health and wellbeing is promoted in ways that are educational – and the extent to which a fully educational agenda exceeds these terms.

Few would dispute that the articulation of a right to education, for *all* children and young people, in *all* circumstances, might appropriately be characterised as bold. And yet, as the analysis undertaken in this chapter might suggest, the very possibility of articulating such a right to education is beset with multiple challenges regarding what such an education might consist in, the translations to which this gives rise, and the ways in which such a call might acknowledge and respect cultural difference. To this extent, the right to education, as articulated in Article 29 and in its ensuing GC, might also be characterised as impossible – impossible, that is, not in the sense that this cannot be attained, but in the sense that its realisation is always yet to come, to be always worked out anew in as yet new and unforeseen circumstances. It is in this sense, therefore, that the right to education is necessarily impossible. But – in so far as this call is in the name of education – this leading out will involve raising critical, experimental and ethical questions and part of the challenge is that this appeal is unlimited. In its effort to ensure that Article 29 is taken up, the GC offers detailed expectations in terms of accountability and these tend toward a centre-periphery account of governance, as we have seen. Given the ethical and empirical difficulties to which this gives rise, it may be more appropriate instead to work with the metaphor of counterpoint rather than that of alignment. Such an openness would encourage mutual exchange regarding significant matters of educational concern in a manner which, according to Brown (2005, p. 74), "complicates a single or dominant theme through the addition of contrasting themes or forces". To this extent, counterpoint:

> promotes an anti hegemonic sensibility and requires a modest and carefully styled embrace of multiplicity in which contrasting elements, featured simultaneously, do not simply war, harmonize, blend, or compete but rather bring out complexity that cannot emerge through a monolithic or single melody.

It is to be hoped that some such "carefully styled embrace of multiplicity" may offer productive ways of engaging the many refractions of Article 29, in ways that promote new forms of dialogue about educational matters of concern.

References

Allwright, D. (2003). Exploratory practice: rethinking practitioner research in language teaching. *Language Teaching Research, 7(2), 113–141.*

Biesta, G. (2011). Disciplines and theory in the academic study of education: A comparative analysis of the Anglo-American and Continental construction of the field. *Pedagogy, Culture and Society, 19*(2), 175–192.

Brown, W. (2005). *Edgework: Critical essays on knowledge and politics*. Princeton University Press.

Darling, J. (1994). *Child-centred education and its critics*. Paul Chapman Publishing.

Education Scotland. (2015). *How good is our school?* (4th ed.). Education Scotland. https://education.gov.scot/improvement/documents/frameworks_selfevaluation/frwk2_nihedithgios/frwk2_hgios4.pdf. Accessed Aug 2019.

General Teaching Council Scotland (GTCS). (2019). *Professional standards*. https://www.gtcs.org.uk/professional-standards/professional-standards.aspx. Accessed 15 Aug 2019.

Hirst, P. H. (1966). Educational theory. In J. W. Tibble (Ed.), *The study of education* (pp. 29–58). Routledge & Kegan Paul.

Holzscheiter, A., Josefsson, J., & Sandin, B. (2019). Child rights governance: An introduction. *Childhood, 26*(3), 271–288.

Hu, A. (2015). The idea of *Bildung* in the current educational discourse: A response to Irene Heidt. *L2 Journal, 7*(4), 17–19.

I'Anson, J. (2016). UNCRC at 25: A critical assessment of achievements and trajectories with reference to educational research. In V. Coppock & J. Gillett-Swan (Eds.), *Children's rights, educational research and the UNCRC* (pp. 17–37). Symposium.

I'Anson, J., & Jasper, A. (2017). *Schooling indifference*. Routledge.

I'Anson, J., Quennerstedt, A., & Robinson, C. (2017). The international economy of children's rights: Issues in translation. *International Journal of Children's Rights, 25*(1), 50–67.

I'Anson, J. (2018). Children's rights. In T. Bryce, W. Humes, D. Gillies, & A. Kennedy (Eds.), *Scottish education* (5th ed.). University of Edinburgh Press.

Jullien, F. (2014). *On the universal, the uniform, the common and the dialogue between cultures*. Polity.

Latour, B. (1999). *Pandora's hope: Essays on the reality of science studies*. Harvard University Press.

Latour, B., & Woolgar, S. (1979). *Laboratory life: The construction of scientific facts*. Princeton University Press.

Law, J. (2009). *Collateral realities*. (December 29, 2009, ver.). www.heterogeneities.net/publications/Law2009CollateralRealities.pdf. Accessed 15 Aug 2019.

Lee, N. (1999). The challenge of childhood: Distributions of childhood's ambiguity in adult institutions. *Childhood, 6*(4), 455–474.

Masschelein, J. (2006). Experience and the limits of governmentality. *Educational Philosophy and Theory, 38*(4), 561–576.

Masschelein, J. (2010a). The idea of critical educational research: Educating the gaze and inviting to go walking. In I. Gurzeev (Ed.), *The possibility/impossibility of a new critical language in education* (pp. 275–291). Sense.

Masschelein, J. (2010b). E-ducating the gaze: The idea of a poor pedagogy. *Ethics and Education, 5*(1), 43–53.

Quennerstedt, A. (2010). Children, but not really humans? Critical reflections on the hampering effect of the "3 p's". *International Journal of Children's Rights, 18*, 619–635.

Quennerstedt, A. (2013). Children's rights research moving into the future – Challenges on the way forward. *International Journal of Children's Rights, 21*(2), 233–247.

Quennerstedt, A., Robinson, C., & I'Anson, J. (2018). The UNCRC – The voice of global consensus on children's rights? *Nordic Journal of Human Rights/Nordisk Tidsskrift for Menneskerettigheter, 38*(1), 38–54.

Readings, B. (1992). Pagans, perverts or primitives? In P. Dhillon & P. Standish (Eds.), *Lyotard: Just education*. Routledge.

Reynaert, D., Bouverne-De Bie, M., & Vandevelde, S. (2012). Between "believers" and "opponents": Critical discussions on children's rights. *International Journal of Children's Rights, 20*(1), 155–168.

Schweisfurth, M. (2011). Learner-centred education in developing country contexts: From solution to problem? *International Journal of Educational Development, 31*(5), 425–432.

Scottish Government. (2012). *A guide to getting it right for every child*. Scottish Government. http://www.scotland.gov.uk/Resource/0039/00394308.pdf. Accessed 15 Aug 2019.

Scottish Government. (2014). *Building the ambition: National practice guidance on early learning and childcare*. Scottish Government. Retrieved August 15, 2019, from: https://education.gov.scot/improvement/Pages/elc1buildingtheambition.aspx. Accessed Aug 2019.

Scottish Government. (2019). *Children's rights: Consultation on incorporating the United Nations Convention on the Rights of the Child into our domestic law in Scotland*. Retrieved August 15, 2019, from: https://www.gov.scot/publications/childrens-rights-consultation-incorporating-uncrc-rights-child-domestic-law-scotland/pages/2/

Spratt, J. (2016). Childhood wellbeing: What role for education? *British Educational Research Journal, 42*(2), 223–239.

Spratt, J. (2017). *Wellbeing, equity and education: A critical analysis of policy discourses of well-being in schools*. Springer.

Stoltz, S. A., & Biesta, G. (2018). Gert Biesta on thinking philosophically about education; Thinking educationally about philosophy in education and educational research. In J. Quay, J. Bleazby, S. Stolz, M. Toscano, & S. Webster (Eds.), *Theory and philosophy in education research: Methodological dialogues*. Routledge.

Thompson, P. (2013). Learner-centred education and "cultural translation". *International Journal of Educational Development, 33*(1), 48–58.

Tisdall, E. K. M. (2015). Children's rights and children's wellbeing: Equivalent policy concepts? *Journal of Social Policy, 44*(4), 807–823.

Tisdall, E. K. M., & Punch, S. (2012). Not so 'new'? Looking critically at childhood studies. *Children's Geographies, 10*(3), 249–264.

United Nations (UN). (1989). *The United Nations Convention on the Rights of the Child (UNCRC)*. General Assembly resolution 44/25, 20 Nov. 1989. U.N. Doc. A/ RES/44/25. http://www.ohchr.org/en/professionalinterest/pages/crc.aspx. Accessed 15 Aug 2019.

United Nations (UN). (2001). *General comment no. 1: The aims of education (Article 29)*. Adopted by the Committee on the Rights of the Child at the Twenty-sixth Session, CRC/GC/2001/1, 17 April 2001. https://www.ohchr.org/EN/Issues/Education/Training/Compilation/Pages/a)GeneralCommentNo1TheAimsofEducation(article29)(2001).aspx. Accessed July 2019.

Young, J. O., & Brunk, C. G. (2012). *The ethics of cultural appropriation*. Wiley-Blackwell.

Chapter 3
"Teaching and Learning Together": One Model of Rights-Centred Secondary Teacher Preparation in the United States

Heather Curl and Alison Cook-Sather

Abstract Perhaps in part because it never ratified the United Nations Convention on the Rights of the Child (UNCRC), the United States neither systematically focuses on children's personalities or talents nor ensures the respect and valuing of students' culture, as specified in Article 29 of the UNCRC. Instead, narrow conceptions of success and the particularly insidious influences of White supremacist and anti-immigrant perspectives undermine the rights outlined in Article 29. Despite these conditions, individual educators attempt to foster rights-centred education that prioritises the perspectives, personalities, and cultures of young people. We present one example of such efforts: "Teaching and Learning Together," which positions secondary students as pedagogical partners to undergraduate, secondary teacher candidates. This project enables deep engagement with the perspectives of students—a necessary foundation for teachers who foster the personalities, talents, and cultures of their students. Providing grounding for appreciation of the rich knowledge and deep insight students and their communities bring—and an understanding of participation in their own education as a right—this program represents one model for developing the capacities among teachers in the United States necessary to realising the goals of Article 29 as an ethical imperative in the absence of any national commitment.

Keywords Student-centred · Rights of the child in the U.S. · Success · Teacher education · Anti-immigrant and White supremacist rhetoric and policy

---

H. Curl (✉)
Antioch University Seattle, Seattle, WA, USA
e-mail: hcurl@antioch.edu

A. Cook-Sather
Bryn Mawr College, Bryn Mawr, PA, USA
e-mail: acooksat@brynmawr.edu

J. Gillett-Swan, N. Thelander (eds.), *Children's Rights from International Educational Perspectives*, Transdisciplinary Perspectives in Educational Research 2, https://doi.org/10.1007/978-3-030-80861-7_3

The Rights of the Child in a U.S. Context

While the United States (U.S.) has ratified Article 2 of the Universal Declaration of Human Rights, which views education as a human right and calls for education to be "directed to the full development of the human personality and to the strengthening of respect for human rights and fundamental freedoms," the U.S. is the only country in the world not to have ratified the United Nations (1989) Convention on the Rights of the Child. Educational policies and practices in the U.S. are therefore not guided by Article 29's mandate that "children's education should develop a child's personality, talents and abilities to the fullest" and "encourage children to respect others, human rights and their own and other cultures," with a particular focus on education's role in "develop[ing] respect for the values and culture of [students'] parents" (United Nations, 1989). They are also not guided by Article 12, which stipulates that students are *entitled* to express their perspectives and be heard. Articles 29 and 12 are key components of the UNCRC framework for children's right to *participate* in their own lives, their own education (Mason, 2005). We argue that, in the absence of national commitment to these tenets, it is a matter of ethical imperative and individual initiative to embed in the U.S. education system "rights-respecting" curricula and pedagogy that include the perspectives, voices, and participation of students (Lundy & Cook-Sather, 2016).

The United States' refusal to ratify the UNCRC is, in part, due to a larger set of underlying premises according to which students, and education, are understood. A hearty commitment to local control (Scribner, 2016; Smolin, 2006) alongside an embrace of a power imbalance between those who "know" (teachers) and those who "learn" (students) prevent U.S. educational policy—and much of practice—from valuing and structuring students' participation in their own learning and education. In contrast, "core principles of both children's rights and student voice call for a kind of respect and shared responsibility—a partnership, in essence—that the traditional hierarchies and power imbalances structured into educational institutions do not easily allow or support" (Lundy & Cook-Sather, 2016, p. 274).

In recent years, we have seen this power imbalance increase and the potential for individual teachers and institutions to support children's rights as articulated in Article 29 become even more difficult to realise. This chapter highlights two of these realities in the U.S.: narrow conceptions of success and anti-immigrant and White supremacist rhetoric and policy. These realities relate directly to the two aspects of Article 29 noted above, that: "children's education should develop a child's personality, talents and abilities to the fullest" and "encourage children to respect others, human rights and their own and other cultures." When educational success is based solely on scores on standardised tests, a child's personality and talents are not a priority. Similarly, encouraging students to respect others' cultures seems counter to national policy and rhetoric that actively devalues, dismisses, and dehumanises certain groups of people.

In this chapter we present an argument for what works against "rights-respecting" education, and we offer one model that strives to work for such education. We first explore how narrow conceptions of success and White supremacist anti-immigrant rhetoric and policy limit education's enactment of the principles articulated in Article 29. We then describe and draw on a program that each of us has led to explore the potential role that teacher education might play in supporting new teachers in creating individual classrooms that resist traditional notions of power within education and challenge the current policies and practices in the United States that limit children's right to realise their potential, as defined by Article 29 in the UNCRC. This chapter is, then, a theoretical exploration that we hope will inspire others to consider what they can do, with or without a formal human rights treaty.

Narrow Conceptions of Success

The negative impacts of No Child Left Behind have been well documented, among them the narrowing of curriculum and pedagogy toward test-friendly content and methods (Crocco & Crostigan, 2007; Kempf, 2016) and a negative impact on teacher-student relationships and teacher professional well-being (Valli & Buese, 2007). In a multi-city study with teachers in the United States and Canada, Kempf (2016) found that "teaching to the test often means teaching the knowledge and skills needed to succeed on tests, as opposed to teaching the knowledge and skills that a test aims to measure", which "can result in the use of a limited variety of teaching and learning strategies" (p. 72).

While the benefits of increased accountability (Jellig, 2013) and a wealth of data (Phelps, 2005) should not be ignored, it is undeniable that the narrow conceptions of success championed by the high-stakes testing movement have made supporting children's right to realise their potential difficult. In particular, the idea that "children's education should develop a child's personality, talents and abilities to the fullest" (United Nations, 1989, Article 29) is counter to the stated priorities in U.S. education policy and practice, including: "to promote student achievement and preparation for global competitiveness by fostering educational excellence and ensuring equal access" (U.S. Department of Education[1]). In practice, this has meant ensuring that students demonstrate their skill or content knowledge in literacy and math in a standardised format that has been demonstrated to discriminate based on class and race (Delgado, 2014).

The rise of high-stakes testing has also narrowed the subject matter offered to students. With the increasingly exclusive focus on those subjects tested, subjects such as art (Baker, 2012; Sabol, 2010) and social studies (Heafner & Fitchett, 2012) are taught less and less. Learning has thus become a set of skills-based activities that can be quantifiably measured, rather than an outcome of curiosity or deep thinking or an extension of natural talents and interests (Crocco & Crostigan, 2007; Kempf,

[1] U.S. Department of Education (Mission) https://www2.ed.gov/about/overview/mission/mission.html

2016). In her recent book, Wexler (2019) argues for increasing content knowledge in schools, since the "federal No Child Left Behind legislation made standardized reading and math scores the yardstick for measuring progress" (p. 7). She notes in particular that access to content knowledge about other countries and cultures is also limited since "the time spent on…social studies decreased" (p. 7).

This focus on narrowly conceived measures of success limits educators' capacity to support children's right to realise their potential, particularly in its exclusion of a child's talents and curiosities when those might be beyond math or literacy. Quantifying students' capacities through standardised tests that privilege certain forms and expressions of knowledge might also limit the development of a child's personality, talents, or abilities to the fullest. The narrowed curriculum (Crocco & Crostigan, 2007) and limited conceptions of success students are taught, and to which they are held accountable, do not begin to address their personalities or capacities, let alone promote their full development especially for those students who have personalities and abilities that better align with abstract thinking, or with talents in the arts.

This reduction of students to how they perform on standardised tests in combination with devaluing social studies education limits our ability to teach students to "live peaceably with one another" and to respect their own and other cultures. Living in community, exploring human rights, and using one's own voice through democratic citizenship are foundational skills clearly articulated in Article 29. Even in districts or states where these goals are explicitly framed as social studies standards (OSPI, 2019), they are increasingly ignored in elementary classrooms due to the persistent focus on literacy and math only (Wexler, 2019). When policy dictates so heavily what *should* be taught (i.e., literacy and math), it becomes harder for teachers to decide what else might be taught beyond those mandates. Like the students with whom they work, teachers cannot develop capacities to be respectful of and responsive to their students' diverse identities, needs, and interests if they are prepared only to shepherd students toward standardised measures of knowledge, capacity, and achievement (Lundy & Cook-Sather, 2016). This is why teacher education serves as a useful liminal space of growth and development (Cook-Sather & Curl, 2016), and a hopeful entry point for future teachers developing a commitment to supporting children's right to realise their potential.

Embracing commitments captured in Article 29's tenets requires new skill development for both teachers and students. Conditioned now to care about a learning opportunity only if it is "on the test," both students and teachers need the chance to practice new ways of teaching and learning that are grounded in human rights and respect for others and that situate students' talents and personalities as central in curricula and pedagogical decisions. As Lundy and Cook-Sather (2016) argue, "For a right-based framework to be taken up and not merely imposed, each differently positioned player within education, including students themselves, needs to develop the dispositions, knowledge and tools necessary to make this shift" (p. 274).

"Teaching and Learning Together", the project we highlight in this discussion, offers one institutional structure, set of commitments, and opportunity through which both students and prospective teachers can develop and deepen these skills.

Because it is integral to the approach to teacher education that we offer at the colleges where the project is situated (Cook-Sather et al., forthcoming), it prepares prospective teachers to foster in their own classrooms, with their own students, an approach to education that develops a child's personality, talents, and abilities, respect for others, human rights, and their own and other cultures, and the capacity and commitment to live peaceably with one another. It therefore also actively works against another set of socio-political forces that currently drive practice: hostile immigration and White supremacist rhetoric and policies.

Hostile Immigration & White Supremacist Rhetoric and Policies

The United States, stained with a founding that includes displacement, murder, and enslavement of non-White peoples, has developed an educational system that mirrors the inequity of its beginning. This system once overtly enacted these inequities through banning education, forcing assimilation and, subsequently, racially segregating schools. It now "egregiously" invests unevenly in public schooling, both within and across states (Baker et al., 2018, p. 23), with funding disparities for vulnerable students as dramatic in some states as in excess of $10,000 per pupil (Baker et al., 2018). The premise of White supremacy, the belief in the superiority of White people and their right to dominate others, underlies both these historical and current practices.

Situated in this history and perpetuation of structural inequity, the United States school system is clearly not committed to the goals articulated in Article 29 of the UNCRC, particularly not as those would manifest in students "respect[ing] others, human rights and their own and other cultures." Such explicit and extreme disparities in valuing and in funding mean that fostering respect for others is undermined by a system that perpetuates the racial and ethnic hierarchies on which the nation was built and that persist today not only in unequal funding but also in anti-immigration and White supremacist rhetoric and action.

Respect for students, families, and cultures, captured in Article 29 as an assertion that "children have a particular responsibility to respect the rights of their parents, and education should aim to develop respect for the values and culture of their parents" (United Nations, 1989), is also largely absent from policy and therefore from much practice. Unfortunately, instead of having access to diverse curricula and respectful representations of their communities, many students in the United States are taught a narrow and inaccurate history of "blind patriotism" (Loewen, 2007, p.6) and are bombarded with negative portrayals of their culture, communities, and parents. Recent attempts to teach a more accurate U.S. history in the wake of George Floyd's murder and the subsequent protests for racial justice have been challenged by state bans against teaching about race and racism in schools (Sawchuk, 2021). In addition, children whose education should be protected via the landmark case *Plyer vs. Doe,* which promises education to every child in the country regardless of citizenship status, instead: are separated from their families (Chotiner, 2019); must deal with the consequences of increased deportation rates (Boehm & Terrio, 2019); are banned from studying the history of their own culture (Cammarato & Romero, 2014); and are required to learn English at times to the detriment of maintaining their home languages, often an important component of the culture of their parents (Davidson & Burson, 2017).

Like the founding principles of the country, these practices and policies are born of a set of racist and nativist attitudes that are essential to name and analyse, given "the ability of public sentiment to influence public policy" (Davidson & Burson, 2017, p. 42). Rather than learn to respect their culture and/or the culture of their families, students have instead been told by the former President of the United States that they come from "sh*thole countries" (Zimmerman, 2018) or by their teachers that they and their families are "illegal" and should be "removed" (Victor, 2019, p. 17). It is difficult to imagine attitudes and expressions more antithetical to respecting others, human rights, and students' own and other cultures.

These racist rhetoric and actions are linked to a rise in both hate crimes (Eligon, 2018) and conflict within schools (Rogers et al., 2017). According to an annual FBI report in 2018, 7100 hate crimes were reported in 2017, and "nearly three out of five were motivated by race and ethnicity" (Eligon, 2018, p. 21). In schools, similar findings indicate a rise in "derogatory remarks about other groups during class discussions" (Rogers et al., 2017, p. vi). In a report called *Teaching and Learning in the Age of Trump* produced by UCLA's Institute for Democracy, Education, and Access, some teachers described how "the political environment 'unleashed' virulently racist, anti-Islamic, anti-Semitic, or homophobic rhetoric in their schools and classrooms" (2017, p. 28). Now, in the wake of so called "Critical Race Theory bans" in Republican led state legislatures across the U.S., some teachers, specifically in Texas, fear that lessons about social studies and current events will be limited "in ways that give a generation of Texas students an incomplete and white-centric view of history and the world around them" (Zou & Kao, 2021, para 3).

Depending, of course, on the context, the idea that students might be taught to "live peacefully" and "respect the cultures of others" is difficult to envision as a reality when such hostile language, beliefs and policies are modelled by leaders and permeate schools and classrooms throughout the United States. The implications for student learning are also stark. Teachers reported that "students who were victims of verbal assaults withdrew from class discussions and sometimes missed class altogether" (Rogers et al., 2017, p. vi). Some have attributed these rises in racial and ethnic violence to "emboldened individuals" who feel "more open and notorious with their racial hatred" (Eligon, 2018, p. 21) due to public rhetoric and overt racist policies.

As the demographics of the nation continue to change, with an increase in non-White students predicted over the next decades (Bryant et al., 2017), we argue that the need has never been greater to fully commit as a nation to the rights of all children. In fact, the specific intentions described in the Convention of the Rights of the Child speak directly to the difficulties many students in the United States face. While the structural inequities described here cannot be solved solely in classrooms or in the teacher education programs that prepare prospective teachers to enter those classrooms, how we prepare teachers to think about, plan for, and respond to students can make a difference. The following section presents one model for supporting teachers in developing the knowledge, skills, and dispositions necessary to combat the tendency for racist perspectives and practices to enter the school and the classroom. This model was not developed to adhere to Article 29 of the UNCRC, since that is not required in the United States, but it was developed with the spirit of Article 29's tenets in mind.

Working from Within: Teacher Education

"Teaching and Learning Together" (TLT) was created in 1995 as an integral component of the secondary teaching methods course both of us have taught at Bryn Mawr and Haverford Colleges[i]. TLT invites secondary students to assume the role of pedagogical consultant to prospective secondary teachers enrolled in the methods course during the semester prior to practice teaching. In this way TLT creates a structure underpinned by respect for students, and it positions them as those with legitimate experiences and important perspectives that should inform the preparation of future teachers. The project has four components, each of which we explain below.

The first component of the project is a weekly email exchange between each prospective teacher enrolled in the college course and a secondary student who attends a local school. Each pair explores topics addressed in weekly seminars at the college (i.e., what makes a good teacher, lesson plan, test, etc.) but also includes topics the pairs feel are relevant to teaching and learning more generally—how students experience the social dynamics at their school, their home communities, and the politics of the country and the wider world. These exchanges afford both prospective teachers and the students with whom they are in dialogue an opportunity to get to know one another, strive to understand their differences of experience and perspective, and develop respect for one another and capacity to communicate across their differences.

The second component is weekly conversations among secondary students convened by school-based educators and held at the students' school. The discussions last for approximately 30 min and are held after school or during lunch. Like the email exchange, these conversations are based on the topics explored in the college seminar. They are audiotaped, uploaded as podcasts, and assigned as required reading to the preservice teachers. This forum affords the secondary students an opportunity to articulate the diversity of their experiences and insights and to develop confidence in presenting those to the prospective teachers with whom they are in dialogue. It also signals to students that their experiences, voices, and perspectives matter—they are part of the curriculum.

The third component is weekly discussions in the college course focused on how the email exchange is going and what preservice teachers are struggling with, learning, and integrating into their plans for practice. This forum requires that the prospective teachers wrestle with their own assumptions about who has knowledge, power, and legitimacy in relation to developing learning and teaching practices and, like the secondary students, it allows them to develop language for naming those in dialogue. It also requires that they develop teaching practices informed by these understandings.

The final component of the project is an end-of-semester analysis paper for which each preservice teacher selects a focus for exploration and draws on and quotes excerpts from the email exchanges, podcasts of discussions among the secondary students, and college-based class discussions. This component of TLT requires prospective teachers to step back from the experience of being in a semester-long dialogue with a student and hearing the perspectives of the whole group of students, treat those perspectives as valid forms of knowledge, and make sense of what they experience in terms of how it will inform their thinking and practice as teachers.

The TLT project is situated within a wider set of assignments for the preservice teachers, including reading theoretical and practical texts, shadowing their student partners at the students' schools for a full school day, and visiting their student partners at home with the school-based educator who facilitates their weekly dialogue. The secondary student participants are selected by the school-based educators with whom we have collaborated. The goal is to recruit a diverse group, including a variety of gender identities, those who are assigned to different tracks, and those who claim different racial, ethnic, and class backgrounds. Students are paid modest stipends for their participation and the school-based teachers are also remunerated. To date, over 250 secondary students and certification candidates have participated in the project. Originally supported by grants from the Ford Foundation and the Arthur Vining Davis Foundations, TLT has been fully supported by Bryn Mawr and Haverford Colleges since 2000 (See Cook-Sather, 2002a, b, 2007, 2009, 2010; Cook-Sather & Curl, 2014, 2016; Cook-Sather et al., forthcoming, for other discussions of this project).

While not expressly designed to meet UNCRC standards, this approach strives to enact tenets of Article 29 in two distinct ways: (1) informing the mindset and beliefs of the preservice teacher; and (2) understanding and practicing education in equity-focused, ecological, and sustainable terms.

TLT fosters the development in secondary teachers of both a mindset and a set of skills that allow and incline them to develop a child's personality, talents, and abilities to the fullest. Because TLT is itself premised on respect for and attention to students' experiences and perspectives, it in turn fosters the development of teachers who value and insist on encouraging children to respect others, human rights, and their own and other cultures. In this way, teacher candidates who participate in TLT approach teaching and learning committed to the importance of developing student personality and perspective and honouring the whole student through relationship. Even as policy and mandates limit these perspectives, these teacher candidates come to their work with this commitment already embedded and so can make decisions within their own school and classroom that foster values and actions articulated in Article 29.

Second, the equity focus and "ecological perspective" (Cook-Sather & Curl, 2014, p.85) embraced and enacted by TLT help pre-service teachers, and, in turn, their students, learn to consider and combat inequities, live peacefully, protect the environment, and respect other people. As we have argued previously (Cook-Sather & Curl, 2014), the project embraces and enacts the notion of ecology in its broadest sense: as a new paradigm for the preparation of teachers (Nolet, 2009) that is not so much "*about* sustainability" or "*for* particular sustainable development outcomes" (2014, p. 87, *emphasis added*). The approach re-conceptualises education *as* teaching sustainability: "nurturing critical, systemic and reflective thinking; creativity; self organisation; and adaptive management" (Sterling, 2004, pp. 56–57). Learning to teach, and then teaching to support students, is a process of developing resilience within teaching-learning relationships in a way that acknowledges and aims to deal with uncertainty (Fazey, 2010). Because "stable structures like equilibrium or homeostasis do not accurately reflect natural systems...[and because] wherever we seek to find constancy we discover change" (Mentz, 2001, pp. 156–157), TLT embraces a "new ecology" that sees sustainability as the preservation and development of life and further capacity for life in and through change.

These shifts in orientation and the development of skills among the pre-service teachers facilitate pedagogical decision making and practices that further support realisation of the tenets captured in Article 29 at the classroom level. A teacher, for instance, who values students' perspectives and seeks to get to know their students or works to build equity-minded, resilient, and sustainable relationships in their classrooms will better attend to students' talents and personalities and ensure that students learn skills to live in ways that are peaceful and respectful of a diversity of people, even when this is not actively prioritised in policy, when districts do not encourage these practices, or when national discourse is anti-immigrant or hostile to people of colour. Participation in TLT ensures that teacher candidates build knowledge about instruction, curricular decisions, and management strategies that are grounded in and that respect student ideas, perspectives, and realities.

Discussion and Concluding Thoughts

Structurally, there are barriers to realising in the U.S. the commitments captured in Article 29's mandates that "children's education should develop a child's personality, talents and abilities to the fullest" and "encourage children to respect others, human rights and their own and other cultures" (United Nations, 1989). Working toward establishing students' (and families') rights in the education system in the absence of a treaty such as the CRC is of paramount importance and could be further advanced beyond individual efforts with the support of legislators, policymakers, and politicians. Such work requires a shift in mindset away from limited conceptions of what measures of success look like (high-stakes testing) and whom success is for (privileged, White Americans) toward recognising and valuing the talents, personalities, and rights of all children and their families. Despite the historical and current realities in the United States and the seemingly uphill battle of working against those, we can still create programs that are true to the spirit of Article 29 and what it articulates and calls for.

The notion that student perspectives, and students themselves, matter and the embrace of an equity-minded and ecological framework for teaching and learning go a long way toward supporting preservice teachers in developing classroom communities and instructional practices that support students to reach their full potential. This individual effort does not change the historical violence, damaging policies, or devaluing of personality and culture so prevalent in our education system, but it creates the space and one model for a different way of being that is true to the spirit and intentions of the Rights of the Child. In the face of dehumanising educational practices and total disregard for the rights and importance of children and young people crossing and within our borders, attending to the mindset and skills of teachers entering classrooms is one way to suspend hopelessness (Curl & Lesnick, 2018) or maintain hope in such darkness. Working teacher by teacher will not fix a system, but it can ensure that we and others maintain commitment to what education can be, what rights children should have. For these reasons we identify the increasing challenge—and stress the concomitant importance—of striving to inspire in prospective teachers the spirit of Article 29 and pedagogical practices informed and guided by that spirit.

References

Baker, R.-A. (2012). The effects of high-stakes testing policy on arts education. *Arts Education Policy Review, 113*(1), 17–25. https://doi.org/10.1080/10632913.2012.626384

Baker, B., Farrie, D., & Sciarra, D. (2018). Is school funding fair? A national report card. *Education Law Center*. https://edlawcenter.org/assets/files/pdfs/publications/Is_School_Funding_Fair_7th_Editi.pdf

Boehm, D., & Terrio, S. (2019). *Illegal encounters: The effect of detention and deportation on young people*. NYU Press.

Bryant, A., Triplett, N., Watson, M., & Lewis, C. (2017). The browning of American public schools: Evidence of increasing racial diversity and the implications for policy, practice, and student outcomes. *Urban Review, 49*(2), 263–278.

Cammarota, J., & Romero, A. (2014). *Raza studies: The public option for educational revolution*. The University of Arizona Press.

Chotiner, I. (2019, July 13). How the stress of separation and detention changes the lives of children. *The New Yorker*. https://www.newyorker.com/news/q-anda/how-the-stress-of-separation-and-detention-changes-the-lives-of-children

Cook-Sather, A. (2002a). Authorizing students' perspectives: Toward trust, dialogue, and change in education. *Educational Researcher, 31*(4), 3–14.

Cook-Sather, A. (2002b). Re(in)forming the conversations: Student position, power, and voice in teacher education. *Radical Teacher, 64*, 21–28.

Cook-Sather, A. (2007). What would happen if we treated students as those with opinions that matter? The benefits to principals and teachers of supporting youth engagement in school. *NASSP Bulletin, 91*(4), 343–362.

Cook-Sather, A. (2009). "I am not afraid to listen": Prospective teachers learning from students to work in city schools. *Theory Into Practice, 48*(3), 176–181.

Cook-Sather, A. (2010). Students as learners and teachers: Taking responsibility, transforming education, and redefining accountability. *Curriculum Inquiry, 40*(4), 555–575.

Cook-Sather, A., & Curl, H. (2014). "I want to listen to my students' lives": Developing an ecological perspective in learning to teach. *Teacher Education Quarterly, 41*(1), 85–103.

Cook-Sather, A., & Curl, H. (2016). Positioning students as teacher educators: Preparing learners to transform schools. In A. Montgomery & I. Kehoe (Eds.), *Reimagining the purpose of schools and educational organisation: Developing critical thinking, agency, beliefs in schools and educational organisations* (pp. 65–76). Springer.

Cook-Sather, A., Curl, H., & Wilson, C. (forthcoming). Intersecting voices: An integrative approach to applying the student voice research framework in teacher education. In M. Brasof & J. Levitan (Eds.), *Student voice research: theory and methods*. Teachers College Press.

Crocco, M. S., & Costigan, A. T. (2007). The narrowing of curriculum and pedagogy in the age of accountability: Urban educators speak out. *Urban Education, 42*(6), 512–535.

Curl, H., & Lesnick, A. (2018). "Beyond fix it or leave it: toward conflict-centered theories of change in education work." *The Sojo Journal, 3*(1), 27–40.

Davidson, T., & Burson, K. (2017). Keep those kids out: Nativism and attitudes toward access to public education for the children of undocumented immigrants. *Journal of Latinos and Education, 16*(1), 41–50. https://doi.org/10.1080/15348431.2016.1179189

Delgado, R. (2014). Standardized testing as discrimination: A reply to Dan Subotnik. *University of Massachusetts Law Review, 9*(1), 98–107. https://scholarship.law.umassd.edu/umlr/vol9/iss1/4

Eligon, J. (2018, November 13). Hate crimes in U.S. increase for the third year in a row, the F.B.I. reports. *The New York Times*, Section A, p. 21. https://www.nytimes.com/2018/11/13/us/hate-crimes-fbi-2017.html

Fazey, I. (2010). Resilience and higher order thinking. *Ecology and Society, 15*(3), 9. http://www.ecologyandsociology.org/vol15/iss3/art9/

Heafner, T. L., & Fitchett, P. G. (2012). Tipping the scales: National trends of declining social studies instructional time in elementary schools. *Journal of Social Studies Research, 36*(2), 190–215.

Jellig, G. (2013, November 12). In defense of NCLB: One school's journey toward intentional practice. *Education Week, 33*(12), 24–28.

Kempf, A. (2016). *The pedagogy of standardized testing: The radical impacts of educational standardization in the US and Canada*. Palgrave Macmillan.

Loewen, J. W. (2007). *Lies my teacher told me: Everything your American history textbook got wrong*. Touchstone.

Lundy, L., & Cook-Sather, A. (2016). Children's rights and student voice: Their intersections and the implications for curriculum and pedagogy. In D. Wyse, L. Hayward, & J. Pandya (Eds.), *The SAGE handbook of curriculum, pedagogy and assessment*, 2v. https://doi.org/10.4135/9781473921405.n17

Mason, M. A. (2005). The U.S. and the international children's rights crusade: Leader or laggard? *Journal of Social History, 38*(4), 955–963. https://www.jstor.org/stable/3790484?seq=1#page_scan_tab_contents

Mentz, S. (2001). Tongues in the storm: Shakespeare, ecological crisis, and the resources of genre. In L. Bruckner & D. Brayton (Eds.), *Ecocritical Shakespeare* (pp. 55–72). Ashgate.

Nolet, V. (2009). Preparing sustainability-literate teachers. *Teachers College Record, 111*(2), 409–442.

Office of Superintendent of Public Instruction (OSPI). (2019, September 17). New social studies standards set for washington K-12 students. *Auburn examiner*. https://auburnexaminer.com/new-social-studies-standards-set-for-washington-k-12-students/
Phelps, R. (2005). *Defending standardized testing*. L. Erlbaum Associates.
Rogers, J., Franke, M., Yun, J. E., Ishimoto, M., Diera, C., Geller, R., Berryman, A., & Brenes, T. (2017). *Teaching and learning in the age of Trump: Increasing stress and hostility in America's high schools*. UCLA's Institute for Democracy, Education, and Access. https://files.eric.ed.gov/fulltext/ED580203.pdf
Sabol, F. R. (2010). *No child left behind: A study of its impact on art education*. Purdue University.
Sawchuk. (2021). https://www.edweek.org/leadership/local-school-boards-are-also-banning-lessons-on-race-heres-how-that-looks-in-7-districts/2021/08
Scribner, C. (2016). *The fight for local control: Schools, suburbs, and American Democracy*. Cornell University Press.
Smolin, D. M. (2006). Overcoming religious objections to the Convention of the Rights of the Child. *The Emory Law Journal, 20*, 83. https://heinonline.org/HOL/LandingPage?handle=hein.journals/emint20&div=11&id=&page=&t=1556652426
Standards. The Office of Superintendent of Public Instruction. https://www.k12.wa.us/student-success/resources-subject-area/social-studies
Sterling, S. (2004). An analysis of sustainability education internationally: Evolution, interpretation, and transformative potential. In J. Blewitt & C. Cullingford (Eds.), *The sustainability curriculum: The challenge for higher education* (pp. 43–62). Earthscan.
United Nations. (1989). *Convention on the Rights of the Child*. https://www.unicef.org/child-rights-convention/convention-text
Valli, L., & Buese, D. (2007). The changing roles of teachers in an era of high-stakes accountability. *American Educational Research Journal, 44*(3), 519–558.
Victor, D. (2019, June 5). Teacher fired over tweets asking to expel immigrants. *The New York Times*, Section A, p. 17. https://www.nytimes.com/2019/06/05/us/teacher-tweets-trump-georgia-clark.html
Wexler, N. (2019). *The knowledge gap: The hidden cause of America's broken education system—And how to fix it*. Penguin Random House.
Zimmerman, J. (2018, January 15). Teaching in Trump's America: Debating with decency isn't easy when the president is profane. *The Philadelphia Inquirer*. https://www.inquirer.com/philly/opinion/commentary/shithole-countries-trump-debate-civil-discourse-20180115.html
Zou, I., & Kao, J. (2021, August 3). Texas teachers say GOP's new social studies law will hinder how an entire generation understands race, history and current events. *The Texas Tribune*. https://www.texastribune.org/2021/08/03/texas-critical-race-theory-social-studies-teachers/

Chapter 4
The Educational Rights of Children with Disability in Australia

Satine Winter and Kate de Bruin

Abstract Children with disabilities' right to an education are articulated through Articles 23 and 28 of the Convention on the Rights for Children (UNCRC) and viewed in conjunction with Article 29. Advances in disability rights and educational practices have meant the interpretation and realisation of disability rights in education do not align with the original text of the UNCRC. We explore and critique disability rights for children *in*, *to*, and *through* the Australian educational context and examine how enacted domestic legislation and policy align with the obligations outlined in the UNCRC. Our analysis of the rights of children with disabilities reveals inconsistencies and conflicts between the articulation of disability rights in the UNCRC and their realisation *in* and *to* education in practice. Moreover, children with disabilities rights are found to be inferior to non-disabled children's rights and lacking in the future vision for education. We recommend the need to update the UNCRC and to use other disability specific Conventions to fully realise disability educational rights.

Keywords Access · Children with disabilities · Education · Educational rights · Inclusion · Legislation · Segregation

---

S. Winter (✉)
James Cook University, Cairns, Australia
e-mail: satine.winter@jcu.edu.au

K. de Bruin
Monash University, Melbourne, Australia
e-mail: catriona.debruin@monash.edu

J. Gillett-Swan, N. Thelander (eds.), *Children's Rights from International Educational Perspectives*, Transdisciplinary Perspectives in Educational Research 2, https://doi.org/10.1007/978-3-030-80861-7_4

Introduction

Children's rights have existed for almost a century with the League of Nations releasing the Declaration on the Rights of the Child in 1924 following the devastation and atrocities of World War I. The League of Nations noted particular groups of children whose rights were considered at risk such as the "hungry", the "sick", and the "backward" (League of Nations, 1924, p. 10). Since that time, special measures to safeguard the rights of vulnerable groups of children, have been successively refined in two international policy documents: the Declaration of the Rights of the Child (United Nations, 1959) and the Convention on the Rights of the Child (UNCRC; United Nations, 1989). Both of these documents were ground-breaking, particularly the UNCRC (United Nations, 1989), which went beyond the aspirational nature of the earlier Declarations and provided binding responsibilities for signatory states.

The UNCRC was written during the United Nations Decade of Disabled Persons and reflected this zeitgeist by becoming the first human rights treaty to use the word "disability" (United Nations, 2003). The UNCRC remains the most widely ratified human rights treaty in history. This treaty has led to some important and substantial improvements in many aspects of children's rights, including in education. Prior to the UNCRC, approximately one in every five children of primary school age was not in school worldwide but, since the UNCRC's implementation, this number has almost halved (UNICEF, 2019). Despite this progress, many children with disabilities around the world continue to be disproportionately denied access to a quality education (Economic and Social Council, 2019), reducing the possibility of the aims of education being realised for these children. Addressing the number of children who remain out of school is vital to achieve the UN's vision of an equitable society in which all humans can be educated and reach their potential.

Issues Identified by the CRC Committee

The UNCRC Committee developed several General Comments to provide interpretation and guidance to State Party signatories. Two General Comments are specifically relevant to discussing the aims of education for children with disability: General Comment 1 on the 'aims of education' (Committee on the Rights of the Child, 2001) and General Comment 9 on "The Rights of Children with Disabilities" (Committee on the Rights of the Child, 2007). In General Comment 9, concerns were raised by the UNCRC Committee about State Parties and the adequacy of domestic legislation to fully recognise, enshrine, and uphold the rights of children with disabilities. The Committee further recognised the potential negation of capacity for children with disabilities to benefit from the aims of education. Similarly, within General Comment 1, the Committee observed a lack of understanding by State Parties on the integrated and complementary nature of rights and provisions for children with disabilities within the UNCRC. In both General Comments, the UN emphasised that educational rights of children with disability articulated in Article 23 of the UNCRC are to be interpreted within the context of all rights in the Convention and not in isolation.

Together, the issues emphasised within these General Comments about lack of educational access and limitations in realising rights in legislation and practice for children with disabilities highlight the need to examine Article 23 more closely in relation to State Parties' interpretation of educational rights and related obligations within their jurisdictions. Accordingly, in our chapter, we undertake an analysis, critique and evaluation of how educational rights are articulated within the UNCRC. Our focus is on school-aged children with disability, providing references to Australia as a case example of how the UNCRC is enacted within domestic policy of a State Party. First, we begin by analysing how disability rights in education are articulated within the Convention itself, and how they differ from the rights articulated for "all" children. Second, we review and critique the efforts to realise educational rights for school students with disability within the case study country of Australia and make particular reference to national disability legislation and policies directly linked to obligations under the UNCRC. Third, we conclude by evaluating the UNCRC as an instrument for achieving the educational entitlements and freedoms intended for all children within the Universal Declaration of Human Rights and in the International Covenants on Human Rights.

Disability and Educational Rights Under the Convention on the Rights of the Child

Educational rights for "all" children within the UNCRC (United Nations, 1989) are specified within Articles 28 and 29. These include the right *to* an education in terms of access, rights *within* education, such as the quality of teaching and provision of support, and also rights *through* education, such to have one's full potential nurtured and to be prepared for life beyond school as a valued and contributing member of a peaceful and cohesive society. Access to an education is a foundational right because it acts as a precursor to the full realisation of both these opportunities and aims. It is an enabler of other human rights. Yet, if educational access is poor, then the aims of education remain unrealised. Therefore, while the majority of the chapter attends to discussion and critique of children's rights *in* and *through* education, examining Article 29 the 'aims of education' in conjunction with Article 23 'children with a disability', we also examine these in light of the foundations laid down in Article 28, the 'right to education'.

The Right to Education for Children with Disability Under the UNCRC

The ‘right to education’ is articulated within Article 28, which places obligations on State Party signatories such as ensuring all children are regularly attending school, not dropping out of school, and provided with compulsory and free primary school education. Article 23 adds additional obligations as special measures for State Party signatories “to ensure that the disabled child has effective access to and receives education”. Together, Articles 23 and 28 are consistent that children with (and without) a disability have entirely the same rights without any limitations. Global monitoring shows that, since the UNCRC came into force, there remain large numbers of children who do not have access to or complete a basic primary education, who do not regularly attend school, or who leave school early (UNESCO, 2018). The majority of these educational access issues are disproportionately associated with developing countries (UNESCO, 2014), pointing to the likelihood that availability of resources may be contributing to the slow progress in these countries, and revealing the need for better international cooperation to assist with this global priority. Significantly, some groups of children are disproportionately affected by these barriers to accessing education, particularly children who are deaf, blind, or on the autism spectrum (UNESCO, 2014), which indicates the need for further examination to understand this phenomenon.

Rights in Education for Children with Disability Under the UNCRC

As ground breaking as it was for the UNCRC to articulate the right of children with disabilities to access education, we identify the special measures for their rights in and through education as problematic as revealed in the wording of Articles 23 and 28. Article 23 outlines a substantially different set of educational rights and aims for these children. Differences in the vision of education for children with and without disability can be seen when comparing the language and rights set out within Articles 23 and 28.

The general rights in education are specified within Article 28 for “all” children, and include obligations on State Parties to ensure that children’s education includes quality through the provision of: financial assistance for support on the basis of need; access to scientific and technical knowledge; access to modern teaching methods; and the elimination of ignorance and illiteracy. These clearly outline a vision for children to become knowledgeable and capable adults through the provision of well-resourced and high-quality teaching. By contrast, Article 23, sets out the special measures State Parties are obliged to provide that characterise educational rights for children with disabilities as “special care” and “assistance” relevant to their “condition”. This characterisation of education as remediation in relation to the characteristics of impairment specifies a substantially different vision to which children with disability are entitled. That vision is less about quality learning to develop clever and capable adults, and more about a therapeutic or medicalised response that implies children with disabilities are limited by their "condition".

The medicalised view of disability within the UNCRC echoes the language used in the antecedent children's rights international policy instruments, beginning with the original terminology of "backward" in the Geneva Declaration (League of Nations, 1924). Since this Declaration, successive policy instruments have contained a medical view of children with disabilities. For example, in Principle 5 from the UN Declaration of the Rights of the Child (United Nations, 1959) it was noted that "The child who is *physically, mentally or socially handicapped* shall be given the *special treatment, education and care required by his particular condition*" (italics added). That language was subsequently repeated within Article 23 from the UNCRC (United Nations, 1989) which specified obligations upon signatory nations to "recognize the right of the *disabled child to special care … which is appropriate to the child's condition* and designed to ensure that the disabled child has access to and received education … conducive to the child's achieving *the fullest possible social integration and individual development*" (italics added). Such an approach to disability has long been criticised and rejected by people with disabilities. It has been decried as serving as an unwelcome euphemism (Gernsbacher et al., 2016), for creating an equivalence between disability and impairment, and for ignoring the role societies and environments play in creating barriers to participation and to learning as is outlined by the social model of disability (Quinn & Degener, 2002). It has also been criticised as justifying the segregation and exclusion of people with disabilities, such as segregation into "special" classes and schools on the basis of needing "special" teachers using "special" strategies (de Bruin, 2020).

While the Convention is meant to be read in its entirely, General Comments 1 and 9 highlight this has not transpired, with State Parties tending to focus on Article 23 in isolation (Committee on the Rights of the Child, 2001, 2007). Since the UNCRC came into force, the UNCRC Committee has gradually shifted their position from a medical model (i.e., therapy) to a social model (i.e., inclusion) of education for children with disabilities. For example, General Comment 9 clarified children's right to an education is both the right to a *quality* education designed to also produce positive educational outcomes rather than therapeutic ones. General Comment 9 also encouraged State Parties to move towards providing an *inclusive* education. However, the Committee still endorsed the continued segregation of students with disabilities on the grounds of economic feasibility for immediate implementation and proposed inclusion be considered as a continuum of options that also encompasses special segregated education. By including segregation as an educational option, the UNCRC Committee was placed at odds with the Committee on the Convention on the Rights of Persons with Disabilities (CRPD) who explicitly rejected this continuum, even though the draft of the CRPD was available and in fact noted in General Comment 9. The discontinuity between these two UN Committees clearly reduced the clarity of obligations for signatories. In 2019, a report to the UN by the High Commissioner for Human Rights clarified that this right is in fact enshrined. The implications of this internal tension, and delay in recognising the right to be included will be considered in terms of the impact on policy enactment within State Party policy in the case study later in the chapter.

Rights Through Education for Children with Disability Under the UNCRC

Article 29 specifies that children have the right to an education promoting their development and potential, their respect for human rights, their sense of identity and affiliation, and their connection to others as well as the environment (United Nations, 1989). The language used in articulating these aims emphasises developing young people to their "fullest potential" through education so they may lead a "responsible life in a free society, in the spirit of understanding, peace, tolerance, equality of sexes, and friendship among all peoples" (United Nations, 1989).

However, within Article 23, the special measures articulated therein imply a narrowed set of aims for children with disability. For example, while Article 29 specifies the right of young people to live a full and satisfying life within society, Article 23 sets the standard much lower, specifying the aim of education for young people with disability merely as achieving the "fullest possible" social integration within the limitations posed by their "condition". In the following section, Australia will be used as a case study example to understand whether the limitations of children with disabilities implied by Article 23 in the UNCRC have influenced domestic legislation and policy for educating children with disabilities.

Critique: A Case Study of Disability and Educational Rights in Australia

Australia is a federation of six states and two territories. The constitutional responsibility for education lies with these states and territories, although the federal government has a role in national legislation, policy, and provision of funding. This means that there are nine governments charged with the responsibility of implementing the UNCRC in Australia. The *Commonwealth of Australia Constitution Act 1900* first identified and paved the way for special laws to be provided for groups of people, however this was limited to "race". The UN has made clear that, within such federated systems, where the State Party has delegated responsibility to regional governments (as is the case in Australia), the State must require these subsidiary governments to both enact legislation consistent with State Party obligations, as well as to implement them (Committee on the Rights of the Child, 2003). Consequently, all nine governments within Australia are responsible for and obligated to uphold and realise the educational rights of children with disabilities through "special laws" including the UNCRC.

The Right to Education in Australia

The right to access an education in Australia is not absolute, with elements of this right distributed across a complex web of instruments. These include the *Australian Education Act* 2013 and the related *Australian Education Regulation* (2013), the Disability Discrimination Act 1992 *(DDA)* and the Disability Standards for Education 2005 *(DSE)* at the federal level, and a host of subordinate state and territory legislation. Strikingly, there is no Commonwealth legislation that preserves the right to access an education in Australia (Attorney-General's Department, n.d.) with the exception of a human rights act in both the Australian Capital Territory (UNICEF Australia, 2018) and Queensland (State of Queensland, 2019). However, each state and territory has legislation that makes education compulsory (Attorney-General's Department, n.d.).

The DDA provides only partial protection of the right to education for students with disabilities to access an education. The Act prohibits schools from denying students access on the basis of their disability, e.g., through denial of enrolment based on discrimination, or discriminatory applications of suspension or expulsion measures, although there are exemptions for schools to discriminate on the basis of "unjustifiable hardship". The DSE interprets the DDA section 22 on education and clarifies that access to schools by students with disability should be free from discrimination through ensuring their access is "on the same basis" (section 2.2) as non-disabled students. The DSE also clarifies that students with disabilities are entitled to "reasonable adjustments" (section 2.2 and Part 3), measures that ensure students can have access to schools and learning on the same basis as their nondisabled peers.

The right to a free education specified within the UNCRC is also not explicitly protected within Australia. However, each state and territory fully resource a fee-free public education system in which any student is legally entitled to apply for enrolment. The UNCRC also places the obligation onto States parties to provide financial assistance on the basis of need to ensure access to an education. Australia has translated this obligation into federal legislation through the *Australian Education Act 2013* and the *Australian Education Regulation 2013*. The Act legislates for the provision of funding by the federal government to both government and non-government schools via the Schooling Resource Standard, a per-student funding estimate of the cost of educating a child which is augmented with extra loadings needed to meet the additional costs of supporting equity for vulnerable students (Australian Education Regulation, 2013). For students with disability, this loading is needs-based and is calculated through the Nationally Consistent Collection of Data on School Students with Disability (NCCD, Australian Education Regulation, 2013; Education Council, 2020). Domestic legislation for needs-based financial assistance to support the access of children with disabilities to an education also exists within state- and territory-based legislation. Each state and territory have legislation and policy with funding models allocating resources schools for providing reasonable adjustments in education, such as the Program for Students with Disabilities (PSD) in Victoria, or the Education Adjustment Program (EAP) in Queensland (de Bruin et al., 2020).

Barriers in Implementation

Many elements of children's rights under the UNCRC are protected within Australian legislation, however collectively they fall short of consistency with the Convention; this has repeatedly been highlighted by the UN in their Lists of Issues to Australia (United Nations, 2019). Researchers have also noted barriers to children's rights are hampered by inconsistencies in legislation across the federation combined with a lack of clarity both in legislation and in schools' understanding of their obligations for children with disabilities thereby creating barriers to educational access (Duncan et al., 2020). These barriers are revealed through schools misunderstanding their obligations and discriminate against students through gatekeeping (refusals or redirections by schools) and restrictive practices by schools (Poed et al., 2020; Lilley, 2013; Walsh & Burton, 2020). Enrolment patterns suggest that gatekeeping and restrictive practices disproportionately affects particular groups of students, such as those on the autism spectrum (de Bruin, 2019).

Rights in Education in Australia

Australian children do not have a clear right to access a quality curriculum delivered through quality teaching consistent with obligations under the CRC. However, there are national policies designed to achieve these. These policies relate to the regulation of authorities who operate on behalf of the government including:

- Australian Curriculum, Assessment and Reporting Authority (ACARA) Act 2008
- The National Disability Insurance Scheme Act 2013 (NDIS).

The right of Australian children with disability to "special care" and "assistance" appropriate to their "condition" in Article 23 are embedded within domestic Australian legislation and policy at both the federal and state level. For example, the DDA (1992) mandates that children with disabilities are entitled to reasonable adjustments to ensure that they learn and participate in schooling on the same basis as their non-disabled peers. These are loosely directed towards children's right to "special care" and "assistance" in terms of accessing support for learning, as they are intended to overcome barriers to learning and participation that children experience as a result of functional impact from a disability. While the Committee has made clear that children with disabilities have a right to receive this "special care" and "assistance" within an *inclusive* education provided through the general education system (Committee on the Rights of the Child, 2007), there is no domestic legislation explicitly specifying this right in Australia.

Article 23 notes that "special care" and "assistance" is to be appropriate to a child's "condition" and to be provided free of charge. At the present time, these elements of educational and financial support for children with disability to learn at school are implemented at both the federal and state levels in quite divergent ways that are complex and interconnected. Within the federal needs-based NCCD model, schools report data on the type and intensity of reasonable adjustments they provide to students who meet the definition of a disability as defined by the DDA (1992). The information is then used to inform the allocation of funds handed to the states (de Bruin et al., 2020). However, at present, these federal funds are redistributed by most states according to their own funding formulae, such as the EAP and the PSD. These formulae only superficially meet the UNCRC obligation of providing financial support for "special care" and "assistance" appropriate to a child's "condition". Under state-based models, children are only eligible to receive assistance if their "condition" is verified by a registered medical practitioner and the degree of functional impairment related to that disability meets explicit and tight eligibility guidelines (de Bruin, 2020). These state-based guidelines for distributing funds are at odds with federal legislation, meaning many children never access funds and schools interpret these guidelines as grounds to refuse enrolment (Commonwealth of Australia, 2016) or deny adjustments (Cologon, 2019).

The right to "special care" in Australian domestic legislation is embedded within legislation that is expressly excluded from educational purposes, the *National Disability Insurance Scheme Act 2013*. The principles of the NDIS clearly state that "special care" as a therapeutic response to children's disability is provided through medical and allied health services as disability support rather than through educational services (Council of Australian Governments (COAG), 2015), highlighting the tension between medicalised responses to children with disabilities and their education. The implications and issues relating to "special care" are twofold and will be discussed in the section below.

Barriers in Implementation

Quality Teaching and Curriculum

There are some barriers and issues in relation to realising the right of Australian children with disability to access a quality curriculum through quality teaching. For example, research has found that many teachers who work with children disabilities implement the national curriculum poorly and use out-of-date practices or even substitute inappropriate alternative curricula with substantially lower expectations than are age-appropriate (Walker et al., 2018). Such teaching practices are in direct conflict with advice from ACARA (2016) and reveal that, despite legislation and policy aligning with the UNCRC to support children's right to quality teaching and quality curriculum, there remains substantial human rights violations and indicates the need for reform.

Special Care and Assistance

The complexity of this web of legislation at both federal and state level means that many students miss out accessing support in the form of "special care" and "assistance" as schools may deny reasonable adjustments. For example, Cologon (2013) noted children with disabilities in Australia experienced refusals to provide the necessary adjustments. Poed (2016) and Poed et al. (2020) identified the persistence of this issue, and observed that legislative complexity and refusals by schools led many parents to rely on the Courts to address discrimination in the provision of reasonable adjustments for children with disabilities.

Additionally, the provision of "special care" is complex because the NDIS is the main provider of therapeutic funding and planning for individuals with disabilities and does not provide support or funding for education or schools. The exclusion of education from NDIS funding places the onus of responsibility for "special care" on education systems and teachers through provision of reasonable adjustments. Consequently, the explicit domestic legislation containing the rights of children to "special care" under Article 23 of the UNCRC does not apply to children's schooling. This highlights the tension between what constitutes therapy and what constitutes education that is the legacy of Article 23.

Inclusive Education

The absence of legislation for inclusive education in Australia has created barriers to its realisation as noted by the Committee on the Rights of the Child (2012, 2019). Indeed, research shows that under the DDA and the DSE, segregation of students with disabilities has actually risen (de Bruin, 2019), indicating that existing anti-discrimination legislation has undermined rather than progressed the inclusion of children with disabilities into the general education system. The UNCRC's language is reflective of "education with care and rights with needs" (Davis et al., 2020, p. 79) is really a translated form of special education, and in Australian education this potentially masquerades under the guise of the NDIS and categorical funding options. It is clear that, continuing to provide medicalised and therapeutic approaches in education through segregated settings, places the aim of education within Australia at stark contrast with the goal of an inclusive education.

Financial Resources

The highly medicalised understanding of disability within the UNCRC has influenced those policies that were written at around the same time as the UNCRC and which relate to financial assistance for "special care" and "assistance" in Australia.

For example, within the state-based funding models, students with disabilities are ineligible for funding until they provide verification of a disability by a medical professional that children fall into a state's "approved" disability category and documentation that the level of functional impact falls within tight eligibility guidelines. These requirements have led to implementation barriers arising from confusion between eligibility for *funding* and eligibility for *reasonable adjustments* with a Senate inquiry finding that adjustments were frequently denied on the basis there was no funding for it, despite all schools receiving throughput funding to support equity (de Bruin et al., 2020). Moreover, the lack of consistency between jurisdictions, whereby each has a funding model that adopts different definitions of disability, contains different categories of recognised disability, and different eligibility criteria for funding thresholds, means that the same child may or may not be eligible for funding or support depending on their address. The lack of consistency also exists between the models and at the state and the federal levels, which influences the way that the states distribute federal funds based on school data through the NCCD and can lead to great inequity and unfairness, meaning that children and their schools miss out on needs-based funds (Fitzsimmons, 2019). Walsh and Burton (2020) suggest that indeed such a breach constitutes a human rights violation for children with disabilities to participate and achieve in education.

A further barrier is that the NDIS, the system expressly charged with the duty of arranging "special care", does not provide funding for education for the provision of educational purposes for children with disabilities. This barrier directly speaks to the problem of having educational rights in education embedded within Article 23 that is essentially focused on health and welfare. The NDIS supports the personhood of people with disabilities under the banner of "choice and control" (Cukalevski, 2019, p. 1), yet Whitburn et al. (2017) highlight tensions within the NDIS relating to the policy problem of education and its overall avoidance of even exploring educational support and assistance in schools. These authors have argued that the intersection between education and service provision, meaning "special care" and "assistance", have continued to be avoided and compounded by competing interests between key stakeholders of the NDIS persistent in perpetuating the medical discourse underpinning this Act and the silenced voices of people with disabilities about their actual needs, wants, and rights realised in education.

Consultation

Within Article 29, the Committee made clear that parents' values were to be respected (Article 29) which in Australian legislation is upheld through the DDA and the DSE. These specify that parents are to be consulted on decisions relating to the education of the child with a disability such as through consultation about adjustments in the classroom or school environment. Children with disabilities are also to be consulted in determining their adjustments under the DSE and this is consistent with their rights under the UNCRC in Article 12. However, Winter (2016) has noted the complexity and tensions between parents' rights and obligations in Australia through policy and practice when advocating for, and supporting, children on the autism spectrum and how parents may need to speak for a child when they are not able to speak for themselves due to their disability. Tancredi (2019) further notes that this process itself is not designed to facilitate quality consultation and riddled with barriers for many children.

Dignity

Children have a right in education to have their dignity preserved when they are being disciplined under Article 28. In Australian legislation, however, there is no right enshrined in law regarding this. Moreover, research suggests that a range of practices are used in schools that enact in fact strip children of their dignity. For example, researchers have found that families of children with disabilities reported their child being suspended multiple times or expelled on grounds of behaviour or physical reasons and even higher numbers of children with disabilities excluded from events or activities in schools (Cologon, 2019) and that a range of practices are widely used that restrict or violate children's right in education to having their dignity preserved while being disciplined (Poed et al., 2020). Recent reports have suggested that these punishments are being meted out to children as young as 5 years old, (Glass, 2017) These rates of expulsion and suspension affect the aim of children with disabilities being "prepared for life beyond school in a free, peaceful and tolerant society" (Article 29) since a lack of participation in education may impact their ability to successfully and fully engage in society beyond school.

Rights Through Education

Within Article 29 of the UNCRC, children's educational rights through education are to have their potential, their respect for human rights, their sense of identity and affiliation, and their connection to others as well as the environment nurtured. In Australia, these are not explicitly legislated however they are partially embedded within the Australian Curriculum (ACARA, 2016). Australia has specified the national aims of education through the decennial declarations that are negotiated by its nine heads of government; the latest of these, the *Alice Springs (Mparntwe) Education Declaration* (Education Council, 2019), was released in 2019. These declarations are not legislative instruments; however, they do inform national and state priorities and set a vision for education in Australia. They are also accompanied by related action plans, which have traditionally provided a roadmap for achieving the national education aims (COAG, 2013) and, in turn, also inform legislation.

For children with disability, the aims of education within Article 23 related to their "preparation for employment and recreation opportunities in a manner conducive to the child's achieving the fullest possible social integration and individual development". Though not protected by Australian legislation, an important component of these rights through education is embedded within the DSE whereby children with a disability have a right to be consulted regarding the reasonable adjustments that they receive. This requirement for consultation is consistent with the child achieving the fullest possible individual development (Article 23) as well as a respect for rights (in this case their own), and their sense of identity (Article 29).

Barriers in Implementation

Several barriers exist in relation to how children's rights through education are realised in Australia. For example, research indicates that student consultation on reasonable adjustments is the exception rather than the norm (Poed et al., 2020; Cologon, 2019; Commonwealth of Australia, 2016) and inaccessible for many students (Tancredi, 2019). Additionally, research suggests that teachers lack confidence and skill in providing access to the Australian curriculum for children with disabilities (Walker et al., 2018; Commonwealth of Australia, 2016), which greatly reduces the potential for these children to have their rights through education in terms of receiving access to critical components of the national curriculum that have been developed to nurture their potential, their respect for human rights, their sense of identity and affiliation, and their connection to others.

Another barrier is that children with disability are not clearly or consistently identified as a priority or a vulnerable population in the vision and goals for Australian education. For example, the *Alice Springs (Mparntwe) Education Declaration* (Education Council, 2019) followed the release of the National School Reform Agreement (NSRA, Council of Australian Governments (COAG), 2018), which specified students with disabilities as a priority equity group, yet the *Mparntwe Declaration* did not include them in their priority equity cohorts. This omission of disability as an equity group exemplifies the conflict and disparity for children with disabilities in being fully seen and included in the vision of education for Australia. Moreover, this omission highlights that Australia still has a long way to go before the national aims for education articulate a vision that includes these most disadvantaged students within the education system, and realises the vision of an equitable society within the UNCRC.

Conclusion

Australia exemplifies several of the issues that the UNCRC committee have noted in relation to the implementation of the UNCRC. Specifically, these issues are apparent in the narrowed focus on special provisions that respond to children' disabilities rather than providing needs-based support to access equitable, high-quality and inclusive education. There are two main points clearly evident from our analysis. The first is that the medical lens in Article 23 has indeed produced an inferior articulation of the rights of children *to* and *in* education. For example, the UNCRC approach to "special care", "assistance", and "condition" was demonstrated throughout numerous Australian legislative and policy instruments which perpetuated a deficit discourse of disability and children in need of specialised services and care rather than in need of (and entitled to) the same high-quality educational opportunities and experiences as their non-disabled peers that can result in their reduced access to their peers and to an appropriate academic curriculum.

It is clear that despite having shifted its position in favour of inclusive education, the UNCRC and its medicalised origins have not been able to shake off the influence of the past. The wording and focus of the UNCRC emphasising "special care" as educational remains as it was, placing it at odds with the CRPD in which there is an explicit definition and right to inclusive education by every child. We therefore assert that the CRPD should be used in preference to the UNCRC for understanding the educational rights of children with disabilities as it provides the strongest and more comprehensive expression of the right to education of children with disabilities in international human rights law (Malaquias, 2020).

The second main point is that the aims of education for children with disabilities contained within Article 23 of the UNCRC are impoverished and narrow, characterising them as holding inferior rights to their nondisabled peers. While the Convention is supposed to be read in its entirety, in practical terms this has not happened at scale, with the Committee noting this repeatedly in their General Comments, as well as in their concluding observations on our case study country of Australia. In Australia and in the rest of the world, the long-term outcomes for children and people with disabilities are poor by many measures including employment, housing, and connection to their communities (UNICEF, 2019). The UN vision for creating respectful, responsible and contributing members of society that are equitable and socially connected is far from a reality for most people with disabilities, suggesting that the special measures within Article 23 may have in fact undermined Article 29. It is high time that the UNCRC is revised and updated so that it can offer a vision for education in which every child's rights and future are equally valued.

References

Attorney-General's Department. (n.d.). *Right to education*. https://www.ag.gov.au/RightsAndProtections/HumanRights/Human-rights-scrutiny/PublicSectorGuidanceSheets/Pages/Righttoeducation.aspx. Accessed 24 Apr 2020.

Australian Curriculum Assessment and Reporting Authority (ACARA). (2016). *NAPLAN*. https://www.nap.edu.au/. Accessed 2 May 2020.

Australian Education Act 2013 (Cth). https://www.legislation.gov.au/Details/C2013A00067. Accessed 3 May 2020.

Australian Education Regulation 2013 (Cth). https://www.legislation.gov.au/Details/F2013L01476. Accessed 3 May 2020.

COAG. (2013). *National education reform agreement* [Online]. http://www.federalfinancial-relations.gov.au/content/npa/national_agreements/past/national-education-agreement.pdf. Accessed 3 May 2020.

COAG. (2015). *Principles to determine the responsibilities of the NDIS and other service systems* [Online]. https://www.coag.gov.au/sites/default/files/communique/NDIS-Principles-to-Determine-Responsibilities-NDIS-and-Other-Service.pdf. Accessed 29 Apr 2020.

COAG. (2018). *National School Reform Agreement* [Online]. https://docs.education.gov.au/system/files/doc/other/national_school_reform_agreement_8.pdf. Accessed 3 May 2020.

Cologon, K. (2013). *Inclusion in education towards equality for students with disability*. https://apo.org.au/node/36129. Accessed 2 May 2020.

Cologon, K. (2019). *Towards inclusive education: A necessary process of transformation*. https://apo.org.au/sites/default/files/resource-files/2019-10/apo-nid265286_1.pdf. Accessed 20 Nov 2020.

Committee on the Rights of the Child. (2001). *General Comment No. 1: Article 29 (1) The aims of education*. [Online]. https://undocs.org/CRC/GC/2001/1. Accessed 20 Apr 2020.

Committee on the Rights of the Child. (2003). *General Comment No. 5: General measures of implementation of the Convention on the Rights of the Child (arts. 4, 42 and 44, para. 6)*. https://undocs.org/CRC/GC/2003/5. Accessed 20 Apr 2020.

Committee on the Rights of the Child. (2007). *General Comment No. 9: The rights of children with disabilities*. [Online]. https://undocs.org/CRC/C/GC/9. Accessed 20 Apr 2020.

Committee on the Rights of the Child. (2012). *Consideration of reports submitted by States parties under article 44 of the Convention*. [Online]. https://www2.ohchr.org/english/bodies/crc/docs/co/CRC_C_AUS_CO_4.pdf. Accessed 3 May 2020.

Committee on the Rights of the Child. (2019). *List of issues in relation to the combined fifth and sixth reports of Australia*. [Online]. https://www.ag.gov.au/RightsAndProtections/HumanRights/United-Nations-Human-Rights-Reporting/Documents/list-of-issues-convention-on-the-rights-of-the-child-australia.PDF. Accessed 3 May 2020.

Commonwealth of Australia. (2016). *Access to real learning: The impact of policy, funding and culture on students with disability*. [Online]. https://www.aph.gov.au/Parliamentary_Business/Committees/Senate/Education_and_Employment/students_with_disability/Report. Accessed 3 May 2020.

Commonwealth of Australia Constitution Act 1900 (Cth). https://www.aph.gov.au/about_parliament/senate/powers_practice_n_procedures/constitution. Accessed 6 July 2020.

Cukalevski, E. (2019). Supporting choice and control – An analysis of the approach taken to legal capacity in Australia's National Disability Insurance Scheme. *Laws, 8*(2), 8.

Davis, J., Gillett-Swan, J., Graham, L. J., & Malaquias, C. (2020). Inclusive education as a human right. In L. Graham (Ed.), *Inclusive education for the 21st century* (pp. 79–99). Allen and Unwin.

de Bruin, K. (2019). The impact of inclusive education reforms on students with disability: An international comparison. *International Journal of Inclusive Education, 23*(7–8), 811–826. https://doi.org/10.1080/13603116.2019.1623327

de Bruin, K. (2020). Does inclusion work? In L. Graham (Ed.), *Inclusive education for the 21st century* (pp. 55–76). Allen and Unwin.

de Bruin, K., Graham, L., & Gallagher, J. (2020). What is the NCCD and what does it mean for my practice? In L. Graham (Ed.), *Inclusive education for the 21st century* (pp. 122–155). Allen and Unwin.

Disability Discrimination Act. (1992) (DDA, Cth). *Australia: Act No. 135 of 1992, Disability Discrimination Act 1992* [Australia], 5 November 1992. https://www.refworld.org/docid/4b4716162.html

Disability Standards for Education. (2005) (DSE, Cth). *Disability Standards for Education 2005*. Australian Government Publishing Service.

Duncan, J., Punch, R., Gauntlett, M., & Talbot-Stokes, R. (2020). Missing the mark or scoring a goal? Achieving non-discrimination for students with disability in primary and secondary education in Australia: A review. *Australian Journal of Education, 64*(1), 54–72.

Economic and Social Council. (2019). *Special edition: Progress towards the Sustainable Development Goals* [Online]. https://undocs.org/E/2019/68. Accessed 20, 2020.

Education Council. (2019). *Alice Springs (Mparntwe) Education Declaration* [Online]. https://docs.education.gov.au/system/files/doc/other/final_-_alice_springs_declaration_-_17_february_2020_security_removed.pdf. Accessed 3 May 2020.

Education Council. (2020). *Nationally consistent collection of data on school students with disability: 2020 Guidelines* [Online]. https://www.nccd.edu.au/sites/default/files/2020_nccd_guidelines.pdf. Accessed 3 May 2020.

Fitzsimmons, C. (2019). *NSW reviewing outdated model for funding students with disabilities*. https://www.smh.com.au/national/nsw/nsw-reviewing-outdated-model-for-funding-students-with-disabilities-20190830-p52mkp.html. Accessed 3 May 2020.

Gernsbacher, M. A., Raimond, A. R., Balinghasay, M. T., & Boston, J. S. (2016). Special needs is an ineffective euphemism. *Cognitive Research: Principles and Implications, 1*(1), 29. https://doi.org/10.1186/s41235-016-0025-4

Glass, D. (2017). *Investigation into Victorian government school expulsion* [Online]. https://assets.ombudsman.vic.gov.au/assets/Reports/Parliamentary-Reports/1-PDF-Report-Files/Investigation-into-Victorian-government-school-expulsions.pdf?mtime=20191218105017. Accessed 3 May 2020.

League of Nations. (1924). Geneva declaration of the rights of the child. *Official Journal, Special Supplement, 21*, 10.

Lilley, R. (2013). *It's an absolute nightmare: Maternal experiences of enrolling children diagnosed with autism in primary school in Sydney, Australia*. https://doi.org/10.1080/09687599.2012.717882. Accessed 20 Feb 2020.

Malaquias, C. (2020). *Submission to the Royal Commission into violence, neglect, abuse and exploitation of people with disability: Response to the education and learning issues paper*. All Means All Australian Alliance for Inclusive Education.

Poed, S. (2016). *Adjustments to curriculum for Australian school-aged students with disabilities: What's reasonable?* PhD thesis, Griffith University, Brisbane.

Poed, S., Cologon, K., & Jackson, R. (2020). Gatekeeping and restrictive practices by Australian mainstream schools: Results of a national survey. *International Journal of Inclusive Education*, 1–14. https://doi.org/10.1080/13603116.2020.1726512

Quinn, G., & Degener T. (2002). *The current use and future potential of United Nations human rights instruments in the context of disability* [Online]. http://repositoriocdpd.net:8080/bitstream/handle/123456789/669/L_QuinnG_UsePotencialInstruments_2002.pdf?sequence=1. Accessed 24 Apr 2020.

State of Queensland Human Rights Act 2019 (QLD). https://www.legislation.qld.gov.au/view/pdf/asmade/act-2019-005. Accessed 4 July 2020.

Tancredi, H. (2019). Meeting obligations to consult students with disability: Methodological considerations and successful elements for consultation. *The Australian Educational Researcher, 47*(2), 201–207.

UNESCO. (2018). *GEM report summary on disability and education* [Online]. https://unesdoc.unesco.org/ark:/48223/pf0000265353. Accessed 22 Apr 2020.
UNICEF. (2019). *For every child, every right: The Convention on the Rights of the Child at a crossroads* https://www.unicef.org/media/61941/file/Convention-rights-child-at-crossroads-2019.pdf. Accessed 20 Apr 2020.
UNICEF Australia. (2018). *The children's report: Australia's NGO coalition report to the United Nations Committee on the Rights of the Child* [Online]. https://www.unicef.org.au/Upload/UNICEF/Media/Documents/Child-Rights-Taskforce-NGO-Coalition-Report-For-UNCRC-LR.pdf. Accessed 22 Apr 2020.
United Nations. (1959). *A/RES/1386(XIV) – E – A/RES/1386(XIV): Declaration of the Rights of the Child* [Online]. https://undocs.org/en/A/RES/1386(XIV). Accessed 2 May 2020.
United Nations. (1989). *Convention on the Rights of the Child.* https://www.ohchr.org/Documents/ProfessionalInterest/crc.pdf. Accessed 2 May 2020.
United Nations. (2003–04). *The United Nations and disabled persons – The first fifty years: 1983–1992* [Online]. https://www.un.org/esa/socdev/enable/dis50y60.htm. Accessed 20 Apr 2020.
United Nations. (2019). *UN Treaty body database: List of Issues – Australia* [Online]. https://tbinternet.ohchr.org/_layouts/15/treatybodyexternal/TBSearch.aspx?Lang=en&TreatyID=5&TreatyID=10&TreatyID=11&DocTypeID=18&DocTypeCategoryID=1. Accessed 2 May 2020.
United Nations Educational, Scientific and Cultural Organization. (2014). *GEM report summary on disabilities and education* [Online]. https://en.unesco.org/gem-report/sites/gem-report/files/GAW2014-Facts-Figures-gmr_0.pdf.pdf. Accessed 22 Apr 2020.
Walker, P. M., Carson, K. L., Jarvis, J. M., & McMillan, J. (2018). How do educators of students with disabilities in specialist settings understand and apply the Australian curriculum framework? *Australasian Journal of Special and Inclusive Education, 42*(2), 111–126.
Walsh, T., & Burton, B. (2020). Queensland's new right to education: What does it mean for children with disabilities? *Alternative Law Journal, 45*(1), 18–24.
Whitburn, B., Moss, J., & O'Mara, J. (2017). The policy problem: The National Disability Insurance Scheme (NDIS) and implications for access to education. *Journal of Education Policy, 32*(4), 467–479.
Winter, S. (2016). *Navigating the battleground: Autism policy and human rights for children with autism spectrum disorders in Australia.* Doctoral dissertation, Griffith University, Brisbane.

Chapter 5
Children's Educational Rights in Poland: Policy, School Realities and Ideological Tensions

Marcin Starnawski, Katarzyna Gawlicz, and Dorota Duda

Abstract While a number of aims listed in Article 29 of the UNCRC have been inscribed in Poland's educational regulations and curricula, criticism of conceptual and practical aspects of their implementation has been voiced, especially by Non-Governmental Organisations (NGOs) and academics. The chapter discusses these barriers to quality education, as well as some aspects of educational access, in the light of Article 28. The analysis highlights *access*, *content*, and *relations* as three fields of inquiry into the relationship between children's rights and education. The discussion explores the priorities of major educational institutions and the extent to which they guarantee equality and diversity. It reflects on gaps and tensions in content substance by examining human rights and environmental education, as well as nationalist and religious exclusions, and by pointing to the compensatory role of NGOs. It provides examples of discriminatory practices that affect in-school interpersonal relations. The chapter considers the politicisation of education, as linked to the right-wing populist and conservative turn, which has aggravated social tensions that destabilise the education system and jeopardise the rights of children.

Keywords Children's rights · Education in Poland · UNCRC Article 28 · UNCRC Article 29 · Discrimination and anti-discrimination in education · Nationalism · Conservative backlash · NGOs

---

M. Starnawski · K. Gawlicz (✉) · D. Duda
Faculty of Applied Studies, University of Lower Silesia, Wrocław, Poland
e-mail: marcin.starnawski@dsw.edu.pl; katarzyna.gawlicz@dsw.edu.pl; dorota_eulalja_duda@wp.pl

J. Gillett-Swan, N. Thelander (eds.), *Children's Rights from International Educational Perspectives*, Transdisciplinary Perspectives in Educational Research 2, https://doi.org/10.1007/978-3-030-80861-7_5

Introduction

Since 2015, under the government of the Law and Justice party (PiS), Poland has seen a turn in its national-development approach. This turn combines a critique of earlier neoliberal economic policies with revindication of the nation-state in the context of EU politics, and a conservative cultural vision. The party leader's claim 'to modernise Poland but not the Polish spirit' epitomised the idea of moving up from semi-peripheral positioning.[1] These shifts affected Poland's education early on. Ideological battles have intensified over nationalism, religion, and sex education. Moreover, a structural reform created both discontent among teachers and parents, and confusion among youth transiting from primary level to secondary level. These circumstances have had a direct impact on the education system's ability to meet the demands contained in the Convention of the Rights of the Child (UNCRC), Articles 28 and 29. The UNCRC provisions are reflected in educational regulations and curricula, but their implementation draws criticism from NGOs and academics, usually in a form of anti-discrimination discourse.

This chapter discusses barriers to effective enactment of Article 29 of the UNCRC, and some aspects of Article 28, in Poland's education system. We draw on a human rights-based approach to education (UNICEF, 2007), which underscores access, quality, and respect in the learning environment—the two latter elements directly linked to Article 29. An early interpretation of the UNCRC distinguished the right *to*, rights *in* and rights *through* education (Verhellen, 1993). Similarly, Quennerstedt's (2015) conceptualisation highlights three aspects of the "right to–rights in" distinction—access, content, and relations—as three fields for exploration. We structure our discussion along these lines, reflecting on aspects of access, gaps and misdirections in content, and discriminatory practices affecting students' interpersonal relations at school.

We also consider the politicisation of education in the context of a broader debate about the organisation and meaning of schooling. Despite a progressive legacy of children's rights struggles pioneered by Janusz Korczak (2017), Poland's pedagogical traditionalism remains strong. Our intention is to outline the conservative-nationalist backlash as reflected in the priorities and school realities of major institutions.

Access to Education: Social Challenges and Political Tensions

In Poland, education is mandatory up to the age of 18, with ca. six million students in 44,000 schools and preschools and over half a million teachers—86% of them in the public sector (GUS, 2019). In 2017, 8-year elementary schooling was reinstated

[1] We draw the notion of the semi-periphery, or semi-peripheral country, from Wallerstein's (2004) world-systems analysis. While this perspective is used in education research (Griffiths & Imre, 2013), a more in-depth discussion goes beyond the scope of this article.

in place of the previous six-plus-three arrangement.[2] Considerable controversy occurred in 2019 due to the 'merger of cohorts', which caused an overdemand for upper-secondary admissions. As teachers became concerned with losing their jobs or began leaving the profession, school staffing shortages arose.[3] Severe understaffing was also reported in vocational education, which had been marginalised during the post-socialist transition in the 1990s by the neoliberal deregulation of industries and due to an expansion of higher education. While the recent reform has stressed the importance of trade schools to rebuild national workforces, parallel changes in higher education have sought to curb massification. Therefore, a return of elitism in education and an even greater reliance on the cultural and social capitals of families may be a possible future scenario.[4]

In relation to Article 28 of the UNCRC, the dynamics described above show how access to education and its institutional layout can be manipulated for the purpose of controlling society's developmental path and its political culture. In addition to introducing educational changes, the government attempted to replace the "intellectual elites", e.g., in the media or the judiciary. Similar leanings towards "illiberal democracy" and the revival of the nation-state have been observed in other right-wing populist movements or regimes across the region, most notably in Hungary (Bonet & Zamorano, 2021; Hidalgo, 2019). While such aspirations are sometimes coupled with a rebuttal of the neoliberal models of growth and globalisation, they trigger nationalist-populist resentments and offer conservative recipes, as seen in Turkey, Brazil, or the post-2016 United States (Devinney & Hartwell, 2020; Fischer, 2020; Nyyssönen & Metsälä, 2020).

The problem of access to education still continues. On the one hand, for a number of years Poland has effectively tackled early leaving from education and training,[5] joining European leaders in this respect (Andrei et al., 2011; Eurostat, 2019; Madalińska-Michalak, 2017). Measures have included staff training in working with children at risk of social exclusion and the introduction of education assistants to both support Romani children in primary and pre-primary facilities, and to facilitate contact between parents and teachers (European Commission, 2013, pp. 42–43). Progress in increasing the attendance of Romani children has been noted (Krzyżanowski, 2018; RPO, 2014). On the other hand, a closer look at

---

[2] The system with 8-year elementary school and post-elementary schooling (general and vocational) had been in place since the 1960s. In 1999, the system was restructured into 6-year elementary school (ISCED 1), 3-year lower-secondary *gimnazjum* (ISCED 2) and upper-secondary general or vocational schooling (ISCED 3). The most recent reform has brought the structure back to the pre-1999 model.

[3] The 'merger of cohorts' paralleled Poland's first nationwide salary-focused teachers' strike in the twenty-first century, and a view that teachers' job satisfaction impacted pupils' learning and well-being was reiterated in the public debate.

[4] The enforced lockdown during the COVID-19 pandemic has revealed disparities in children's access to digital tools, skills, and learning environments at home and in the capacity of schools to provide online education (Cichy & Helak, 2021).

[5] *Early school leaving* is measured among young adults (aged 18–24) who have only completed ISCED-2-level education or less (European Commission, 2013).

statistics reveals that around 5% of children aged 6–17 have remained outside the schooling system, including the mandatory pre-primary year (GUS, 2019), with primary school dropout significantly responsible for this proportion (Madalińska-Michalak, 2017).

A recent challenge concerns the increasing numbers of foreign students, most notably from Ukraine. Integrative measures, such as additional Polish language instruction or language assistants, have been launched. However, teachers lack the necessary knowledge and skills to work with multi-ethnic groups and migrant students (Hajduk-Gawron, 2018). In some locations, municipality-managed programs and teacher-initiated professional learning communities serve as an aid to immigrant students and school staff (Bucko, 2019).

Another trend that has been gaining currency in Poland in recent years is out-of-school education, regarded as an alternative form of compulsory education (Czuba-Wąsowska & Mańko, 2011, pp. 77–78). Rather than a child's right, it tends to be interpreted as an expression of respect for a parents' right to decide about their children's education and upbringing, which is enshrined in Poland's Constitution. Apart from individualised instruction based on assessments issued by Psychological and Counselling Centres, out-of-school education takes two forms. One is home schooling, popular with religious families (Kucharska, 2014) and parents of exceptionally gifted children (Giercarz-Borkowska, 2019). The other type includes informal educational settings established by parents, which are referred to as democratic or free schools. Their growing popularity indicates that a species of parentocracy has emerged (Brown, 1994), where children's education predominantly depends on their parents' resources and wishes. In this case, parents' decisions are driven by a desire to protect children against an authoritarian public school system which is accused of disrespecting children and squandering their potential. Admittedly, parental withdrawal from the system is not in itself a violation of the UNCRC's Article 29(1). However, these new forms of education remain accessible only to families with sufficient cultural and economic capitals and, as such, bring together children from similar social backgrounds. Thus, paradoxically, while criticising injustices of the public system, democratic or free schools may actually be falling short of their ambition to prepare children to live in diverse societies.

Access and Content: Institutions' Priorities

In Poland, public responsibility for children's rights interventions rests primarily with the Ministry of National Education, the Ombudsman for Children (RPD) and the Commissioner for Human Rights (RPO). Another major institution is the Centre for Development in Education (ORE), whose responsibilities include providing professional development for teachers and assistance to school administrations. A study based on a full-year monitoring (961 entries) of the websites of the Ministry, the RPD, and the ORE in 2015, showed that only a tiny proportion of online information offered by these institutions was related to rights. While the Ministry focused mostly on socio-economic inequalities and the situation of students with disabilities, it shared little information on children's rights in this respect. The study also showed limited governmental information on multicultural education. While the rights of immigrant and refugee children were covered by some entries, the situation of Romani students was not addressed at all. The Ministry website contained almost no materials on religious freedom, gender equality, or the prevention of homophobia. The analysis indicated that activities of the ORE had been much more aligned with the anti-discrimination perspective than those of the Ministry, though still with deficits in the areas of religious freedom, gender, and sexuality (Chustecka, 2016, pp. 95–97).

Among the initiatives of the RPD, the most prominent were those focused on children and adolescents with chronic diseases and disabilities, including specialised pedagogies, transportation, and the elimination of architectural barriers, which increased access to education for students with motor impairments. Unlike the three other educational institutions, the RPD used the language of children's rights, emphasising the child's agency and dignity. The office showed concern with educational opportunities of children from rural and economically disadvantaged communities. They issued a statement against hate speech (jointly with the RPO), encouraging the Ministry to introduce anti-discrimination education with a particular focus on students who were not Polish citizens: refugees and other migrants. At the same time, the RPD did not attend to gender, sexuality, and religion (Chustecka, 2016, pp. 97–98). Other institutions are remarkably reluctant to consider the full array of issues highlighted in Article 29 of the UNCRC, particularly its provisions concerning tolerance, gender equality, and religious diversity. However, the pursuits of the current (2015–2021) RPO, Adam Bodnar, not only fill gaps in the efforts of other agencies but also promote greater progress in quality education.

The Content of Education: Gaps and Tensions

Quennerstedt (2015) defines educational content as facts, skills, and values taught at school, along with pedagogical actions. This definition partly overlaps with Verhellen's (1993) discussion on teaching *about* rights and *respecting* them in everyday school life. The selection of content and pedagogy are central to Article 29(1). Educational content is also subject to ideological debates on what young people learn and, consequently, what kinds of identities they develop. Polish schools are rife with such tensions, particularly in the contexts of religion, sexuality, and patriotism. In this section, we refer to Article 29 provisions to discuss the kinds of educational content that are either marginalised or prone to conflicting interpretations. We indicate when such omissions and/or inconsistencies may result in discrimination.

Across educational levels, educational content is specified in core curricula laid out by the Ministry of Education. A study of the core curricula and 55 textbooks in four subjects (History, Polish, Civics, and Formation for Family Life) registered little information on discrimination and the situation of minorities, ways to counter prejudice, and support measures for stigmatised individuals and groups (Abramowicz, 2011, p. 295). In a study of textbook discourses of national identity, Popow (2015) noted inadequate representations of women and working classes, while other studies confirmed the persistence of cultural stereotypes (Chmura-Rutkowska et al., 2016; Kielak et al., 2016). We now consider educational content in four specific areas: human rights education, religious instruction, nationality, and ecology in the context of Article 29(1).

Education About Human Rights

Article 29(1)(b) of the UNCRC stipulates that education should be directed to "the development of respect for human rights and fundamental freedoms." The core curricula assign teaching about human and children's rights to Civics classes, starting from the 4th grade of elementary school and throughout secondary school. Curricula for preschool and grades 1–3 of elementary school only stipulate that students should be familiarised with the idea that all people have rights and duties, without explicitly referencing human and children's rights. Although some teachers discuss the notion of rights with students at these lower levels as well, the omission of this topic in the legally binding curricula contradicts provisions of the UNCRC and of several other international legal instruments adopted by Poland (Kozak, 2014, pp. 47–50). Nonetheless, a recent UNESCO report shows that 95% of children have heard of children's rights and that the school remains the primary source of information in this regard (Falkowska & Telusiewicz-Pacak, 2019, p. 21). While students express a preference for learning about their rights during dedicated lessons and from invited experts, approximately one third of respondents claim that they would like to do so through practice, such as through participation in decision-making processes (Falkowska & Telusiewicz-Pacak, 2019, p. 41). However, schools frequently fail to provide such opportunities. While most teachers recognise positive effects of education on children's rights, as many as 17% claim that it results in "an excessive focus on one's own needs," and 10% insist that it leads to "children's arrogant behaviour" (Falkowska & Telusiewicz-Pacak, 2019, p. 55). Coupled with the possibility that teachers are not trained to teach rights (Kozak, 2014), these figures raise doubts about whether teachers actually understand the spirit of the UNCRC and the principles of children's citizenship.

Religious Instruction and Practices

Although the Constitution of the Republic of Poland stipulates the separation of church and state, the public education system in Poland is permeated with the Roman Catholic religion. The Preamble of the Education Law points to the importance of Christianity, stating that "teaching and education, which respect the Christian value system, are based on the universal principles of ethics."[6] Religious instruction is provided as a non-mandatory subject and almost exclusively concerns Roman Catholicism,[7] with lay teachers or priests[8] paid by the state. While a non-mandatory ethics course can be selected instead of, or along with, religion classes, controversies persist. Issues include the non-provision of ethics classes in many schools, insufficient information on the opt-in/out procedure for religious classes, informal ways of discouraging students from enrolling in ethics classes,[9] a competitive relationship between the two subjects and the ideological supremacy of a single religious tradition (Anczyk & Grzymała-Moszczyńska, 2018; Freedom from Religion Foundation, 2017; Madalińska-Michalak & Jeżowski, 2018). Article 14 of the UNCRC is typically referred to in such instances, along with the constitutional provisions on the freedom of religion and conscience. Analysis of media reports reveals that Catholicism-related practices permeate everyday life in educational institutions, far beyond religious instruction classes. Masses, prayers, and spiritual retreats are held in school buildings and during lesson time; crucifixes are placed on classroom walls next to the national emblems, while celebrations such as Halloween may be banned as incongruent with the faith (Rawłuszko, 2016). This kind of structural discrimination may lead to stigmatisation and bullying of students who do not embrace the dominant religion. All such cases directly contravene the provisions of Article 29(1)(d) of the UNCRC.

The ideological influence of the Roman Catholic Church also extends to other subjects, such as sex education. Sex education is taught as part of an optional course called 'Formation for Family Life'. Its curriculum equates family with heterosexual marriage. Recommended textbooks provide stereotyped and incorrect information on homosexuality (Abramowicz, 2011, pp. 239–249) and young people do not consider this subject a good source of information on sexuality at all (Bieńko et al., 2016). At the same time, researchers and educators point to notoriously persistent problems connected with inadequate sexual education, such as children's exposure to pornography, which becomes a means of education (Bieńko et al., 2016; Pyżalski et al., 2019), and a high rate of teenage pregnancies. The Roman Catholic church and conservative organisations see even this restricted form of sex education as

[6] http://isap.sejm.gov.pl/isap.nsf/download.xsp/WDU20170000059/U/D20170059Lj.pdf (Accessed June 20, 2020).

[7] A school survey (RPO, 2015) showed that in-school minority religious instruction was provided in 4% of schools, inter-school classes were organised for students from 8% of schools, while nothing of this kind was offered in the remaining 88% of schools.

[8] Graduates of seminaries or theology departments and educators who have completed catechetics courses at theology departments are eligible to teach religion at schools. All of them are required to hold general teaching qualifications.

[9] Formally, it is possible to take both ethics and religion classes, but choosing ethics is typically seen as a rejection of religious instruction by students or parents (in case of younger pupils). As one report states: "Teachers sometimes discourage [students] from participating in ethics classes, for example by saying that the course may be scheduled very late during the day, such as the eighth or even the ninth lesson hour" (Freedom from Religion Foundation, 2017, p. 7).

'demoralising' and 'sexualising' children, and attempt to curb it further (e.g., a draft law that would effectively criminalise sex education was submitted to Parliament in 2019[10]).

Nationalism

Nationalism is pervasive in Poland's educational content in the form of ethnocentric ideas about a homogeneous nation with a glorious past, a pattern recorded across Central and Eastern Europe (Kamusella, 2010). While earlier studies indicated that nationalism coloured textbooks and teachers' attitudes (Jaskulowski & Surmiak, 2015; Popow, 2015), the situation seems to have worsened recently. As in many other parts of Europe, the humanitarian crisis of 2015 and the growth of anti-refugee and anti-Muslim resentment made up an important context of this deterioration. However, distinctive to Central European states was their rejection of the relocation mechanism, and this non-solidarity policy was reflected in Poland's public discourse (Bobako, 2018) and strong prejudice (Goodwin & Raines, 2017; Pousther, 2016). In October and November 2015, cases of teachers publicly expressing racist content were reported (Rawłuszko, 2016).[11] The nationalist radicalisation of youth is rising, which poses the question of young people's indoctrination produced by an interplay of school and other socialisation spaces, such as online communication, football fan groups and street demonstrations of far-right organisations. Members of the latter, especially of the All-Polish Youth and the National-Radical Camp, have made several successful attempts to offer extracurricular activities within schools (Woźnicki, 2016; Giedrys, 2017). This trend seems to be absent in Western European contexts, as reflected in a recent paper by the Radicalisation Awareness Network (Krasenberg et al., 2019). It acknowledges the classroom presence of the far-right extremism at the level of individuals' views, but does not envisage the possibility of the school administration and staff actually *inviting* far-right activists to interact with students.

The instances of tolerating or promoting extreme nationalism in schools imply a breach of Article 29 in relation to "the spirit of understanding, peace, tolerance, equality of sexes and friendship among all peoples, ethnic, national and religious groups" (1)(d), as well as to "the development of respect for … civilizations different from his or her own" (1)(c). However, one may argue that a patriotic orientation of schools, even when ethnocentric and under authoritarian pressures (Cervinkova

---

[10] Submitted by the *Stop paedophilia* citizens' initiative and supported by ca. 265,000 citizens, the draft stipulates 3-year imprisonment for any professionals (including educators) who promote or approve of any sexual activity undertaken by a minor.

[11] These cases included a high-school teacher posting neo-Nazi materials on Facebook, a lower-secondary school physics teacher who assigned an exercise depicting refugees in a dehumanising way and a priest teaching religion in elementary school who spoke against Muslims at an anti-immigration rally (Rawłuszko, 2016, pp. 128–32).

& Rudnicki, 2019), conforms with the rest of Article 29(1)(c), that is, "respect for the child's parents, his or her own cultural identity, language and values, for the national values of the country in which the child is living." The problematic nature of this provision lies in that it lends itself to essentialist interpretations of "cultural identity" or "values of the country." Alternative views or experiences of children from minority communities may be marginalised in textbooks and classrooms. "Respect for the child's parents" becomes quite a questionable notion if family upbringing strengthens xenophobic dispositions. Polish schools tend to show weakness in this regard and seem unprepared to tackle the problem in ways proposed by the 'democracy labs' model outlined by the Western anti-radicalisation experts referred to above. Another problematic aspect is the ambiguous notion of civilisational difference, which may also generate essentialist understandings of 'us/them', potentially feeding racist imagery. In short, while Polish schools fall short of meeting the UNCRC's provisions and sometimes go against them, the UNCRC itself seems insufficient in countering the state-supported nationalistic tendencies.

The Development of Respect for the Natural Environment

Article 29(1)(e) of the UNCRC highlights the importance of ecological awareness. Elements of environmental education are included in Polish curricula for all grades, yet it remains rather superficial in practice. The Commissioner for Human Rights has recommended developing a specific climate crisis curriculum, but the Ministry has rejected this, claiming that the relevant content is already covered (RPO, 2020). Indeed, teachers incorporate aspects of environmental and global education into their instruction, but they lack a broader, critical perspective on it (Jasikowska et al., 2015, pp. 147–148). Polish activists of the Youth Climate Strike regard the current curricula as inadequate and call for their modification (Jurszo, 2019). Additionally, this theme is not free from political and economic tensions. Some of Poland's regions still depend on coal mining, which is supported for the sake of national energy sovereignty. The reasons for deficiencies in environmental education might, again, be traced back to a broader context, namely the country's historical and contemporary status and development trajectory.

Filling the Gaps Through Non-Governmental Initiatives

Various programs in anti-racism, human rights, sex education, media literacy (aimed at countering susceptibility to fake news), global education and ecology are offered to schools by NGOs to fill the perceived curriculum gaps. Organisations reach out to individual schools and teachers, providing them with information and teaching materials, skill development, and volunteer support. Some of their activities ameliorate access conditions, as in the case of the Nomada Association in Wrocław, which works with immigrant Romani children, including illiterate teenagers. Other projects focus on school democracy, as does the Poznań-based Astrid Lindgren Institute for Early Childhood Development. The youth-run *Pontoon* group of sexuality educators offers workshops and counselling. Such initiatives contribute to the fulfilment of the UNCRC's principles and often serve as avenues to civic engagement for young people themselves. However, subject to the economic volatility of grant-based funding, the good will of school administrators and public opinion pressures, these actions remain on the fringes of the education system rather than constituting its integral component.

Relations: Exclusion and Discrimination

As an aspect of children's rights in education, interpersonal relations are crucial to students' experience of school and learning about social life (Quennerstedt, 2015). Positive interpersonal relations form a critical context for developing the child's personality, talents and abilities (Article 29(1)(a) of the UNCRC) and his/her capacity to live responsibly in a free society (Article 29(1)(d)). Article 29 concerns gaining "life skills" to make decisions, solve conflicts, take responsibility, think critically, and act on the world in accordance with human rights (UNCRC, 2001, pp. 2–4). Such skills can only be acquired in a school that functions as a democratic space of participation, mutual respect, and openness towards diversity, where everyone feels welcome. For many Polish students this is not the case. A recent study found that only 53% of the participants aged 15–17 enjoyed going to school (Falkowska & Telusiewicz-Pacak, 2019), while merely 60% of 15-year-olds felt that they belonged at school (OECD, 2019). Statistics convey a worrying picture of Polish students' mental health: increasing numbers of children suffer from mental and behavioural disorders; the suicide rate is above the EU average; and children and youth express dissatisfaction with their lives (Falkowska & Telusiewicz-Pacak, 2019; OECD, 2019; Szredzińska, 2017, p. 113). The school's negative impact should not be underestimated.

More specifically, students have a limited sense of inclusion in the life of their class community. They assess their influence on school regulations, trips, the organisation of space, or electing students' representatives as lower than desired and, indeed, lesser than their teachers claim it is (Falkowska & Telusiewicz-Pacak, 2019, p. 44). Fixed curricula, standardised exams, and teacher dominance in learning environments hamper students' influence on the content and organisation of instruction. While there are student councils that could serve as a platform for children's voice in school, they tend not to be considered partners, and their role in decision-making is restricted to insignificant issues. This may explain students' meagre interest in these bodies (Ziółkowski, 2014).

Some students feel stigmatised. Previous research indicates that non-heterosexual students, non-Catholics and members of ethnic minorities are especially prone to find themselves "strangers" at school (Gawlicz & Starnawski, 2013). Quennerstedt

(2015, p. 206) argues that protecting students from discrimination and violence is the responsibility that schools must fulfil in order to retain students' status as rights holders. Certain systemic developments have targeted discriminatory practices at Polish schools. In 2013, the Ministry of Education amended a regulation on educational superintendence, making it mandatory for educational institutions to implement activities aimed at countering discrimination. Such activities were to be reported by teachers and the school administration as part of school evaluation. This regulation could be seen as a step towards monitoring the practical enactment of Article 29, as well as a tool for protecting and enforcing its provisions, especially with regard to respect for human rights and religious, cultural and individual differences, as well as the principle of tolerance (Article 29(1), points b, c and d). Nonetheless, analysis of selected records in the System of Evaluation showed that school staff tended to marginalise, overlook, or misrepresent the issue (Jonczy-Adamska & Rawłuszko, 2015). The most commonly, albeit infrequently, reported activities concerned economic status and disability, while those focused on other categories (gender, race, ethnicity/nationality, religion, age, sexual orientation, political views) appeared in fewer than 10% of evaluations, with sexual orientation and political views barely present (Jonczy-Adamska & Rawłuszko, 2015). The requirement to report anti-discrimination activities was removed from the regulation in 2017, which suggests that the Ministry downplays the importance of practices targeting discrimination at school.

Violence is another critical aspect in this context. A study of almost 11,000 students in 185 schools indicated that 10% of students (15% in elementary schools) experienced bullying, with certain forms of verbal violence reported by one-fifth to over half of the respondents (Przewłocka, 2015, pp. 34–36). While children and youth experience physical, sexual, or relational peer violence at all levels of schooling, they assert that teachers disregard it and are unable to prevent it (Nowakowska & Przewłocka, 2015). In the case of 14-year-old Dominik Szymański, the lack of teachers' reaction to homophobic bullying caused the boy to commit suicide (Chustecka, 2016, pp. 173–175). Some cases of violence committed by teachers have been reported too. In a widely-publicised incident, a teacher taped the mouths of 5- and 6-year-olds (Rawłuszko, 2016, p. 114), but multiple other cases of teachers humiliating their students have also been reported to the RPD. A news outlet has documented 18 cases of physical abuse of schoolchildren by priest-teachers over the past 15 years, some resulting in lenient sentences (Sidorski, 2019).

Non-heterosexual students are a group particularly targeted by discriminatory practices. A survey of 2666 LGBTA[12] people aged 13–19 revealed that school was the place where the respondents most frequently experienced violent attacks, with school peers being the most frequent perpetrators (Świder & Winiewski, 2017, pp. 132–133). A recent qualitative study of LGBT graduates has analysed the exclusion of non-heterosexual identities in schools. The authors have argued that staff members, if not perpetrators of homophobic violence themselves, are poorly

[12] LGBTA refers to Lesbian, Gay, Bisexual, Transgender, and Asexual persons.

prepared to respond to homophobic violence (Pogorzelska & Rudnicki, 2020). Unsatisfactory relations between non-heterosexual students and their peers and teachers may contribute to the fact that a third of those young people assess their lives negatively, more than 70% feel lonely, and almost as many contemplate suicide (Świder & Winiewski, 2017, p. 134). In-school homophobia persists in an atmosphere bred by the Roman-Catholic bishops (e.g., the notorious 'rainbow plague' expression), the discourse of conservative politicians, and mob aggression against LGBT marches in various Polish cities. It represents group-based discrimination and hinders the realisation of Article 29(1)(a), which promotes the child's fullest development. Indeed, it destroys the humanity of both victims and aggressors, and prevents the spirit of trust and understanding from being cultivated and appreciated.

Conclusion

The enactment of children's educational rights in Poland is embroiled in conflicting claims about children's well-being. While tensions over the organisation and meaning of education are universal, they tend to belong to specific debates on a country's or region's historical-structural trajectory and aspirations of its population. These tensions and debates are where the question of children's rights is enmeshed in various contested issues: from nationhood, democracy, and equality to family, identity, and individual freedoms.

Using the conceptual lenses of access, content, and relations, our analysis reveals some critical patterns. In access, the persistent underfunding of schools may strengthen elitism, whereby educational opportunities hinge on the economic capacities and social networks of families, including resources to organise autonomous schools or home instruction. Further research should determine how the recent reforms such as those described in the chapter, affect the educational chances and choices of young people, especially from the upper-secondary level on. The observed mistrust in Poland's public education system stems from concerns about the content and methods of teaching in general, but religion-related tensions are particularly salient, owing primarily to fundamentalist interventions that mirror trends seen in the United States, for example. Nationalist and xenophobic tendencies have been met with responses, mainly from NGOs, which operate parallel to the schooling system and the official curriculum.

The efficacy of these alternative efforts can be explored further by investigating how their purposes relate to national and local realities. This relationship is where there might be gaps in the global circulation of educational ideas. For instance, can multicultural or global education concepts be easily transplanted from North-Western societies (with unique histories of capitalism, colonial expansion, and migration, such as the U.K.) to less "central" zones of the world-system, in this case to post-socialist Central and Eastern Europe torn between centuries of lagging-behind and the contemporary ambitions? As mentioned above, challenges in environmental education are another example of this tension. Both cases draw attention to how national policies structure and thematise education in the context of global economic pressures.

Perhaps it is in the third sphere—that of school interpersonal relations—that the children's rights perspective may have the most promising prospects, given that each new generation has their unique concerns and interests in transforming the world. For example, international youth initiatives on climate change have already exerted pressure to revise the 'aims of education'. And while reports on hate and bullying provide alarming information, personal relations tend to transgress prejudice. Visions of morality and identity enforced by the state and religion have already proven inadequate to many young people's lived experiences. Therefore, regardless of the current restrictions on the agency and participation of children and youth, we should expect to hear their voice. In the current climate, these voices may resonate stronger than ever before.

Acknowledgements The research was supported with funding from the National Science Centre, Poland (project no. 2014/13/D/HS6/01896).

References

Abramowicz, M. (Ed.). (2011). *Wielka nieobecna—o edukacji antydyskryminacyjnej w systemie edukacji formalnej w Polsce: Raport z badań*. TEA.

Anczyk, A., & Grzymała-Moszczyńska, J. (2018). Religious discrimination discourse in the mono-cultural school: The case of Poland. *British Journal of Religious Education, 40*(2), 182–193. https://doi.org/10.1080/01416200.2016.1209457

Andrei, T., Teodorescu, D., & Oancea, B. (2011). Characteristics and causes of school dropout in the countries of the European Union. *Procedia – Social and Behavioral Sciences, 28*, 328–332. https://doi.org/10.1016/j.sbspro.2011.11.062

Bieńko, M., Izdebski, Z., & Wąż, K. (2016). *Kontrola realizacji prawa młodzieży do edukacji seksualnej. Realizacja zajęć wychowania do życia w rodzinie. Perspektywa uczennic/uczniów i dyrektorów/dyrektorek szkół. Skrót raportu z badań jakościowych*. Federacja na rzecz Kobiet i Planowania Rodziny; Ponton Grupa Edukatorów Seksualnych. https://rownosc.info/media/uploads/raport_skrot_prawo_do_edukacji_seksualnej_ponton_2016.pdf

Bobako, M. (2018). Semi-peripheral Islamophobias: The political diversity of anti-Muslim discourses in Poland. *Patterns of Prejudice, 52*(5), 448–460. https://doi.org/10.1080/0031322X.2018.1490112

Bonet, L., & Zamorano, M. M. (2021). Cultural policies in illiberal democracies: A conceptual framework based on the Polish and Hungarian governing experiences. *International Journal of Cultural Policy, 27*(5), 559–573. https://doi.org/10.1080/10286632.2020.1806829

Brown, P. (1994). Education and the ideology of parentocracy. In M. J. Halstead (Ed.), *Parental choice and education: Principles, policy and practice* (pp. 51–67). Kogan Page.

Bucko, D. (2019). Wspomaganie rozwoju nauczycieli uczących dzieci z doświadczeniem migracji. *Kwartalnik Polonicum, 31*(32), 113–120.

Cervinkova, H., & Rudnicki, P. (2019). Neoliberalism, neo-conservatism, authoritarianism: The politics of public education in Poland. *The Journal of Critical Education Policy Studies, 17*(2), 1–23.

Chmura-Rutkowska, I., Duda, M., Mazurek, M., & Sołtysiak-Łuczak, A. (Eds.). (2016). *Gender w podręcznikach. Projekt badawczy. Raport*. Feminoteka.

Chustecka, M. (2016). Perspektywa antydyskryminacyjna w działaniach instytucji publicznych. In M. Chustecka, E. Kielak, & M. Rawłuszko (Eds.), *Edukacja antydyskryminacyjna. Ostatni dzwonek! O deficytach system edukacji formalnej w obszarze przeciwdziałania dyskryminacji i przemocy motywowanej uprzedzeniami* (pp. 40–98). TEA.

Cichy, H., & Helak, M. (2021). *Usługi publiczne w kryzysie: Edukacja do zmiany*. Polityka Insight.

Czuba-Wąsowska, M., & Mańko, K. (2011). *Egzekucja obowiązków szkolnego i nauki. Zagadnienia prawne. Teoria i praktyka*. Wolters Kluwer.

Devinney, T. M., & Hartwell, C. A. (2020). Varieties of populism. *Global Strategy Journal, 10*, 32–66. https://doi.org/10.1002/gsj.1373

European Commission. (2013). *Reducing early school leaving: Key messages and policy support (Final Report of the Thematic Working Group on Early School Leaving)*. https://ec.europa.eu/education/content/reducing-early-school-leaving-key-messages-and-policy-support_en

Eurostat. (2019). *Early leavers from education and training*. https://ec.europa.eu/eurostat/statistics-explained/index.php/Early_leavers_from_education_and_training

Falkowska, E., & Telusiewicz-Pacak, A. (2019). *Prawa dziecka z perspektywy dzieci, rodziców i nauczycieli: Raport z badań*. UNICEF Polska.

Fischer, A. M. (2020). The dark sides of social policy: From neoliberalism to resurgent right-wing populism. *Development and Change, 51*(2), 371–397. https://doi.org/10.1111/dech.12577

Freedom from Religion Foundation. (2017). *Dyskryminacja dzieci niewierzących i nieuczestniczących w lekcjach religii*. https://wolnoscodreligii.pl/app/uploads/2019/04/Raport-badania-ankietowe-2017.pdf

Gawlicz, K., & Starnawski, M. (2013). Areas of discrimination and marginalisation in school and preschool education in Poland. In M. Starnawski, P. Rudnicki, M. Nowak-Dziemianowicz, & Associates (Eds.), *Educational change and challenges in Poland and the Czech Republic after 1989* (pp. 39–52). WN DSW.

Giedrys, G. (2017, January 23). Młodzież Wszechopolska z pogadanką w szkole. Burza w sieci. *Wyborcza.pl*. https://torun.wyborcza.pl/torun/1,48723,21280984,mlodziez-wszechpolska-z-pogadanka-w-szkole-burza-w-sieci.html

Giercarz-Borkowska, M. (2019). *Edukacja domowa jako alternatywa edukacyjna dla dzieci zdolnych*. Teksty.

Goodwin, M., & Raines, T. (2017). *What do Europeans think about Muslim immigration?* Chatham House. https://www.chathamhouse.org/expert/comment/what-do-europeans-think-about-muslim-immigration#.

Griffiths, T. G., & Imre, R. (2013). *Mass education, global capital, and the world: The theoretical lenses of István Mészáros and Immanuel Wallerstein*. Palgrave Macmillan.

GUS. (2019). *Education in the 2018/2019 school year: Statistics Poland*. Statistical Office in Gdansk.

Hajduk-Gawron, W. (2018). Uczniowie cudzoziemscy w polskim systemie edukacyjnym—doświadczenia śląskich szkół z perspektywy osób przyjmowanych i środowiska przyjmującego. *Postscriptum Polonistyczne, 2*(22), 187–203.

Hidalgo, O. (2019). Religious backgrounds of illiberal democracy in Central and Eastern Europe. *Religion and Society in Central and Eastern Europe, 12*(1), 3–21. https://doi.org/10.20413/rascee.2019.12.1.3-21

Jasikowska, K., Pająk-Ważna, E., & Klarenbach, M. (2015). *Edukacja globalna w Małopolsce. Podmioty—Praktyki—Konteksty*. Impuls.

Jaskulowski, K., & Surmiak, A. (2015). Teaching history, teaching nationalism: A qualitative study of history teachers in a Polish post-industrial town. *Critical Studies in Education, 58*, 36. https://doi.org/10.1080/17508487.2015.1117006

Jonczy-Adamska, M., & Rawłuszko, M. (2015). Dyskryminacja i działania antydyskryminacyjne w szkołach na podstawie danych Systemu Ewaluacji Oświaty. In K. Gawlicz, P. Rudnicki, & M. Starnawski (Eds.), *Dyskryminacja w szkole—obecność nieusprawiedliwiona. O budowaniu edukacji antydyskryminacyjnej w systemie edukacji formalnej w Polsce*. TEA.

Jurszo, R. (2019, November 29). *Młodzieżowy Strajk Klimatyczny ma głęboki sens. Czego nie rozumieją prawicowi publicyści*. OKO.Press. https://oko.press/mlodziezowy-strajk-klimatyczny-ma-gleboki-sens-czego-nie-rozumieja-prawicowi-publicysci/

Kamusella, T. (2010). School history atlases as instruments of nation-state making and maintenance: A remark on the invisibility of ideology in popular education. *Journal of Educational Media, Memory, and Society, 2*(1), 113–138. https://doi.org/10.3167/jemms.2010.020107

Kielak, E., Cieślikowska, D., & Kudarewska, A. (Eds.). (2016). *Edukacja globalna w podręcznikach do geografii i wiedzy o społeczeństwie. Raport z analizy wybranych podręczników szkolnych pod kątem założeń edukacji globalnej*. Grupa Zagranica.

Korczak, J. (2017). *A child's right to respect*. (S.G. Bye, Trans.). Rzecznik Praw Dziecka.

Kozak, M. (2014). *Edukacja na rzecz praw człowieka w szkole wyższej*. Impuls.

Krasenberg, J., Lenos, S., & Sterkenburg, N. (2019). *RAN EDU Academy: Far-right extremism in the classroom. Ex Post Paper*. RAN Centre of Excellence and the RAN EDU Working Group. https://ec.europa.eu/home-affairs/sites/homeaffairs/files/what-we-do/networks/radicalisation_awareness_network/about-ran/ran-edu/docs/ran_edu_academy_far-right_extremism_in_classroom_berlin_13-14_062019_en.pdf

Krzyżanowski, P. J. (2018). Realizacja rządowego programu integracji społeczności romskiej w Polsce na przykładzie województwa lubuskiego. *Polityka i Społeczeństwo, 16*(2), 130–141. https://doi.org/10.15584/polispol.2018.2.9

Kucharska, A. (2014). Dlaczego edukacja domowa? Aksjologiczne uzasadnienia edukacji bez szkoły. *Wychowanie w Rodzinie, 10*(2), 205–224.

Madalińska-Michalak, J. (2017). Zjawisko przedwczesnego kończenia nauki i jego ograniczanie. *Studia Edukacyjne, 43*, 81–97. https://doi.org/10.1016/j.sbspro.2011.11.062

Madalińska-Michalak, J. M., & Jeżowski, A. J. (2018). Etyka i religia jako przedmioty nauczania: Konkurencyjność czy komplementarność? *Forum Oświatowe, 30*(2), 219–241.

Nowakowska, A., & Przewłocka, J. (2015). *Szkoła oczami uczniów: Relacje z nauczycielami i kolegami oraz przemoc szkolna*. IBE.

Nyyssönen, H., & Metsälä, J. (2020). Liberal democracy and its current illiberal critique: The emperor's new clothes? *Europe-Asia Studies, 73*, 273. https://doi.org/10.1080/09668136.2020.1815654

OECD. (2019). *PISA 2018 results (volume III): What school life means for students' lives*. OECD Publishing. https://doi.org/10.1787/acd78851-en

Pogorzelska, M., & Rudnicki, P. (2020). *Przecież jesteśmy! Homofobiczna przemoc w polskich szkołach narracje gejów i lesbijek*. Impuls.

Popow, M. (2015). *Kategoria narodu w dyskursie edukacyjnym. Analiza procesów konstruowania tożsamości w podręcznikach szkolnych*. WN UAM.

Pousther, J. (2016). *European opinions of the refugee crisis in 5 charts*. Pew Research Center. https://www.pewresearch.org/fact-tank/2016/09/16/european-opinions-of-the-refugee-crisis-in-5-charts/

Przewłocka, J. (2015). *Bezpieczeństwo uczniów i klimat społeczny w polskich szkołach. Raport z badania*. IBE.

Pyżalski, J., Zdrodowska, A., Tomczyk, Ł., & Abramczuk, K. (2019). *Polskie badanie EU Kids Online 2018*. WN UAM.

Quennerstedt, A. (2015). Education and children's rights. In W. Vandenhole, E. Desmet, D. Reynaert, & S. Lembrechts (Eds.), *Routledge international handbook of children's rights studies* (pp. 201–215). Routledge.

Rawłuszko, M. (2016). Dyskryminacja w szkole na podstawie doniesień medialnych. In M. Chustecka, E. Kielak, & M. Rawłuszko (Eds.), *Edukacja antydyskryminacyjna. Ostatni dzwonek! O deficytach system edukacji formalnej w obszarze przeciwdziałania dyskryminacji i przemocy motywowanej uprzedzeniami*. TEA.

RPO. (2014). *Działania Rzecznika Praw Obywatelskich na rzecz mniejszości romskiej w województwie małopolskim. Raport z wizytacji osiedli romskich*. Biuro Rzecznika Praw Obywatelskich.

RPO. (2015). *Dostępność lekcji religii wyznań mniejszościowych i lekcji etyki w ramach systemu edukacji szkolnej. Analiza i zalecenia* (Vol. 6). Biuletyn Rzecznika Praw Obywatelskich.

RPO. (2020, January 24). *Kryzys klimatyczny ma związek z prawami człowieka—Przyznaje resort edukacji*. https://www.rpo.gov.pl/pl/content/kryzys-klimatyczny-zwiazany-z-prawami-czlowieka-przyznaje-men-rpo

Sidorski, A. (2019). *Księża biją dzieci. 18 przykładów*. OKO Press.

Świder, M., & Winiewski, M. (Eds.). (2017). *Situation of LGBTA persons in Poland: 2015–2016 report*. Campaign Against Homophobia.

Szredzińska, R. (2017). Zdrowie dzieci i młodzieży. *Dziecko Krzywdzone. Teoria, Badania, Praktyka, 16*(1), 94–131.

UNCRC. (2001). *General comment no. 1 (2001): Article 29 (1): The aims of education* (CRC/GC/2001/1). https://www.refworld.org/docid/4538834d2.html

UNICEF. (2007). *A human rights-based approach to education for all: A framework for the realization of children's right to education and rights within education*. UNICEF, UNESCO. https://unesdoc.unesco.org/ark:/48223/pf0000154861

Verhellen, E. (1993). Children's rights and education: A three-track legally binding imperative. *School Psychology International, 14*(3), 199–208. https://doi.org/10.1177/0143034393143002

Wallerstein, I. (2004). *World-systems analysis: An introduction*. Duke University Press.

Woźnicki, Ł. (2016, March 17) "Wielki przełom". Dyrektor wpuściła do szkoły ONR. Człowiek z falangą wystąpił przed uczniami. *Wyborcza.pl*. https://wyborcza.pl/1,75398,19778799,wielki-przelom-dyrektor-wpuscila-do-szkoly-onr-czlowiek-z.html

Ziółkowski, P. (2014). *Samorząd uczniowski—idee, uwarunkowania i doświadczenia*. Wydawnictwo Uczelniane Wyższej Szkoły Gospodarki w Bydgoszczy.

Chapter 6
Children's Education: From a Right to a Capability

Elisabetta Biffi and Chiara Carla Montà

Abstract As stated in Article 29 of the UNCRC, the goal of education is to prepare children for a responsible life in a free society. However, recent international agendas and strategy documents (such as the United Nations 2030 Agenda for Sustainable Development) have emphasised the need to develop a more equal and just – more so than a freer – society, while continuing to identify education as a key pillar of human development. In light of this background, the present chapter offers a theoretical analysis of the role of education in human social development, exploring possible connections between children's rights studies and the capabilities approach. It refers to the terms of the UNCRC to suggest that children's capabilities need to be conceptualised on their own terms.

Keywords Children's rights · Capabilities · Sustainable development · Education

Children's Right to Education and Sustainable Development

Article 29 of the UNCRC (1989) is of far-reaching importance: it promotes the innate human dignity and inalienable rights of all children, while recognising their individual developmental needs and capacity for development. General Comment No. 1 of the Committee of the Rights of the Child (2001) offers a more in-depth understanding of the article, stating that education embraces the broad range of life experiences and learning processes that enable children, individually and collectively, to develop their personality, talents and mental and physical abilities to their fullest potential. The 'aim of education', according to Article 29, is to prepare

---

E. Biffi (✉) · C. C. Montà
University of Milano-Bicocca, Milan, Italy
e-mail: elisabetta.biffi@unimib.it; c.monta@campus.unimib.it

J. Gillett-Swan, N. Thelander (eds.), *Children's Rights from International Educational Perspectives*, Transdisciplinary Perspectives in Educational Research 2, https://doi.org/10.1007/978-3-030-80861-7_6

children for a responsible life in a free society. To this end, General Comment No.1 (2001) lists certain fundamental skills that every child needs to have, in order to face the challenges she/he will be confronted with in life, such as: literacy and numeracy; the ability to make well-balanced decisions; to resolve conflicts in a non-violent manner; and to develop a healthy lifestyle, good social relationships, responsibility, critical thinking, creative talents, and other abilities which give children the tools needed to pursue their options in life. This implies the need for a holistic and integrated approach to education that values the different ways in which people learn, think, feel, and act. In sum, the overall goal of education is to promote children's ability and opportunity to participate fully and responsibly in a free society.

This brings us to the *UN 2030 Agenda for Sustainable Development*, which defines the bases for ensuring children's full participation in society and offering them a nurturing environment where they can fully realise their rights and capabilities, outcomes viewed as crucial to the very survival of humanity. Education is key to achieving such goals, both in keeping with the vision of the UNCRC and because it is seen as an essential prerequisite for human development and flourishing. Indeed, the Agenda states that:

> We commit to providing inclusive and equitable quality education at all levels – early childhood, primary, secondary, tertiary, technical and vocational training. All people, irrespective of sex, age, race or ethnicity, and persons with disabilities, migrants, indigenous peoples, children and youth, especially those in vulnerable situations, should have access to life-long learning opportunities that help them to acquire the knowledge and skills needed to exploit opportunities and to participate fully in society. We will strive to provide children and youth with a nurturing environment for the full realization of their rights and capabilities, helping our countries to reap the demographic dividend, including through safe schools and cohesive communities and families. (UN Resolution A/RES/70/1, p. 7)

The Agenda acknowledges that economic resources alone will not ensure adequate conditions for human development; nor can mere recognition of human rights bring about the sustainability, inclusion, and human dignity called for in the document's sustainable development goals (SDGs). This position is confirmed by data from the UNICEF report *Building the Future. Children and Sustainable Development Goals in Rich Countries* (UNICEF, 2017), which assesses children's well-being in relation to sustainable development across 41 countries in the EU and OECD. The UNICEF report underlines that neither legislative frameworks nor economic prosperity are sufficient to ensure a good quality of life and wellness for the children of a country. It is essential to foster a high-quality general education framework.

Moss' (2007, p. 9) work on the role of early childhood education in building a democratic society also suggests that thinking of educational services as democratic is the outcome of a conscious choice and requires countries to act at five different levels:

- "a clear entitlement to access to services for children as citizens";
- "a funding system that enables all children to exercise their entitlement";
- "a framework curriculum that defines broad values and goals but allows local interpretation";
- "a fully integrated early childhood policy";

- "a well-educated and well-paid workforce for all young children"; and
- "active policies to reduce poverty and inequality".

Moss proposes that schools[1] may be viewed either as institutions for the education of children of all ages or as structures whose aim is to produce spaces of sharing and learning where adults and children can build a community together. According to the latter view, schools are places of education not only for children, who represent the heart of a school, but also for the adults involved. This will be even more the case in schools that succeed in developing a democratic ethos that values the sharing of opinions and points of view and/or establishing a democratic system for managing school life.

From another perspective, the focus of the SDGs on equitable development and of policy in general on *leaving no one behind* (Adamson, 2010) draws our attention to inequalities in multiple domains, including not only wealth or the formal recognition of rights, but also health and education, voice and political participation. Long-term development goals may only be achieved by attending to children and their specific needs, and creating the life conditions, through education, that allow people (children) to realise their potentialities and existential projects. These preliminary considerations prompt a specific focus on the role of children in our contemporary society, a role that is closely related to the concept of childhood embedded in our political and cultural worldview (Biffi, 2018).

Education as *Right*, Education as *Just*

Investing in children has been a recurrent feature of an ongoing process of liberation, protection, and emancipation (Lindsay, 1992) that began in the 1800s. Early steps to protect children were advocated by the philanthropic movement and then pursued by society more broadly, leading to the introduction of specific legislation such as the *Children's Act* of 1908. Literature in the form of novels such as those of Charles Dickens told of an underworld in which children and women were exposed to ill treatment and appalling living conditions. Social reformers turned their attention to issues of poverty and came to realise that children were unable to transform their status alone. Hence the 1908 Act, which drew together existing legislation and made improvements in several areas to protect the poorest and most vulnerable children in society. The Act was designed to prevent cruelty towards children, protect the life of infants, put a system in place for dealing with juvenile offenders, and provide a legal basis for reform and industrial schools. Children had been neglected for centuries, but now parents or other child-minders who ill-treated or neglected

[1] Schools in this context encompass all levels of education, including ECEC, and educational institutions in general. Our focus here is on children's schooling, given that the UNCRC exclusively concerns minors. For background on how these issues have been addressed in relation to higher education, see: Davids & Waghid, 2016; Evans et al., 2017; Gale & Tranter, 2011; Singh, 2011.

the young could be prosecuted. This Act played a key part in shaping the acceptance that parents and the state are obliged to take responsibility for children, a step towards recognising childhood as distinct from adulthood and thereby establishing the rights of the child.

The implicit reason for protecting children was recognition of the risks associated with neglect, exploitation, and harsh punishment, which included premature death and sickness in adulthood, thus producing individuals who were unable to contribute to society or viewed as a burden. Hence, children were protected as future adults. The push to emancipate children gained further momentum in the twentieth century thanks to the *discovery of childhood* (Ariès, 1968), facilitated by scientific advances in the fields of psychology, anthropology, psychoanalysis, and pedagogy showing that childhood is not a mere transition phase, functional to producing adulthood, but a specific category of existence that is meaningful in its own right and also profoundly influences adulthood. These scientific advances and the related cultural shift paved the way for the child protection movement, for which the *Geneva Declaration* of 1924 represented a first milestone. Several years went by before the General Assembly approved the *Declaration of the Rights of the Child* on the 20 November 1959, a document that laid greater onus to comply on the signatory countries: not yet from a statutory perspective, but at least from an ethical and political point of view.

Most recently, in our contemporary era, the *United Nations Convention on the Rights of the Child, UNCRC* of 1989, which is binding on the signatory nations, at last accorded full citizenship status to children. The UNCRC ushered in a culture of childhood and children's rights (Moro, 1991), fostering a novel, more emancipated perspective on childhood, and offering a framework for the development of child policies. However, it should be noted that this cultural departure was again mainly economically driven. A clear example is the continuous highlighting of the economic cost of failing to protect children, and thereby "leaving them behind" (Adamson, 2010, p.4). For example, a note on the *Rights of the Child* (UN General Assembly 2006), citing an earlier WHO (2000) report on violence, emphasised the economic motives for protecting children from violence: the cost of violence against children (in terms of post-traumatic therapy and reduced performance in adulthood) is socially and economically higher than that of prevention and protection measures.

Liberals across different historical periods have always supported investing in education, first and foremost for reasons of cost-effectiveness. Societies that can rely on quality educational systems increase their future chances of having competent adults, deemed from the liberal perspective to be more productive adults and therefore as making a greater contribution to society. Investing in education generates *human capital* and this is socially and economically advantageous (Becker et al., 1964). On these grounds, many studies have focused on the need for *quality* education beginning in early childhood because, in economic terms, quality education is associated with greater productivity in adulthood and a lesser need to invest in remedial action (Buzzelli, 2015; Heckman, 2007). Heckman (2007) for example argues that investing in programs earlier in children's lives is more cost-effective than intervention later in the life cycle.

In sum, within the contemporary debate on the recognition of children as citizens (Deardorff, Kiwan, & Park, 2018), which is a core concept in the UNCRC, calls for active participation by children are still set off by an inability to abandon adult-centric perspective viewing child policies as a means of defending children as adult capital. This ambiguity also features in leading social justice theories concerning children. For example, in the work of Rawls (1971), although education is not explicitly treated, it is implicitly viewed as a means of producing adults who are able to contribute to economic development.

Rawls developed his theory of justice within the field of political philosophy and ethics. His key concern was the socially just way to distribute goods in a society. His pre-eminently political theory was informed by the social contract tradition and drew on an artificial device termed the *original position* to explain how principles of justice are decided upon. Scholars from other traditions argue that Rawls' primary goods approach – which focuses on general-purpose goods, such as income and wealth, opportunities and liberties, and the social good of self-respect – overlooks human diversity (Sen, 1980), excluding – for example – the disabled and children, and even women.

Instead, the capability approach (CA) to social justice, which is the framework underpinning the SDGs in UN Agenda 2030, was originally proposed by Amartya Sen and subsequently developed by Martha Nussbaum. It is an economic theory first put forward in the 1980s as an alternative approach to welfare economics. Sen and Nussbaum drew together ideas that had been excluded from or poorly developed in traditional approaches. Their core focus is on what a person can do and be in a given society, therefore on what they are capable of. This vision of development takes into consideration the complexity of contemporary reality and differences among human beings and does not see a country's GDP as the only or main indicator of its level of development.

The SDGs emphasise concepts such as sustainability, equality, inclusion, and human dignity, which since the late twentieth century have increasingly been seen as important, in light of evidence that economic prosperity is not the sole indicator of development. Nor does the formal recognition of rights mean that subjects actually enjoy them. Hence, the SDGs, in addition to rights, emphasise the opportunities available to individuals and include aspects of quality of life – such as wellbeing and personal life planning – among the markers of development. This represents a departure from the neo-liberal and neo-positivist view of quality that came to the fore in the 1980s and 1990s and was informed by particular notions of management and accountability. Ultimately, the SDGs are underpinned by a holistic perspective on the life of an individual and its multiple interrelated dimensions.

Nussbaum (2010) views profit and rights (Hammarberg, 2008a) as instrumental to the promotion of liberty and democracy, and not as mere ends in themselves. The ultimate aim of global development is to create conditions allowing individuals to enjoy full and creative lives, while developing their potential and living a life that they value and that reflects their human dignity. To this end, Sen (2000) speaks of the capability to transform goods and resources into the freedom to pursue one's own objectives, to plan a life according to what one values. Human dignity demands the opportunity to attain a high level of capacities. Hence fostering capacities as possibilities from which to choose implies fostering freedom. Unlike Sen, Nussbaum (2000, 2010) identified a list of central capabilities of which a political order, to be considered decent, needs to guarantee at least a minimum level to all citizens. The core capabilities that should be supported by all democracies are: life; bodily health; bodily integrity; senses, imagination and thought; emotions; practical reason; affiliation; other species; play and control over one's environment (Nussbaum, 2011, pp. 33–34).

As this list makes clear, education is not one of the capabilities envisaged by Nussbaum, but this does not denote a lack of interest, on the contrary: education in the CA represents even more than a capability, as it is the key prerequisite condition for the development of all capabilities (Nussbaum, 2010).

The CA features its own unique discussions on the child. Sen (2011) often refers to his own childhood to justify his positions and offer examples, but he never discusses the role of children in a just society (Macleod, 2010). Nussbaum's main contribution on the theme of childhood from a CA perspective is an essay co-authored with Rosalind Dixon (Nussbaum & Dixon, 2012). Here, the authors argue that the main treaties on social justice, which were informed by the contract tradition, underestimate the role of children, on account of their vulnerability and their need of care (Nussbaum & Dixon, 2012, p. 563). They suggest viewing childhood as a specific category rather than the "negative" image of adulthood. In other words, as what adulthood is not. Yet, even this essay is ambiguous, in the sense that it still conceptualises children as future adults, characterised primarily by the potential to grow. "The starting point for the CA is the fact that human beings come into the world with a variety of inchoate capacities that need development" (Nussbaum & Dixon, 2012, p. 563). Furthermore, the perspective outlined by Nussbaum and Dixon (2012), clearly implies a cost-effectiveness rationale for investments on education albeit within a more complex view of the role of children.

There are two main contemporary manners of considering education and educational services. The first one views education as a mere technical practice, so a space and time in which technologies can be applied to produce determinate outcomes; the second one views educational services as competing businesses in a private market (Moss, 2007). Technologies, scientific progress, and business are surely important components when thinking of education. However, while these are only some of the aspects that need to be considered, they tend to be dominant, they aspire to be absolute. This leads us to the need to see education as something more than a means of enhancing social productivity and obtaining certain outcomes.

Coming back to our earlier reference to the Capability Approach and the 2030 Agenda, it should be noted that the latter reflects the awareness – which since the 1980s has increasingly informed international agendas and strategies, at different levels and in different domains (an example in the field of education policy would be the Bologna Process) – of the interrelated nature of education, quality, and policy. Indeed, contemporary education policy is focused on enhancing the quality of education and assessing its social and economic, impact. This is not unique to education: as observed above, even policies designed to protect children from violence and informed by a rights perspective are often initially prompted by analyses of the economic costs of violence.

However, when focusing on the economic motive for investing in education it might be viewed as weak, from at least a couple of different angles. First, because, as Robeyns points out, an instrumental view of education values skills and knowledge "only in so far as they contribute (directly and indirectly) to expected economic productivity" (Robeyns, 2006, p. 73). This means that state investment in competences that are not directly productive, such as the arts, could not be justified. Second, a vision of education limited to the "economic impact factor" fails to take into account the role of education in individual lives, in terms of enhancing "individual agency".

This last consideration represents a crucial turning point for the analysis of children's education in contemporary society. It allows us to connect the concept of "education" with a broader notion of human existence across the lifespan. The opportunity to define one's own personal learning and development process is thus an integral part of the educational process itself, crucially fostering self-definition and self-construction right from the early years. However, a key question remains: "What kind of education are we talking about?" An education focused on making profit or on fostering a more inclusive type of citizenship?

The opening of Nussbaum's (2010) *Not for profit* denounces the "silent crises of education" that, in the long run, will damage the future of democracy. The imaginative, creative aspect of education and that of rigorous critical thought are losing ground, because countries are opting to pursue short-term profit by promoting the development of sought-after practical skills. So, the question is whether education is preparing young people for meaningful lives – and indeed whether it is truly preparing them for employment? A meaningful life implies being able to participate in decisions concerning oneself and other people – this is what democracy entails. On the one hand, the capacity to think critically and imagine the experience of others is key to democracy. On the other hand, economic wealth is also valuable, as is scientific and technological knowledge. Nussbaum resolves this apparent contradiction between education for profit and education for citizenship by pointing out that a flourishing economy requires the same skills that support citizenship, but views them from within a different paradigm; a paradigm in which education is not seen in functionalistic terms but in terms of promoting human flourishing.

General human flourishing requires participation on the part of citizens with the capacity to actively contribute to human development. It requires citizens who are prepared to play an active role in society, from a democratic perspective:

> Social justice education is both a process and a goal. The goal of social justice education is full and equal participation of all groups in society that is mutually shaped to meet their needs. Social justice includes a vision of society in which the distribution of resources is equitable, and all members are physically and psychologically safe and secure. We envision a society in which individuals are both self-determining (able to develop their full capacities), and interdependent (capable of interacting democratically with others). (Bell, 1997, p. 3)

Based on Moss' earlier mentioned theorising about early childhood education and democracy, we may identify four levels of community action that constitute "proof" of a democratisation process within educational institutions: decision making, evaluation, contesting dominant discourses, and opening up to change (Moss, 2007, p. 12). These are all democratic practices that may only be learned by doing, that is, they are learnt through direct experience. Teachers and educators require specific training if they are to offer democratically oriented educational experience throughout early childhood education and school years.

There is further level of education that democratic institutions need to deliver, which entails learning to live in an intergenerational community. This means, among other aspects, learning how to manage the inevitable "power relations" dynamics between adults and children. The concept that educational experience invariably features power in terms of an unequal relationship between the adult and the child, whatever the nature of the tie (parent-child, teacher-pupil and so on) was brilliantly theorised by Michael Foucault. According to his concept of the *dispositif* (1975), even a school is a system that includes dimensions of power, control, punishment, and reward. Instead of ignoring these dimensions, with a view to defending the "purity" of the educational relationship, it is crucial for both adults and children to learn to address these complex and ambiguous dimensions, approaching them from a democratic perspective. When schools are thought of as offering training in the workings of democracy, experiencing a "lower power position" can afford children the opportunity to learn how to use their voices, how to constructively enact their rights to the benefit of the entire community. And the same will be true for adults.

Implementing this kind of participatory approach is a complex undertaking:

> Participation is based on the idea that reality is not objective, that culture is a constantly evolving product of society, that individual knowledge is only partial; and that in order to construct a project, everyone's point of view is relevant in dialogue with those of others, within a framework of shared values. The idea of participation is founded on these concepts: and in our opinion, so, too, is democracy itself. (Cagliari et al., 2004, p. 29)

Via such a participatory process, ECEC and schools can share with the broader local community an alternative "culture of childhood", in which children are seen as active citizens contributing to what Moss has defined as "contesting dominant discourses" (Moss, 2007): all educational institutions, given the leading role of education in the development of a flourishing human society, can make a significant contribution to encouraging critical thinking, thus counteracting the tendency to a-critically accept mainstream perspectives.

Conclusion: The Right to Be Educated in One's Own Rights

Finally, there is another aspect that we should address in our analysis of the common ground between the capability approach and children's rights perspectives: the broad range of issues related to education as a right includes the right to be educated in one's own rights. Social justice requires human rights education (Brantefors et al., 2019), yet this has not been systemically delivered in schools, but rather has been left up to the efforts of non-governmental organisations (Covell, 2013). In contrast, Article 4 of the UNCRC demands that the signatory states take all appropriate measures to implement the rights recognised by the Convention. This means that education should be viewed as empowering both children and adults, but especially children because it gives them the opportunity to become aware of their own rights, which in turn can help them to learn how to participate in a democratic society and make their own personal contribution to human development.

This approach underpins the international strategy adopted by the UNESCO, as defined in the document *Education 2030 Agenda*. Specifically, the Education 2030 Framework for Action refers to Goal 4. Target 4.7 of the Sustainable Development Goals, and indicates that by 2030 all learners should be in a position to "acquire knowledge and skills needed to promote sustainable development, including among others through education for sustainable development and sustainable lifestyles, human rights, gender equality, promotion of a culture of peace and non-violence, global citizenship, and appreciation of cultural diversity and of culture's contribution to sustainable development" (SDG 4.7).

The Education 2030 Agenda bases UNESCO's entire strategy on the idea that in order to promote sustainable development, it is necessary to learn what human sustainable development is. The possibility to enact one's own rights relies, initially, on helping children to learn how they can enact their rights in the *here and now*. Rather than general discourses on the importance of children's rights, the Agenda stresses the need for a specific educational focus on the themes of human and children's rights. To translate these themes into concrete, everyday practice, the UNESCO Agenda proposes a strategy focused on the interconnection between the local and the global. While the UNCRC defines a global framework for children's rights, it is only by contributing to the definition of local procedures that children can live out their role as "social actors".

This means that education needs to fulfil at least three essential tasks:

First, it should *help children to develop critical thinking abilities*. The CA suggests reflecting, even on rights themselves, from a critical perspective, inquiring into their meanings in people's concrete, everyday lives. Hence, even education in children's rights needs to be rethought, and not viewed as a linear information process but as a complex dialogical process of co-construction between adults and children. Because content alone is not enough to create democratic, empowering classroom settings or to prepare students to become active agents of social justice in their lives and communities (Hackman, 2005). This because education in social justice is the "root" of teaching and schooling in a democratic society (Ayers et al., 2009) a kind of joint teaching and learning, in which children and adults are invited to critique, understand, and create new systems in line with the 2030 Sustainable Development Goals. This means creating educational communities that are aware of their identities and connections with others, but that are able to think critically and interact, and continually negotiate with the broader economic, historical, and cultural context.

Second, it should *help children to define what life is worthy of being lived.* This requires the adults to define educational tasks that incorporate ethics and key ethical themes into the overall educational framework. Within the fields of knowledge and topics viewed as necessary for the education of children, integrating a children's-rights-based approach (Gillett-Swan & Coppock, 2016) with CA will require adults to view ethical issues as core, as a prerequisite for allowing the children to reflect on values, on what is valuable from their perspective. The right to be educated in one's own rights entails helping children to identify by themselves what is right and what is not, within the course of a shared process of constructing values via dialogue between adults and children. This is closely related to the debate on "the best interest of the child" (Hammarberg, 2008b), which is still striving to move away from an 'adult centred perspective' and to develop a sharper focus on children and their stories. It also intersects with the debate on 'child participation' in terms of looking at how the demands of rights, equality and justice can be met via children's active participation in the everyday life of their communities, while always keeping their best interest in mind (Brantefors et al., 2019; Percy-Smith & Thomas, 2010).

Finally, education should *help children to contribute to defining their rights.* Ultimately, the main challenge for adult educators who wish to adopt a children's rights-based approach integrated with CA is to learn to view the child as the leading expert in his/her own citizenship status. "(…)social justice education encourages students to take an active role in their own education and supports teachers in creating empowering, democratic, and critical educational environments". (Hackman, 2005, p. 103) This point is crucial because it implies training children to see and understand and, when necessary, to challenge what they have in front of them, to be agents in their own lives and of their own rights. This means that all educational institutions and settings should provide the conditions necessary for children to take active part in their decision-making and democratisation processes. Ultimately, democratic participation is a citizenship right that is crucial to fighting oppression and injustice, and a means of fostering diversity.

This chapter has briefly outlined the complex challenge inherent in educating children about their rights via a capability approach, rather than an exhaustive treatment of the topic in hand. Our aim was to offer a theoretical starting point that will require translation into practice. Children's range of capabilities can only be measured in terms of concrete, everyday actions, and indeed we are all called to engage directly with experience: from the ordinary citizen, to teachers, local government officials, and the politicians in charge of developing the international strategies from which our reflections in this chapter began.

References

Adamson, P. (2010). *The children left behind: A league table of inequality in child Well-being in the world's rich countries. Innocenti Report Card 9*. UNICEF.

Ariès, P. (1968). *Padri e figli nell'Europa medievale e moderna, trad. it. Trad. it*. Roma-Bari.

Ayers, W., Quinn, T. M., & Stovall, D. (2009). *Handbook of social justice in education*. Retrieved from https://books.google.it/books?hl=it&lr=&id=oZaNAgAAQBAJ&oi=fnd&pg=PP1&dq=Handbook+of+social+justice+in+education.&ots=Rw-miTCclu&sig=CHPv5SeRAWSZfRMyChPt2KA9lmU#v=onepage&q=Handbookofsocialjusticeineducation.&f=false.

Becker, G. M., DeGroot, M. H., & Marschak, J. (1964). Measuring utility by a single-response sequential method. *Behavioral Science, 9*(3), 226–232.

Bell, L. (1997). Theoretical foundations for social justice education. In M. Adams, P. Griffin, & L. Bell (Eds.), *Teaching for diversity and social justice: A sourcebook*. Routledge.

Biffi, E. (2018). Cosa può fare ed essere un bambino oggi? Riflessioni pedagogiche sul contributo dell'infanzia nella società contemporanea. *Pedagogia Oggi, 16*(2), 205–225.

Brantefors, L., Tellgren, B., & Thelander, N. (2019). Human rights education as democratic education. *The International Journal of Children's Rights, 27*, 694–718. https://doi.org/10.1163/15718182-02704007

Buzzelli, C. A. (2015). The capabilities approach: Rethinking agency, freedom, and capital in early education. *Contemporary Issues in Early Childhood, 16*(3), 203–213. https://doi.org/10.1177/1463949115600030

Cagliari, P., Barozzi, A., & Giudici, C. (2004). Thoughts, theories and experiences for an educational project with participation. *Children in Europe, 6*, 28–30.

Covell, K. (2013). Children's human rights education as a means to social justice: A case study from England. *Revista Internacional de Educación Para La Justicia Social, 2*(1), 35–48. Retrieved from http://www.rinace.net/riejs/numeros/vol2-num1/art2.pdf

Davids, N., & Waghid, Y. (2016). Higher education as a pedagogical site for citizenship education. *Education, Citizenship and Social Justice, 11*(1), 34–43. https://doi.org/10.1177/1746197915626079

Deardorff, D. K., Kiwan, D., & Park, S.-Y. (2018). *Global citizenship education: Taking it local*. https://unesdoc.unesco.org/ark:/48223/pf0000265456

Evans, N. J., Broido, E. M., Brown, K. R., & Wilke, A. K. (2017). *Disability in higher education: A social justice approach*. Wiley.

Foucault, M. (1975). *Discipline and punish: The birth of the prison*. Vintage Books.

Gale, T., & Tranter, D. (2011). Social justice in Australian higher education policy: An historical and conceptual account of student participation. *Critical Studies in Education, 52*(1), 29–46.

Gillett-Swan, J., & Coppock, V. (2016). *Children's rights, educational research and the UNCRC*. Symposium Books Ltd..

Hackman, H. W. (2005). Five essential components for social justice education. *Equity & Excellence in Education, 38*(2), 103–109. https://doi.org/10.1080/10665680590935034

Hammarberg, T. (2008a). *No real development without human rights*. Lecture on the interrelationship between development and human rights when implementing the UN Millennium Development Goals. Retrieved from https://rm.coe.int/16806daa59

Hammarberg, T. (2008b). *The principle of the best interest of the child – What it means and what it demands from adults*. Retrieved from https://rm.coe.int/16806da95d

Heckman, J. J. (2007). The economics, technology, and neuroscience of human capability formation. *Proceedings of the National Academy of Sciences, 104*(33), 13250–13255. https://doi.org/10.1073/pnas.0701362104

Lindsay, M. (1992). *Highlight: An introduction to children's rights*. National Children's Bureau.

Macleod, C. M. (2010). Primary goods, capabilities, and children. In H. Brighouse & I. Robeyns (Eds.), *Measuring justice: Primary goods and capabilities* (pp. 174–192). Cambridge University Press.

Moro, A. C. (1991). *Il bambino è un Cittadino. Conquista di libertà e itinerari formativi: la Convenzione dell'ONU e la sua attuazione*. Mursia.
Moss, P. (2007). Bringing politics into the nursery: Early childhood education as a democratic practice. *European Early Childhood Education Research Journal, 15*(1), 5–20. https://doi.org/10.1080/13502930601046620
Nussbaum, M. (2000). Women's capabilities and social justice. *Journal of Human Development, 1*(2), 219–247.
Nussbaum, M. C. (2010). *Not for profit: Why democracy needs the humanities* (Vol. 2). Princeton University Press.
Nussbaum, M. (2011). *Creating capabilities: The human development approach*. The Belknap Press of Harvard University Press.
Nussbaum, M. C., & Dixon, R. (2012). *Children's rights and a capabilities approach: The question of special priority* (No. 384). Retrieved from http://www.law.uchicago.edu/academics/publiclaw/index.html
Percy-Smith, B., & Thomas, N. (2010). *A handbook of children's participation: Perspectives from theory and practice*. Routledge.
Rawls, J. (1971). *A Theory of justice*. Harvard University Press. https://doi.org/10.2307/j.ctvjf9z6v
Robeyns, I. (2006). Three models of education: Rights, capabilities and human capital. *Theory and Research in Education, 4*(1), 69–84.
Sen, A. (1980). Equality of what? In S. McMurrin (Ed.), *Tanner lectures on human values, Volume 1*. Cambridge University Press.
Sen, A. (2000). *Social exclusion: Concept, application and scrutiny*. Office of Environment and Social Development, Asian Development Bank, Social Development Papers.
Sen, A. (2011). *La libertà individuale come impegno sociale*. Laterza.
Singh, M. (2011). The place of social justice in higher education and social change discourses. *Compare: A Journal of Comparative and International Education, 41*(4), 481–494.
UN General Assembly. (2006). Rights of the child. *Note/by the Secretary-General*. A/61/299. https://www.refworld.org/docid/453780fe0.html
UNICEF. (2017). Building the future: Children and the sustainable development goals in rich countries. In Innocenti Report Card (Vol. 14). *Florence: UNICEF Office of Research - Innocenti*. https://doi.org/10.1016/0022-0248(94)91042-1
World Health Organization. (2000). The World health report: 2000: Health systems: improving performance. *World Health Organization*. https://apps.who.int/iris/handle/10665/42281

Chapter 7
It Takes a Village to Overcome School Failure and Dropout: Innovative Educational Practices Promoting Children's Educational Rights in Portugal

Joana Lúcio and Fátima Antunes

Abstract As part of a wider research project analysing practices, voices, and pathways of inclusive education, this chapter discusses factors supporting the construction of inclusive educational practices that interrupt the school failure-dropout cycle and favour educational remobilisation. In order to understand these practices, a framework discussing barriers to access and participation in education provides conceptual tools to explore some analytical dimensions. The empirical basis for this chapter is a multi-case study analysing intervention on school failure and dropout, by mapping the points of view of actors engaged in ten different contexts (in the framework of two nation-wide programs) across the Portuguese territory. These actors contribute to the understanding of the processes, rationales and partnerships that support such practices. This contribution seeks to further the discussion about children's right to education, specifically the role education has in fostering equality with identity, valuing the child's socio-economic background and their position within a community (Article 29 of the UNCRC). As we focus on the local dimension of inclusive educational practices, we discuss the community's role in developing, implementing and evaluating said practices. In addition, we address how these practices negotiate children's community and cultural identity, while also exposing them to different cultures and values.

Keywords Inclusive education · Socio-educational practices · School failure · School dropout · Children's rights

J. Lúcio (✉) · F. Antunes
CIEd – Research Centre on Education, Institute of Education, University of Minho, Braga, Portugal
e-mail: joana.lucio@ie.uminho.pt; fantunes@ie.uminho.pt

J. Gillett-Swan, N. Thelander (eds.), *Children's Rights from International Educational Perspectives*, Transdisciplinary Perspectives in Educational Research 2, https://doi.org/10.1007/978-3-030-80861-7_7

Introduction

School failure and dropout have become educational and socio-political problems in almost every country, impacting many children and young people over an increasingly longer period of the life cycle (Ramirez & Boli, 1987; Perrenoud, 2000; Macedo et al., 2015), and in contexts where the school was instituted as the primary instance of socialisation (Candeias, 2009). The European Union (EU), in the Education and Training 2010 Program (Council of the European Union, 2002), has set as a goal that no more than 10% of young people leave school before the completion of compulsory education. School failure[1] and dropout have, therefore, acquired higher priority, visibility, and centrality (socio-politically, academically, scientifically, and educationally), across EU member states, although modified by each country's historical and institutional pathways and resources. Portugal is one of the EU Member States with the highest rates of early school leaving, but is also one that has significantly reduced these rates over the last decades (Eurostat, 2019). Social cohesion, democratisation, and educational inclusion (i.e., participation in school and learning) are parameters that guide socio-educational policies and practices aimed at overcoming school failure and dropout. Nevertheless, scientific, academic, and educational knowledge and debate open up the space and challenge researchers to question the theoretical and empirical basis of these policies and practices, and to discuss their contribution to the understanding of the educational processes involved.

Project *EDUPLACES/Educating places: practices, voices and pathways of inclusive education* highlights the points of view of the actors engaged in successful socio-educational practices, and proposes to answer two research questions: (1) which processes, factors, and actors contribute the most, from the subjects' perspective, to overcome school failure and dropout, and (2) what processes and factors support the disruption of the school failure-dropout downward spiral, and promote the remobilisation of young people towards learning and educational success? In this sense, this project also proposes a discussion on how these so-called successful practices contribute to the empowerment and inclusion of marginalised groups, which is, after all, a discussion about education as an instrument of social justice (Singh, 2015) and equity (Balsera et al., 2016).

We are interested in understanding relationships between individuals and institutional and cultural contexts, like schools, families and communities, as well as how these contexts shape (and are shaped by) relationships of power, identity, and agency. In this sense, we look for articulating issues proposed by critical and socio-cultural theories in order to discuss how, in micro-level interactions, people can build, reproduce, and challenge structural relationships of meaning and power.

[1] According to Psacharopoulos (2007), school failure "may mean that a school system is failing to provide services conducing to learning, or that a student is failing to advance to the next grade and eventually becomes a drop out" (p. 4). For *EDUPLACES*' intents and purposes, the definition of school failure was more strictly connected with that of "[g]rade repetition or retention, also known as flunking" (Psacharopoulos, 2007, p. 5)

We conceive schools as sites of action, negotiation, and conflict, where inequality and difference are built day after day around "cultural tools, resources, and identities (both within and across communities)" (Lewis & Moje, 2003, p. 1992); where social justice remains at stake through socio-educational practices that contribute to maintain or to overcome institutional, dispositional and situational barriers to children and youth participating in learning and school. These theoretical and methodological orientations integrate a perspective about seeing "the world through the eyes of the dispossessed and act against the ideological and institutional processes and forms that reproduce oppressive conditions". The project underscores the aim of contributing "to challenge existing educational and social inequalities and to create curricula and teaching that are more socially just" (Apple, 2018, pp. 688, 686).

Because socio-educational practices that are aimed at overcoming school failure and dropout can be argued to contribute to social justice and inclusion (educational and otherwise), this chapter takes on the challenge of analysing them through the lens of the UN Convention on the Rights of the Child (United Nations, 1989) and, more specifically, that of the right to education/educational success. Inclusive socio-educational practices will subsequently promote children's educational rights, should they be successful in overcoming school failure and dropout. While the research project's goals were wider (as alluded in the methodology section below), the focus of this chapter is mostly to discuss some concepts emerging from data analysis that hope to provide a frame for evidencing the impacts these inclusive practices have on school participation. We begin by presenting the theoretical and epistemological framework supporting this research on socio-educational practices aimed at overcoming school failure and dropout, focusing on what types of barriers to participation in education and learning are identified in the literature. We will then briefly address project *EDUPLACES*' methodological pathway, followed by some findings and participants' voices.

A School of One's Own: A Framework on Overcoming Barriers to Participation in Education and Learning

Appropriating the same questioning proposed by Sverdlick (2019), we ask: what meanings does the right to education take on in socio-educational practices aimed at overcoming barriers to participation in learning and school? In 2018 in Portugal, the real school enrolment rate of young people aged 15–17 was 79.3%, while early school leaving affected around 12% of young people (less than 10% of girls) between 18 and 24 years old (Eurostat, 2019). In this context, the obvious and strongest sense linking the practices studied with the right to education is precisely because they address and challenge its *effectiveness*. The socio-educational practices analysed by project *EDUPLACES* seek to "produce meaningful and valuable learning experiences for all" (Sverdlick, 2019, p. 6), given that a fundamental human right cannot be partially fulfilled, and therefore school failure and dropout are a manifestation of its *unfulfillment*. Since research clearly points out that school failure and dropout begin as school disengagement does, at an early point of school pathways, and are fuelled and reinforced by institutional day-to-day routines and relationships. Overcoming them begins with policies and practices that build a school of one's own, and commits a village (all of society) with the wellbeing of any one and all children (Dale, 2010; Baroutsis et al., 2016; Gillett-Swan & Sargeant, 2018). In its 2014 report regarding the Portuguese situation, the Committee on the Rights of the Child noted that "the recession and the current financial and economic crisis are taking their toll on families and on public social investment, including on the prospects of implementing the Convention [United Nations Convention on the Rights of the Child, or the UNCRC]", by "increasing the risk of children being exposed to poverty and affecting the enjoyment of many of the rights contained in the Convention, including health, education and social protection" (United Nations, 2014, p. 3).

According to available research, socio-educational practices developed in territory-based initiatives can be oriented in many ways – from a palliative intervention to the promotion of equal opportunities, from a "more education" based strategy to a pedagogy that "allow[s] connections to be made between pupil's experience and the curriculum (…) articulating the connections and disconnections between home and school" (Power, 2008, p. 34). We share the same understanding as De Witte et al. (2013, p. 15), that school dropout constitutes "an indication and origin of fundamental inequities", mobilising attention to participation in school and learning "as a right of citizens that is to be safeguarded in any democracy" (Smeyers & Depaepe, 2006; Dorn, 1996).

The conceptualisation of a problem in terms of *barriers* to participation in education has been developed, with some exceptions (Booth & Ainscow, 2002; Arnaiz Sánchez et al., 2019), especially in analyses of sectors and audiences that are distinct from those in compulsory education. Concerning the *participation* category, and following ongoing discussions, we adopt Booth and Ainscow's proposal (2002, p. 3): "Participation means learning together with others and collaborating with them on shared learning experiences. It requires active commitment to learning and having a say in how education is experienced. More deeply, it's about being recognized, accepted and valued for yourself". In this perspective, our understanding of "inclusive education" closely follows that recently proposed by Messiou (2017, p. 148) when she argues that it concerns "all children's presence, participation and achievement". However, the quality of the educational experience and of learning processes has been given a relative political priority and thus very uneven achievements and outcomes for the various audiences involved (Haug, 2017).

One of the first, if not the first, formulations of the problem of barriers to participation and learning/cultural transmission in the education system is proposed by Ruth Ekstrom (1972) in *Barriers to Women's Participation in Post-Secondary Education. A Review of the Literature*. Here, Ekstrom (1972, p.1) suggests *barriers* consist of "factors that work to exclude", and identifies three categories:

institutional (internal to institutions, such as admission practices, educational provision, or staff attitudes); *situational* (specific life situations including social expectations and pressures, or family responsibilities); *dispositional* (constructed by social experience, from fear of failure to attitude towards intellectual work or appreciation of educational goals, academic aspirations and expectations).

Decades later, Long and Mejia (2016) discuss a broader version of the *institutional barriers* category of this typology. In the context of a debate on the diversity of target audiences in education, inclusion and participation of under-represented population groups in engineering courses, the authors consider the following triad as central: socio-cultural deficit perspective, low expectations, and impoverished learning and stimulation (Long & Mejia, 2016, p. 3). Also a problem is *Restrictive* (selective) curricula – that is, those that assume that students have acquired a pattern of learning prerequisites that is far from being the norm and heavily penalises those with weaker prior academic learning, many times coincidental with underrepresented or newcomer segments. Insufficiently diverse institutional (and societal) *models*, the erasure (in the textbooks and reference texts) of the history and contribution of the various collectives to society constitute other institutional barriers to the identification of underrepresented groups with learning proposals. To adapt, these subjects "must appear to accept existing norms and not openly resist or challenge them" (Tonso, 1996, p. 224), and identifying with an unfamiliar context and activities is much more difficult for underrepresented students (Mejia et al., 2015).

Debating the complex relationship between school and social justice and its contradictory position in relation to socio-educational inequalities, Power argues that successive "generations" of education policies (redistribution, recognition, and representation) have fallen short of expectations in reducing inequalities and social injustices, either because the causes are insufficiently recognised, or because the interventions directed at them neglect the socio-educational processes that may challenge them. In this sense, while refusing that "unequal educational outcomes can be explained only in terms of the misrecognition" (Power & Frandji, 2010, p. 394), the author argues that certain compensatory-oriented educational policies cannot only fail but aggravate forms of inequality and cultural discrimination: "From this perspective, it is not that the redistribution was insufficient, but rather that it is premised on a deficit view of inner-city families and their communities. Indeed, from this angle, a politics of redistribution constitutes in itself a form of cultural injustice" (Power, 2012, p. 480). It is not simply a matter of recognising, but of facing the circumstances, which, from the author's perspective, involves developing pedagogical proposals and practices oriented towards contextualising the curriculum. This course of action implies establishing strong connections between academic knowledge and common, everyday experience, changing learning activities and pathways without changing its goals (Power, 2008, p. 35; Morais & Neves, 2009).

Building a sense for academic work, as well as the competent exercise of the student craft (Perrenoud, 1995) and calibrated adherence to the student role (Apple & King, 1977), are necessary and not guaranteed at the outset. These conditions and experiences are hampered in the case of audiences who are socio-economically and educationally disadvantaged by the lack of opportunities to discuss and grasp the relevance of activities, and to build a connection with their values, cultures, practices and daily lives. According to Mejia et al. (2015), successful permanence in school for underrepresented groups requires that teachers and educators favour a positive perception of their ability to succeed and a perspective on their role as students and graduates in a way that does not clash with their cultural identity. Members of underrepresented groups can experience isolation, anxiety, alienation, and reduced performance when the disadvantages they experience remain hidden. Institutional modes of functioning remain oblivious to the disadvantages and asymmetries of cultural and emotional knowledge, conditions, and resources among audiences in understanding, interacting with, negotiating and appropriately responding to institutional expectations.

It was equally central – to the study of socio-educational practices aimed at overcoming barriers to participation in learning and school – to problematise the school-family-community relationship as a relationship between cultures, which involves the individual/collective and academic/non-academic aspects, and constitutes a "power relation" that "can contribute to reinforce, maintain or mitigate social inequalities and cultural differences" (Silva, 2010, p. 450).

Methodology

Project *EDUPLACES/Educating places: practices, voices and pathways of inclusive education* (PTDC/MHC-CED/3775/2014), ongoing between June 2016 and November 2019, was a multi-case study of ten socio-educational practices, involving 18 researchers associated with four Portuguese research centres and universities. The ten socio-educational practices took place in as many different contexts, located in four Portuguese municipalities (three in the north and one in the south of the country). Each practice was developed within one of two national government programs (one school-based and one community-based) aimed at overcoming school failure and dropout.

The selection of the programs that frame the practices under study was the first step of the investigative process. These are the most enduring national government programs focused on intervention against school failure and dropout (both in force, at the start of project *EDUPLACES*, for over 15 years), located in territories with vulnerable and disadvantaged populations, and both presuppose interactions between the school and the community. Two criteria governed the selection of projects (within which the practices under study are developed): accessibility (namely, availability of information) and outcomes. These outcomes – that is, the impact of the projects on the populations, according to intervention objectives – were measured in two ways:

1. For the community-based program, each of the selected projects placed in the upper tier for the program's 2016–2018 funding application (35.6% approval rate): four of the five projects have been in place since 2010 and had been selected for a third round of funding. The fifth one had initiated a year prior and placed first in said application round. Three projects had a 'global rate of school success' higher than the program's average (74%), while the fourth scored 73%;
2. For the school-based program, each of the six selected projects had, according to the program's report for 2014–2015, received the following formal assessment: 'in 2014–15, [name of school group] successfully Reached/Exceeded the general goals.'

Following contact with the teams responsible for the projects in question and their agreement to collaborate with project *EDUPLACES*, 11 socio-educational practices were identified as successful by the institutional leaders of the projects that framed them. The process of indicating one practice was not linear: in some cases, those responsible did not find it difficult to elect a particular practice (a certain aspect or dimension of the intervention carried out by the project) as the one that most contributed to overcoming the potential failure and/or dropout of disadvantaged children and young people. In other cases, selection proved to be more problematic, eventually falling on an articulated set of dimensions, which was given an aggregating designation.

The practice selection process was supported by semi-directive interviews with institutional leaders of the promoting projects and by documentary analysis of the information available about the contexts, projects, target audiences, and practices, but also about the framing government programs, in an effort to triangulate data. This stage of the investigative process, which led to the constitution of a Portfolio of Practices (definition of the set of practices under study and collection and processing of data characterising them), was supported by two fundamental instruments of data aggregation and analysis: the *Descriptive Note* and the *Selection Criteria Grid*.

In early 2018, one of the projects promoted by the national school-based program terminated its collaboration protocol with project *EDUPLACES* due to institutional constraints. For this reason, from the second year of research onwards (2017–2018), the project contemplates ten practices. The second year of the project was aimed at the development of Practice Monographs which included (in addition to previously collected data) a broad set of information on the views of actors directly involved in the practices under study: teachers/professionals, parents/families, children/young people, and institutional partners. This data was collected through semi-directive interviews (10), focus groups (37), questionnaires (82) and observation. As highlighted in the following section, this chapter draws exclusively upon data stemming from the focus groups, and particularly those involving children and young people.

In the third and final year (2018–2019), the focus was on characterising atypical academic pathways and exploring innovative dimensions of the practices. For the first objective, a panel of 15 young people (participating in semi-directive biographical interviews) was constituted, featuring subjects who had a history of interaction with seven of the practices being studied, and who had been identified by the institutional leaders as having, at some point, experienced failure and/or dropout, and were completing (or had completed) successful school pathways. For the second objective, teachers and professionals involved in three of the practices being studied participated in focus groups to explore whether/to what extent these practices constitute Learning Communities/Communities of Practice, by reference to their professional exercise and development.

Overcoming School Failure and Dropout: Inclusion and Children's Rights in Education, in Their Own Words

The year 2019 marked the 30th anniversary of the UNCRC. At the time of publication, all UN member countries except the USA subscribe to the UNCRC. In its current form, the UNCRC (United Nations, 1989) contains 54 articles relating to the specific needs and rights of children, including the right to life, a name and an identity, to be raised within a family or cultural group, and to participate fully in family, cultural, and social life.

Two UNCRC articles emerge as particularly pertinent for thinking about the "right to education" issues and, in this sense, the research objectives proposed by project *EDUPLACES*: Article 28, entitled 'Provision of Education', and Article 29, entitled 'Aims of Education'. The first invokes (among other things) the importance of organising different education systems, which should be public and accessible to all children, and the importance of fostering regular school attendance and reducing dropout rates. From the point of view of providing education, the UNCRC defines the role of the state as ensuring accessibility, diversity, and adequacy of socio-educational offerings, as well as the promotion of schooling. The second of these two articles defines the importance of respect for human rights and fundamental freedoms, respect for the family, cultural identity and values of the child's origin, and the importance of preparing for the assumption of the responsibilities inherent to life in society. From the point of view of the 'aims of education', the UNCRC defines that education is intended to promote the development and personality of the child, preparing them for an active adult life in society, and inculcating respect for their parents, their identity, their language and cultural values, as well as the cultures and values of the Other (i.e. "that/those who is/are different from myself and/or my community").

The challenge framing this chapter is to explore how the practices under study (a) reflect diverse and accessible forms of organisation of education, and (b) value the cultures and beliefs of origin of the children and young people who are their target audience, simultaneously exposing them to cultures and values different from their own. For the discussion of the first aspect, we recall the definition of "social innovation" (Moulaert et al., 2013, p. 1): data from the first year of research showed that, as an intention, the innovation dimension of these socio-educational practices has yet to be fulfilled, especially as regards the participation of families, but also of children and young people themselves, in the context of the practices under study. Regarding social relations, these practices seemed to have a positive effect at the organisational level (internal dynamics and relations with other organisations), but not so much at the community level, as they seemed to foster the creation of spaces and/or times and procedures for interaction. Even so, there were no specific mentions to either participation in educational decisions or the encouragement of joint work.

With regard to the second aspect, which refers to the 'local' dimension of these inclusive socio-educational practices, community participation seemed to be based more on a governance logic, in which the decision-maker consults some more or less strategic partners – still very far from effective co-construction (Klein et al., 2013), involving various local actors with the ability to decide and influence.

The 47 sources that constitute the core *corpus* of this research, (37 focus groups and ten interviews with teachers/professionals, parents/families, children/young people, and institutional partners) were subjected to content analysis using the NVivo 12 software and an *a priori* category grid (or tree), consisting of 22 items: five categories/dimensions and 17 subcategories. The basis of this category tree was the conceptual framework and the research question framing the project's second year: which factors, processes, rationales and partnerships most contribute to overcoming (institutional/socio-cultural, situational, and dispositional) barriers to participation in school and learning, and promote change (Ekstrom, 1972; Lynch & O'Riordan, 1998; Roosmaa & Saar, 2017).

Considering the overall data, the most frequently mentioned "processes contributing to overcome barriers" are related to *Pedagogy, Curriculum, and Evaluation* (297 references in 37 sources), *Interactions between Schools, Families and Communities* (216 references in 38 sources) and *Stability of intervention teams – Strong and continuous relationships* (103 references in 23 sources).

When we consider the various types of voices heard separately, interesting contrasts emerge. Teachers/professionals follow the global trend with regard to the "processes contributing to overcome barriers" to learning and school participation that they value most, and most often identify with the practices in which they participate. In turn, parents seem to value the impact of practices at the *school-family-community interactions* level (91 references) rather than at the level of *pedagogy, curriculum and evaluation* (45). This seems to suggest that these actors recognise the practices in which they are involved as making a significant contribution to communication, translation and negotiation with the school (and in some cases other relevant local entities). The surveyed institutional partners tend to highlight the contribution of *partnerships* (34 references) to overcoming barriers to educational success. This seems to indicate that they recognise themselves in their institutional role, as having knowledge, input and commitment to practice. They also highlight "processes" related to *school-family-community interactions* (27) and *pedagogy, curriculum and evaluation* (22). Finally, children/young people most often refer to "processes" related to *pedagogy, curriculum and evaluation* (64 references), *learning the student craft* (35) and *student participation* (27). This seems to indicate that, in some cases, they see the practices in which they participate as showing a certain concern with the creation of spaces, times, activities and procedures that promote their participation in the decision-making process regarding learning contents, themes, activities, performance and rules. Participants in one of the focus groups for one community-based practice were asked about the type of support they received from the practice's staff. One child said they were advised "to behave better in school and study more". Another child stated that the conversations with, and support from, the practice's staff had been an incentive to improve their results: "I had more negatives [scores bellow the passing grade] before, I had five negatives. In the first term I had five negatives, then Ursula [member of staff] talked to me…and now I had two negatives". When asked about how they had started their engagement with the practice, one boy participating in one school-based practice stated that the initiative had been his, as he wished to "improve my attitude, my work and everything, and my life in this school".

In two mediation practices developed within community-based projects and located in the north (N_CB_1 and N_CB_2), the voices of teachers and professionals, parents, and partners aligned in terms of the dimensions of the intervention that are seen as contributing the most to overcoming school failure and dropout. In both practices, it is the voices of children and young people that "clash". Participants in N_CB_1 value the practice's contribution in learning the student craft. Participants in N_CB_2 recognise the importance of the stability of intervention teams, and how this fosters strong and sustained relationships that enhance educational success. One participant in the children/young people's focus group for N_CB_1 spoke of the impact the practice has had on their overall conduct: "This is like, we came here to distract [ourselves], if this was to end, we would have nothing to do, we would always be out there screwing up, and here we are fine." When asked about how their experience in school differed from their experience in the practice, participants in the children/young people's focus group for N_CB_2 said: "Here they give us affection and it's easy to be together and in school no, everyone turns their faces away from us", with another participant adding, "[They respect us] and we respect them".

The practices where *school-family-community interactions* emerge as the most relevant (most frequently mentioned) "process contributing to overcome barriers" to educational success – such as the two mediation practices mentioned above – seemed to focus their intervention on the "distance" or the relationship between (the cultures of) school-families-communities (Silva, 2010). The orientation to mobilise institutional resources to support the exercise of the student craft and the student role, to diversify proposals, and to monitor learning progress, or to expand times and spaces of communication and negotiation between the school and families contributes to reinforcing elements of *institutional habitus* (Bourdieu & Passeron, 1970; Reay et al., 2001; Araneda-Guirriman et al., 2017) – organisational practices, academic expectations, conceptions of educational success, and academic performance rules – that favour the lengthening of young people's educational pathways and the mitigation of the effects of barriers to their participation in education (Tarabini et al., 2015). Children and young people engaging in N_CB_1 reported that teachers treat them differently and that some are racist. The practice had improved their relationship with the school, teachers and peers, as well as school performance. All of them attached great importance to the project in which the practice is being developed, describing it as a space of friendship, occupation of free time and as "a second home". Children and young people participating in N_CB_2 reported many difficulties in complying with the demands imposed by the school, identifying discriminatory attitudes, and valuing the proximity work and adjustment effort developed by the practice.

Closing Remarks

Seeking to articulate some queries offered by educational socio-cultural and critical theories, this research project aimed to emphasize perspectives from disadvantaged children and young people, parents and families, their teachers, and other professionals. The information gathered from this wide range of actors – who hold various statuses, interests, and motivations – seems to highlight on the one hand, the focus of the intervention in overcoming barriers (of different natures and origins) to children and young people's participation in learning and school. On the other hand, while these actors acknowledge that these practices contribute to overcoming barriers that hinder children and young people's schooling, the question remains whether these practices have broken down some, or any, of these barriers.

In certain practices, procedures or devices are tested that alter professional relationships and exercises, or interfere with power relations between school and family and/or community cultures. They negotiate, for example, certain class/subject attendance rules for girls, or response to evaluation requirements, but also because the interaction between institutional agents and parents and families is intensified. To this extent, these practices challenge the *institutional habitus* (Tarabini et al., 2015). In this sense, these practices seem to alter the effects of certain barriers that influence the school paths of the children/young people they reach. They thus hold a certain potential for contextualised and localised challenge, but also for creating a repertoire of institutional practices favourable to overcoming barriers to the participation of all children and young people in learning and school.

So, the research discussed in this chapter suggests that practices of Study Support, Mediation, Student Grouping, and Pedagogical Differentiation can generate repertoires of organised collective pedagogical action that:

- create integrative and ambivalent educational contexts (e.g. more time to learn and to progress with individual activities and goals or group projects, in the class they belong to, in a special class that is "our own", in a group and support room, sometimes with good involvement of parents and families);
- support empowering pedagogical relationships (which generate confidence and autonomy, expand options and horizons of action, and support decisions by young people and their families);

- interfere in power relationships (build trust, open spaces for the neighbourhood to be present at the school and the school in the neighbourhood, and facilitate communication and negotiation between professionals, parents and communities).

We return to the two questions framing this chapter – to discuss whether the socio-educational practices aimed at overcoming school failure and dropout analysed by project *EDUPLACES* (a) reflect diverse and accessible forms of organisation education, and (b) value the cultures and beliefs of the children and young people who are their target audience while exposing them to other cultures and values. The tentative and hypothetical answer to the first question, suggested by the compiled data, is that these practices interfere with institutional functioning, for example, by responding to *pedagogical deficits* or promoting learning opportunities that favour the competent exercise of the *student craft* and the *student role.* In this sense, they influence the overcoming of these barriers, regarding the educational pathways of the children and young people that participate in them. As for the second question, data seems to confirm how (some of) these practices contribute to fulfilling the 'aims of education' established in the UNCRC (and particularly Article 29). They not only seek to help children and young people respond to the demands of the school, but they adopt an integrative and ecological approach to their development, undertaking a crucial task of socio-educational mediation in promoting children and young people's educational rights. In terms of participation, data analysis offers some insights into whether or not these inclusive practices are preparing children and young people for a responsible life in a democratic society. While in some practices, participation is mostly engagement – that is, children and young people's voluntary enrolment in the proposed activities – in others, the impact is somewhat deeper. At the individual level, both parents and families, and children and young people report on the practices' impact on the students' willingness to learn, their persistence, their ability to delay gratification, their self-confidence, and their overall sense of responsibility towards school and learning. At the group level, and particularly for Mediation practices (mainly N_CB_1 and N_CB_2), there are some accounts of the practices' impacts in terms of a shift in parents' and families' perceived value of education and schooling. There is a growing interest in their children's academic pathways and outcomes, and also daily activities, with an increasing proactivity to overcome underqualification and unemployment. The picture presented by this research endeavour, however narrow, is certainly promising.

Acknowledgements The data presented in this chapter is the outcome of the joint work of the *EDUPLACES* research team: Fátima Antunes (coord.), Almerindo J. Afonso, Armando Loureiro, Carlos Gomes, Emília Vilarinho, Esmeraldina Veloso, Fátima L. Carvalho, Isabel Costa, Isabel Menezes, Joana Lúcio, José Augusto Palhares, José Pedro Amorim, Manuel António Silva, Marta Rodrigues, Raquel R. Monteiro, Rosanna Barros, Tiago Neves, and Virgínio Sá.

This research is funded by National Funds through FCT – Foundation for Science and Technology (Portugal), in the context of project PTDC/MHC-CED/3775/2014. This research is funded by CIEd – Research Centre on Education, project UID/CED/01661/2019, Institute of Education, University of Minho, through national funds of FCT/MCTES-PT.

References

Apple, M. W. (2018). Critical curriculum studies and the concrete problems of curriculum policy and practice. *Journal of Curriculum Studies, 50*(6), 685–690. https://doi.org/10.1080/00220272.2018.1537373

Apple, M. W., & King, N. R. (1977). What do schools teach? *Curriculum Inquiry, 6*(4), 341–358.

Araneda-Guirriman, C., Pedraja-Rejas, L., & Rodríguez-Ponce, E. (2017). Desafíos de la educación superior en el contexto de la masificación: un análisis conceptual desde el habitus institucional. *Revista Espacios, 38*(60), 19–30.

Arnaiz Sánchez, P., De Haro-Rodríguez, R., & Maldonado Martínez, R. (2019). Barriers to student learning and participation in an inclusive school as perceived by future education professionals. *Journal of New Approaches in Educational Research, 8*(1), 18–24. https://www.learntechlib.org/p/207145/

Balsera, M. R., Dorsi, D., Termes, A., Bonal, X., Verger, A., & Diaz, J. G. (2016). Private actors and the right to education. *Compare: A Journal of Comparative and International Education, 46*(6), 976–1000. https://doi.org/10.1080/03057925.2016.1207939

Baroutsis, A., McGregor, G., & Mills, M. (2016). Pedagogic voice: Student voice in teaching and engagement pedagogies. *Pedagogy, Culture and Society, 24*(1), 123–140.

Booth, T., & Ainscow, M. (2002). *Index for inclusion: Developing learning and participation in schools*. Centre for Studies on Inclusive Education (CSIE).

Bourdieu, P., & Passeron, J.-C. (1970). *A Reprodução: Elements for a theory of the education system*. Francisco Alves. Vega.

Candeias, A. (2009). *Educação, Estado e Mercado no século XX. Apontamentos sobre o caso português numa perspectiva comparada*. Edições Colibri/FCSH-UNL.

Council of the European Union. (2002). Detailed work programme on the follow-up of the objectives of Education and training systems in Europe (2002/C 142/01). *Official Journal of the European Communities of 14.6.2002*, C142/1–C142/22.

Dale, R. (2010). Early school leaving. Lessons from research for policy makers. *NESSE Report*. http://hdl.voced.edu.au/10707/218243

De Witte, K., Cabus, S., Thyssen, G., Groot, W., & Van den Brink, H. (2013). A critical review of the literatures on school dropout. *Educational Research Review, 10*, 13–28.

Dorn, S. (1996). *Creating the dropout: An institutional and social history of school*. Praeger Publishers.

Ekstrom, R.B. (1972). *Barriers to women's participation in post-secondary education. A review of the literature*. https://eric.ed.gov/?id=ED072368

Eurostat. (2019). *Early leavers from education and training. Statistics explained*. http://ec.europa.eu/eurostat/statistics-explained/index.php/Early_leavers_from_education_and_training

Gillett-Swan, J. K., & Sargeant, J. (2018). Voice inclusive practice, digital literacy and children's participatory rights. *Children & Society, 32*(1), 38–49.

Haug, P. (2017). Understanding inclusive education: Ideals and reality. *Scandinavian Journal of Disability Research, 19*(3), 206–217.

Klein, J.-L., Fontan, J.-M., Harrisson, D., & Lévesque, B. (2013). The Québec model: A social innovation system founded on cooperation and consensus building. In F. Moulaert, D. MacCallum, A. Mehmood, & A. Hamdouch (Eds.), *The international handbook on social innovation: Collective action, social learning and transdisciplinary research* (pp. 371–383). Edward Elgar Publishing.

Lewis, C., & Moje, E. B. (2003). Sociocultural perspectives meet critical theories. *International Journal of Learning, 10*, 1979–1995.

Long, L. L., & Mejia, J. A. (2016). Conversations about diversity: Institutional barriers for underrepresented engineering students. *The Journal of Engineering Education, 105*(2), 211–218. https://doi.org/10.1002/jee.20114

Lynch, K., & O'Riordan, C. (1998). Inequality in higher education: A study of class barriers. *British Journal of Sociology of Education, 19*(4), 445–478. https://doi.org/10.1080/0142569980190401

Macedo, E., Araújo, H. C., Magalhães, A., & Rocha, C. (2015). A construção do abandono escolar precoce como conceito político: Uma análise na sociologia da educação. *Profesorado, Revista de Curriculum y Formación del Profesorado, 19*(3), 28–42.
Mejia, J. A., Drake, D., & Wilson-Lopez, A. (2015). Changes in Latino/a adolescents' engineering self-efficacy and perceptions of engineering after addressing authentic engineering design challenges. In *Proceedings of the American Society for Engineering Education annual conference* (pp. 1–14).
Messiou, K. (2017). Research in the field of inclusive education: Time for a rethink? *International Journal of Inclusive Education, 21*(2), 146–159. https://doi.org/10.1080/13603116.2016.1223184
Morais, A. M., & Neves, I. P. (2009). Textos e contextos educativos que promovem aprendizagem – optimização de um modelo de prática pedagógica. *Revista Portuguesa de Educação, 22*(2), 5–28.
Moulaert, F., MacCallum, D., & Hillier, J. (2013). Social innovation: Intuition, precept, concept, theory and practice. In F. Moulaert, D. MacCallum, A. Mehmood, & A. Hamdouch (Eds.), *The international handbook on social innovation: Collective action, social learning and transdisciplinary research* (pp. 13–24). Edward Elgar Publishing.
Perrenoud, P. (1995). *Ofício do Aluno e Sentido do Trabalho Escolar*. Porto Editora.
Perrenoud, P. (2000). *Pedagogia Diferenciada. Das Intenções à Acção*. Artmed Editora.
Power, S. (2008). How should we respond to the continuing failure of compensatory education. *Orbis Scholae, 2*(2), 19–38.
Power, S. (2012). From redistribution to recognition to representation: Social injustice and the changing politics of education. *Globalisation, Societies and Education, 10*(4), 473–492.
Power, S., & Frandji, D. (2010). Education markets, the new politics of recognition and the increasing fatalism towards inequality. *Journal of Education Policy, 25*(3), 385–396.
Psacharopoulos, G. (2007). *The costs of school failure a feasibility study*. European Expert Network on Economics of Education.
Ramirez, F. O., & Boli, J. (1987). The political construction of mass schooling: European origins and worldwide institutionalization. *Sociology of Education, 60*(1), 2–17.
Reay, D., David, M., & Ball, S. (2001). Making a difference? Institutional habituses and higher education choice. *Sociological Research Online, 5*(4), 1–12.
Roosmaa, E.-L., & Saar, E. (2017). Adults who do not want to participate in learning: A cross-national European analysis of their perceived barriers. *International Journal of Lifelong Education, 36*(3), 254–277.
Silva, P. (2010). Análise sociológica da relação escola-família: um roteiro sobre o caso português. *Sociologia, 20*, 443–464.
Singh, K. (2015). Safeguarding education as public good and regulating private providers. *Social Change, 45*(2), 308–323. https://doi.org/10.1177/0049085715574322
Smeyers, P., & Depaepe, M. (2006). On the rhetoric of 'what works.' Contextualizing educational research and the picture of performativity. In P. Smeyers & M. Depaepe (Eds.), *Educational research: Why 'what works' doesn't work* (pp. 1–16). Springer.
Sverdlick, I. (2019). Inclusión educativa y derecho a la educación: La disputa de los sentidos. *Archivos Analíticos de Políticas Educativas, 27*(26). https://doi.org/10.14507/epaa.27.3197
Tarabini, A., Curran, M., Montes, A., & Parcerisa, L. (2015). School engagement as an antidote of early school leaving: Exploring the role of the Institutional Habitus. *PRO, 19*, 196–212.
Tonso, K. L. (1996). The impact of cultural norms on women. *Journal of Engineering Education, 85*(3), 217–225.
United Nations. (1989). *United Nations convention on the rights of the child*. http://www.ohchr.org/Documents/ProfessionalInterest/crc.pdf
United Nations. (2014). *Concluding observations on the third and fourth periodic reports of Portugal*. http://tbinternet.ohcrc.org/_layouts/treatybodyexternal/Download.aspx?symbolno=Crc/C/Prt/Co/3-4&Lang=En

Chapter 8
The Education of First Nations Children in Australian Educational Contexts: Some Children Are More Equal Than Others

Grace O'Brien

Abstract It has been highlighted by the international community and the United Nations Committee on the Rights of the Child that the Australian federal government has ostensibly neglected the rights of First Nations children in Australia. Although there have been some improvements across a range of economic and social determinants, alliance with First Nations peoples is critical to eliminate socio-economic disadvantage across all sectors for First Nations children. First Nations organisations and Communities have expressed that responses to adversity experienced by many First Nations children have so far been overlooked by the Australian government. This chapter investigates the rights of First Nations children from an educational perspective, examining the ways in which current political and social structures in Australia inadvertently or purposely disadvantage First Nations children. By continuing to privilege Eurocentric systems of education in mainstream schooling the rights of First Nations children are continually being disregarded. Nakata's, Cultural Interface is used to explore the unequal treatment experienced by First Nations children in educational settings and identifies the ways in which inequality may be reinforced by non-Indigenous educators who lack cultural capacity.

Keywords First Nations children · Inequality · Rights · Education · Incarceration

G. O'Brien (✉)
Queensland University of Technology, Brisbane, QLD, Australia
e-mail: g8.obrien@qut.edu.au

J. Gillett-Swan, N. Thelander (eds.), *Children's Rights from International Educational Perspectives*, Transdisciplinary Perspectives in Educational Research 2, https://doi.org/10.1007/978-3-030-80861-7_8

Introduction

Historically, many First Nations peoples of Australia have had negative experiences at school, and many and have endured high levels of discrimination (Hayes et al., 2009) across all education sectors (Ockenden, 2014). Education policies and practices continue to impact upon First Nations peoples' connection to the education system and some parents view schools to be authoritarian, punitive, and racist environments. Nevertheless, parents of First Nations children want them to gain the skills and knowledges that will support their children to learn, achieve and participate fully within Australian society, while also being strong in cultural knowledge and connected with their identity (Tripcony, 2010). Article 29(1a) and (1c) stipulate that a child's culture and identity should be at the centre of their learning. Too often, this is not occurring within Australian educational contexts and it is often voiced that the current education 'system' is impenetrable for some First Nations students (Bodkin-Andrews & Carlson, 2016; Social Justice Report, 2005).

This chapter speaks to two key issues fundamental to the rights of First Nations children in education. Firstly, the examination of educational rights of First Nations children with respect to the enactment of Article 29 under the United Nations, Convention of the Rights of the Child (UNCRC). Enactment of Article 29 requires that the Australian government ensures First Nations children reach the highest possible standards of educational achievement (United Nations, 1989). A brief case study is provided which identifies that urgent and critical reform is required for breaches of Human Rights for First Nations children in Australia. An increasing volume of international literature indicates that those from minority groups, particularly young males who are excluded from schools are more likely to enter into the criminal justice system (Owusu-Bempah et al., 2014). While there is international literature addressing the school to prison pipeline (Mallet, 2017; Mittleman, 2017; Raufu, 2017) there is minimal literature addressing the link between these two phenomena in Australia. The chapter then critiques why the implementation of Article 29 may be difficult in current Australian education contexts. In Australian mainstream schooling, a majority of educators are non-Indigenous and there appears to be an explicit lack of understanding about how to implement Indigenous Knowledges and perspectives into the school curriculum (Castagno & Brayboy, 2008). Nakata's theory of The Cultural Interface will be used to examine Article 29 with respect to education for First Nations children.

Interpretation of Article 29 – The Rights of First Nations Children (Australia)

Australia is one of the only Western countries in the world without a Federal government Human Rights Act or Bill of Rights. The critical nature and significance of protecting the rights of the most vulnerable within Australian society is emphasised as, "Australia is exceptional in that we have few constitutional protections for human rights" (Triggs, 2017, p. 11). Nonetheless, the states of Queensland and Victoria, and the Australian Capital Territory have indeed superseded the Commonwealth of Australia with each having independently adopted a Human Rights Act. Although Australia ratified the UNCRC and agreed to incorporate its provisions into law, First Nations peoples of Australia have too often witnessed blatant disregard and removal of their human and legal rights (Behrendt, 2012).

In 2007, the Commonwealth Government of Australia suspended the *Racial Discrimination Act 1975* under the Northern Territory Emergency Response intervention. First Nations families and children were subjected to discriminatory laws and trial by media regarding their living conditions and unsubstantiated accusations of harm to children. The majority of these claims were later discounted following further investigations. This had a profound and debilitating impact on the lives of First Nations peoples in remote communities in the Northern Territory.

In 2009, the Federal government amended the *Social Security Act 1999* which would see a direct link between school attendance and the ability to receive welfare support, affecting predominantly First Nations peoples in Northern Territory and Northern Queensland (Cowling, 2009). In 2011, the Northern Territory government also made changes to the *Education Act*, complementing the Federal government's stance on quarantining welfare support payments for non-compliant parents of the Commonwealth government's *School Enrolment through Welfare Reform Measure* (*SEAM*). Australia witnessed how easily laws and Acts could be changed to suit the political will of those in power and subsequently disadvantage First Nations peoples. The right to an equitable education from early childhood significantly affects future life opportunities for First Nations children of Australia. Have we as a nation, the political will, or the social and cultural mechanisms in place, for the rights of First Nations children to be achieved at a national level in the twenty-first century?

The UNCRC has two specific articles that are committed to supporting a child's right to education – Articles 28 and 29, focus on the provision of education for all children. Woolley (2009) maintains that 1989 UNCRC Articles are "not specific to Indigenous children, but the entire Convention is applicable to this sub-group and is one of the first international treaties to specifically address Indigenous children's rights (Articles 17, 29, and 30)."

To understand this argument more fully it is important to unpack what Article 29 embodies in relation to the rights of First Nations children and the Australian education system. Although Article 29(1a) seeks to promote "the development of the child's personality, talents and mental and physical abilities to their fullest potential", Behrendt et al. (2009) suggest that systemic racism is still a huge problem within educational institutions. As such, associated mental and physical health aspects may contribute to the disengagement and exclusion of some young First Nations people from education. Indeed, some educators have minimal explicit comprehension of the historical impacts, or the contemporary policies and practices that have shaped the education and social landscape for First Nations peoples (Duthie, 2019; O'Brien & Trudgett, 2018).

Since the late 1960's reports of First Nations disadvantage in education came to the fore, and many government policies surfaced to address the inequitable and disparate educational outcomes being experienced by First Nations children (Patrick & Moodie, 2016). While it is interesting to note that educational policies around culturally responsive frameworks in schools do exist specifically to support embedding of First Nations perspectives within our national curriculum (White et al., 2013), everyday application of these policies, for the most part, are rarely actualised within schools or classrooms. Consequently, those who work within an educational environment may not have the practical capacity to implement equitable educational rights for First Nations children within existing operating structures (Booth, 2014; Turner et al., 2017). Therefore, the ability to achieve opportunities for First Nations children to reach their full potential according to Article 29 may be hindered dramatically (Ma Rhea et al., 2012; Shipp, 2013).

Similarly, the interpretation of Article 29(1b) cannot be considered in cultural, social, or political isolation. Across Australia's states and territories, the enforcement of unjust policies has rendered many First Nations peoples powerless within their own nation state (Kearney, 2019). Clearly, Australian educators must consider the broader political, socio-economic, and cultural implications under Article 29(c), as well as the United Nations Declaration on the Rights of Indigenous Peoples in policy interpretation and praxis. Understanding these rights is fundamental to provide equitable educational opportunities ensuring the wellbeing of First Nations children in our classrooms.

Australian Government Response – Closing the Gap

A statement released in 2017 by the then UN Special Rapporteur indicated Australia did not have a particularly good record across economic and social provisions when it came to Human Rights matters for First Nations peoples (Tauli-Corpuz, 2017). This record can be witnessed in the political and socio-economic legacies that continue to affect contemporary education, employment, health, and housing, high incarceration rates and mortality rates of First Nations peoples (Department of Prime Minister and Cabinet, 2019). In 2008, Closing the Gap (CTG) reforms were established by the Council of Australian Governments (COAG) and were intended to reduce disparity between First Nations peoples and non-Indigenous Australians across several social and economic determinants (Social Justice Report, 2008, 2009).

Relative to education, in 2019 the CTG report indicated that there were still substantial gaps in educational outcomes for First Nations children, particularly in very remote areas, and results varied considerably according to geographical location throughout Australian states and territories. Across year levels one through to ten, attendance at school for First Nations children remained considerably lower than that of their non-Indigenous counterparts and First Nations children in very remote areas had the lowest attendance rates "at up to 16 percentage points lower than that for Indigenous children in other areas" (Department of Prime Minister and

Cabinet, 2019, p. 45). The Prime Minister's response to the CTG targets in 2016 acknowledged that, "the original target to ensure access for all Indigenous four-year-old's in remote communities to early childhood education expired unmet in 2013" (Department of Prime Minister and Cabinet, 2016, p. 12). This target was then revised to 95% by 2025 and, according to data released in 2019, this target would be met within the prescribed timeframe. Clearly, there is an issue with the CTG policy.

Considering the Cultural Implications – Power and Hegemonic Practices

The State and the education system are inextricably linked and exist to produce citizens who can deliver the economic outcomes required to govern, as well as support the political machinations of those who hold power. Indisputably, many First Nations peoples are consistently excluded (Hogarth, 2018; Miller, 2015) from engaging in any cross-cultural dialogue, which seeks to shift the balance of power and create opportunities to move forward within the schooling system. Promisingly, some schools are working in partnership with First Nations communities families and children to deliver culturally appropriate education (Sarra et al., 2018). These partnerships can be seen in programs such as the Stronger Smarter Program[1] or the Pedagogy of Difference project in Townsville, Queensland, which aims to draw upon the knowledge and aspirations of First Nations children and include these in the development and delivery of culturally appropriate curriculum. Pursuant on the implementation of Article 29(1c), the State agrees to:

> The development of respect for the child's parents, his or her own cultural identity, language and values, for the national values of the country in which the child is living, the country from which he or she may originate, and for civilizations different from his or her own.

In Australia there are structural barriers which thwart the aspirations to achieve UNCRC developments, particularly for minority groups, such as First Nations peoples who make up just over 3% of Australia's total population (Australian Bureau of Statistics, 2016). Eurocentric practices continue to shape systems of government as well as the Australian Curriculum presented in the nation's schools. This is despite mounting evidence that successful outcomes in education for First Nations children transpires when Indigenous Knowledges and perspectives are embedded into the curriculum and when schools provide culturally safe spaces for First Nations children to thrive (Lewthwaite et al., 2015).

While Article 29(1c) explicitly advocates for the rights of all children to express their cultural identity, languages and values within an educational context, some

[1] The Stronger Smarter Program is a national program that supports educators to provide innovative and dynamic approaches and processes in the area of Indigenous education that are supported by high expectations relationships.

parents of First Nations children concede that educational institutions tend to remain places of inequality. Indicating that, schools lack inclusion of First Nations "ways of knowing, ways of being and ways of doing" (Martin, 2003, p. 211). Thereby, precluding First Nations children from participating, which demonstrates the difficulty of practical application of Article 29(1c). Although education is a right of all individuals, in an Orwellian twist[2] (Orwell, 1946) it appears that in the current Australian schooling system, some children are more equal than others.

Exclusionary practices such as the denial of a right to education up until the early 1970's, or the delivery of sub-standard education in dormitory missions for First Nations children has affected generations of First Nations peoples (Blake, 2001). The legacy of colonialist settler policies and practices which prevailed well into the 1970s meant that sub-standard education for First Nations peoples was, in principle, readily accepted by many of those in power and within mainstream society (Behrendt, 2012). Previously enforced discriminatory policies targeting First Nations peoples directly, included segregation onto missions and reserves, assimilation, as well as the stolen generations where First Nations children were indiscriminately removed from their parents and communities (Allison, 2014). As such, many First Nations peoples still experience an element of distrust of government institutions and their agents, including those employed within the education system (Davis, 2006; Habibis et al., 2016).

The political, social and economic structural power throughout Australia's "nation building" has had an antithetical effect on the rights of many First Nations peoples' lives, including the fundamental right to education. Continued hegemonic practices contributes to the preservation of inequitable ideological agendas within educational institutions and this may have a decidedly negative impact upon the individual power and agency of First Nations children, which Article 29(1c) seeks to endorse. Indeed, preclusion of First Nations cultural capital whether deliberate or not (Walter, 2010; Xu, 2018) in institutions such as schools can lead to a significant loss of cultural agency and feelings of alienation for many First Nations children. The inability of some educators to set aside their power and authority and enter a space where shared inquiry takes place has stymied progress from occurring within educational sectors, such as schools (Lukes, 2004).

McAllan (2013) argues that, "Australia's education system is one of the most powerful institutional mechanisms in constructing and maintaining white-dominated social hegemony" (p. 4). The argument is persuasive and controversial and challenges educators to consider why the education system continues to maintain the privileges of a 'white' dominant society and set the knowledge parameters for all people. We can see the problem of the attainability of the provisions set out under Article 29 for First Nations children.

Article 29(1d) identifies that there needs to be preparation of the child to meet their responsibilities in a 'free' society. As educators we must recognise that in

---

[2] Dystopian author George Orwell noted that, within society, there are those whose past existence is expunged from public record and memory, and this is reinforced by modern repressive governments.

some capacity First Nations peoples may believe that freedom is non-existent and that resistance to dominant institutional practices by First Nations peoples has been ongoing since settler colonisation (Gillan et al., 2017; Morgan, 2015). The transformative potential for improving educational outcomes for First Nations children, is undeniable, but on whose terms? First Nations peoples must be able to openly critique structures of education at the cultural interface (Nakata, 2002) and question how and why those in positions of power negate or 'shut-down' critical conversations that seek to challenge the prevailing status quo.

Briefly, Article 29(1e) stipulates that the development of respect for the natural environment is vital. Even so, we can see the education system is upheld by neo-liberalist principles (Savage, 2017; Tait, 2019) that are binary and dualistic to the natural environment and are therefore not necessarily supportive or symbiotic with First Nations peoples principles of 'being'. One could say that the actual structure of the school system is the antithesis of nature and it is not a natural environment at all but sets up a hierarchy of power. For First Nations peoples, collective nature and connection to family and community, and culture and land may more clearly define and represent respect for the natural environment (Lohoar et al., 2014).

Agency, Education and the Lived Reality of First Nations Boys

Nakata's (2007a) theoretical framework explores the contested space between Eurocentric and Indigenous Knowledge systems, which he describes as the Cultural Interface, establishing three foundational principles. The first is the contested space; the second is Indigenous agency, and thirdly, the tensions that are "created between Indigenous and non-Indigenous dualities" (Nakata, 2007b, p. 12). Nakata's (2007b) theoretical philosophy allows examination of the ways that young First Nations children are positioned within education and challenges the invisibility of privilege and 'whiteness' within these dominant structural systems.

A lack of inclusion of Indigenous Knowledges and perspectives in schools, and the lack of cultural capacity of educators in Australia needs to be addressed (Harrison, 2011; Hart et al., 2012). The Australian Institute for Teaching and School Leadership (AITSL)[3] (2011) promotes important strategies for teachers to develop their professional practice across all stages of their teaching career. Three pivotal areas to support inclusive practices within their professional standards framework are:

> 1.4 Strategies for Teaching Aboriginal and Torres Strait Islander Students: which supports teachers to demonstrate a broad knowledge and understanding of culture, cultural identity and linguistic background of students from Aboriginal and Torres Strait Islander backgrounds.

[3]AITSL provides structured opportunities for pre-service teachers to consider and undertake in practice the work of teaching, to relate the practice to knowledge and understanding they are developing in their program, and to demonstrate a positive impact on student learning.

2.4 Understand and Respect Aboriginal and Torres Strait Islander Peoples histories, cultures and languages, and

4.1 Support Student Participation by supporting inclusive student participation and engagement in classroom activities.

Although cross-curricula priorities do exist, quite often their implementation is not forthcoming by teachers who struggle to understand how to put these strategies into practice (Craven et al., 2007). Privileging colonialist ontologies, epistemologies and power structures demonstrates that the relevance of Indigenous Knowledges within the curricula are often de-valued or denied (Fabelo et al., 2011; Rose, 2012). "Othering" and stereotyping First Nations children continues through intentional or unintentional discourses that take place within schools and classrooms daily. The following case study briefly highlights the disturbing findings of the Royal Commission conducted in 2016 into the welfare and the education of young First Nations peoples incarcerated within the Don Dale Youth Detention Centre (DDYDC) in the Northern Territory of Australia.

Case Study – Don Dale Youth Detention Centre

Across Australia, young First Nations males experience high exclusion rates from schools and are over-represented in the juvenile justice system. There has been minimal discussion of the school to prison pipeline within Australia up until recently, and too often, the rights of First Nations children in Australian schooling contexts are overlooked. All people regardless of age have the indisputable right to respect and fundamental freedoms. In 2016, the Australian Broadcasting Commission's (ABC) *Four Corners* reported on the appalling treatment of young males (98% of whom identified as First Nations children) in the Northern Territory Don Dale Youth Detention Centre (DDYDC). Images of a First Nations teenager, Dylan Voller, being restrained and 'spit hooded' by security staff at the centre were officially released. According to an ABC media report by Meldrum-Hannah and Worthington (2016) a detention guard indicated that Voller had been placed in a restraint chair on at least three separate occasions. It is understood that from the age of just 11 years old Voller had been incarcerated for varied offences for substantial periods in the facility. During this time, he received little to no formal education, contravening his fundamental human rights.

This footage led to an immediate public outcry within the wider Australian community and internationally. Public pressure and extensive reporting by media agencies (Aikman, 2016; Meade, 2016) resulted in the then Prime Minister of Australia, calling for an urgent royal commission into the mistreatment and lack of care of young people in the Detention Centre. Many other young males in the DDYDC were also subjected to continued and deliberate ongoing abuses by security staff, which included teargassing, strip searches, excessive control and humiliation.

Shortly after the airing of the footage Mr. Alvaro Pop and Professor Megan Davis (2016), both members of the United Nations Permanent Forum on Indigenous Issues, denounced the brutality and inhumane treatment inflicted upon the children in this facility.

As a signatory to the UNCRC and the Declaration on the Rights of Indigenous peoples, Lundy et al. (2017) claim that Australia's integration of the UNCRC principles are not methodical across states, and a child rights-based approach was not always explicit. In the DDYDC, the inhumane treatment perpetrated upon First Nations children was confirmed through the findings presented by the Commissioners' investigations. The Royal Commission into the Protection and Detention of Children in the Northern Territory (RCPDCNT) resulted in 227 recommendations, all of which were agreed to in full, or in principle by the Northern Territory government. Disturbingly, these recommendations were only accepted in principle by the Federal government. The findings indicated a breach of human rights and lack of duty of care for children and demonstrated that contraventions of the United Nations Convention on the Rights of the Child had occurred. These findings were also inconsistent with the Youth Justice Act of Northern Territory.

It is important to restate that at the time 98% of juveniles in Don Dale were First Nations boys. Of the 227 recommendations, 15 related to inadequate provision of educational opportunities for young people within the correctional facility. Findings 13 and 14 in *Education in Detention* identified that children were not given any transition support into mainstream schooling once they left the centre and neither was there any readily shared access by schools to children's educational records, resulting in greater difficulties for children to re-integrate back into mainstream schooling upon their release (RCPDCNT, 2017). Within the DDYDC, the commission also found that children were being punished excessively and suspended or excluded from the school (within detention) without adequate behaviour management plans in place to support student re-entry into the classroom (RCPDCNT, 2017). Despite the findings and recommendations, there has been no substantial legal reform and there have been no charges laid against any of the perpetrators who carried out these acts against boys incarcerated in the centre. The State has a legal and moral obligation to ensure respect for the human rights, fundamental freedoms and dignity for all children and yet in this instance for First Nations boys this did not occur.

The UNCRC principles in relation to Article 29 are not protected under an Australian legal context. The Don Dale case study highlights the difficulties of ensuring that Australian, state and territorial governments take responsibility for the protection of the rights of those children who continue to experience juvenile incarceration, the majority being First Nations young males. Currently the Australian Children's Commissioners and Guardians are demanding that children's rights are protected when in custody, and that the rehabilitation of children who are incarcerated remains a critical priority.

Manoeuvring Cultural Identity Constructs – Looking Forward

For First Nations children, their journey of learning is located within a contested space (Nakata, 2007a, b) as soon as they enter the school gate. Nakata (2002) considers this contested space as the intersection of Western and First Nations knowledge domains. Summerville and Hokanson (2013) explain that:

> It is also important to note that Aboriginal people often traverse dual macrosystems; the traditional Aboriginal macrosystem with its own set of rights and responsibilities, ideology, social values and mores, and the dominant macrosystem (p. 17).

Nakata's (2002) Cultural Interface theory allows interrogation of different knowledge systems. Parents of First Nations children struggle to maintain their children's cultural identity within school settings. Knowing your identity and where you are from is critical for the self-empowerment of First Nations children and highlights the importance and acknowledgement of Article 29(1) (Jackson-Barrett & Lee-Hammond, 2018; SNAICC, 2012). Culture is fundamental to the lives of First Nations peoples and is affirmed by the UNCRC as a critical human right outlined in many human rights documents. While some parents encourage their children to adopt a First Nations standpoint of being, knowing and doing, they also acknowledge that their children are in a place of learning that privileges Western ontologies and epistemologies above all other knowledge systems (Martin, 2003). Nakata (2007a, b) maintains that this dichotomy can be addressed positively if we consider the relational opportunities that can improve social structures for First Nations children as emphasised in Article 29(1d), rather than simply focussing on the tensions that occur within this contested space.

Nakata (2018a, b) suggests that, "decolonising approaches centralise Indigenous ways of knowing, being and doing in an effort to deal with the dominant Western presence in the way we now understand Indigenous realities" (p.5). He insists that the way forward is "by reclaiming and reconstructing Indigenous traditions subjugated by colonialism" (Nakata, 2018a, b, p. 5). Tuck and Yang (2012) highlight that "decolonisation is not a swappable term for other things we want to do to improve our societies and our schools" (p. 3). Educators must look beyond merely including metaphorical discourses of decolonisation within their teaching practice. But how do non-Indigenous educators seek to address and implement equitable opportunities for First Nations children in schools when they lack the cultural capacity to do so? More importantly, what about the perspectives of First Nations children and their families? In concurrence with Article 29(1c) families of First Nations children have a unique position from which they understand the educational process as it applies to their children and it is within this space First Nations voices must be heard.

Culture, Curriculum and the Rights of First Nations Children

First Nations children who attend school must carefully navigate between two cultural constructs. The first being the construction of their Indigeneity and how this is viewed and either accepted or rejected by the dominant majority. The second requires negotiation through Eurocentric education systems and finding suitable pathways that enable them to engage with the dominant mainstream structures of schooling whilst keeping their culture intact (Shipp, 2013). The enculturation of First Nations children into Eurocentricism is therefore seen to be highly problematic in relation to the enactment of Article 29.

In contrast, many non-Indigenous children do not have to consider navigating these two cultural constructs and are considered at an advantage at the commencement of their schooling experience (O'Brien, 2019; O'Brien & Trudgett, 2018). Nevertheless, First Nations children are aware that this duality is always present. By providing a culturally safe environment and by enacting Article 29(1a) teachers can support First Nations children to feel a sense of belonging and connectedness to school (Krakouer & Meston, 2015; Macfarlane et al., 2007). Cultural safety is grounded in three tenets – reflection, recognition and respect (Nursing Council of New Zealand, 2011). In Australia, the implementation of these tenets has been adopted within the domains of health and education. To provide a culturally safe environment within schools and classrooms educators must make relational connections with Community,[4] acknowledge and understand the historical and contemporary issues faced by First Nations peoples and use authentic resources that relate to local First Nations communities where possible. This can have enormous benefits for the self-efficacy and agency of First Nations children (McLaughlin et al., 2008; Purdie et al., 2000).

O'Brien and Trudgett (2018) suggest that there have been some encouraging advances by individual schools who have established meaningful relationships and partnerships with their local First Nations communities. Nevertheless, current and future educators should be supported with opportunities for professional learning to take place in this space. Therefore, understanding the critical nature of the rights of all children to achieve their highest educational potential and to realise that this cannot occur without ratification and collective action to apply these rights in all extents of education, particularly for those children who are marginalised.

More positively, First Nations Community schools[5] and some mainstream schools are focussing upon the revitalisation of First Nations languages, for example the Yugambeh Language Program and Mossman State School language program, are both supported by the State Library of Queensland. There is also inclusion of

---

[4] "Community" refers to individual First Nations Communities within Australia.

[5] First Nations Community Schools refers to independent schools that are autonomous, focus upon Indigenous education, have a governing body comprising of members of the Community in which the school is located, is responsible for staffing, curriculum, school buildings, staff housing, and financial accountability.

First Nations languages in the Australian Curriculum and Reporting Authority Framework. Promisingly, we can see that UNCRC Article 29(1c) and the UNDRIP Articles 8(1), 11(1) and specifically Article 13(1), which specifies the right to "revitalise, use, develop and transmit to future generations their histories, languages, oral traditions, philosophies, writing systems and literatures, and to designate and retain their own names for communities, places and persons". These examples demonstrate that First Nations languages are beginning to be included in learning as an enshrined right of First Nations children.

It is not enough that educators solely engage with culturally responsive best practice, they must also understand how deep-seated constructs of power and oppression maintained within political and educational structures continue to adversely affect many First Nations children of Australia. For educators, the challenge is to disrupt these dominant power structures and ensure that socially just practices are embedded within educational policy and subsequently into praxis. Educators must identify, and continue to contest and challenge, inequitable practices within systems of education from a social justice and human rights perspective.

Conclusion

This chapter has discussed some of the ways that Article 29 is fundamental to ensuring that First Nations children within Australia are receiving the opportunities to excel from the very beginning of their educational journey. As educators we are responsible for understanding and engaging with education (teaching and learning) from a human rights and social justice position. The interpretation of the components of Article 29 has shown that colonially imposed systems and practices have had an overwhelming influence on Australia's First Nations peoples since invasion and colonisation. Policy implementation for First Nations peoples in the past and present has a direct bearing on whether the United Nations Convention on the Rights of the Child is being implemented within Australia. Further discussion is required by Australian politicians, governments and agents of social change in relation to the establishment of a Human Rights Act (Gerber & Castan, 2013) that will protect all Australians, including those who are most vulnerable and marginalised (Behrendt et al., 2009).

This chapter highlighted a notable lack of cultural capacity by some educators as to the everyday occurrences affecting First Nations children and their families. Its resolution requires substantially more than educators possessing cultural capacity, it also necessitates critical understanding and acceptance of the historical and contemporary issues continuing to affect First Nations peoples. Reducing educational disparity should be a priority for federal, state and territory governments in alignment with Article 29. The parameters of power and agency of First Nations children and their families is still being determined by non-Indigenous people within the education system and many other sectors of Australian society. These parameters present a critical barrier to the positive transformation of the current status of the Australian education system for First Nations children. First Nations children have a right to a quality education and a right to their cultural identity, emancipation and self-determination in the process (Articles 28, 29, 30).

References

Aikman, A. (2016, July 28). NT government moves to ban spit hoods and restraint chairs. *The Australian*. Retrieved November 17, 2019, from https://www.theaustralian.com.au/news/nation/nt-youths-may-be-moved-from-dondale-to-wickham-point/news-story/b9119482dc97401f25b565fc288f636d

Allison, F. (2014). A limited right to equality: Evaluating the effectiveness of racial discrimination law for Indigenous Australians through an access to justice lens. *Australian Indigenous Law Review, 17*(2), 3–25.

Australian Bureau of Statistics. (2016). *Census of Population and Housing: Reflecting Australia - Stories from the Census, 2016*. Canberra: Commonwealth of Australia.

Australian Institute for Teaching and School Leadership. (2011). *Australian professional standards for teachers*. AIHW.

Behrendt, L. (2012). Aboriginal sovereignty: A practical roadmap. In J. Evans, A. Genovese, A. Reilly, & P. Wolfe (Eds.), *Sovereignty: Frontiers of possibility* (pp. 163–177). University of Hawaii Press.

Behrendt, L., Cuneen, C., Libesman, T., & Quiggan, R. (2009). *Indigenous legal relations in Australia*. Oxford University Press.

Blake, T. (2001). *A dumping ground: a history of the Cherbourg settlement*. St Lucia, Qld: University of Queensland Press.

Bodkin-Andrews, G., & Carlson, B. (2016). The legacy of racism and Indigenous Australian identity within education. *Race Ethnicity and Education, 19*(4), 784–807.

Booth, S. (2014). *Teaching Aboriginal curriculum content in Australian high schools*. Retrieved March 13, 2020, from https://ro.ecu.edu.au/cgi/viewcontent.cgi?article=2523&context=theses

Castagno, A., & Brayboy, B. (2008). Culturally responsive schooling for Indigenous youth: A review of the literature. *Review of Educational Research, 78*(4), 941–993. https://doi.org/10.3102/0034654308323036

Cowling, S. (2009). *Suspending welfare payments to promote school attendance: Strange logic, unlikely outcomes and a better way*. Paper presented to the ACOSS National Conference, 2–3 April, 2009, Sydney. Retrieved March 12, 2020 http://www.childrenyoungpeopleandfamilies.org.au/data/assets/pdf_file/0015/71106/Cowling_-_ACOSS_2009.pdf

Craven, R., Bodkin-Andrews, G., & Yeung, A. (2007). *A Model for success for aboriginal students: Paper presented at the australian association for research in education, Freemantle*. Retrieved from http://www.aare.edu.au/07pap/cra07433.pdf

Davis, M. (2006). A culture of disrespect: Indigenous peoples and Australian public institutions. *University of Technology Sydney Law Review, 8*, 137–154.

Department of Prime Minister and Cabinet. (2016). *Closing the gap: Prime Minister's report 2016*. Commonwealth of Australia.

Department of Prime Minister and Cabinet. (2019). *Closing the gap: Prime Minister's report 2019*. Commonwealth of Australia.

Duthie, D. (2019). Embedding Indigenous knowledges and cultural safety in social work curricula: Commentary on "Creating a culturally safe space when teaching Aboriginal content in social work: A scoping review". *Australian Social Work, 72*(1), 113–116. https://doi.org/10.1080/0312407X.2018.1534978

Fabelo, T., Thompson, M. D., Plotkin, M., Carmichael, D., Marchbanks, M. P., & Booth, E. A. (2011). *Breaking schools' rules: A Statewide study of how school discipline relates to students' success and juvenile justice involvement*. Council of State Governments Justice Center.

Gerber, P., & Castan, M. (2013). *Contemporary perspectives on human rights law in Australia*. Thomson Reuters Professional Australia.
Gillan, K., Mellor, S., & Krakouer, J. (2017). *The case for urgency: Advocating for indigenous voice in education*. ACER Press, Australian Council for Educational Research.
Habibis, D., Taylor, P., Walter, M., & Elder, C. (2016). Repositioning the racial gaze: Aboriginal perspectives on race, race relations and governance. *Social Inclusion, 4*(1), 57–67.
Harrison, N. (2011). *Teaching and learning in aboriginal education*. Second edition, South Melbourne: Oxford University Press.
Hart, V., Whatman, S., McLaughlin, J., & Sharma-Brymer, V. (2012). Preservice teachers' pedagogical relationships and experiences of embedding indigenous Australian knowledge in teaching practicum. *Compare, 42*(5), 703–723.
Hayes, D., Johnston, K., Morris, K., Power, K., & Roberts, D. (2009). Difficult dialogue: Conversations with Aboriginal parents and caregivers. *The Australian Journal of Indigenous Education, 38*, 55–64.
Hogarth, M. (2018). Talkin' bout a revolution: The call for transformation and reform in Indigenous education. *Australian Educational Researcher, 45*(5), 663–674. https://doi.org/10.1007/s13384-018-0277-8
Jackson-Barret, E., & Lee-Hammond, L. (2018). Strengthening identities and involvement of Aboriginal children through learning on Country. *Australian Journal of Teacher Education, 43*(6), 85–104. https://doi.org/10.14221/ajte.2018v43n6.6
Kearney, A. (2019). Interculturalism and responsive reflexivity in a settler colonial context. *Religion, 10*(3). https://doi.org/10.3390/rel10030199
Krakouer, J., & Meston, T. (2015). Review of Thelma Perso and Colleen Hayward, teaching indigenous students: Cultural awareness and classroom strategies for improving learning outcomes. *Australian Journal of Education, 59*(3), 329–331.
Lewthwaite, B., Osborne, B., Lloyd, N., Llewellyn, L., Boon, H., Webber, T., Laffin, G., Kemp, C., Day, C., Wills, J., & Harrison, M. (2015). Seeking a pedagogy of difference: What Aboriginal students and their parents in North Queensland say about teaching and their learning. *Australian Journal of Teacher Education (Online), 40*(5), 132–159.
Lohoar, S., Butera, N., & Kennedy, E. (2014). *Strengths of Australian Aboriginal cultural practices in family life and child rearing*. Child Family Community Australia, Australian Institute of Family Studies (AIFS).
Lukes, S. (2004). Power A Radical View, 2ed. Basingstoke: Palgrave Macmillan Ltd.
Lundy, L., Kilkelly, U., & Byrne, B. (2017). Incorporation of the United Nations Convention on the Rights of the Child in Law: A comparative review. In U. Kilkelly & L. Lundy (Eds.), *Children's rights (The library of essays on family rights)* (Vol. 1, p. 223). Routledge.
Ma Rhea, Z., Anderson, P., & Atkinson, B. (2012). *Improving teaching in Aboriginal and Torres Strait Islander education: Australian professional standards for teachers*. Australian Institute for Teaching and School Leadership (AITSL).
Macfarlane, A., Glynn, T., Cavanagh, T., & Bateman, S. (2007). Creating culturally safe schools for Māori students. *Australian Journal of Indigenous Education, 36*, 65–76.
Mallet, C. (2017). The School-to-Prison Pipeline: Disproportionate Impact on Vulnerable Children and Adolescents. *Education and Urban Society, 49*(6), 563–592.
Martin, K. (2003). Ways of knowing, being and doing: A theoretical framework and methods for Indigenous and Indigenist research. *Journal of Australian Studies, 27*(76), 203–214.
McAllan, F. (2013). *Speaking-writing with Aboriginal and settler interrelations*. Cambridge Scholars Publishing.
McLaughlin, J., Whatman, S., Katona, M., & Ross, R. (2008). Indigenous knowledge and effective parent/school partnerships: insights and issues from 4 school case studies. In Indigenous Studies and Indigenous Knowledge Conference, 2008-07-02 - 2008-07-04. (Unpublished).
Meade, A. (2016, July 26). Abuse of teenage prisoners in NT detention: How Four Corners got the story. *The Guardian*. Retrieved July 26, 2016, from Hunter, F. (2016, July 26). Malcolm

Turnbull calls royal commission into youth abuse at Northern Territory's Don Dale detention centre. *Sydney Morning Herald*. Retrieved November 11, 2019 from https://www.smh.com.au/politics/federal/prime-minister-malcolm-turnbullcalls-royal-commission-into-youth-detention-abuse-at-don-dale-detention-centre20160726-gqdm7x.html

Meldrum-Hannah, C., & Worthington, E. (2016, July 26). Evidence of 'torture' of children held in Don Dale detention centre uncovered by Four Corners. *ABC News*. Retrieved November 14, 2019 from http://www.abc.net.au/news/2016-07-25/four-cornersevidence-of-kids-tear-gas-in-don-dale-prison/7656128

Miller, M. (2015). Consultation with Aboriginal and Torres Strait Islander people in early childhood education: The impact of colonial discourses. *The Australian Educational Researcher, 42*(5), 549–565. https://doi.org/10.1007/s13384-015-0186-z

Mittleman, J. (2017). "A School-to-Prison Pipeline? Locating the Link Between Exclusionary School Discipline and Juvenile Justice Contact," Working Papers wp17- 14-ff, Princeton University, Woodrow Wilson School of Public and International Affairs, Centre for Research on Child Wellbeing.

Morgan, B. (2015). *A submission to the House of Representatives Standing Committee on Indigenous Affairs Inquiry into Educational Opportunities for Aboriginal and Torres Strait Islander Students*. Wollotuka Institute University of Newcastle.

Nakata, M. (2002). Indigenous knowledge and the cultural interface: Underlying issues at the intersection of knowledge and information systems. *IFLA Journal, 28*(5/6), 1–11.

Nakata, M. (2007a). *Disciplining the savages savaging the disciplines*. Aboriginal Studies Press.

Nakata, M. (2007b). The cultural interface. *The Australian Journal of Indigenous Education, 36*, 7–14.

Nakata, M. (2018a). Difficult dialogues in the South: Questions about practice. *The Australian Journal of Indigenous Education, 47*(1), 1–7.

Nakata, S. (2018b). The infantilisation of indigenous Australians: A problem for democracy. *Griffith Review, 60*, 104–116.

Nursing Council of New Zealand. (2011). *Guidelines for Cultural Safety, the Treaty of Waitangi and Maori Health in Nursing Education and Practice*. Wellington, NZ.

O'Brien, G. (2019). *Educational experiences of young Indigenous males in Queensland: Disrupting the school to prison pipeline*. Unpublished doctoral dissertation. University of Technology Sydney, Centre for the Advancement of Indigenous Knowledges, Sydney.

O'Brien, G., & Trudgett, M. (2018). School house to big house. *The Australian Journal of Indigenous Education, 49*(1), 98–106. https://doi.org/10.1017/jie.2018.13

Ockenden, L. (2014). *Positive learning environments for Indigenous children and young people. Closing the Gap Resource Sheet No. 33*. Australian Institute of Health and Welfare.

Orwell, G. (1946). *Animal farm*. Harcourt, Brace & World.

Owusu-Bempah, A., Kanters, S., Druyts, E., Toor, K., Muldoon, K., Farquhar, J., & Mills, E. (2014). Years of life lost to incarceration: Inequities between Aboriginal and non-Aboriginal Canadians. *BMC Public Health, 14*(1), 585–585.

Patrick, R., & Moodie, N. (2016). Indigenous education policy discourses in Australia: Rethinking the problem. In T. Barkatsas & A. Bertram (Eds.), *Global learning in the 21st century* (pp. 165–184). Sense Publishers.

Pop, A., & Davis, M. (2016). *Statement by the Permanent Forum on Indigenous Issues on the Don Dale Youth Detention Centre (NT, Australia)*. UNDESA Division for Social Inclusive Development Indigenous Peoples. Retrieved October 30, 2019 from https://www.un.org/development/desa/indigenouspeoples/news/2016/08/statementby-the-permanent-forum-on-indigenous-issues-on-the-don-dale-youth-detentioncenter-nt-australia/

Purdie, N., Tripcony, P., Boulton-Lewis, G., Fanshawe, J., & Gunstone, A. (2000). *Positive self-identity for Indigenous students and its relationship to school outcomes*. Department of Education, Training and Youth Affairs.

Raufu, A. (2017). School-to-Prison Pipeline: Impact of School Discipline on African American Students. *Journal of Education & Social Policy, 7*(1), 47–53.

Rose, M. (2012). The 'silent apartheid' as the practioner's blindspot. In *Aboriginal and Torres Strait Islander Education: An introduction for the teaching profession* (pp. 64–80). Cambridge University Press.

Royal Commission into the Protection and Detention of Children in the Northern Territory. (2017). *Attorney-General for Australia*. Government of Australia.

Sarra, C., Spillman, D., Jackson, C., Davis, J., & Bray, J. (2018). High-expectations relationships: A foundation for enacting high expectations in all Australian schools. *Australian Journal of Indigenous Education*, 1–14. https://doi.org/10.1017/jie.2018.10

Savage, G. C. (2017). Neoliberalism, education and curriculum. In B. Gobby & R. Walker (Eds.), *Powers of curriculum: Sociological perspectives on education*. Oxford University Press.

Shipp, C. (2013). Bringing Aboriginal and Torres Strait Islander perspectives into the classroom: Why and how. *Literacy Learning: The Middle Years, 21*(3), 24–29.

SNAICC. (2012). *Aboriginal and Torres Strait Islander children's cultural needs*. Australian Government Department of Families and Housing, Community Services and Indigenous Affairs (FaHCSIA), Australia.

Social Justice Report 2004. (2005). Sydney: Human Rights and Equal Opportunity Commission.

Social Justice Report 2008. (2009). *Report of the Aboriginal and Torres Strait Islander Social Justice Commissioner to the Attorney-General as required by section 46C(1)(a) Human Rights and Equal Opportunity Commission Act 1986*. Human Rights and Equal Opportunity Commission.

Summerville, J., & Hokanson, J. (2013). *Cultural Perspectives on Learning: Building the foundations for working with Aboriginal & Torres Strait Islander children and families*. Child Australia & Shift Consulting Group Pty Ltd: Darwin.

Tait, G. (2019). *Making sense of mass education* (3rd ed.). Cambridge University Press.

Tauli-Corpuz, V. (2017). *UN Special rapporteur: Self-determination is key to addressing aboriginal and torres strait islander disadvantage*. Office of the High Commissioner for Human Rights.

Triggs, G. (2017). The protection of human rights and the idea of a "fair go" in Australia today. *Redress, 26*(1), 8–15.

Tripcony, P. (2010). *Indigenous children and youth: Issues and underlying factors*. Background paper to presentation by Dr Penny Tripcony, Child Protection Peak Ltd.

Tuck, E., & Yang, W. (2012). Decolonization is not a metaphor. *Decolonization: Indigeneity, Education & Society, 1*(1), 1–40.

Turner, A., Wilson, K., & Wilks, J. (2017). Aboriginal community engagement in primary schooling: Promoting learning through a cross- cultural lens. *Australian Journal of Teacher Education (Online), 42*(11), 96–116.

UN General Assembly. *United Nations declaration on the rights of Indigenous peoples: Resolution/ adopted by the General Assembly, 2 October 2007, A/RES/61/295*. Retrieved November 11, 2019 from https://www.refworld.org/docid/471355a82.html

United Nations. (1989). *Convention on the rights of the child*. Geneva, Switzerland.

Walter, M. (2010). *Understanding methodologies: Indigenous research methodologies*. Master Class 2010, University of Tasmania & IRMMM. Retrieved November 12, 2019 http://www.isrn.qut.edu.au/research/documents/UnderstandingMethodologiesandIndigenousMethodologies2011.pdf

White, S., Ma Rhea, Z., Anderson, P., & Atkinson, B. (2013). *A unit outline and content for professional learning units to support teachers in meeting Focus Areas 1.4 and 2.4 – Teacher professional development in Indigenous education curriculum: Curriculum development unit for the Australian Institute of Teaching and School Leadership (AITSL)*. Monash University.

Woolley, S. L. (2009). The rights of Indigenous children around the world – Still far from a reality. *Global Child Health, 94*(5), 397–400.

Xu, D. (2018). *Indigenous cultural capital: Postcolonial narratives in Australian children's literature*. Retrieved August 17, 2018 from https://ebookcentral.proquest.com

Chapter 9
Ability-Grouping and Rights-Based Education in the Neoliberal Era: An Irresolvable Combination?

Nerida Spina, Jess Harris, and Felicia Jaremus

Abstract Ability-based groupings have long been a contentious issue within schooling. Neoliberal imaginaries, which position parents as 'consumers' within the education marketplace, however, have intensified the development of school structures that use student assessment data to determine student "ability". These categories are used group students by ability so that teaching can be directed at improving publicly-reported student outcomes on high-stakes standardised tests. This chapter uses a critical theoretical approach, informed by the United Nations Convention on the Rights of the Child (Article 29) to examine implications of ability-based groupings in one regional secondary school in Australia. A vignette, based on a range of data from this school, illustrates how these kinds of school structures influence pedagogical practices, access to knowledge and expectations for students. In so doing, we identify how these school structures (re)construct inequities for students and limit some students' opportunities to 'develop their personality, talents and mental and physical abilities to their fullest potential'.

Keywords Ability-grouping · Data · Streaming · Tracking · Inequity · Education · Australia

N. Spina (✉)
Queensland University of Technology, Brisbane, QLD, Australia
e-mail: n.spina@qut.edu.au

J. Harris · F. Jaremus
University of Newcastle, Newcastle, NSW, Australia
e-mail: jess.harris@newcastle.edu.au; felicia.jaremus@newcastle.edu.au

J. Gillett-Swan, N. Thelander (eds.), *Children's Rights from International Educational Perspectives*, Transdisciplinary Perspectives in Educational Research 2, https://doi.org/10.1007/978-3-030-80861-7_9

Introduction

Despite being widespread in subject areas like secondary mathematics and English, ability-based student grouping remains a highly contentious practice (e.g., Kulikand & Kulik, 1987; Rist, 1970). Yet, there is evidence that, in an era of competition, school choice, and high stakes testing, this set of practices is intensifying relatively uncontested (e.g., Francis et al., 2019).

This chapter examines how ability-based streaming curtails the capacity of schools to meet central tenets of the United Nations Convention on the Rights of the Child [hereafter, UNCRC] (United Nations, 1989), in particular Article 29. The chapter begins by outlining the logics of neoliberal education reform and establishes how this context has prompted schools to structure class groupings based on student achievement data. We consider how neoliberal imaginaries, in which parents are constituted as "consumers" with a right to choose schools, can amplify structural inequities. We then present a vignette (Ely et al., 1997) from one school to demonstrate how the political and sociocultural landscape of education influences school structures and can create barriers for rights-informed schooling. In the concluding sections, we present evidence that calls into question whether schools using ability-based structures can meet students' rights to an education that allows them to develop their "personality, talents and mental and physical abilities to their fullest potential" (United Nations, 1989, Article 29 1(a)). We conclude with a discussion of UNCRC Article 29 and consider how neoliberal education systems create challenges for rights-based education in terms of human dignity and development of the whole person.

Competing Pressures in the School Marketplace

School systems across Australia and internationally face increasing pressure to demonstrate ongoing improvement in rankings on local and global league tables (Sellar et al., 2017). System authorities filter this pressure to schools through accountability measures, designed to encourage increased student performance on standardised testing measures, like Australia's National Assessment Program for Literacy and Numeracy (NAPLAN). Introduced in 2008, NAPLAN was developed to measure and report on student achievement in literacy and numeracy. The introduction of NAPLAN, and the associated national *MySchool* website, which reports school NAPLAN outcomes, has been widely critiqued (Gorur, 2015; Mills, 2015). While public reporting of school achievement data was justified as providing information to support school choice (Gillard, 2010), the literature shows that this is really only possible for families with sufficient cultural and economic capital to choose a school (Kenway, 2013; Mills, 2015). As Elwood and Lundy's (2010) work in the UK demonstrates, the substantial impact such standardised assessment regimes have had on education systems, the links to children's rights have rarely been made.

Over recent decades, school systems throughout the global north have encouraged market-driven logics of school choice, resulting in higher levels of competition between schools and increased scrutiny from systems and from certain caregivers hoping to select the "best" school for their child[ren] (Kenway, 2013). While promoted as a "tide that lifts all boats" (Hoxby, 2003), research cautions that policies promoting school choice and competition do not result in improved learning outcomes for all students (Kenway, 2013; Mills, 2015), nor do they ensure rights for all (Elwood & Lundy, 2010). Striking evidence of the potential fragmentation of schooling has been seen in the US (Lipman, 2004) and England (West & Hind, 2007), where such policies have prompted increases in between- and within-school segregation. As such, students from low socio-economic backgrounds, ethnic and linguistic minorities, and those with disabilities are being turned away from "high-performing" schools (West & Hind, 2007) and grouped into "low ability" classes (Connolly et al., 2019).

Ability-based grouping, using data from high-stakes standardised tests is commonly referred to as "tracking" in the US, "setting" in the UK, and "streaming" in Australia, the term used in this chapter. In our wider program of research with a network of schools (Harris et al., 2018), we found a twofold logic for implementing streaming. First, the schools believed that separating students in this way would assist teachers to target activities to improve student achievement data; and second, they believed it afforded strong promotional opportunities, in particular, marketing extension classes to families seeking to maximise their child[ren]'s academic success (Spina, 2019). Central to this logic is a number of assumptions, including that student ability in any given subject is fixed, and/or that teachers are better able to support individuals in a class of students with a narrower range of achievement levels, and that this practice will boost student achievement (Johnston & Wildy, 2016; Slavin, 1990). These assumptions are challenged by research that demonstrates ability is plastic and heavily influenced by sociocultural factors (Boaler, 2005; Rist, 1970).

Elwood and Lundy's (2010) work in the UK indicates that links between school responses to public assessment regimes and children's rights have rarely been made. Despite neoliberal education policy reforms leading to a focus on evidence-based policy and practice being taken up in schools (Spina, 2020), an analysis of multiple national legislative initiatives found that the UN's focus on human rights education had limited impact on school-based policies and practices (Robinson et al., 2020).

However, practices such as streaming appear at odds with perspectives that view education as a human right, with the capacity to transform inequities and unjust social relations. Critical theorists such as Freire (1972) advocated for an approach to teaching that would liberate and ultimately enable the oppressed to "regain their humanity" (p. 48). Critical theory conceives of human rights as being related to "those conditions that are necessary for human emancipation… [and that operate] on a personal, cultural and systemic level" (Keet, 2007, p. 202). Giroux (1984) draws on the work of Freire to argue that understanding who controls access to knowledge and knowing is critical because "only then can the oppressed recognise the ideological distortions that influence and shape their understanding of social and political reality" (p. 132).

Similarly, contemporary scholars (Apple, 2016; Luke, 2018) have highlighted how education constructs social relations, including access to knowledge, skills and values. They indicate that school knowledge, and its transmission through pedagogic choices is not neutral. Rather, it works to position different subjects—in this case, students—within wider power relations. Giroux (1984) noted that education based on respect for human rights requires recognition of the connection of pedagogy to agency, control over the production of knowledge, and power relations. Such education must equip all students with the knowledge and skills necessary to become "more fully human" (Freire, 1972). This theoretical approach has been adopted in human rights education scholarship to examine how "freedom, knowledge, rights and power as a counter-narrative to the dominant discourse" (Dunkerly-Bean, 2013, p. 40) can be realised through education.

The Research

We provide a vignette on a large, regional Australian secondary school, Glenbrook North High (pseudonym), serving 1200 students from years 7–12, to illustrate effects of schools' structures based on student attainment data. Approximately 70% of students' families are classified as being in the bottom half of socio-economic disadvantage (according to *MySchool*). Drawing from data collected over a 3-year period, this vignette presents the 'complex dimensions' of what has been learned about the structures at Glenbrook North High (Ely et al., 1997, p.70).

In 2013–14, Glenbrook North High's leadership team expressed concern around the school's results on NAPLAN and the trend for local parents of high-achieving students to enrol their children in 'better performing' secondary schools. In 2014, NAPLAN results placed Glenbrook North below the national average in more than half of the domains tested. In response, the leadership team decided to implement a new structure where students in Junior Secondary (Years 7–9) would be allocated into streamed classes on the basis of their NAPLAN results and, to a lesser extent, primary school report card data.

The classes included a "Middle" class of students with average attainment; an "Elite" class for high-achieving students, and a "Basic" class for students who had achieved "low" NAPLAN results. In anonymising our data, we have assigned names for these class groups that represent class titles frequently assigned in schools. Class groups stayed together for 'core' subject areas of English, mathematics, science, and social sciences. Students, therefore, who excelled in one area of learning but overall had average attainment would not be given the opportunity to join the Elite class.

Streamed classes were marketed to prospective parents at information evenings and via promotional material, including the school website and enrolment information packs. The Elite class was described as offering high-performing students opportunities to deepen their learning via extension activities and independent inquiry. At the other end of the spectrum, the Basic class was described as providing an overt focus on fundamental literacy and numeracy skills through direct instruction and revision of prior learning. The Middle class was described as utilising a range of pedagogies – some direct instruction, some independent inquiry, and so forth. While there were similarities between classes, including the curriculum followed, this vignette highlights substantial differences in pedagogical approaches and expectations for students, particularly between Elite and Basic classes. In so doing, we raise questions about how this structure relates to the UNCRC's goals of equity and education that provides all students with the opportunity to develop their "personality, talents and mental and physical abilities to their fullest potential" as per Article 29 (United Nations, 1989).

Methodology

Research presented in this chapter draws on in-depth interviews with all 12 Junior Secondary teachers at Glenbrook High and 16 50-min classroom observations across each stream. Interviews with teachers occurred after classroom observations, with questions relating to teachers' perceptions of class allocations; pedagogy in different classes; and perceived benefits and drawbacks of the structure in its second year of implementation. Interviews lasted between 40 min and 1 h, providing time to discuss the observed lesson, including pedagogical choices. The classroom observation protocol included a description of the class layout, and detailed observation notes about pedagogy, teacher talk, and interactions with students. These notes were used as prompts in interviews to discuss specific pedagogies employed in each class.

While students' perspectives on teaching and learning were sought as part of a wider research project in which this work is situated (Harris et al., 2018), the views of Glenbrook students were not sought with respect to classroom streaming. We have previously documented the importance of listening to the voices of learners, teachers and the wider community in supporting ethical approaches that adopt a rights-based approach education system. That is not the focus of the current chapter.

This vignette examines pedagogies employed in Elite and Basic class lessons. Our initial research question was: "how are classroom groupings enabling or constraining teachers' abilities to ensure equal access to curriculum and pedagogy, on the same basis"? Data were analysed using critical theory, which has been used extensively in the field of education (Apple, 2012a, b: Giroux, 1984; Luke, 2018.

Critical theories are grounded in understanding socio-cultural contexts, power relations and contradictions in education. Apple (2012a, b), for instance, has written extensively on oppression of marginalised groups through inequitable access to the curriculum. Luke (2018), similarly, applied critical perspectives to understand how pedagogies are applied unevenly so as to (re)produce inequalities. These scholars have shown that curriculum, pedagogy and assessment are deeply political, with the capacity to replicate privilege, and to curb equal access to knowledge. In the tradition of critical education research, we examined the pedagogical practices of teachers in Elite and Basic classrooms to examine how access to knowledge differed across class groupings.

In the following sections, we set out key differences identified by researchers and teachers between Elite and Basic classes. We draw primarily on the words of teachers to illustrate variations between classes, which reflected researchers' observations. We focus on the Elite and Basic classes as a means of exemplifying stark differences, revealing how marketisation and school competition can lead to the development of within school structures that provide unequal access to knowledge and stifle the rights of some students. As the vignette illustrates, these structures created a dichotomy between Elite and Basic classes that was evident in pedagogical approaches and the discursive construction of students in these groups.

Vignette: Streamed Classes as a Form of Structural Inequality

Elite Class

The observed Elite classes provided rich opportunities for students to co-construct knowledge and engage in problem solving and deep thinking about concepts. In our observations, we noted that teachers used subject-specific vocabulary, led substantive discussions about curriculum concepts and made links to locally relevant happenings. An example of a questions posed by an Elite class teacher is, "Has anyone heard of "de-amalgamation" [of local city councils]?"

This question occurred in a Year 8 Elite English class, to which a local newspaper editor had been invited to speak with students about journalism and writing. Students were engaged in discussions of local issues and given opportunities to ask their teacher and the editor questions. Students' questions ranged from the mechanics of writing to the financial viability of printed news in contemporary times. This example was one of many we observed in which students were encouraged to engage in deep discussion of issues and the curriculum in ways that linked to their knowledge and interests beyond the classroom.

We observed numerous Elite lessons where teachers encouraged students to actively discuss curriculum content and make connections between their learning in the classroom and their lived experiences. We also saw teachers engaging in extended conversations with student groups and individuals. It was evident in teacher interviews that this collaborative, socio-constructivist approach to learning was planned specifically for Elite classes, who were deemed 'easier' to engage in substantive discussion. For example, one teacher reported:

> I think collaborative learning is so much easier with an Elite class group of students than it is in a Middle or Basic class because they're ability group[ed]. They're all of a reasonably high level… So probably the grouping – and even though it might not always be group activities that they're doing, they're still interacting. I hear them teach each other, "oh what do you mean by that?"

In interviews, teachers talked about their high expectations of Elite students, and their perception that students had high expectations of themselves. They explained that they intentionally planned lessons that encouraged students to explore their own interests, passions and talents. Frequent classroom interactions meant teachers were cognisant of students' interests, and sought to expand on this in lessons:

> The... thing that works well in my class is just having group discussions, putting questions to the class, getting them to think about it. We get this amazing range of ideas that the students bring to the class. We can then – once I've gauged their interest, I can then go to them and say, we're looking at natural disasters, what sort of things do you want to learn about? ... They come to class and basically present some of their ideas so then I can go and make sure that that's where we're going with the lessons.

Students in Elite classes spent a great deal of time engaged in knowledge co-construction and deep learning. For example, in the lesson involving the local newspaper editor, observation notes included comments such as "Engaging and locally relevant content – 100% of students are listening quietly" and "some turn to look through examples of newspapers that [editor] has bought in". Teachers articulated that significant time on task was possible as students were engaged and on-task. One teacher commented:

> I think for my class – obviously their results are wonderful because behaviour was [great] – I teach a non-streamed class once a week and behaviour is such an issue that I just think, "how are they learning"? Whereas I've never had a behaviour problem in that class ever, ever, ever.

Teachers demonstrated a clear commitment to the students in Elite classes, who were viewed as likely to achieve future academic success:

> The expectations are far higher. I'm constantly talking to them about what happens in Year 11 and 12. I constantly can talk to them about university – you will do this – whereas in other classes that can't be the case.

There was also a focus on personalising the learning of students in Elite classes, with one teacher reporting that she made sure that every lesson included time to work with individual students to "check with them, see where they're at, gauge what level they're at, whether they're coping, whether they've got any questions". What was evident in our observations and in teachers' interviews was the focus on delivering high quality instructional practices such as using formative assessment, providing quality feedback, and planning for deep intellectual engagement with curriculum content. This pedagogical approach is consistent with rights to an education that assists with developing students "personality, talents and mental and physical abilities to their fullest potential" (United Nations, 1989, Article 29 1(a)).

Basic Class

In stark contrast, we observed that teachers in Basic classes tended towards highly structured tasks, involving lower-order thinking, and a focus on classroom management. Task completion was a focus of Basic lessons, with less emphasis on extending student learning. As one teacher said:

> It's great if you're in the [Elite] class, you get a lot more opportunities to extend – or I expect you do – to extend the learner, and less time, I imagine, being distracted from the teaching in the room.

In contrast to Elite classes, Basic classes were characterised by 'busy work' such as worksheets and games. Comparing two year 8 English classes illustrates this distinction. The Elite class described above, where students talked with their teacher and a local newspaper editor about academic and political issues was vastly different to a year 8 Basic English lesson that required students to rearrange the letters in the word "skateboard" to find smaller words, with the goal of increasing students' vocabulary. This whole-class activity saw students calling out words they identified; the teacher would write these on the board so other students could copy the words into workbooks. The teacher indicated she had intentionally selected the word "skateboard" because she hoped to draw on students' interests in her teaching. However, the connection with student interests was superficial and did not provide any opportunity for students to extend their learning, make new links with prior knowledge, or engage in an intellectually meaningful way (for example, analysing skating culture).

Another Basic class we observed [year 8 Maths] was taken up with students completing a worksheet on calculating rates. Early in the lesson, we noted that the teacher asked if students knew about rates and one student provided the example of buying petrol [gas] for a car. This answer was rejected, however, by the teacher's comment that "you have got to have your hand up". Around 20 minutes into the lesson we observed a drop in student engagement, noting that:

> very few students were looking at the board where the teacher was demonstrating how to calculate rates. Teacher says that the first person to correctly copy what he has written on the board will receive a sticker. A student [girl] says "I'm stuck sir". The teacher talks to another student. She copies the answer on the board and later receives a sticker.

The didactic approaches observed in Basic classes did not provide students with opportunities to make connections between their existing knowledge and the curriculum, clarify misunderstandings, or engage in conversation about content. Instead, a common feature of the pedagogies on offer was carrying out procedural work, like copying information into books, and completing worksheets. In our interviews, teachers reported that this pedagogical approach was intended to minimise time available for students to work independently, which could lead to disruptive behaviour. One teacher said, "we can't necessarily do independent [work]. We don't do it. I read it for them, they follow along, I do the notes, they might copy it".

Our observations and interviews also revealed substantially different teacher expectations for students in Elite and Basic classes. In Basic classes, we observed no conversations with students about their futures, and limited evidence of teachers trying to establish the significance of students' learning or engaging them in collaborative knowledge construction. Teachers' expectations for student achievement were lower, and described as "slower learning, academically", causing teachers to have "lower expectations of academic results".

Comparisons of achievement, and the potential for disruptions from learning, caused significant stress for Basic class teachers. They shared the view that students in Basic classes were more likely to have "behaviour problems". As one of the teachers described:

> ... I think you've got to be really aware of having all the kids that might have the behaviour difficulties, behaviour problems and how they're seen as group...and how difficult they are to manage.

A common classroom management strategy was the use of rewards to encourage participation. One teacher said, "I try different things, so different activities, different games that they compete against their friends.... like relay races with worksheets... they get a mark and so many points [when they complete a] worksheet. Whoever gets the most points gets a prize..." This approach was part of a broader strategy of breaking up lessons into short segments, often 5–10 min in duration. Teachers reported asking students to do one or two activities (for example, on a worksheet) before stopping for a break or reward:

> I don't know if there's any one technique that actually works overall well with them... You try and keep them as motivated as possible and just a variety of teaching to keep it flowing smoothly; that way they don't stagnate and get off task... I tend to do everything in small chunks.

While pedagogical approaches were intended to minimise individual input, we observed resistance from students, including attempts to shift classroom dynamics and engage in discussion. For example, in the English lesson where students were asked to think of small words from the word "skateboard", one student offered the word "bard", saying she had learned it in a poetry lesson the previous year. After a brief discussion, we noted the teachers' attention quickly shifted to two disruptive students at the back of the classroom. The opportunity to engage in an extended discussion that linked the student's prior knowledge to the activity was lost as the teachers' focus moved to behaviour management. The focus on busy work, basic skills didactic teaching and classroom management represented the dominant approach towards pedagogy in Basic classes, with students given little opportunity to deeply engage with the work.

Drawing on the critical scholarship of Luke (2018) and Apple (2016) helps to identify how differences in expectations and access to knowledge within this school structure operates as a conserving force that reproduces social and cultural inequities. To return to the rights outlined in Article 29, the class structures should ensure that the best interests of children are prioritised and that equal access is made available–not only to education itself, but also to opportunities for progress and success. The opportunities for students to engage with knowledge and extend their learning were limited, particularly when compared with the opportunities for those in the Elite class.

Discussion: The Better Gets Better, the Worst Gets Worse

Contrasts in the pedagogical approaches and expectations for students in Elite and Basic classes were stark. Students in Elite classes were encouraged to engage in intellectually challenging discussions about curriculum and given the opportunity to engage with complex language and concepts. In contrast, Basic classes were typified by tightly controlled activities, direct instruction, short whole-class activities, worksheets and rewards.

Article 29(a) of the UNCRC (1989) states that education should be directed to "the development of the child's personality, talents and mental and physical abilities to their fullest potential" (p. 9). The socio-constructivist pedagogical approaches observed in the Elite classes saw teachers extending the learning of individual students by encouraging them to construct links with their knowledge, talents and abilities beyond the classroom. The didactic approaches prominent in Basic classes, on the other hand, offered limited opportunities for students to develop their individual personality, talents and abilities, or to access curriculum on an equal basis. The Basic lessons we observed included a dominance of lower-order tasks, recollection and repetition of basic information. While teachers in Basic classes used this approach to limit disruptive behaviour, it was likely to have *limited* students' engagement in lessons, and further slowed academic progress (cf. Newmann et al., 2001).

Article 29(b) affirms the importance of the human rights enshrined in the Charter of the United Nations, the preamble to which states that "[we the peoples of the United Nations determined] to reaffirm faith in fundamental human rights, in the dignity and worth of the human person…" (United Nations, 1989, Article 29b). The nature of class timetables and structures meant that all students were aware of the ability-based groupings at Glenbrook North.

We draw on the words of Aung San Suu Kyi, Winner of the Nobel Peace Prize (1991), who wrote that "respect for human dignity implies commitment to creating conditions under which individuals can develop a sense of self-worth and security. True dignity comes with an assurance of one's ability to rise" (United Nations, 2002). In reflecting on the differences in pedagogical approaches between Basic and Elite classes, we were concerned about the potential impact this structural inequality might have on the human dignity of both students and teachers. We believe this is an area of schooling that requires much more rights-focused research, particularly in the current era of evidence-based decision making (Spina, 2020).

Being designated as a low-ability student creates almost insurmountable barriers (Loveless, 2016), making it structurally impossible to 'catch up'. Boaler's (2005) follow-up research with young adults who had been grouped during their school years revealed that their belief that classification as 'low-attainment' had significant long-term effects on factors such as students' incomes, occupations and psychology, with some describing grouping as a form of psychological prison. A significant body of literature has documented harmful psychological effects for students of being placed in lower streamed classes over an extended period of time (e.g.,

Loveless, 2013; Oakes, 2005), indicating students in the Basic class were at risk of experiencing adverse effects on self-concept and academic self-efficacy beliefs.

This is alarming when we consider that students from disadvantaged social groups are consistently overrepresented in low-ability groups, in some situations even when achievement is controlled for (Muijs & Dunne, 2010; Connolly et al., 2019). Structural responses to competition within and between schools, thus have the potential to promote greater inequity for those students whose interests have not been previously served by traditional education. Factors such as disability, language, refugee, Indigeneity and socio-economic status are implicated in achievement gaps (e.g., Apple, 2012a, b; Gillborn & Youdell, 2000; Luke, 2018). Critical theoretical perspectives draw attention to how differential access to curriculum and pedagogy can restrict the rights of specific groups of students. As Apple (2012a, b) notes, when official knowledge and pedagogy are rationed through ability-based groupings, "divisions strongly rooted in racializing and class-based structures [are] not simply mirrored in the schools. They actually [are] produced in these institutions" (p. 230).

At Glenbrook North, disparities in student achievement gains were clearly recognised by teachers, who stated in interviews:

> Definitely the Elite Classes definitely benefit the most out of the situation. The Basic Class I think it's disadvantaged, because they can – they move slower... and then they even move slower ...

Another teacher summarised the situation as "the better gets better and the worst get worse". What was concerning for teachers was that the opportunities afforded to students in Elite Classes were being denied to those who were in greatest need of access to content knowledge, dignity, and human development. In analysing the operation of power and the reproduction on unequal access to knowledge, we identified that structures created to raise standards, were most damaging for the least advantaged students. As this vignette illustrates, structuring for inequality as a response to neoliberal pressures represents a significant challenge to rights-based education.

Conclusion

This chapter presented a vignette of Glenbrook North High's approach to streaming to improve performance in the education marketplace. Specifically, we illustrated how growing pressures to increase standardised test scores and compete with local schools for their "market share" of students (Harris et al., 2018), led to the adoption of structures that appear to benefit high-performing students and disadvantage those students deemed to be low-ability. In so doing, we have demonstrated how neoliberal imaginaries create significant barriers for rights-informed education, by creating conditions in which schools provide students with inequitable access to knowledge and reproduce adopt inequitable grouping structures. While this chapter focuses on a single school, it raises questions about whether ability-based grouping within the current neoliberal climate could ever be concomitant with rights-based education.

We have illustrated how streaming violates the educational rights of students in lower streamed classes to develop their personality, talents and mental and physical abilities to their fullest potential (United Nations, 1989, Article 29 1(a)). Starkly different pedagogies, classroom management and intellectual opportunities were manifestations of this violation. Indeed, recent guidelines for equitable student grouping, developed as part of a large UK study (Francis et al., 2019) – including making grouping subject specific, applying high expectations to all groups and ensuring groups receive the same curriculum – were not evident in the practices observed at Glenbrook North. Francis et al.'s (2019) guidelines for 'best practice' groupings provide a promising model for how Glenbrook North could improve the rights of students, particularly those in low-achievement groups.

Slee (2019) argues that the 'ethic of competitive individualism' that sits behind neoliberal policies "subverts aspirations for inclusive education" (p. 7). Interviews with educators at Glenbrook North highlighted their concerns about comparison and competition. Their response to this pressure was to devise strategies to attract high-achieving students to the school, and to extend their learning across all areas of the curriculum. The focus on high-achieving students, however, raises concerns about residualisation for those students who are not already the highest achievers, and those whose caregivers do not have the privilege of choosing their child(ren)'s school because of their cultural or economic capital. As there are currently no national or state policies on ability-based grouping in Australia (Johnston & Wildy, 2016), school leaders are free to decide whether, and how, grouping practices are enacted. In this context, competition to attract and extend high-achieving students through ability-based groupings have resulted in "nested" forms of inequality within and between schools (Spina, 2019).

Elwood and Lundy's (2010) work in the UK drew attention to the link between the educational assessment policies that governments put in place, and the responsibility of governments as signatories to human rights treaties, including the UNCRC. Using a similar framework to analyse school structuring responses to large-scale standardised assessment regimes, it is apparent that under these conditions, not all students as rights-holders have equal access to knowledge, or participation. Critical education theorists have mounted a strong case that education must attend to matters of justice by adopting critical pedagogies, and critiquing the kinds of practices that "ration" (Gillborn & Youdell, 2000) education. Elwood and Lundy (2010) argue that one way forward is employing the "moral coinage of rights" to encourage policy change. Developing "children's rights standards" (p. 350) provides a way of thinking through how schools ensure the delivery of rights through the way that education is structured and delivered.

To end on a more positive note, grouping by student achievement is not a necessary or inevitable school structure. There are numerous countries around the world (such as Finland and Japan) where grouping students by ability is not a common practice. While differentiating instruction for individuals and groups of students is common in schools, it is important to consider structuring practices from a rights-based perspective. For example, teaching using fluid groupings of students that change over time and adjusts to accommodate the changing needs of learners can ensure parity of participation and increase more equitable access to knowledge (Hart & Drummond, 2014). According to Boaler (2005), such systems rely on a belief, supported by plasticity research, that high quality instructional practices can support all students to develop their "personality, talents and mental and physical abilities to their fullest potential" (United Nations, 1989, Article 29).

References

Apple, M. W. (2012a). *Knowledge, power, and education: The selected works of Michael W. Apple*. Routledge.

Apple, M. W. (2012b). *Education and power*. Routledge.

Apple, M. W. (2016). Challenging the epistomological fog: The roles of the scholar/activist in education. *European Educational Research Journal, 15*(5), 505–515.

Boaler, J. (2005). The 'psychological prisons' from which they never escaped: The role of ability grouping in reproducing social class inequalities. *Forum, 47*(2&3), 135–143.

Connolly, P., Taylor, B., Francis, B., Archer, L., Hodgen, J., Mazenod, A., & Tereshchenko, A. (2019). The misallocation of students to academic sets in maths: A study of secondary schools in England. *British Educational Research Journal, 45*(4), 873–897. https://doi.org/10.1002/berj.3530

Dunkerly-Bean, J. (2013). Reading the world in the word: The possibilities for literacy instruction framed within human rights education. *Language and Literacy, 15*(2), 40–55.

Elwood, J., & Lundy, L. (2010). Revisioning assessment through a children's rights approach: Implications for policy, process and practice. *Research Papers in Education, 25*(3), 335–353. https://doi.org/10.1080/02671522.2010.498150

Ely, M., Anzul, M., Downing, M., & Vinz, R. (1997). *On writing qualitative research*. Falmer Press.

Francis, B., Taylor, B., & Tereshchenko, A. (2019). *Reassessing 'ability' grouping*. Routledge.

Freire, P. (1972). *Pedagogy of the oppressed*. Penguin.

Gillard, J. (2010). *A future fair for all – School funding in Australia – Address to Sydney Institute* [Press release]. Retrieved from https://ministers.employment.gov.au/gillard/future-fair-all-school-funding-australia-address-sydney-institute

Gillborn, D., & Youdell, D. (2000). *Rationing education: Policy, practice, reform and equity*. Open University Press.

Giroux, H. A. (1984). *Ideology, culture, and the process of schooling*. Temple University Press.

Gorur, R. (2015). The performative politics of NAPLAN and MySchool. In B. Lingard, G. Thompson, & S. Sellar (Eds.), *National testing in schools* (pp. 30–43). Routledge.

Harris, J., Carrington, S., & Ainscow, M. (2018). *Promoting equity in schools: Collaboration, inquiry and ethical leadership*. Routledge.

Hart, S., & Drummond, M. J. (2014). Learning without limits: Constructing a pedagogy free from determinist beliefs about ability. In *The SAGE handbook of special education: Two volume set* (pp. 439–458). SAGE Publications.

Hoxby, C. M. (2003). School choice and school productivity: Could school choice be a tide that lifts all boats? In *The economics of school choice* (pp. 287–342). University of Chicago Press.

Johnston, O., & Wildy, H. (2016). The effects of streaming in the secondary school on learning outcomes for Australian students–A review of the international literature. *Australian Journal of Education, 60*(1), 42–59.

Keet, A. (2007). *Human rights education or human rights in education: A conceptual analysis.* (Doctor of Education Dissertation, University of Pretoria). https://repository.up.ac.za/bitstream/handle/2263/25653/Complete.pdf?sequence=8&isAllowed=y

Kenway, J. (2013). Challenging inequality in Australian schools: Gonski and beyond. *Discourse: Studies in the Cultural Politics of Education, 34*(2), 286–308. https://doi.org/10.1080/01596306.2013.770254

Kulikand, J. A., & Kulik, C. (1987). Effects of ability grouping on student achievement. *Equity and Excellence in Education, 23*(1–2), 22–30. https://doi.org/10.1080/1066568870230105

Lipman, P. (2004). *High-stakes education: Inequality, globalisation, and urban school reform.* Routledge Falmer.

Loveless, T. (2013). *How well are American students learning? The 2013 Brown Center report on American education, (3)*2. Washington, DC: Brookings Institution. Retrieved from http://www.brookings.edu/~/media/research/files/reports/2013/03/18%20brown%20center%20loveless/2013%20brown%20center%20report%20web.pdf

Loveless, T. (2016). Tracking in middle school. *Education for upward mobility, 216–232.*

Luke, A. (2018). *Critical literacy, schooling, and social justice: The selected works of Allan Luke.* Routledge.

Mills, C. (2015). Implications of the My School website for disadvantaged communities: A Bourdieuian analysis. *Educational Philosophy and Theory, 47*(2), 146–158.

Muijs, D., & Dunne, M. (2010). Setting by ability – Or is it? A quantitative study of determinants of set placement in English secondary schools. *Educational Research, 52*(4), 391–407.

Newmann, F. M., Bryk, A. S., & Nagaoka, J. K. (2001). *Authentic Intellectual Work and Standardized Tests: Conflict or Coexistence? Improving Chicago's Schools.* Consortium on Chicago School Research.

Oakes, J. (2005). *Keeping track.* Yale University Press.

Rist, R. (1970). Student social class and teacher expectations: The self-fulfilling prophecy in ghetto education. *Harvard Educational Review, 40*(3), 411–451.

Robinson, C., Phillips, L., & Quennerstedt, A. (2020). Human rights education: Developing a theoretical understanding of teachers' responsibilities. *Educational Review, 72*(2), 220–241. https://doi.org/10.1080/00131911.2018.1495182

Sellar, S., Thompson, G., & Rutkowski, D. (2017). *The global education race: Taking the measure of PISA and international testing.* Brush Education.

Slavin, R. E. (1990). Achievement effects of ability grouping in secondary schools: A best-evidence synthesis. *Review of Educational Research, 60*(3), 471–499.

Slee, R. (2019). Belonging in an age of exclusion. *International Journal of Inclusive Education, 23*(9), 909–922.

Spina, N. (2019). 'Once upon a time': Examining ability grouping and differentiation practices in cultures of evidence-based decision-making. *Cambridge Journal of Education, 49*(3), 329–348.

Spina, N. (2020). *Data culture and the organisation of teachers' work: An institutional ethnography.* Routledge.

United Nations. (1989). *Convention on the rights of the child.* Geneva: United Nations. Retrieved from: https://downloads.unicef.org.uk/wp-content/uploads/2016/08/unicef-convention-rights-child-uncrc.pdf?_ga=2.163599994.47948641.1579048141-336807963.1579048141

United Nations. (2002). *Human development report 2002: Deepening democracy in a fragmented world.* : Oxford University Press. Retrieved from http://hdr.undp.org/sites/default/files/reports/263/hdr_2002_en_complete.pdf

West, A., & Hind, A. (2007). School choice in London, England: Characteristics of students in different types of secondary schools. *Peabody Journal of Education, 82*(2–3), 498–529.

Chapter 10
Participation and Social Exclusion – Are They Mutually Exclusive Phenomena?

Julia Häbig, Enikö Zala-Mezö, Pascale Herzig, and Daniela Müller-Kuhn

Abstract The local education laws in Switzerland mandated the implementation of the rights of the child which includes student participation. Through a comparative case study, our aim was to achieve a better understanding of how participation could be put into practice. While we sought out narratives and situations in which participation took place, in one school we discovered many tendencies towards social exclusion. Children and teenagers reported in interviews and group discussions experiencing humiliation and exclusion, which is contrary to Article 29. In this chapter, the concepts of social exclusion and participation will be introduced and connected. Different perspectives of teachers and students will be combined to demonstrate how different attitudes, beliefs and actions sustain an exclusionary school culture. We conclude that participation is a counteragent of social exclusion and an essential condition to implementing Article 29 embedded in a thorough school improvement process, where all actors collectively construct meaningful student participation.

Keywords Student participation · Social exclusion · Children's rights · School improvement

Introduction

Many cantons in Switzerland have integrated the United Nations Convention on the Rights of the Child (UNCRC) into their local school law. In the Canton of Zurich for example, students are given the opportunity to participate in decisions that

---

The original version of this chapter was previously published non-open access. A Correction to this chapter is available at https://doi.org/10.1007/978-3-030-80861-7_19

J. Häbig (✉) · E. Zala-Mezö · P. Herzig · D. Müller-Kuhn
Zurich University of Teacher Education, Zurich, Switzerland
e-mail: julia.haebig@phzh.ch; enikoe.zala@phzh.ch; pascale.herzig@phzh.ch; daniela.mueller@phzh.ch

J. Gillett-Swan, N. Thelander (eds.), *Children's Rights from International Educational Perspectives*, Transdisciplinary Perspectives in Educational Research 2, https://doi.org/10.1007/978-3-030-80861-7_10

concern them (Kantonsrat des Kantons Zürich, 2005).[1] Participation, which results as a consequence when applying the Rights of the Child, is associated with many positive effects. It can increase a student's motivation and thereby facilitate their learning processes and it can improve the relationship between teachers and students (Howley & Tannehill, 2014; Rudduck, 2007). Participation is also related to wellbeing and has a positive impact on students' health or social behaviour in school (Anderson & Graham, 2016; Fletcher et al., 2015). Consequently, participation can lead to a more constructive school climate, and can be considered an important factor in school life and an aim of school improvement. However, school climate is also influenced by social exclusion with studies showing that exclusionary processes highly impact school climate and student well-being (Razer et al., 2013; Vanderbilt & Augustyn, 2010). In our research, we sought to better understand how the local school law is implemented in schools and how student participation is embedded in school life (Häbig et al., 2019; Müller-Kuhn et al., 2021; Zala-Mezö et al., 2018). In the example we present here, students and teachers in one school reported numerous narratives representing social exclusion, in addition to answers they provided about the participatory situation. This experience drove us to question how participation and social exclusion relate to one other and is the focus for this chapter.

The following research questions were examined: Which elements of social exclusion could be detected in this school? (How) are these elements related to participation?

In this chapter, we will first relate the concepts of participation and social exclusion to one other before defining the context and parameters of the study. In the presentation of results, examples of social exclusion will be identified alongside how beliefs and attitudes of students and teachers are interrelated and create an exclusionary school culture. We illustrate how social exclusion constitutes a barrier to enact Article 29 of the Convention on the Rights of the Child in school.

Participation and Social Exclusion – Two Phenomena Influencing School Climate

Participation

Participation occurs when "students are offered the possibility of forming and expressing their opinions, getting involved in decisions, and actively influencing school life" (Zala-Mezö et al., 2020, p. 3). We consider participation as a continuum "starting from an informed decision not to participate and ending in full and equal

[1] "In the multilingual and federally structured Switzerland the 26 cantons have the primary responsibility for education. Compulsory education is largely rooted in the cantons and local municipalities. In post-compulsory education the cantons and the federal authorities each have their own responsibilities." (Swiss Conference of Cantonal Ministers of Education, n.d.).

participation" (Gal, 2015, p. 457) – and not as a dichotomous (yes/no) category. It also involves negotiation among the members of the school community. Realising participation therefore requires respect of individual needs on the one hand, but draws on the idea of collectivity on the other (Gal & Faedi Duramy, 2015). The views and needs of students and teachers regarding learning and school life must be considered and negotiated. Niemi and Kiilakoski's (2020, p. 986) definition highlights this aspect of participation in "understand[ing] participation as a relational concept that exists between an individual and a larger social entity, such as a group, class, family or a society." Their differentiation between political and social participation is helpful to study participation in school life. Political participation means "making an impact, influencing the community, taking part in decision-making and taking responsibility", which depends on social participation understood as "a sense of community, belonging, membership and positive social interdependence" (Niemi & Kiilakoski, 2020, p. 986).

Participation is related to many positive effects, such as increased self-efficacy, feelings of self-worth and belonging (Ryan & Deci, 2000; Howley & Tannehill, 2014; Rudduck, 2007), and positive self-image (Niemi & Kiilakoski, 2020). Participation can also be considered a goal of school improvement. But it can also be a means to carry out school improvement, where students are central actors.

School improvement is a collective, socially and interactively constructed process (Zala-Mezö et al., 2020) allowing for changes in everyday school life. International law, like children's rights, formulate clear expectations considering participation of students. Despite the clear expectations, it cannot specify precisely how to implement the law. Implementation happens in schools as part of a school improvement process. Students can valuably support the improvement (Pekrul & Levin, 2007) and there are numerous benefits of integrating students in school improvement (Rudduck, 2007). For example, students can display an enhanced commitment to learning and to school, and teachers' knowledge of students is transformed which leads to better teacher-student relationships.

Thus, participation can have great influence on school life, school climate, and school culture. However, asking students to participate in decisions within schools is a relatively new phenomenon resulting from the juridification of human rights (Lundy, 2007). Schools are known as traditionally hierarchical institutions, assessing qualifications and producing various kinds of inequality (Simons & Masschelein, 2016). Exclusion, still existing in many schools, is a result of hierarchical and power-based culture, which is neither compatible with the non-discrimination right (Article 2) nor with Article 29 that requests tolerance.

Social Exclusion

Social exclusion broadly focuses on relationships between individuals or groups and mainstream society. Individuals or groups are "socially 'excluded' when they lack effective participation in key activities or benefits of the society in which they live" (Razer et al., 2013, p. 1152). The work of Peters and Besley (2014), when referring to Foucault, highlights the constructive nature of exclusion characterised by a given society. Accordingly, exclusion is the result of "social construction that discursively created human beings as subjects or non-subjects, as human or something less than human, as abnormal" (Peters & Besley, 2014, p. 101).

In school life, exclusion applies not only to students being excluded in the sense of dropping out of the school system but can also refer to students being excluded from the class or school community. Two concrete forms of social exclusion are described by Chiffriller and colleagues: "being rejected and being ignored" (Chiffriller et al., 2015, p. 2). While "rejection is a form of exclusion that is active, direct, and explicit; it involves collaborating with others to marginalize someone, [...] being ignored is a form of exclusion that is passive, indirect, and implicit; it includes not acknowledging an individual in a social setting" (Chiffriller et al., 2015, p. 4). Link and Phelan (2001) describe four components of social exclusion: labelling somebody as different; stereotyping by attributing a negative association; using the negative characterisation for separation; and provoking status loss and discrimination.

By creating an environment where students are able to develop a sense of self-efficacy, self-worth, and belonging, schools can play an important role in "reducing vulnerability to social exclusion" (Razer et al., 2013, p. 1153). At the same time, it is essential for children's rights (Article 29). Crucial actions for schools to take to avoid exclusion are fostering the formation of positive relationships and analysing students' needs in order to meet these needs. Razer and colleagues highlight the importance of the quality of relationships between teachers and students and mention involvement as a key element: "Since social exclusion is essentially a relationship and the process through which this relationship takes shape, interrupting the cycle of exclusion must focus on changing relationships that give concrete expression to respect, solidarity, and involvement" (Razer et al., 2013, p. 1164).

A frequent form of social exclusion in school is bullying, which traditionally is analysed relating to individual traits of the persons involved, focusing on characteristics of aggressor and victim (Thornberg & Delby, 2019). Another approach is to conceive it as a phenomenon, that is "inherently social" (Rawlings, 2019, p. 5), and which can be considered "a means of social positioning" (Thornberg & Delby, 2019, p. 155). If it is conceived as such, conditions that lie within the school structure, such as inappropriate school rules for students or an orientation towards standardised tests (Razer et al., 2013) as well as reactions on the part of teachers and students, are important for how social exclusion will be treated in the long run by schools and teachers. Rawlings (2019) examined how teachers and students frame violence with words and thereby construct a reality where the gravity of an incident is diminished. She describes the reactions of both sides to a case of physical violence. The incident is downplayed by students who mentioned other cases, which they classified as not serious because "we knew it was a joke" (Rawlings, 2019, p. 11), or argued that the victim deserved it. Teachers reacted similarly and ultimately "teachers and students both reached the same conclusion—that this event was not 'bullying'" (Rawlings, 2019, p. 15). It seems that norms of school culture result in shared behavioural patterns. If students' and teachers' reactions when faced with violence consist of passive acceptance, this helps aggressors produce "complicity or advocacy" (Rawlings, 2019, p.5). Thornberg and Delby (2019) demonstrate the great influence of teachers' behaviour. The researchers deduce factors that – from a student perspective – are considered as supporting bullying. They identify rule diffusion and absence of clear consequences following rule breaking as one important condition that supports bullying instead of stopping it.

Downplaying an incident and not defining it as a harmful act makes intervention both unnecessary and impossible. Collectively constructing norms that allow problems to be raised would make schools a safer place (Razer et al., 2013). Schools failing to notice harmful actions do not provide psychological safety for their members (Edmondson & Lei, 2014). Accordingly, such exclusionary tendencies are embedded in school cultures and significant efforts are needed to overcome negative routines.

Participation as a Means to Alter Exclusionary School Culture?

In the following section we will elaborate on how participation and social exclusion influence one other in school. Several studies identify positive effects of participation, making it a factor that can reduce social exclusion. Mager and Nowak's (2012) review of several studies on the effects of student participation indicates more positive relationships among peers as a result of student participation. It also highlights positive outcomes regarding school climate: "Nearly half of the cases [...] indicated improvements in school climate, a better atmosphere in class, improved discipline among students, less bullying or less racism" (Mager & Nowak, 2012, p. 37).

An Australian study on the relation between having a say and well-being demonstrates that "having a say and being listened to supported student well-being by fostering a sense of equality, feeling respected, safe, and valued" (Anderson & Graham, 2016, p. 359). That study illustrates the important role of informal participation:

> Our results provide specific examples of informal participation, and highlight that meaningful participation not only includes having voice in the public or political domain of school life, but also being able to voice preferences in relation to personal needs and identity. (Anderson & Graham, 2016, p. 360)

Studies that examine participation also talk about bullying, which is an often-studied form of exclusion. That student participation and bullying are negatively connected was shown by Ahlström (2010, p. 97), finding "in schools with a higher level of student participation [...] the level of perceived bullying among the students was lower than in schools with a lower level of participation." Låftman et al. (2017) also identify factors on class- and school-levels that correlate with bullying in schools. The authors assume that the degree to which students can participate in decision-making in class correlates to the rate of bullying. In their study of students aged 15–16 years, less bullying occurred in classes where students could participate in decision-making (Låftman et al., 2017, p. 158).

The broader question of how student voice can change school climate was examined by Voight (2015). A student voice program (SVP) implemented in a school led to an improvement in school climate. In the program, over the course of several weeks, students of different grades analysed problems or issues that concerned them in school and worked together with teachers on finding solutions. "The SVP group process of identifying issues, investigating their root causes, and advocating for changes resulted in the implementation of several climate-friendly policies and practices" (Voight, 2015, p. 319), including an anti-bullying campaign. Acosta et al. (2019) conclude that the relation also works in the reverse direction: "School climate can either promote or minimize bullying behaviour and is associated with the development of social skills" (p. 201).

All these findings support the assumption that participation and social exclusion can be considered counteragents (see Fig. 10.1). If exclusion is understood as a social phenomenon, participation is a means to prevent it. The definition of participation highlights the importance of negotiating all needs and interests, and consideration of all perspectives. Student diversity should be seen and responded to in an appropriate way. It needs "a strategy and process involving the transformation of schools to cater for all children" (Peters & Besley, 2014, p. 109). Enhancing participation can be a strategy to alter an exclusionary school culture. This requires that hierarchical power differences – between teachers and students and among peers — are reduced. One way is to allow and encourage students to present their needs and take part in decisions. To do so teachers and students must have a serious interest in considering the needs and opinions of the other group to avoid tokenistic involvement (Lundy, 2007, 2018). Conversely, social exclusion can be viewed as a phenomenon that clearly plays on the 'vertical' line of social relationships, since a driver for social exclusion is to reach a stronger position to maintain power over others. This is why exclusion increases power differences instead of resolving them.

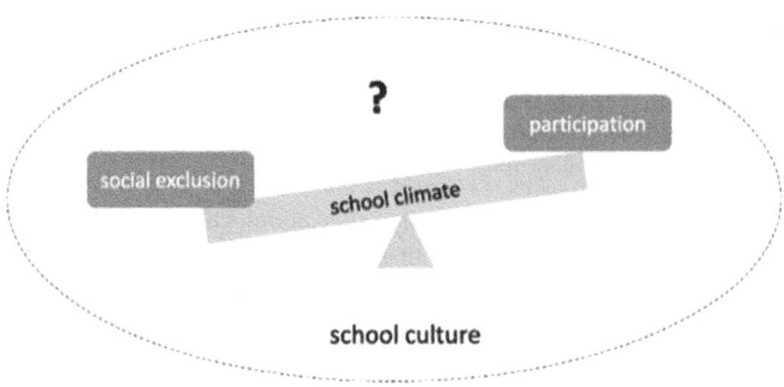

Fig. 10.1 Social exclusion and participation as elements affecting school climate and forming school culture

Given the relationship between social exclusion and participation, the following study sought to illustrate how the two phenomena interact in one school. The research questions were: Which elements of social exclusion could be detected in this school? (How) are these elements related to participation?

Examining Student Participation

Data used in this chapter is drawn from the study "Strengthen participation – improve schools"[2] conducted in Switzerland between 2016 and 2019. The study analysed how schools realised student participation, and how participation related to school improvement processes and structures within schools. Five schools participated in the larger study. This chapter focuses on information from one school and was analysed following a single case study design (Yin, 2009). It is a comprehensive school[3] with students aged 4–15 years. The school is situated in a rural town with approximately 400 students of different social backgrounds (families of varying migration backgrounds and socio-economic status). This school's two principals showed a high interest in the topic of participation and tried to implement it as a school improvement process.

The present chapter uses qualitative data from students and teachers to investigate the interaction of participation and social exclusion. Structured interviews were conducted with selected teachers (n = 8) and students (n = 3) who were particularly responsible for participation, for example a student holding a position within student parliament. Also, separate group discussions were held with students and teachers, where participants were invited to discuss the topic of participation. Two group discussions with eight teachers in each group and eight group discussions with four to eight students were held. Data were analysed using qualitative content analysis (Kuckartz, 2014). Interviews and group discussions were screened to select relevant sections categorised as "social exclusion" and "understanding of participation". Quotations will be used to illustrate findings.

Perspectives of Students and Teachers

Findings are divided into two parts. First, examples of social exclusion reported by students in group discussions and interviews are described. Analysing these concrete situations, mechanisms, and conditions that support social exclusion are identified, pointing to its social character. Then, second, teachers' beliefs and attitudes towards participation are related to the phenomenon of social exclusion to identify

[2] The project was financially supported by the Mercator Foundation Switzerland.

[3] Comprehensive schools include primary and secondary education in one schoolhouse.

how participation and social exclusion interact. Since school improvement is understood as a collective, socially and interactively constructed process, central actors in it are the teachers whose beliefs and attitudes shape their actions (Biesta et al., 2015).

Exclusion as Part of Everyday School Life – Examples of Social Exclusion

Social exclusion forms part of everyday school life in the examined school. Findings indicate that phenomena such as making fun of others — which the students themselves refer to as "bullying"[4] —occurs in everyday school life. There are however differences between individual classes — some have bigger problems than others. A girl, Kerstin,[5] aged 15, states: "There is always a kid that is being bullied for a week. It is being bullied for a week and then it will be another kid that will be bullied."

What is striking is that this student considers these tendencies as quite normal, accepting them as an unchangeable circumstance in the context of this school, which is an indication that it is not a single but frequent experience reflecting the school culture. The girl in this interview describes the risk of being bullied but also states, even though insults and ridicule are normal, that does not mean that a climate of fear exists in her school:

Interviewer: And you personally, when you wake up in the morning, do you like going to school or rather not?

Kerstin: It depends, there are weeks or days when you think, no, I don't want to go to school because the day before something has happened. But in our class so far nothing has occurred that you would really say I don't have any motivation to go to school, I am afraid to go to school because this or that could happen. I personally have never experienced that. Ok, there are days that I think I don't want to go because somebody could be insulting me. But then I tell myself, hey, just let it happen because if you don't get upset about it, they will start to get bored annoying you.

This student, although she does not have personal experiences, has developed a coping strategy, confirming that the risk and fear of being insulted is real. Interestingly the strategy is not actively seeking help but rather ignoring.

In her subsequent explanation she elaborates on the character of harassment she has experienced in school and differentiates between "real bullying" and only making fun of others. Despite trivialising the potential harassment, she seems to suffer from it because it means that one cannot freely express an opinion:

Kerstin: Sometimes you cannot openly say what you think, and I find this is a pity. We are in 2017 and you can state your opinion without fear that something happens. But espe-

---

[4] It is noted that the word "bullying" is frequently used by students for naming any kind of exclusion. Their understanding is not necessarily the same as official and conceptualised definitions (e.g., Rawlings, 2019).

[5] Names are anonymised.

cially in school you must be careful, oh what did I say, I cannot speak up openly because the consequence is that I will be harassed or something like that.

Interviewer: Fear of the reaction of the teachers or the group?

Kerstin: More from the peers. Well, we have never bullied somebody because for example the father was unemployed. In that case maybe for a month you are being laughed at but then it is forgotten.

While in her former description she denies that she is "afraid to go to school", she reveals an atmosphere of fear from the possible reaction of her peers, being somewhat inconsistent in her statements. Her description of the situation also displays a certain insecurity of how to handle this problem: On the one hand, she does not simply accept the situation as it is, clearly stating her opinion, "I find this is a pity". On the other hand, she does describe ways to deal with it.

As demonstrated in the example above, one form of exclusion is laughing at others. This laughing is also described by a group of students, aged 7–9:

Gina: It is laughing at others which simply is

Sarah: A bit stupid and

Larry: Yes, or if somebody

Gina: In our class there is a lot of laughing at others.

Larry: And if somebody falls and cries but the others don't notice it then everybody starts laughing. If later they realise that he is crying they say oh I am sorry, I did not want to make fun of you. [...]

Melina: Sometimes you simply must laugh because it looks funny.

[...]

Gina: But it is not meant to be mean.

Larry: And then later they always say sorry, I didn't mean to do that.

Laughing at others seems to be a common practice in this class. In the described incident, several students take advantage of the weakness of a student that has hurt himself and make fun of it. The students are divided in their positions — they clearly dislike the described behaviour of making fun of others by stating that it is "simply a bit stupid". But they justify it by taking the perspective of the ones who laugh. This description of the situation does not make clear if the excuses of those who laugh at others are to be taken seriously or if it is tokenism. The girls describing the situation do not exhibit empathy or take the perspective of the one who has fallen but describe the reaction of having to laugh as natural: "sometimes you simply have to laugh because it looks funny". With this sentence, Melina lays open that she might also belong to the group that laughs in such a case, receiving immediate support from Gina and Larry, who explain that such behaviour is not meant to be mean.

Another example stems from another class, aged 10–12, illustrating how students explain making fun of others and the dynamic involved.

Maria: There is a girl, Cinthia, it is mostly her who starts bullying someone. And then others join in and start laughing and then they start.

Kathrin: Her intention only is that others laugh about it.

Priska: Yes, and she wants to show off with that. For example, if she is bullying Hannes then she feels cool.

Kathrin: She hits him.

Priska: Then she feels that she is cool.

The citation shows that the students perceive one girl to be often the instigator. This naming can itself be seen as a form of social exclusion (Link & Phelan, 2001). Perpetrator and victim roles appear easily interchangeable. The students describe her motivation as a search for admiration from her peers. Here, a reason why Hannes becomes her target is not mentioned, which makes it appear somehow random who becomes a victim. Most importantly, it seems to be the effect it has on the others: that Cinthia can show off with her behaviour. She gets attention and recognition from the group, which makes her social position strong. This example shows the very social character of exclusion: it is meant as an action to be seen and praised by others.

A further example from students aged 8 illustrates how the process of social exclusion, including labelling, stereotyping, and discriminating as described by Link and Phelan (2001), is applied by students in a group discussion.

Lynn: And the teacher's job is to take care that nobody is shouting. [...]
Marc: And that, you must respect each other, for example. And that you don't, hm, if you are talking to each other all the time.
Lynn: Like Noel and Nico sometimes.
Several students: (laughing)
Noel: But we haven't been talking now for a long time.
Lynn: Yes, but before you have always been talking.
Noel: Yeah, sometimes.

Speaking about disturbing behaviour during class, a student names two other students, Noel and Nico, who have been disruptive by talking to each other. She labels them as the disturbers, attributing the negative behaviour to them. By exposing them to the entire group she separates them and the reaction of the others — laughing — provokes a certain loss of status.

How Teachers Perceive Participation – Beliefs and Attitudes

These descriptions of incidents that can be classified as social exclusion will now be contrasted with the teachers' beliefs and attitudes concerning participation. These beliefs were deduced from group discussions where teachers talked about the topic of participation.

The first example illustrates how teachers promote a hierarchical relationship in school where students are meant to follow the rules and directives teachers set. This hierarchy stands in conflict with participation:

Tina: Especially kids that repeatedly search for a stage, a moment to stick out and attract attention in a negative way, they are better integrated if it is clear: this is what we are doing at the moment.
[...]
Daria: And my impression is that students do have difficulties to integrate. They also do have to learn to do what they are told [by the teachers] and often this is what they are not so good at. And then it is difficult if you open up too fast and the kids still do have problems following instructions and accepting that this is the aim we are following at the moment. [...] And I think you cannot function well as a class if you don't learn to subordinate yourself.

Tina describes that there are students who seek opportunities to obtain attention from the rest of the group by exposing themselves in a negative light. In this way, she applies the same pattern as the students, naming and blaming a "disturbing" student group for misusing situations offering participation. In her view, such students need clear instructions from a teacher. The elaboration from Daria shows that students should subordinate themselves into the hierarchical structure of school where teachers decide. Such hierarchical structures make it complicated to realise participation, which she refers to as "opening up".

The second example illustrates how the students' suggestion to define topics, which should be discussed in student parliament, is foiled by the teacher. This teacher leads the student parliament of 7 to 9-year-olds and complains that students have no ideas for what they should work on. Shortly after, she describes a situation where students tried to participate but they chose — in her opinion — the wrong topic.

> *Sandra:* In my grade level we have to push on topics. [...] We once really reached the point where we had to say, stop, it can't be that way. Then it became a bit like a blaming-circle. Something was stolen from someone; who did observe something, like that. And we had to say, no, it can't be that, this instrument [student parliament] is not suitable for that. So, you had to put the brakes on the students and say, look, what is meant is not simply a call to find the perpetrator or something. Actually, what is meant is finding topics [to work on for the student parliament]. And that is also really hard to understand for the young students – what belongs there? [...] It is too much for them when they have to bring in own, new topics.

Students experienced theft — a strong form of violence among peers — and wanted to stop it. They used the same pattern described in the previous section and looked for persons to blame when something went wrong. The teacher senses that this social practice is not helpful in solving the problem and that the "blaming-circle" makes things even worse. But she is helpless and not able to redirect the process in a constructive way. Her solution is to stop the process and define the need of the students as inadequate or illegitimate for student parliament. In this way, it becomes clear that student parliament in her view is an "instrument" with its own rules that are defined by adults, including which topics are suitable. Young students in particular are seen as unable to fulfil these requirements of defining suitable topics. By attributing this weak position to students, the teacher uses her power and stops any further negotiation to deal with the problem members of the student parliament brought up.

Discussion

Since Foucault (Peters & Besley, 2014), exclusion is understood as a social phenomenon based on the discourse of a given society. This social constructivist understanding of exclusion (Rawlings, 2019) is demonstrated at the school level within the case study described in this chapter. Widespread exclusion forms part of this school's culture (Acosta et al., 2019) and reduces the rights of students to experience human dignity and a safe, non-violent school environment, as described in Article 29. Three main observations regarding exclusionary tendencies were made:

First, signals of mitigating the harmfulness of social exclusion (Thornberg & Delby, 2019) were found in different interview situations (single and group interviews). Certain forms of exclusion are considered normal in everyday school life. A student expressed she does not fear going to school while describing her coping strategies to deal with insults. Therefore, the experience of exclusion is a real risk in this school.

Second, this normality is a sign of the frequency of exclusionary tendencies and students do not often actively seek help to stop these tendencies. Why they fail to ask for help was not an objective of the study so we may only speculate. It is possible they had attempted to obtain help unsuccessfully in the past, which only made situations worse. Students accept insults or even react similarly with exclusion: they ignore or name (Chiffriller et al., 2015) and blame the perpetrators, becoming perpetrators themselves.

Third, the construction of exclusion is interwoven. There are many actors — teachers and students — involved and they appear in different constellations again and again. There is a clear pattern of excluding persons where the reason for exclusion is explained by behaviours of the excluded (Hills & Stewart, 2005). In this way, the socially constructed character of exclusion is particularly visible.

In the theoretical background we demonstrated exclusion and participation are counterparts. Many definitions (e.g., Razer et al., 2013) of exclusion are based on understandings of failing participation. This seems appropriate especially if participation is considered as social participation, conceived as a positive social interdependence and that has to be guaranteed first before decision making can take place (Niemi & Kiilakoski, 2020). The clear connection between social exclusion and participation evident across different data sources in the analysed case proves this relationship and explains why interviewees reported examples of social exclusion instead of participation.

Conclusion

Exclusion, forming a social phenomenon and being a pattern that many actors support, cannot be changed through a single intervention. A starting point to alter exclusionary school culture is to think of participation as a broader concept that cannot only be realised in institutionalised forms such as a student parliament. Participation is a way for the school community to deal with problems requiring corresponding attitudes from students and teachers.

Students in the analysed school are not helpless, as the examples demonstrate. They exercise power in a competing way, building hierarchical relationships. The question is how students can have the opportunity to change this power culture to a participative culture and build positive relationships. To be able to do so they need adults that are sensitive to students' needs and actively stop tendencies of exclusion. First of all, teachers should start to alter their own behaviour.

Before being able to change one's own beliefs and attitudes, one has to be conscious of them. A possibility to make existing beliefs and behaviour of teachers and students in school visible is to feedback research results like these and stimulate discussions about similar situations from different perspectives. Often, neither teachers nor students are aware of the culture they are part of and actively form. In the presented study feeding back the research results helped to identify situations of exclusion but also of participation. Already the fact of holding up a mirror, if done in a thoughtful way from the researchers' side, can have an effect and stimulate a shift from a culture marked by enacting power over others to a participative culture based on feelings of belonging.

References

Acosta, J., Chinman, M., Ebener, P., Malone, P. S., Phillips, A., & Wilks, A. (2019). Understanding the relationship between perceived school climate and bullying: A mediator analysis. *Journal of School Violence, 18*(2), 200–215. https://doi.org/10.1080/15388220.2018.1453820

Ahlström, B. (2010). Student participation and school success — The relationship between participation, grades and bullying among 9th grade students in Sweden. *Education Inquiry, 1*(2), 97–115. https://doi.org/10.3402/edui.v1i2.21935

Anderson, D. L., & Graham, A. P. (2016). Improving student wellbeing: Having a say at school. *School Effectiveness and School Improvement, 27*(3), 348–366. https://doi.org/10.1080/09243453.2015.1084336

Biesta, G., Priestley, M., & Robinson, S. (2015). The role of beliefs in teacher agency. *Teachers and Teaching, 21*(6), 624–640. https://doi.org/10.1080/13540602.2015.1044325

Chiffriller, S. H., Kangos, K. A., & Milone, L. (2015). What elementary students experience outside of the classroom: Children's responses to social exclusion. *Journal of School Counseling, 13*(1). Retrieved March 22, 2020, from: https://eric.ed.gov/?id=EJ1051101

Edmondson, A. C., & Lei, Z. (2014). Psychological safety: The history, renaissance, and future of an interpersonal construct. *Annual Review of Organizational Psychology and Organizational Behavior, 1*(1), 23–43. https://doi.org/10.1146/annurev-orgpsych-031413-091305

Fletcher, A., Fitzgerald-Yau, N., Wiggins, M., Viner, R. M., & Bonell, C. (2015). Involving young people in changing their school environment to make it safer. Findings from a process evaluation in English secondary schools. *Health Education, 115*(3), 322–338. https://doi.org/10.1108/HE-04-2014-0063

Gal, T. (2015). From social exclusion to child-inclusive politics: Toward an ecological model of child participation. In T. Gal & B. Faedi Duramy (Eds.), *International perspectives and empirical findings on child participation. From social exclusion to child-inclusive policies* (pp. 451–465). Oxford University Press.

Gal, T., & Faedi Duramy, B. (2015). Enhancing capacities for child participation: Introduction. In T. Gal & B. Faedi Duramy (Eds.), *International perspectives and empirical findings on child participation. From social exclusion to child-inclusive policies* (pp. 1–16). Oxford University Press.

Häbig, J., Zala-Mezö, E., Müller-Kuhn, D., & Strauss, N.-C. (2019). 'Im normalen Leben funktioniert das auch nicht' Rekonstruktionen des kollektiven Verständnisses von Schülerinnen- und Schülerpartizipation. In S. Hauser & N. Nell-Tuor (Eds.), *Sprache und Partizipation im Schulfeld*. Bern, Switzerland, Hep Verlag.

Hills, J., & Stewart, K. (2005). *A more equal society? New labour, poverty, inequality and exclusion*. The Policy Press.

Howley, D., & Tannehill, D. (2014). Crazy ideas: Student involvement in negotiating and implementing the physical education curriculum in the Irish senior cycle. *The Physical Educator, 71*(3), 391–416.

Kantonsrat des Kantons Zürich. (2005). *Volksschulgesetz, Zürich*. http://www2.zhlex.zh.ch/appl/zhlex_r.nsf/0/13EF955B1682B079C12573B50025B2CC/$file/412.100_7.2.05_59.pdf. Accessed 22 Mar 2020.

Kuckartz, U. (2014). *Qualitative inhaltsanalyse. Methoden, praxis, computerunterstützung* (2nd ed.). Beltz Juventa Publishing.

Låftman, S. B., Östberg, V., & Modin, B. (2017). School climate and exposure to bullying: A multilevel study. *School Effectiveness and School Improvement, 28*(1), 153–164. https://doi.org/10.1080/09243453.2016.1253591

Link, B. G., & Phelan, J. C. (2001). Conceptualizing stigma. *Annual Review of Sociology, 27*(1), 363–385. https://doi.org/10.1146/annurev.soc.27.1.363

Lundy, L. (2007). Voice' is not enough: Conceptualising article 12 of the United Nations convention on the rights of the child. *British Educational Research Journal, 33*(6), 927–942. https://doi.org/10.1080/01411920701657033

Lundy, L. (2018). In defence of tokenism? Implementing children's right to participate in collective decision-making. *Childhood, 25*(3), 340–354. https://doi.org/10.1177/0907568218777292

Mager, U., & Nowak, P. (2012). Effects of student participation in decision making at school. A systematic review and synthesis of empirical research. *Educational Research Review, 7*(1), 38–61.

Müller-Kuhn, D., Herzig, P., Häbig, J., & Zala-Mezö, E. (2021). Student participation in everyday school life—Linking different perspectives. *Zeitschrift für Bildungsforschung, 11*(1). https://doi.org/10.1007/s35834-021-00296-5

Niemi, R., & Kiilakoski, T. (2020). "I learned to cooperate with my friends and there were no quarrels": Pupils' experiences of participation in a multidisciplinary learning module. *Scandinavian Journal of Educational Research, 64*(7), 984–998. https://doi.org/10.1080/00313831.2019.1639817

Pekrul, S., & Levin, B. (2007). Building student voice for school improvement. In D. Thiessen & A. Cook-Sather (Eds.), *International handbook of student experience in elementary and secondary school* (pp. 711–726). Springer.

Peters, M. A., & Besley, T. A. C. (2014). Social exclusion/inclusion: Foucault's analytics of exclusion, the political ecology of social inclusion and the legitimation of inclusive education. *Open Review of Educational Research, 1*(1), 99–115. https://doi.org/10.1080/23265507.2014.972439

Rawlings, V. (2019). "It's not bullying", "It's just a joke": Teacher and student discursive manoeuvres around gendered violence. *British Educational Research Journal, 0*(online first). https://doi.org/10.1002/berj.3521.

Razer, M., Friedman, V. J., & Warshofsky, B. (2013). Schools as agents of social exclusion and inclusion. *International Journal of Inclusive Education, 17*(11), 1152–1170. https://doi.org/10.1080/13603116.2012.742145

Rudduck, J. (2007). Student voice, student engagement, and school reform. In D. Thiessen & A. Cook-Sather (Eds.), *International handbook of student experience in elementary and secondary school* (pp. 587–610). Springer.

Ryan, R. M., & Deci, E. L. (2000). Self-determination theory and the facilitation of intrinsic motivation, social development, and Well-being. *American Psychologist, 55*(1), 68–78. https://doi.org/10.1037/0003-066X.55.1.68

Simons, M., & Masschelein, J. (2016). Gouvernementale, politische und pädagogische Subjektivierung: Foucault mit Rancière. In R. Casale, H.-C. Koller, & N. Ricken (Eds.), *Das pädagogische und das politische* (pp. 165–188). Ferdinand Schoningh Publishing. https://doi.org/10.30965/9783657782680_011

Swiss Conference of Cantonal Ministers of Education. (n.d.). http://www.edk.ch/dyn/11586.php. Accessed 22 Mar 2020.

Thornberg, R., & Delby, H. (2019). How do secondary school students explain bullying? *Educational Research, 61*(2), 142–160. https://doi.org/10.1080/00131881.2019.1600376

Vanderbilt, D., & Augustyn, M. (2010). The effects of bullying. *Paediatrics and Child Health, 20*(7), 315–320. https://doi.org/10.1016/j.paed.2010.03.008

Voight, A. (2015). Student voice for school-climate improvement: A case study of an urban middle school. *Journal of Community & Applied Social Psychology, 25*(4), 310–326. https://doi.org/10.1002/casp.2216

Yin, R. K. (2009). *Case study research: Design and methods* (4th ed.). SAGE.

Zala-Mezö, E., Strauss, N.-C., Herzig, P., Müller-Kuhn, D., Häbig, J., & Kuster, R. (2018). Der Komplexität von Schulentwicklung methodisch begegnen: Das Projekt 'Partizipation stärken—Schule entwickeln'. In E. Zala-Mezö, N.-C. Strauss, & J. Häbig (Eds.), *Dimensionen von Schulentwicklung. Verständnis, Veränderung und Vielfalt eines Phänomens* (pp. 15–59). Waxmann.

Zala-Mezö, E., Datnow, A., Müller-Kuhn, D., & Häbig, J. (2020). Feeding back research results – Changes in principal and teacher narratives about student participation. *Studies in Educational Evaluation, 65*, 1–10. https://doi.org/10.1016/j.stueduc.2020.100848

Chapter 11
Education Rights and the Convergence of Provision and Participation

Michael Wyness

Abstract The chapter explores the meaning and significance of participation as it relates to children's rights to schooling and education. Articles 28 and 29 of the UNCRC offer a more detailed and refined version of earlier declarations of children's rights focusing on the duties of adults, institutions and states to provide for children's schooling. Proponents and opponents of children's rights, on the other hand, have focused attention on one of the major departures from these earlier declarations, the capacity of children themselves to participate in these processes of provision. Articles 12 to 15 in different ways underpin children's entitlements to participate in various aspects of their lives, including their schooling. There is the potential for some disagreement and conflict between children's participatory rights and the rights provided for by others. This chapter explores convergences rather than disagreements between rights to provision and participation and draws on Thomson and Holdsworth's typology of children's educational participation. This typology broadens categories of participation to include children's co-presence or attendance at school as well as more conventional notions of participation, such as democratic participation and community activism. Two cases are used to illustrate the range and complexity of children's school participation.

Keywords Participation · Provision · Inter-dependence · Co-presence · Community activism

---

M. Wyness (✉)
Education Studies, University of Warwick, Coventry, UK
e-mail: m.wyness@warwick.ac.uk

J. Gillett-Swan, N. Thelander (eds.), *Children's Rights from International Educational Perspectives*, Transdisciplinary Perspectives in Educational Research 2, https://doi.org/10.1007/978-3-030-80861-7_11

Introduction

In this chapter I discuss two of the key features of the UN Convention on the Rights of the Child (UNCRC) as it applies to education. Two dominant and potentially conflictual principles of the UNCRC are children's right to provision and their right to participation (Invernizzie, 2005; Alderson, 2008). In most instances provision is the dominant force. Children are being provided for by others, part of what Archard (2015, p. 72) refers to as the "caretaker thesis", where "adults may paternalistically choose for children" on the basis of lack of experience and cognitive capacity. Children are the responsibilities of parents, teachers, organisations and states. Schools, in particular, are involved in securing the moral, intellectual, and social wellbeing of children. The key education provision articles of UNCRC are Articles 28 and 29 focusing on access and quality respectively. Article 28 emphasises the registration and completion of primary education by all children and the promotion of access to secondary and higher education. Article 29 emphases responsibilities that states and organisations have for improving educational quality and standards for all children. Both articles converge with other global educational commitments through the Millennium and Sustainable Development goals and the UNESCO's Education for All initiative. There is thus a powerful global discourse on improving access to schools and the quality of formal education.

While articles on provision suggest that decisions are made by adults on the nature of children's schooling, the concept of participation implies that children may have some input. Articles 12 to 15 in different ways focus more on rights in terms of children taking ownership of decisions that affect them in relation to their schooling. Thus Article 12 refers to conditional forms of voice (Wyness, 2019). Children are put in positions where they articulate their interests. While the agenda for children's participation is heavily circumscribed by adults, these interests may not always coincide with the interests of adult educators. Article 13 extends the idea that children have a right to knowledge and information. The advent of digital technology in some respects complicates the capacity of adults to regulate children's access to knowledge and there is potential for children's digital capacities to be in conflict with adults' responsibilities to protect children from 'harmful' data (Livingstone et al., 2018). Article 15 focuses on children's right to more collective forms of participation. Again, UNCRC accommodates the individualistic nature of learning within a more globalised education system. In this sense, we can see a possible tension between the curriculum, the pedagogies and the regulations that are handed down to children, what might be collectively referred to as the provision of educational structures, and the rights of children both individually and collectively to challenge this provision.

There is also a fundamental clash between provision and participation, in terms of the globalising forces of mass compulsory schooling, and more localised combinations of schooling and labour. On the one hand, education is viewed as a global common good to be handed down to children irrespective of localised factors. On the other hand, localised ideas and practices may not always converge with this form of provision. At the level of children's rights what we are saying here is that the global push for universal school access and completion has the effect of marginalising commitments that children have contributing towards domestic and local economies and thus participating in other ways within their communities. We need to be careful when conflating work with voiced based conceptions of participation: in many cases children's family and social obligations offer few opportunities for them to take part in decision-making processes, particularly over their economic responsibilities (Banks, 2007). Participation at these local levels is broadened to include children making significant contributions to their families and communities. Nevertheless, research suggests that, at the very least, some working children are able reflect on the relative advantages of paid work as well school attendance (Boyden et al., 2016; Kluttz, 2015; Woodhead, 1999).

While there is the potential for conflict between 'provision' and 'participation', I want to move away from a more bifurcated model of children's rights to education and explore the relationship between the provision of schooling and the participation of pupils. I want to argue that children's right to participation, a critical feature of the UNCRC, is integral to their provision and protection. Alderson (2008) in her analysis of children's rights provides one version of this argument. Rather than focus on the separate nature of the categories 'provision' and 'participation', she argues for their interdependency. Children are in a much stronger position to make suggestions about their schooling if the education system provides them with sufficient opportunities to participate.

Moreover, the interdependency of provision and participation can be conceptualised in terms of rights 'to', 'in' and 'through' education (Osler & Vincent, 2003; Verhellen, 2000). Article 28 focus on rights to education with an emphasis on all children having access to schooling (Osler & Vincent, 2003, p. 2000). Article 29 extends the notion of provision to focus more on the quality of schooling in the way that key aim of the school is to "develop the child's personality, talents and mental and physical abilities to their fullest potential" (United Nations, 1989, Article 29). This converges with both rights 'through' and 'in' education. Rights 'through' education focuses on the inclusion of rights within the curriculum and the idea that teachers should have respect for their pupils. Rights 'in' education connects with Article 12 and the idea of children having a say on various aspects of their schooling and being protected in school from forms of discrimination. Both reinforce the idea that children become more knowledgeable rights holders as pupils and citizens within their schools (Osler & Vincent, 2003).

There are also some issues with the way that the UNCRC offers participation in terms of voice. Despite the possibilities of children's participation offered across articles 12–15, most of the focus has been on Article 12, a conditional form of voice. Here there is some recognition of children's capacity to formulate an opinion and that this recognition is extended in terms of adults and institutions giving "due weight" to these perspectives based on children's "age and maturity". In effect, Article 12 is about consultation, a framework within which older children respond to arrangements put in place for them by adults. This is quite a limiting conception of children's participation. Arguably, we need to extend our conception of what counts as children's participation. In this chapter I want to frame children's participation by taking account of the diversity of ways in which children contribute to the wellbeing of themselves and those around them. Rather than focus on the tension between adult provision and children's participation it might be worth exploring 'provision' and 'participation' as part of a broader conception of children's participation. I set out this broader conception of participation and offer illustrations through two case studies that illustrate the diverse and context bound nature of children's educational participation.

Defining Participation

Thomas (2007, p. 199) defines participation as "taking part in an activity, or specifically to taking part in decision-making. It can also refer either to a process or to an outcome". There are two parts to participation here, the act of taking part in something, which, within the context of schooling, is generally viewed as uncontroversial. The second part focuses more on decision-making in terms of children being actors within decision-making processes. Drawing on this broader conception of participation within an educational context incorporates the provision of schooling, allowing children to participate in decision-making processes as part of a more democratic conception of schooling. Similarly, Thomson and Holdsworth's (2003) notion of student participation incorporates provision *within* the category of participation and goes beyond the dominant conception of participation to emerge from the UNCRC. Instead of offering a single definition, they set out a five-fold typology of student participation which incorporates provision and participation, "taking part" and decision-making processes. Importantly, each conception of participation is contextualised, that is, political, economic, and cultural factors shape the meaning of children's participation within specific contexts.

Being Physically Present in School (P1)

Within the context of truancy and issues of access to school, children's presence in school becomes a significant means and outcome in terms of children's participation. We referred earlier to a global political commitment to improving the registration and completion of children's schooling. Economic and cultural factors still restrict the capacity of some children to attend school, particularly in Southern Asia and Sub Saharan Africa. In the latter case despite global commitments to ensure that all children have completed primary and secondary schooling by 2030, 20% of children still drop out of school (UNESCO, 2018; United Nations, 2015); school attendance is a critical form of student participation. Children's participation in school is shaped by children's capacity to attend school regularly. Participation relates to Article 28 of UNCRC in terms of access to schooling. Participation becomes a form of *pupil co-presence*.

Involved in School Activities (P2)

Participation takes the form of children engaging in tasks and activities with other children in class and in school. The context here is schools where there are issues with engagement and significant numbers of disaffected children (Allan & Duckworth, 2018). Children participate in that they are on-task in the classroom. The issue of any absence of pupil participation here revolves around children struggling to engage with the curriculum and the school structures. Participation connects with Article 29 of UNCRC in that issues of engagement relate to the quality of schooling for children. Participation here equates with *pupil engagement.*

Involved in Formal School Decision Making (P3)

Participation comes close to Arnot and Reay's (2007, p. 319), concept of code talk where "(p)upils describe(d) their identities as learners, their confidence, the processes of inclusion in learning, and the degree of control they have over the selection, sequencing, pacing and evaluation of knowledge". In terms of school practice there are a range of forms of participation here from general consultation through to children's participation in school councils. There is a strong element of adult regulation here with participatory initiatives fitting in with school structures approximating to liberal democratic forms of political structures (Wyness, 2009). This takes us close to Article 12 of the UNCRC. Pupil participation here can be viewed in terms of *formal democratic processes.*

Children's Initiation of Ad Hoc Forms of Participation (P4)

Participatory initiatives are more ad hoc and less formal, therefore less likely to be structured by the school. Participation approximates more to forms of deliberative democracy with groups of children working alongside groups of teachers generating an agenda for change within the school (Cockburn, 2005). Participation here may also extend outside of the school, with pupils making various connections with their local communities. We can refer to this as *pupil centred deliberative participation.*

Community and Social Activism Through the School (P5)

These forms of participation are likely to be initiated and run by the children themselves. But whereas pupil-centred forms focus on school-related matters and are an end in themselves, community and social activism is more 'political', more challenging here with the school used as a means through which children are mobilised into action. One example of this mobilisation was the recent demonstrations by pupils of climate change, where children in 1600 cities across the globe walked out of their schools to protest on environmental issues (Haynes, 2019). Pupil participation here equates with forms of *political mobilisation*.

In the following case studies I want to explore the nature of these distinctive forms of educational participation. Issues of access to school and physical attendance are often associated with 'provision'. Firstly, I draw on an empirical study of a school in an economically deprived area, in illustrating the significance of access and attendance as a form of children's participation. Secondly, I focus more on the relationships between the different models of participation. While conventional wisdom would view co-presence (P1) as a necessary condition of the other four forms of participation, in the second case study I will briefly discuss the possibility of community activism among children (P5) as a precondition of co-presence (P1).

Participation as Co-Presence: The Case of One English School

Co-presence is an issue within Western contexts. While extreme poverty is an underlying cause of provision problems in the global South, poverty is also an underpinning factor in restricting children's capacities to attend school in parts of the UK. Recent research on Scottish secondary schools provides little evidence to support the notion that adults in school take seriously the perspectives that children have of their school provision (Cairns et al., 2018). According to the authors, the weakness of participatory opportunities in school is often a consequence of an overbearing paternalism, an emphasis on adult 'provision' that marginalises any attempts by children to have some say in the nature of this provision. However, Cairns et al. (2018) argue that in some instances children are not only deprived of an active voice in school, their entitlement to provision is itself compromised. They refer to the draconian nature of some of the punishments in school that restricted children's access to education because they were sometimes removed from class or excluded from school. Thus, children in some instances struggle to participates at all levels.

Henry Fields offers an interesting example of a school in an affluent country with similar issues in relation participation, but where the issue of co-presence is largely an effect of broader economic and social factors. Despite mass compulsory schooling being a well-established norm and practice in England for over a century, there are still areas of deprivation where pupil participation is partly about children having access to schooling. Contemporary analysis has focused on the social, economic and sometimes cultural barriers to children's school attendance (Wainwright & Marandet, 2017). This is compounded by a culture of performativity, where schools are assessed in terms of tangible outcomes (Ball, 2003). One such measure of educational accountability is the level of school absence at classroom and school level. League tables are constructed in order to identify a school or classroom's attendance record in percentage terms with lower percentages signalling a failure of the part of the school or the relevant teacher.

Henry Fields was a small secondary school of 715 pupils, situated in a deprived part of an English midlands city (1). Around half (48%) of the children were on the pupil premium and entitled to free schools (2). 40% of the pupils were designated as multiply deprived, considerably higher than the national average of 12.4% in secondary schools (DfE, 2018). Half of all pupils were from ethnic minorities with around a third taking English as a second language. The school regularly took in children from refugee and migrant families and had a consistent population of Romany children who intermittently attended the school. The school also took in children who had been excluded from other schools.

One of the initiatives developed by the school to manage a variegated and challenging school population was the introduction of a cadre of 15 associate teachers (AT), unqualified support staff, who among other things, mediated between the school and the home. The ethos of the school was relational: children's behavioural and learning problems were viewed as 'social' in nature. Supporting parents was a way of helping kids to engage with the school. Participation at this level was about engaging with parents to ensure children attend the school on a regular basis. The associate teachers had responsibilities for developing links with parents. This was seen as a precondition of children's school presence and participation. As the head clearly stated:

> One of the really successful things about this work is that you separate out which kids have a significant special educational need, something diagnosable, and which are kids not making enough progress for a variety of reasons. We would have had kids in the past on the SEN register who were two years behind in their reading age. The reason they're two years behind is because their attendance was only 50%. They haven't really got a special need – they need to be at school more (Head teacher).

Attendance was a crucial issue at the school and pupil absenteeism seen as a major barrier to other forms of children's participation in school. Earlier inspection reports highlighted the relatively low level of pupil attendance. At the same time later reports commended the school management for tackling what was seen by staff as an entrenched problem. One of the strategies used to improve rates of participation was to commission (AT) to reach out to parents by picking up students from home, where there had been problems of attendance in the past. For some ATs, bringing children into the school on a regular basis was part of an arrangement with parents. As one AT stated, "I go out and pick them up, see the family…put them on a personalised timetable…Put them onto six week plans. We do absolutely anything to get children into school" (AT 4). For other staff, home visits were ad hoc:

> there have been times when students haven't come into school and parents haven't phoned in, so we have just gone out and knocked on the door: 'Oh, how is he doing?' Which is good as it shows the school's idea that we care so much. I think it is better to be proactive (AT 8)

In some respects the concept of pupil participation here follows a developmental trajectory. Issues of school democracy, pupil engagement and consultation presuppose an earlier period where children establish patterns for regularly attending schools. While the school viewed co-presence as a form of participation, they were also engaging with pupils at level 3 of the typology. As with most of other schools in the UK, there were more structured forums for children to participate in terms of forums for the discussion of school rules as well as a number of ad hoc groups set up where children had limited decision-making powers. However, the starting point for many of the teachers was getting children into school. In referring to participation in this school the teachers focussed on the importance of co-presence. There was an acute awareness of poverty, unemployment, chronic illness and homelessness as factors that hampered children's ability to participate in school. As one teacher stated:

> What the school tries to achieve is to become a community…Obviously as a school we have targets that we have got to meet. We have exam grades that we have got to get. But we can't focus on that because as you know, if a child can't learn in the classroom, there's loads of other stuff going on in the emotional world. They just won't focus. It's just a barrier. Who wants to hear about geography when you haven't got anywhere to live that night. That's what we are sometimes up against (Individualised Learning Manager).

In returning to the issue of educational rights, what we argue here is that children have a right to attend school; a right to be provided for; and in more affluent regions globally, there are considerable obstacles to ensuring participation as co-presence.

Community Activism as a Precondition of Co-Presence

The first case illustrates the significance of co-presence as a form of children's participation. We also referred to the potential for other categories of participation to come in to play once co-presence has been established. I want to now turn to the relationship between the different categories of pupil participation. In a conventional sense Thompson and Holdsworth's (2003) typology can be applied in developmental terms. For example, model 3 is a less pupil-centred version than models 4 and 5. We might see this developmentalism in both psycho-social, hierarchical, and practical terms. In more formal psychological terms, children need to develop in and through attendance and engagement at school in order to participate later. Development here is cognitive, social, and emotional. Children's involvement in formal education from ever earlier ages, such as nursery school, is viewed as a way of developing children's capacities later in primary school (GPE, 2015; Moss, 2014). Children need to be in school before they can participate. Provision is a necessary precondition of later participation. Thus co-presence provides a starting point and a context within which children are able to engage with others in school. This engagement is often viewed as a precursor to children's involvement in formal democratic processes within school. Children at the upper end of primary or elementary school are developmentally ready to take on more responsibilities as participants within the classroom and the school.

In hierarchical terms there are parallels with Hart's ladder of participation (1997), where participation gradually becomes more sophisticated and children become more engaged with the structures of participation as they move up the ladder. From P3 to P5 there are increasing levels of pupil autonomy and space. P3 locates children in more structured and adult modes of voice. P4 and P5 are more pupil focused and less structured by adults. Children are in a position to initiate participation; children are also in a position to make stronger links between the school and the wider community (P5).

The relationship between the different participation models can be interpreted in less obvious ways. We can invert the conventional relationship between the models and challenge the power of developmentalism. The general accretion of capacities as children grow up which developmentalism assumes, takes little account of the social and economic contexts of children. Moreover, we can also challenge the hierarchical relationship which views 'co-presence' and 'engagement' as preconditions of later more advanced forms of participation. Perhaps we can focus on children's participation outside of an educational context. The global child labour discourse, for example, focuses on the way that children's work impedes children's development because it restricts their access to schooling. Article 32 of the UNCRC legitimates the approach in emphasising that children's economic activities potentially compromise their schooling and thus their capacity to participate in terms of participation modes 1 and 2. However, issues of children's provision are contested locally. One example of this are child workers mobilising support among themselves and others locally in order to promote school structures which take account of their work responsibilities.

The Case of the African Movement of Working Children and Youth (AMWCY)

The AMWCY (2016) was set up in 1994 within four African countries. By 2015, 27 African countries were involved incorporating around 3000 grass roots organisations. The commitment that the movement had towards working children was framed in terms of rights. Three categories of rights were invoked: a right to work and health; educational and social rights and ontological rights. The first two categories are normally in opposition. Thus the UNCRC largely endorses education and rejects work. However, we might see both of these realms of children's lives working in tandem. While there is research that challenges labour on health and social grounds, the AMWCY encapsulates the view that, in some respects, participation is a precondition of provision (Kana et al., 2010; Woldehanna et al., 2008). In other words, for children here to have better access to education, they need to organise themselves as a group that can put pressure on educationalists and politicians to provide them with more appropriate and accessible schooling. Thus, in terms of the Thompson and Holdsworth's (2003) typology, community activism (P5) is a precondition of co-presence (P1).

There are two important dimensions to this: first in temporal terms many children have to work in order to supplement the resources needed for school attendance. There is a temporal inversion of the conventional idea that children attend school before they are in a position to undertake paid work. Work becomes a precondition of children being able to continue their schooling (Twum-Danso, 2009) Here we might broaden the definition of children's participation to incorporate forms of work or labour. A dominant global discourse on labour excludes the work that children undertake as legitimate forms of activities for children (Sinha, 2003). However, I would argue that work may be viewed as an often necessary feature of children's lives, in the sense that children take part in material activities that improve the wellbeing of others around them as well as themselves. Participation is material as well as discursive (Wyness, 2013). A second political dimension focuses on the role that various organisations play in mobilising support for children to work and learn. While AMWCY is important as a movement for the legitimising of children's right to work as well as their right to education, it also adopts the view that work is not an alternative to school, it runs in parallel through children's lives. Various "Learn to Earn" initiatives have been set up globally. In Bangladesh, for example, *Basic Education for the Hard to Reach Urban Children,* was a project set up in 1996 with employers and parents working together to set up learning centres within close proximity to where children work (Child Friendly Cities, n.d.). The aim was to encourage working children to engage more with schooling, offering them at least 2 h tuition per day.

In these terms the developmental process is reversed with political mobilisation a precondition rather than an effect of *appropriate* provision and engagement. AMWCY can be viewed as a form of child participation with educational ends among others. Arguably, we can bring it in line with P5, a political movement populated by children and supported by various adult institutions. One of its aims is the promotion of children's rights to work and education. Moreover, AMWCY is committed to mobilising support among children their families and communities, as well as local employers and politicians. Children here are helping to mobilise support for safe and respectful access to schools for child workers.

Discussion and Conclusion

The UN Convention on the Rights of the Child (1989) and its relationship with children's schooling tends to be conceptualised in terms of two broad categories of rights: provision and protection rights where states and organisations take responsibility for children's formal education, and participation rights where children themselves have a say in their schooling. The former is normally seen as a precondition of the latter. Educational rights are defined globally in terms of mass compulsory schooling handed down to children and their families irrespective of cultural and social context. The UN Convention narrowly offers participation as regulated activities that give children more of a say in their lives. Within an educational context children's participation comes into operation *once* children are committed to mass compulsory schooling.

In this chapter I have argued that children's educational participation is contested and context bound. While there is now a global commitment to ensuring that children have rights to participate, the nature of this participation is shaped by global and local economic, cultural and social factors. I have also broken down the separation of educational provision from educational participation by exploring the relationship between the two forms of rights. Drawing on Thomson and Holdsworth's (2003) typology of pupil participation, I have incorporated 'provision' within a broader framework of participation. In this chapter I drew on two case studies in illustrating a more complicated relationship between different forms of participation.

In the first case I outlined a school within an affluent country where there was a typical hierarchical and developmental relationship between the different forms of participation. However, what was unusual about this case was the extent to which co-presence, the first level of pupil participation, became an end in itself, rather than simply a mundane precursor to the business of participating at levels 2 and 3. Participation here was about being in a position to 'take part', which despite the internalisation of compulsory schooling as a taken-for grated norm, was a particular challenge for a significant minority of children within this school.

The second case challenged the view that co-presence was always a precondition of other productive and more sophisticated forms of participation. The focus here is on children's paid work and the way that this can be redefined, challenging the delegitimised status of children's work, viewing it as a routinised and in some instances essential feature of family and community life. Work here becomes a form of children's participation in two ways. First, children's work is about engaging in community activities contributing to the material wellbeing of themselves, their families and their communities. It can also be connected with Thompson and Holdsworth's (2003) higher form of participation in a second way. Children are involved in mobilising political support through AMWCY to have their work recognised as a right alongside the right to education. While the dominant global discourse rejects the work or labour that children undertake, and this position is legitimated by the UNCRC, we can view work as a precondition of schooling and therefore an integral part of the educational project in many countries.

Notes

1. The methodology was a qualitative case study of a single school involving interviews with various school participants. The empirical focus was one secondary school in a deprived area. This was an in-depth analysis of various participants' understandings of home-school practices including managers, teachers, pupils and parents. For more detail see Wyness and Lang (2016).
2. The pupil premium refers to funding given to English schools on the basis of the numbers of pupils from disadvantaged backgrounds.

References

The African Movement of Working Children and Youth (AMWCY). (2016). http://www.maejt.org/page%20anglais/English%20about%20us%20history.htm consulted June 2019.

Alderson, P. (2008). *Young children's rights, exploring beliefs, principles and practice* (2nd ed.). Jessica Kingsley.

Allan, D., & Duckworth, V. (2018). Voices of disaffection disengaged and disruptive youths or agents of change and self-empowerment? *British Journal of Special Education, 45*(1), 43–60.

Archard, D. (2015). *Children: Rights and childhood* (3rd ed.). Routledge.

Arnot, M., & Reay, D. (2007). A sociology of pedagogic voice: Power, inequality and pupil consultation. *Discourse: Studies in the cultural politics of education, 28*(3), 311–325.

Ball, S. (2003). The teacher's soul and the terrors of performativity. *Journal of Education Policy, 18*(2), 215–228.

Banks, C. (2007). The discourse of children's rights in Bangladesh: International norms and local definitions. *International Journal of Children's Rights, 15*(3 & 4), 391–414.

Boyden, J., Porter, C., & Zharkovic, I. (2016). Balancing school and work with new opportunities: Changes in children's gendered time use in Ethiopia (2006–2013). *Young Lives,* Working Paper 1612.

Cairns, L., Byrne, S., Davis, J., Johnson, R., Konstantoni, K., & Kustatcher, M. (2018). Children's rights to education – Where is the weight for children's views? *International Journal of Children's Rights, 26*(1), 38–60.

Child Friendly Cities. (n.d.). *Basic education for the hard to reach urban children (BEHTRUC) in Dhaka, Chittagong, Khulna, Rajshahi, Barisal and Sylhet.* http://www.childfriendlycities.org/en/to-learn-more/examples-of-cfc-initiatives/bangladesh

Cockburn, T. (2005). Children's participation in social policy: Inclusion, chimera or authenticity? *Social Policy and Society, 4*(2), 109–120.

Department for Education (DfE). (2018). *Schools, pupils and their characteristics.* https://assets.publishing.service.gov.uk/government/uploads/system/uploads/attachment_data/file/719226/Schools_Pupils_and_their_Characteristics_2018_Main_Text.pdf. Accessed May 2019.

Global Partnership for Education (GPE). (2015). *FACTSHEET – Early childhood care and education*. http://www.globalpartnership.org/focus-areas/early-childhood-care-and-education

Hart, R. (1997). *Children's participation: The theory and practice of involving young citizens in community development and environmental care*. Earthscan.

Haynes, S. (2019). Students from 1,600 cities just walked out of school to protest climate change. It could be Greta Thunberg's biggest strike yet, *Time,* May 24th.

Invernizzie, A. (2005). Perspectives on children's work in the Algarve (Portugal) and their implications for social policy. *Critical Social Policy, 25*(2), 198–222.

Kana, M., Phoumin, H., & Seiichi, F. (2010). Does child labour have a negative impact on child education and health? A case study in rural Cambodia. *Oxford Development Studies, 38*(3), 357–382.

Kluttz, J. (2015). Reevaluating the relationship between education and child labour using the capabilities approach: Policy and implications for inequality in Cambodia. *Theory and Research in Education, 13*(2), 165–179.

Livingstone, S., Mascheroni, G., & Staksrud, E. (2018). European research on children's internet use: Assessing the past and anticipating the future. *New Media and Society, 20*(3), 1103–1122.

Moss, P. (2014). Early childhood policy in England 1997–2013: Anatomy of a missed opportunity. *International Journal of Early Years Education, 22*(4), 346–358.

Osler, A., & Vincent, K. (2003). *Girls and exclusion: Rethinking the agenda*. Routledge.

Sinha, S. (2003). Schools as institutions for the elimination of child labour: The experience of the M.V. Foundation in the Ranga Reddy District. In N. Kabeer, G. Nambissan, & R. Subrahmanian (Eds.), *Child labour and the right to education in South Asia*. Sage.

Thomas, N. (2007). Towards a theory of children's participation. *International Journal of Children's Rights, 15*(2), 199–218.

Thomson, P., & Holdsworth, R. (2003). Theorising change in the educational "field": Re-readings of 'student participation' projects. *International Journal of Leadership in Education, 6*(4), 371–391.

Twum-Danso, A. (2009). Reciprocity, respect and responsibility: The 3Rs underlying parent–child relationships in Ghana and the implications for children's rights. *International Journal of Children's Rights, 17*(3), 415–432.

United Nations (UN). (1989). *Convention on the rights of the child.* UN.

United Nations (UN). (2015). *Millennium development goals report 2014.* United Nations.

UNESCO. (2018). *Education for sustainable development goals: Learning objectives.* https://unesdoc.unesco.org/ark:/48223/pf0000247444

Verhellen, E. (2000). Children's rights and education. In A. Osler (Ed.), *Citizenship and democracy in schools* (pp. 33–43). Trentham.

Wainwright, E., & Marandet, E. (2017). Education, parenting and family: The social geographies of family learning. *British Educational Research Journal, 43*(2), 213–229.

Woldehanna, T., Jones, N., & Tefera, B. (2008). The invisibility of children's paid and unpaid work. *Childhood, 15*(2), 177–201.

Woodhead, M. (1999). Combating child labour: Listen to what the children say. *Childhood, 6*(1), 27–50.

Wyness, M. (2013). Global standards and deficit childhoods: the contested meaning of children's participation. *Children's Geographies, 11*(3), 340–353.

Wyness, M. (2019). *Childhood and society* (3rd ed.). Palgrave.

Wyness, M. (2009). Children representing children: Participation and the problem of diversity in UK youth councils. *Childhood, 16*(4), 535–552.

Wyness, M., & Lang, P. (2016). The social and emotional dimensions of schooling; a case study in challenging the barriers to learning. *British Educational Research Journal, 42*(6), 1041–1055.

Chapter 12
Small Voices Bring Big Messages. Experiences of Student Voice and Inclusion in Spanish Schools

Noelia Ceballos, Teresa Susinos, and Ángela Saiz-Linares

Abstract This paper sets up a dialogue between Article 29 and Article 12 of the Convention of the Rights of the Child. A research that seeks to broaden the students voice and to promote school improvements following a critical model of participation is analysed. The project was carried out in 11 education schools in Cantabria (Spain) from early childhood to secondary levels. The methodological framework is based on Participatory Qualitative Research. The results are organized according to three key aspects: (1) Can all children participate? We will focus on our research concerning how age, capacity or any individual trait does not limit the right of participation. (2) Has everyone "the right to express their views freely"? It is analysed which were the most relevant improvement proposals for the children and how innovative methodologies can be used successfully for children to express important ideas, even if orality is not yet developed. (3) Has everyone the right to participate "in all matters affecting the child"? The paper concludes by affirming the necessity to develop student voice as a democratic day-to-day practice in schools and as a feasible path to approach children's rights in a way that leads to real participation.

Keywords Convention on the rights of the child · Right to education · Inclusive education · Student democratic participation

Introduction

In this text, we will set up a dialogue between Article 29, which focuses on the 'aims of education', and Article 12, which focuses on the 'right to participation' (United Nations Convention on the Rights of the Child, 1989). For this purpose, we use the results from our research in 11 schools on student voice and the substantive content

N. Ceballos · T. Susinos · Á. Saiz-Linares (✉)
University of Cantabria, Santander, Cantabria, Spain
e-mail: ceballosn@unican.es; susinost@unican.es; saizla@unican.es

J. Gillett-Swan, N. Thelander (eds.), *Children's Rights from International Educational Perspectives*, Transdisciplinary Perspectives in Educational Research 2, https://doi.org/10.1007/978-3-030-80861-7_12

of these articles. As known, the Convention is structured around 54 articles that set out the rights of children in various areas: economic, social, cultural, civil, and political. These articles are grouped under four general principles, with the right to be heard being one of these, together with non-discrimination, best interest of the child and right to life survival and development. Even so, it is recognised that there is interdependence between the articles, such that the proposals and actions aimed at implementing a particular right are interwoven with others.

Children's right to education not only concerns access (Article 28) but also its content. One of the objectives of the Convention is the holistic development of children to their fullest potential (29 (1) (a)), which includes: instilling respect for human rights (29 (1) (b)); enhancing their sense of identity and belonging (29 (1) (c)); their integration into society and interaction with others (29 (1) (d)); and their integration with the environment (29 (1) (e)). The content of Article 29 implies a statement of the principles that should govern all educational processes, so education must be provided in a way that respects children and allows them to express their opinion freely (Article 12) and participate in school life. Therefore, in this work we attempt to build bridges between the theoretical formulation of the articles regarding the right of children to education and school practices that have the democratic participation of children as a guiding principle (Gillett-Swan & Coppock, 2016; Lundy, 2007). We also intend to discuss and illustrate what is expressed so succinctly in the aforementioned Article 12, providing insights to the issues raised from the results of our research. To do this, we make use of an investigation conducted in Spanish schools (in Cantabria) over 4 years with funding from the Spanish Ministry of Education. When we analyse the participatory culture of schools through the lens of Articles 29 and 12, it reveals the existence of processes and practices in schools that deny the principles defined in these articles. For this reason, the purpose of this project was to promote and analyse diverse initiatives involving the inclusive participation of students in school life consistent with a critical Student Voice model (Ceballos et al., 2019; Saiz et al., 2019; Susinos, 2019; Susinos & Ceballos, 2012; Susinos & Haya, 2014; Susinos et al., 2018).

From a methodological point of view, the research follows the qualitative tradition (Beach et al., 2018) and adopts a participatory focus (Aldridge, 2015; Groundwater-Smith et al., 2015; Nind, 2014; Bergold & Thomas, 2012). This approach allows a thorough understanding of the dynamics of democratic participation in schools to be obtained and how to address school change and improvement based on active listening to the students.

The project has been carried out in all levels of compulsory education – Infant, Primary and Secondary Education – as well as in the so-called "second-chance programmes". This breadth has allowed for the implementation and analysis of student voice initiatives in a total of 11 schools throughout the autonomous community of Cantabria located in both rural and urban areas.

The remainder of the chapter is built around a number of vignettes extracted from this body of research and that come primarily from field observations or interviews. Article 12 of the Convention will act as the guiding thread of this text which will allow us to organise the selected passages to initiate the dialogue between how the characteristics and aims of education are defined in the Convention (Article 29) and the school practices that allow them to experience the right to participate and have a voice of their own (Article 12). For this purpose, the ways that teaching processes and pedagogical methods have been configured in each of the experiences to achieve the full development of the entire student body, and to prepare them for a "responsible life in a free society, in the spirit of understanding, peace, tolerance, equality of sexes" (Article 29(d)) are shown.

By doing this, the intention is to show patterns of action in schools that are consistent with the contents of the Convention. Therefore, the objective is to establish bridges between theory and practice to ensure that children's right to participation is effective and also understandable for teachers (Jerome, 2016; Lundy, 2012). However, the research also raises some additional questions regarding what is expressed in the Convention that arise from a positioning based on a critical student voice approach, as will be shown below.

Can all Children Participate?

> States Parties shall assure to the child who is capable of forming his or her own views the right to express those views freely in all matters affecting the child, the views of the child being given due weight in accordance with the age and maturity of the child (United Nations Convention on the Rights of the Child, 1989, Article 12)

Article 28 of the Convention promulgates the right of all children, without exception, to education. However, beyond access, there are processes and practices in schools that negate the principles defined in Article 29. We are referring to practices which, depending on age, ability, origin or gender, relegate some students and groups to some form of segregation, exclusion, or silence. Clearly, any discriminatory practice contradicts the article.

In this vein, we find the first contradiction at the beginning of Article 12 that school practice must resolve on a day-to-day basis. On the one hand, the Convention recognises the ability of children to form their own opinions, confirms their right to express them and urges countries to undertake significant participation actions with all children of "*any age, within the family, community and schools, paying particular attention to girls and children in disadvantaged or marginalized situations*" (Committee on the Rights of the Child, 2018, p.5). But, on the other hand, the text excludes those children who "cannot" form their own views, without specifying in any way what these exclusion criteria are (Gillett-Swan, 2019; Shier, 2019).

There is therefore evidence of a gap between the formal language of the text and the recommendation for action, with ambiguity created by avoiding the definition of criteria relating to children that might be discriminatory, but at the same time accepting the possibility that some of them are not "*capable of forming his or her own views*".

This wording implicitly recognises the fact that certain groups, such as those considered to have special educational needs or minority ethnic and cultural groups, often end up being excluded from these participatory processes when a deficit view of children's inherent capabilities is adopted (Gillett-Swan & Sargeant, 2018; Lindley et al., 2011). This vision was attempted to be overcome through GC12 (2009), where it is recognised that "States parties should presume that a child has the capacity to form her or his own views and recognize that she or he has the right to express them; it is not up to the child to first prove her or his capacity" (United Nations, 2009).

Our research is aligned with the principles of educational inclusion understood as the development of policies and practices that allow all students, without exception, to have a presence, participate and be successful in school (Ainscow, 2001; Thomson & Hall, 2015). This implies the recognition of the right to access education (Article 28), but especially to maximise the child's ability to participate fully and responsibly in a free society (Article 29).

To illustrate this principle, we will describe experiences in a public school with students in the second and sixth years of primary education (7 and 12 years old, respectively) who carry out a joint research of the different school spaces using the photovoice methodology (Susinos et al., 2019). They analyse their use and occupation, reflecting on the activities they usually perform in these places, the relationships developed and the resources they find there to enable them to carry out different actions (Ceballos & Susinos, 2019). The selected fragment corresponds to the observation of the joint assembly that sets the beginning of the project, in which the teachers present the experience to the students (Image 12.1):

If we confined ourselves to the statement in the Article 12 that specifies maturity and capacity as criteria to be able to exercise the child's right to be heard, this vignette would invite us to ask if the difficulties experienced by S. justify his/her participation being limited or revoked.

Article 29 highlights the requirement that education must pursue the development of each child's personality, their natural gifts and ability, recognising the fact that each child has unique characteristics, interests and abilities and also their own learning needs. The ultimate purpose of education must therefore be the all-round development of all students to their fullest potential (Article 29 (a)). Consequently, in our project the question we considered most pertinent was: how can we listen to all students without exception based on the recognition of their right to participate?

The teacher realises that S. (7 years old) is crying. The teacher hugs him/her and says, "I know that new things are a bit overwhelming, but you'll soon see that we have a good time." H. (12 years old) proposes to the teacher that S. take a picture now to see if he/she likes it. [...]. At the end of the assembly, the teacher explains to me that S. has difficulties with literacy and is in the process of educational psychology evaluation. [When working partners are formed for the photovoice activity] J. (12 years old) slaps S. on the back when they sit together. The teacher says that S. also wanted to be with two classmates. S. "It's just that I find it a bit more difficult." (Fragment of the observation diary)

Image 12.1 Fragment of the observation diary. Can all children participate?

How can we listen to S. if oral and written language is not a vehicle of expression with which he/she feels competent?

In the process of answering our question, two decisions emerged. The first relates to the choice of participatory methodologies that do not impose the use of oral and written language as the only vehicle of expression (Gillett-Swan & Sargeant, 2018). We chose the photovoice strategy in order to offer the opportunity to use a common and accessible language for students that allowed access to the interpretations and meanings of all students (Wang, 2003; Prins, 2010). This methodology made it possible for us to: record and visualise the ideas, concerns, and interpretations of students through images; use photographs as objects of analysis; for the construction of knowledge through dialogue, reflection, and intersubjectivity; and, finally, have a means of sharing our ideas with others. The second decision dealt with the need to establish educational self-help among peers. The forming of pairs was left to the school children, who grouped freely, with the sole constraint that they were to work with a student from the other class.

The question that began with S. resurfaces in different moments of this experience. How can we listen to all students without exception based on the recognition of their right to participate? During the implementation of the photovoice strategy, we found that there was a group of students who were not present in a considerable number of work sessions. These students of Roma ethnicity[1] have a high rate of absenteeism, which makes their presence and involvement in the proposal difficult. Again, the question arises: how can we listen to these students who show a high degree of absenteeism? Three principal actions were undertaken. First, we made educational times more flexible, and some of the key work sessions, such as the sharing and dialogue about the images, were postponed until these students were present. Since it was not possible to know about attendance in advance, this presented a challenge for the organisation of the school times, which was prone to be rigid. In this way, the inclusive imperative was given greater priority than the pressure of school times. A second action was linked to the creation of heterogeneous groups. The initial choice of these students to work together was not very viable since it was common for them not to coincide, which meant that they were unable to make progress in the work. After negotiation with them, it was agreed that they would join other groups, always respecting their ability to choose who they wanted to work with. Finally, each work group generated minutes of their work sessions, so that when the students who had been missing joined in, they could check the record of what had happened and the tasks in progress.

[1]The Roma is the main ethnic minority in Spain. The presence of students from this minority is a common feature of the schools participating in this project. Although the schooling of students in Compulsory stages is practically complete (Fundación Secretariado General Gitano, 2013), we find high percentages of absenteeism and premature abandonment: 64% of Roma students do not complete compulsory studies (Fundación Secretariado General Gitano, 2013), which is more pressing in Roma girls (Cárdenas-Rodríguez et al., 2019). This makes them a disadvantaged group at risk of social and educational exclusion.

Finally, we would like to highlight that the protagonists of this experience are students of different ages (6 and 12 years old). Due to this age difference, and in order to avoid an imbalance of power favouring those who were older, various elements of the democratic dialogue were emphasised in the experience (active listening, respect for everyone's proposals, etc.).

This example taken from an observation is in line with the report on Article 12, which emphasises not imposing any age limit on the child's right to express his or her opinion. Although, as we have already pointed out, the various statements and reports make use of ambiguous and contradictory language: it seems contrary to the stated purpose that participatory action is limited "in accordance with the age and maturity of the child" (Committee on the Rights of the Child, 2009, p. 11).

In short, the educational processes undertaken must promote the spirit and educational principles of the Convention on the Rights of the Child, especially those of Article 29, making schools into exceptional spaces for learning and exercising their rights in everyday experiences (Article 29). This requires the rethinking of existing proposals based on inclusive principles in order to guarantee the participation and success of all students, regardless of their characteristics and needs.

Has Everyone "The Right to Express Their Views Freely"?

This consideration refers to the child's right to express their ideas without pressure, manipulation or influence, as well as the choice to share them or not (Committee on the Rights of the Child, 2009). Similarly, in the last report for Spain by the Committee on the Rights of the Child in 2018, discussing the right of the child to be heard, the Committee recommends that the State:

> Ensure that the inclusion and participation of children is not merely symbolic, but that their opinions are genuinely heard and duly taken into account. (p. 6).

This aim is in line with the definition of participation in our project, which refers to the different practices that allow children to be able to make decisions and take effective action in relation to their reality and the world in which they live. Participation, as a collective action based on inclusive deliberation, must be accessible to everyone and should eventually become a daily democracy, incorporated into the day-to-day routine of schools as an alternative form of school governance (Susinos, 2019).

The child's ability to participate fully and responsibly in a free society requires learning that occurs in action. Therefore, schools must be configured as spaces to learn about democracy within a democratic context. This full adoption of the principles of Article 29 requires a review of educational practices and the redefining of existing spaces to promote the child's participation in school life, as part of the learning process and the experience of exercising their rights. It is therefore clearly insufficient to implement cosmetic solutions or those that are limited to incorporating these purposes into the theoretical provisions without promoting more profound transformations.

One of the nearest children (from now on referred to as Mario) talks about me – "she's a show-off" – while laughing at the surnames of some of his classmates. It is one of them who makes the comments and the two or three next to him who laugh [...] The tutor reviews everything they have said and explains that the group as a whole must choose five proposals: five which they agree to take to the management team. The tutor, regrouping the ideas, begins the process of asking them to vote. [...] I realise that Mario determines what the others should vote. Each time the tutor reads a proposal, he tells them whether they should vote for it or not and the others, except for one, do as he says even if they say they want to vote otherwise. [When they propose to vote for the proposal to bring together the infants and primary education playground areas] Mario comments to his companions that he rejects the idea: "No, let's smash their faces in." [...] Games: When Mario hears this, he says, "We already play," and he tells his classmates not to raise their hands because they already do that. [...] Cooking: One of the children next to Mario raises his hand. Mario looks at him and says, "No! What for?" The boy keeps his hand raised to vote yes. [...] Cooking: One of the children next to Mario raises his hand. Mario looks at him and says, "No! What for?" The boy keeps his hand raised to vote yes. [RESISTANCE]

Image 12.2 Fragment of the observation diary. Everyone has "the right to express their views freely"

Protecting this right to express their opinion freely requires a combination of strategies to ensure that all children, without exception, have the opportunity to express their point of view. That is, it is about preventing a person or group from dominating the process of debate, which is something that tends to occur, as we show in the vignette above (Image 12.2).

The example selected relates to a student participation experience that involves all the students in a public School (2–12 years) which aims to improve the school playground.[2] The fragment we present is taken from an observation of the democratic deliberation phase carried out in a primary classroom. In the situation shown, a voting system has been developed, prior to deliberative debate, to encourage decision-making on everyone's proposals. Mario sets himself up as a leader of the process and exhibits an attitude of authority over the rest from the beginning, trying to modify the votes of his peers to suit his own interests and getting several children to vote in a way that is contrary to their wishes. Thus, we see how the pressure of the group is, in many cases, more important than individual and/or common priorities and how voting systems do not guarantee deliberative democratic processes. These tendencies are especially common in the traditional delegated systems of student participation that are in use in schools, and that is why it is essential to

[2] The school playground is the area that is available to students for free play which is used for between 20 and 30 minutes of the school day.

implant participation practices in the daily life of children that go beyond formal representation systems.

This and other experiences connected with student participation initiatives have taught us that in order to facilitate inclusive deliberative processes that take into account all opinions it is advisable to start by opening up spaces that allow the individual expression of each voice. This prevents a person or group from dominating in the subsequent debate. Additionally, the domain of democratic deliberation entails ensuring that the proposals individually drawn up are subsequently debated, justified and defended publicly so that the group can finally choose one of the proposals for improvement that, in essence, represents an improvement for the common good (Della-Porta, 2005; Englund, 2006; Lundy, 2007; Ross, 2012; Thompson, 2008). Furthermore, the method of expressing their opinions is important, since we have also learned that the use of diverse and creative consultation mechanisms (not always supported by verbal language) allows us to expand the possibilities of participation, connecting with the communicative affinities of each student.

Thus, for example, in other research carried out in the Infant Education stage (0–6 years) a common question emerged: what happens when children do not possess oral language skills? The challenge we faced was to recognise the existence of other non-verbal methods of communication involving body language, crying, facial expressions, noises and movements (Clark & Moss, 2011; Ghirotto & Mazzoni, 2013; Ceballos et al., 2016). Faced with this challenge, we understood the need to devote a prolonged period of time to attentive listening and to use different strategies to create a dialogue between different perspectives that allow us to gain more in-depth knowledge of the needs and preferences of the children. We also reviewed the role of adults (teachers and families) as facilitators. The fundamental challenge is to prevent the adult's perspective and (over-)interpretation from being imposed on the needs and interests of the children. This inclusion of an increasingly heterogeneous repertoire of devices enables more heterogeneous forms of understanding, expression and interaction and, therefore, recognition of a greater diversity of capacities, interests and learning rhythms.

In the following table we extract the participation strategies that have been tested in the different schools and that ensure the inclusive qualities mentioned: all opinions are heard and respected, priorities and needs are analysed together, decisions are adopted based on consensus after dialogic processes of discussion, etc. (Ceballos et al., 2019) (Table 12.1).

Has Everyone the Right to Participate "in all Matters Affecting the Child"?

In Article 29, when defining educational purposes and principles, the all-round development of students in all their dimensions is made explicit. This is not a process that is isolated or out of context but is connected to the characteristics and needs of their local community, without losing sight of global issues. In this way,

Table 12.1 Participation strategies

Deliberate together, make decisions	Discuss, argue about shared issues	Find out the opinions of others
•Classroom assemblies •School assemblie	•Watching videos/films and later discussion (cinema forum)	•Interviews with classmates, teachers •Dialogue with informal groups
Have an informed opinion	**Consult non-verbal children**	**Anonymous student expression** **Free expression of the influence of peers or adults**
•Interview with key informants •A guest in class •Information search	•Observation •Mediated consultation: through families and teachers •Documentation	•Suggestion box •Surveys •Online questionnaire •Video booth •Wandering or walking methods

Non-discursive strategies to communicate ideas	Manage common decisions	Communicate the experience, report	Propose improvements to adults or institutions
•Photos, photo-documentation •Photovoice •Slogans •The sculpture •Incomplete phrases ("What I like about you is …") •Creation of visual stories •Drawing, comic, etc.	•Appoint secretaries, coordinators •Public panel of proposals for all students •Minutes, summary of collective agreements •Decalogue of the researcher	•Blog about the experience •Presentation to families •Create a video •Exposure to the educational community based on graphic productions •School magazine •Classroom/school blog •Research report •Social media	•Interview with policy makers •Written letter to the head •Presentation to the school board

education and the exercise of their rights is not limited by closed, restricted and/or predetermined curricula. The curriculum must have a direct relationship with the child's social, cultural, environmental, and economic framework and with their present and future needs. On this basis, we find a new challenge in the implementation of Article 12. This dimension of Article 12 leads us to reflect on the issues that are the subject of dialogue with children. The statement emphasises administrative and judicial aspects. However, in the subsequent report, these areas of participation are expanded, with special mention of the school and education.

> In all educational environments, including educational programs in the early years, the active role of children in a participatory learning environment should be promoted (Committee on the Rights of the Child, 2009, p.26).

Similarly, we find among the recommendations that the Committee made to Spain (2018), the need to "conduct programmes and awareness-raising activities to promote the meaningful and empowered participation of all children, at any age, within the family, community and schools".

This confronts us with one of the constant challenges within the critical student voice perspective: the establishment of a participation agenda that responds to the needs and preferences of children as opposed to the imposition of an adult agenda (Shier, 2019). This leads us to ask ourselves which issues are subject to participation in schools, and if they are significant for children (Bourke & Loveridge, 2018; Fielding & Bragg, 2003; Rudduck, 2007; Powell et al., 2018).

In this section, we are in a position to reflect on the issues which form the basis of the improvement projects chosen by the students and which are therefore on the agenda of our research. We present the activity undertaken in a public school with students in the fifth year (11 years old). In this experience students are invited to discuss and make proposals for improving life in the classroom through the following consultation question: what are the things that you would like to improve in your class?[3] To give their answer, the students were organised in groups of four to five children who took part in a dialogue, negotiated and agreed on their proposals (Image 12.3).

We have selected the minutes for two groups from different classrooms because they allow us to reflect on two key ideas. The first set of minutes present us with a list of classroom rules, written in prohibition mode, which faithfully include the rules that the teacher imposes in the classroom. These students have tried to give what they think is the "right answer". Although the teacher gave them freedom, by choosing an open question, these students reproduced what they have learned about

Things we want to improve in class:
-Don't mix the paint pots in class
-Tidy up the puzzles afterwards
-Don't get up to mischief when the teacher leaves
-Don't make noise when the teacher is explaining something

Things we should improve in class:
-We would like to be able to choose the homework
-When we finish, we would like to be left to do what we want
-Organise the games
-Put things in the cubby holes
-When it's our turn to be leader for the day, we would like to be able to change the tortoise whenever we want
-Organise the cubby holes

Image 12.3 Examples of student responses

[3]This experience has been documented in detail in the book, *When everyone counts. Experiences of student participation in schools.*, edited by Susinos et al. (2018).

their schooling: giving adults a single answer, the result of reproducing what teachers have previously told them.

In the second set of minutes we find three recurring issues in the students' demands: the improvement of coexistence in the classroom, and especially compliance with the rules; modification of certain aspects of the organisation of the classroom ("leader for the day"[4]); and the ability to choose the activities they can carry out in their "free" time.[5]

This experience allows us to reflect on some general trends in the improvement projects proposed by the students. We find initiatives that focus on improving the school curriculum or school organisation less frequently raised, consistent with previous research (Bragg, 2007; Cox & Robinson, 2008; Grace et al., 2019). What stand out are the projects aimed at improving spaces in the school, both the physical aspects (architecture, accessibility and school playground) and coexistence (in the classroom and the playground).

A second recurring issue is related to educational organisation and management, the coexistence of students being the most common and visible in school life. Meanwhile, other issues, such as a representative decision-making system, school projects or financial management, seem to be hidden or considered unattainable by students, limiting their ability to make decisions about these political and governance aspects.

Finally, few projects are undertaken that have the curriculum as an area of participation and improvement. However, there are examples that illustrate negotiation processes involving some of the aspects of the curriculum that have encouraged students to develop critical questions about the world and what they learn by undertaking research projects led by the students themselves. These initiatives are found more frequently in the infant and primary education than in secondary education. An example is found in School 9, which addresses the improvement of the neighbourhood undertaken in a primary school class. It is necessary to highlight how students identify the needs of their local community (Article 29 (c)), but also how they give answers relating to global problems. Thus, one of the proposals of the students for the improvement of their neighbourhood was the care and development of green areas and environmental care practices (Article 29 (e)). After choosing the improvement project, students undertake and lead a research process that concludes with the delivery of a dossier to the town hall with their proposals for improvement (Susinos et al., 2018).

[4] It is common in the classrooms to find students responsible for certain tasks: watering the plants, writing the date, and organising the materials, etc.. This figure of the leader of the day rotates among the students.

[5] Students refer to that time that passes between the end of one activity and the beginning of the next in which they can choose between playing, reading, etc..

Discussion

In this article we show how there is a need to find ways for the real implementation of the rhetoric on the rights of the child, more specifically with reference to the right to education (Article 28 and Article 29) and its connection with the right to participation, in the context of children's daily lives. In particular, this work focuses on the experiences in several primary and secondary schools that have participated in a research project aimed at promoting the student voice. Through several participation vignettes selected from this investigation, we have analysed how schools have redefined their practices and structures to assume the principles of Article 29, as well as the core elements that make up Article 12 of the Convention. The following essential questions arise from an analysis of this article: Can all children participate? Can they freely express their opinions? Can they really intervene in all matters affecting them?

Paragraph 1 of Article 29 emphasises the point that the right of children to education not only concerns access (Article 28) but also the content and principles that govern the educational process itself and that these should be aligned with the general principles of the convention: non-discrimination (Article 2), the best interests of the child (Article 3), the right to life, survival and development (Article 6) and the right of the child to express their opinion and that this is given due weight (Article 12). We conclude that it is essential that participation be truly universal and that we need to ensure that there are no a priori restrictions in relation to the age or other qualities of children (Article 2). Any discriminatory practice is in contradiction of Articles 28 and 29, which recognise the right to education and the development of all students to their fullest potential. It is necessary to overcome a deficiency-based vision of childhood as a waiting time before adulthood to recognise the agency of children and their ability to make decisions in educational and school improvement processes (Rudduck & Flutter, 2007; James & Prout, 2015, Shier 2019; Susinos & Haya, 2014).

Participation also requires ensuring that everyone can freely express their opinion. For this, we must begin by recognising that the voice of students is not homogeneous and ensure that all opinions can be heard (not only those of a few students with greater social and cultural capital). The full adoption of Article 29 requires a review of educational practices and the redefining of existing spaces to promote the child's participation in school life. We need to respect the right of children to express their ideas without being pressured or their words manipulated, avoiding practices by adults that are no more than tokenism (Lundy, 2007; Gillett-Swan & Sargeant, 2018).

Finally, we have verified that the participation of students in such a way that they intervene on all matters affecting them is still very much limited by the pressures of a traditionally very top-down school culture. As can be seen from the principles of Article 29, educational proposals must be directly related to the child's social, cultural, environmental and economic framework and their present and future needs.

As we have seen, students make recommendations to improve their schools that are on the conservative side and tend not to contradict the school ethos.

We can therefore conclude that the advancement of the right to participation included in the Convention requires its incorporation into daily practices that carefully address the limitations we have identified so that participation is inclusive and does not become another dividing practice in schools.

References

Ainscow, M. (2001). *Desarrollo de escuelas inclusivas. Ideas, propuestas y experiencias para mejorar las instituciones escolares*. Narcea.

Aldridge, J. (2015). *Participatory research: Working with vulnerable groups in research and practice*. The Policy Press.

Beach, D., Bagley, C., & Marquez, S. (2018). *The handbook of ethnography of education*. Wiley.

Bergold, J., & Thomas, S. (2012). Participatory research methods: A methodological approach in motion. *Historical Social Research, 37*(4), 142–191–222.

Bourke, R., & Loveridge, J. (2018). *Radical collegiality through student voice: Educational experience, policy and practice*. Springer.

Bragg, S. (2007). Student voice and governmentality: The production of enterprising subjects? *Discourse, 28*(3), 343–358.

Cárdenas-Rodríguez, R., Terrón-Caro, T., & Gimeno, M. (2019). Educación Primaria y alumnas gitanas. Análisis de las barreras sociales en contextos de exclusión. *Revista de Investigación Educativa, 37*(1), 75–91.

Ceballos, N., Calvo, A., & Haya, I. (2019). Student consultation strategies as a lever for school improvement. Results of a collaborative study. *Cultura y Educación, 31*(4), 780–813.

Ceballos, N., & Susinos, T. (2019). Me gusta "la selva" porque es un sitio salvaje, donde me puedo esconder»: el uso de la fotografía participativa en las geografías de la infancia. *Documents d'anàlisi geogràfica, 65*(1), 43–67.

Ceballos, N., Susinos, T., & Saiz, Á. (2016). How can we improve through pupil participation? An infants school experience. *Journal of Research in Special Educational Needs, 16*(1), 583–586.

Clark, A., & Moss, P. (2011). *Listening to young children: The mosaic approach*. Jessica Kingsley Publishers.

Cox, S., & Robinson-Pant, A. (2008). Power, participation and decision making in the primary classroom: Children as action researchers. *Educational Action Research, 16*(4), 457–468.

Della-Porta, D. (2005). Deliberation in movement: Why and how to study deliberative democracy and social movements. *Acta politica, 40*(3), 336–350.

Englund, T. (2006). Deliberative communication: a pragmatist proposal. *Journal of Curriculum Studies, 38*(5), 503–520.

Fielding, M., & Bragg, S. (2003). *Students as researchers. Making a difference*. Pearson.

Fundación Secretariado General Gitano. (2013). *El alumnado gitano en secundaria: un estudio comparado*. Madrid: Ministerio de Educación.

Ghirotto, L., & Mazzoni, V. (2013). Being part, being involved: The adult's role and child participation in an early childhood learning context. *International Journal of Early Years Education, 21*(4), 300–308.

Gillett-Swan, J. (2019). No child should be sacrificed for the "greater good" of a school or "best interests" of majority. This is what child rights is about. *EduResearch Matters*. https://www.aare.edu.au/blog/?p=3757. Accessed 20 Feb 2020.

Gillett-Swan, J., & Sargeant, J. (2018). Assuring children's human right to freedom of opinion and expression in education. *International Journal of Speech-Language Pathology, 20*(1), 120–127.

Gillett-Swan, J., & Coppock, V. (Eds.). (2016). *Children's rights, educational research and the UNCRC: Past, present and future*. Symposium Books.

Grace, R., Knight, J., Baird, K., Ng, J., Shier, H., Wise, S., Fattore, T., McClean, T., Bonser, G., Judd-Lam, S., & Kemp, L. (2019). Where are the silences? A scoping review of child participatory research literature in the context of the Australian service system. *Children Australia, 1*, 1–15.

Groundwater-Smith, S., Dockett, S., & Bottrell, D. (2015). *Participatory research with children and young people*. Sage.

James, A., & Prout, A. (2015). *Constructing and reconstructing childhood*. Routledge.

Jerome, L. (2016). Interpreting children's rights education: Three perspectives and three roles for teachers. *Citizenship, Social and Economics Education, 15*(2), 143–156.

Lindley, E., Brinkhuis, R., & Verhaou, L. (2011). Too young to vave a voice? In S. Miles & M. Ainscow (Eds.), *Responding to diversity in schools* (pp. 81–90). Routledge.

Lundy, L. (2007). "Voice" is not enough: Conceptualising article 12 of the United Nations convention on the rights of the child. *British Educational Research Journal, 33*, 927–942.

Lundy, L. (2012). Children's rights and educational policy in Europe: The implementation of the United Nations convention on the rights of the child. *Oxford Review of Education, 38*(4), 393–411.

Nind, M. (2014). *What is inclusive research?* Bloomsbury Academic.

Powell, M., McArthur, M., Chalmers, J., Graham, A., Moore, T., Spriggs, M., & Taplin, S. (2018). Sensitive topics in social research involving children. *International Journal of Social Research Methodology, 21*(6), 647–660.

Prins, E. (2010). Participatory photography: A tool for empowerment or surveillance? *Action Research, 8*(4), 426–443.

Ross, A. (2012). Education for active citizenship: Practices, policies, promises. *International Journal of Progressive Education, 8*(3), 7–14.

Rudduck, J. (2007). Student voice, student engagement, and school reform. In D. Thiessen & A. Cook-Sather (Eds.), *International handbook of student experience in elementary and secondary school* (pp. 587–610). Springer.

Rudduck, J., & Flutter, J. (2007). *Cómo mejorar tu centro escolar dando la voz al alumnado*. Morata.

Saiz-Linares, Á., Rodríguez-Hoyos, C., & Susinos-Rada, T. (2019). 'I think we are still very directive': Teachers' discourses on democratic student participation. *British Educational Research Journal, 45*(1), 83–98.

Shier, H. (2019). Student voice and children's rights: Power, empowerment, and "protagonismo". In M. A. Peters (Ed.), *Encyclopedia of teacher education* (pp. 1–6). Springer Nature.

Susinos, T. (2019). Is participation a "sick word"? New insights about student democratic participation in light of some research with Spanish schools. In J. Allan, V. Harwood, & C. Jorgensen (Eds.), *World year book 2020. School governance: Closing the gap in education*. Routledge.

Susinos, T., Calvo, A., Rodríguez, C., & Saiz, Á. (2019). ICT for inclusion. A student voice research project in Spain. *Magis, 11*(23), 39–54.

Susinos, T., & Ceballos, N. (2012). Voz del alumnado y presencia participativa en la vida escolar. *Apuntes para una cartografía de la voz del alumnado en la mejora educativa. Revista de educación, 359*, 24–44.

Susinos, T., Ceballos, N., & Saiz, A. (2018). *Cuando todos cuentan. Experiencias de participación de estudiantes en las escuelas*. La Muralla.

Susinos, T., & Haya, I. (2014). Developing student voice and participatory pedagogy: A case study in a Spanish primary school. *Cambridge Journal of Education, 44*(3), 385–399.

Thompson, D. (2008). Deliberative democratic theory and empirical political science. *Annual Review of Political Science, 11*, 497–520.

Thomson, P., & Hall, C. (2015). "Everyone can imagine their own Gellert": The democratic artist and "inclusion" in primary and nursery classrooms. *Education 3–13, 43*(4), 420–432.

United Nations. (1989). *Convention on the rights of the child*. Retrieved from https://www.unicef.org/crc/

United Nations. (2009). General comment no. 12. *The right of the child to be heard.*
United Nations. (2018). Comité de los Derechos de la infancia. *Observaciones finales sobre los informes periódicos quinto y sexto combinados de España.*
Wang, C. (2003). Using photovoice as a participatory assessment and issue selection tool: A case study with the homeless in Ann Arbor. In M. Minkler & N. Wallerstein (Eds.), *Community-based participatory research for health* (pp. 179–196). Jossey-Bass.

Chapter 13
Inclusive and Exclusionary Practices Concerning a Child's Voice in Preschool: The Perspectives and Experiences of Polish Student Teachers

Anna Babicka-Wirkus

Abstract This chapter describes inclusive and exclusionary practices concerning children's voices. These practices were reconstructed based on the experiences of Polish student teachers who have completed their professional training in preschools. Qualitative methods were used for data collection and analysis. The aim of this chapter is to analyse the reconstructed inclusive and exclusionary practices through Jacques Rancière's prism of the *distribution of the sensible*. This category allows for the evaluation of different ways of expressing voice. In the dominant school discourse, voices can be defined as significant (usually it is the teacher's voice) and as clatter or chatter (often the child's voice is perceived this way). Such a division is typical for educational institutions but hidden under the veil of political correctness and teachers' assurances that they respect children's rights to freedom of speech and opinion. Being aware of this division, especially by future teachers, is important for the implementation of the 'aims of education' and children's rights culture in educational institutions.

Keywords Children's rights · Child's voice · Inclusive practices · Exclusionary practices · Preschool · Student teachers

Introduction

Teachers, as agents of educational institutions, play an important role in implementing children's rights (Brantefors et al., 2019; Osler & Starkey, 2010). According to General Comment No. 1 regarding the 'aims of education' (United Nations, 2001),

A. Babicka-Wirkus (✉)
Pomeranian University in Słupsk, Słupsk, Poland
e-mail: anna.babicka-wirkus@apsl.edu.pl

J. Gillett-Swan, N. Thelander (eds.), *Children's Rights from International Educational Perspectives*, Transdisciplinary Perspectives in Educational Research 2, https://doi.org/10.1007/978-3-030-80861-7_13

"children should (...) learn about human rights by seeing human rights standards implemented in practice, whether at home, in school, or within the community". Human rights education is important for shaping children's motivations and actions. According to Article 29(1)(b) of the Convention on the Rights of the Child (UNCRC) education should be directed towards respect for human rights and fundamental freedoms (United Nations, 1989). After all, freedom of expression and opinion is a fundamental human right. From this perspective, it is interesting to consider how student teachers perceive practices relating to human rights that occur in preschools, especially those that concern children's voice and expression. Given that human rights in educational practice are often embedded in social relationships and interactions (Brantefors et al., 2019), investigating the ways children's voice is included or excluded in education is fundamental to understanding human rights in the context of early childhood. The way participatory practices relating to children's voice are reconstructed by student teachers is important for two reasons. First of all, it indirectly shows their sensitivity to the issues of respecting children's rights when children express their views in preschool. These sensitivities appear to be based on their knowledge, experience, and views (Sargeant & Gillett-Swan, 2019). Secondly, it refers to their understanding of the idea that all children have the right to speak on matters important to them.

This chapter analyses the experiences and practices of Polish student teachers who have completed their professional training in preschools. The collected empirical material relating to children's voice in the preschool is analysed using the concept of Ranciere's *distribution of the sensible* (1999, 2004), in which the voice, its use, hearing, and understanding are very important.

Children's Right to Speak as a Key Aspect of Creating Educational Discourse in Preschool

Children have an inherent right and ability to take part in a serious discussion and all the decision-making concerning their life (Harris & Manatakis, 2013; Sargeant & Gillett-Swan, 2019). Children are experts of their own lives as well as active constructors of meanings (Biesta, 2011; Harris & Manatakis, 2013; MacNaughton et al., 2003). Perceiving a child as an active actor of social reality is reflected in General Comment No. 1 and General Comment No. 12. According to these recommendations, respecting the child's right to be heard and to participate in the decision-making process on the issues that are important to them are important objectives of education (United Nations, 2001, 2009). According to Article 29(1) of the UNCRC (United Nations, 1989), children's education should be directed towards a holistic development as a human being and 'the development of respect for human rights and fundamental freedoms' (Article 29(1)(b)). One of the fundamental freedoms is the right of the child to speak up on all matters concerning them (Article 12 of the UNCRC). This right is defined in General Comment No. 12, according to which the voice of the child is heard and taken seriously by adults (United Nations, 2009). However, in the educational reality, the voice of the child is often ignored and inaudible (Messiou & Ainscow, 2015), which fosters a culture of silence in school (Jones & Welch, 2010; Lewis, 2010). The culture of silence is rooted in the perception of the child as an entity whose opinions are less significant than those of adults (Jones & Welch, 2010). This culture is not based on the Voice-Inclusive Practice (VIP) described by Sargeant and Gillett-Swan (2019), which promotes an active involvement of all parties in the education process. Voice-Inclusive Practice is about pupils and teachers, and is important for shaping an educational environment centred around respect for the rights of the child, where human rights are not a school subject but a "*subject field* that goes beyond subject boundaries in all educational activities" (Brantefors et al., 2019, p. 699, *emphasis in original*).

Respect for the rights of the child in terms of creating conditions for the practice of free speech is, therefore, a key factor in individual and social development because by using their voice, children learn how to be active agents of change in their environment (Marshall, 2006; Rudduck, 2007; Ribaeus & Skånfors, 2019). However, according to Lundy (2007), allowing children to express their opinion is not in itself an exercise of the right stipulated in Article 12 of the UNCRC. This right requires allowing children to speak up and respecting their decision to remain silent (Jones & Welch, 2010; Bligh, 2011). It is also important to listen to children and pay attention to their views, and to ensure that they are genuinely involved in the decision-making process concerning matters important to them (Lundy, 2007). Children should feel that their opinions matter and are indeed taken into account by their teachers and other members of educational institutions (Perry-Hazan, 2015; Ribaeus & Skånfors, 2019). Taking children's views into account and consulting them on issues that are relevant to them is a key aspect of participation and realisation of democratic education based on children's rights (James & James, 2012; Lansdown, 2011; McIntyre et al., 2005; Ribaeus & Skånfors, 2019; Rudduck, 2007; Simó Gil et al., 2017).

Providing children with the conditions indicated by Lundy (2007) to exercise the right to their views makes them active creators of the preschool discourse. This discourse, as understood by Rancière (1999), is created by entities whose voice is heard, understood and treated with due seriousness. Human ability to speak is reflected in Rancière's philosophy, which demands equality between people in a hierarchical society. According to the French philosopher, "the human child is first of all a speaking being" (Rancière, 1991, p. 11). Therefore, in the process of education, children should not be restricted in their ability to speak out and express themselves. Ensuring that children use their voice and express themselves freely makes it possible to establish a relationship between two equal subjects – the pupil and the teacher because, according to Rancière (1991), they both have equal intelligence as human beings. While discussing Rancière's views on education, Masschelein and Simons (2011, p. 163) conclude: "It is the school where we could call *democratic* moments can arise, where teachers and pupils are exposed to each other as equals in relation to a book, a text, a thing". However, the reality of many educational institutions is different and although, paradoxically, they are designed for children, the opinions and postulates of the youngest usually give way to the "wisdom" of the elderly, i.e. the teachers. According to Rancière (1991), such a situation results from a pedagogical myth that there are two types of intelligence at school: an inferior and a superior one. The first, in principle, is typical for pupils, who have less knowledge and experience. The second characterises teachers, whose knowledge and experience are greater, which makes their views more important than those of the pupils and that is the reason why they occupy a privileged position in educational institutions.

The existing inequality between the position of the pupil and the teacher in preschool, as well as in school, is related to inclusive and exclusionary practices concerning the child's voice and its meaning (Warzecha, 2002; Friedman et al., 2004). Inclusive practices are based on the approach and methods used by teachers, which involve providing all pupils with access to and full participation in education. Myck-Wayne and Pierson (2019), referring to the inclusive practices concerning children with disabilities, claim that these activities enable pupils to practice independence. Ensuring the implementation of Article 12 of the UNCRC by including the voices of all children in the main discourse of preschool enables them to have a sense of agency. It is important to support children's development so that they may reach their full potential (Article 29 of the UNCRC).

Exclusionary practices result in a lack of effective participation of pupils in the educational environment. They include actions taken by teachers to exclude certain persons or groups (pupils) from a particular environment or certain practices. According to Razer et al. (2013), such actions lead to pupils' failure and anxiety, which have repercussions on the teachers who use exclusionary practices, causing them to have similar feelings. This creates a cycle of exclusion, which can have serious consequences in terms of helplessness and lack of support, both among pupils and teachers.

Both inclusive and exclusionary practices take place in preschool. The scope of their application largely depends on the views of a teacher and the culture of a given educational institution (Babicka-Wirkus, 2019; Sargeant & Gillett-Swan, 2019). In many Polish schools this culture is based on the exclusion of the child's voice from important aspects of these institutions, as it is based on a popular Polish saying: *children and fish have no voice*[1] (Babicka-Wirkus, 2018, p. 63). This proverb reflects the approach of many social circles to the views of children, which are often irrelevant to the decisions made by adults and teachers (Babicka-Wirkus, 2018).

The child's right to express their views is not a privilege that can be taken away. Instead, it is a claim that must be respected by States Parties and adults. Referring to Rancière's (2004) concept of the *distribution of the sensible*, this right, as well as many other children's rights, is often part of what is not visible in the dominant discourse of educational institutions. According to Rancière (2004, p. 14), "distribution of the sensible is the system of the self-evident fact of sense perception that simultaneously discloses the existence of something in common and the

[1] English equivalent: Children should be seen and not heard.

delimitations that define the respective parts and position within it". The distribution of the sensible is a process of distribution of space, time, places, identities, a meaningful voice and noise, something that is visible, and something invisible (Rancière, 1999, 2004). Through this practice, what is shared and what is excluded are established at the same time. Thus, the distribution of the sensible corresponds to inclusive and exclusionary practices in preschool and school.

In Rancière's theory (1999), the force behind the distribution of the sensible is the police, which is responsible for establishing the distribution of the sensible and for preventing its potential changes. In educational institutions, this police order is often represented by teachers whose attitude towards their pupil is based on the perception of the child as an incomplete subject – the learner (Biesta, 2011), whose views are not taken into account when deciding on important aspects of preschool or school operations. However, there are also transformative teachers working in educational institutions who, through their actions, distort the established process of the distribution of the sensible (Babicka-Wirkus, 2019). Teachers play a significant role in introducing children into the role of active and conscious citizens. Education for democracy and in democracy, by creating an appropriate environment in the first stages of formal education, is crucial for the development of critically thinking and acting subjects/citizens, which is one of the main international educational aims (Article 29 of the UNCRC). In this context, teachers' attitudes towards respecting children's right to speak are crucial as they are the basis for the design and implementation of the education and learning process of young people. Experiencing the work of transformative teachers, who are sensitive to the pupil's voice (Fielding, 2004), by student teachers is an important element in developing their views on the role and place of the child and the child's voice in education.

Methodological Background

This chapter focuses on a part of a larger project that investigated children's rights in everyday preschool life and the dilemmas of student teachers related to respecting children's rights.[2] The aim of this study was to recognise the meanings that student teachers of early childhood and elementary education give to children's rights and the role these rights play in everyday preschool life. The issue of reviewing the respondents' knowledge of children's rights was also significant. For this reason, a qualitative approach was adopted in the study, which allowed to identify the student teachers' real opinions and views on this matter (Creswell & Creswell, 2017). In order to fulfil the above-mentioned objectives, the participants were asked for written answers to the following questions: What is your attitude to the saying "children and fish have no voice"? How often does this reflect in the preschool

[2] The study was conducted in June 2017 by Maria Groenwald from the University of Gdańsk and the author of this article.

training?; What do children's rights mean to you?; In your opinion, which children's rights are most significant in preschool and early school training?

The student teachers wrote down the answers to the above-mentioned questions, which were read out to them at intervals. Thus, they did not know all the questions right from the beginning of the study, so that their answers would not be influenced by other questions. By answering the questions, the student teachers described the practices that they encountered during their training in preschools. The descriptions of their experiences reflected the discourse of children's rights that shapes relations in preschools. This chapter presents only a fragment of this discourse, which refers to the inclusive and exclusionary practices concerning the child's voice in preschool.

The research was conducted at two Polish universities. The research group consisted of 76 female student teachers of the following specialisations: early childhood education (51 student teachers from the University of Gdańsk) and elementary education (26 student teachers from the Pomeranian University in Słupsk) who had completed at least one professional training in a preschool. The respondents were students of pedagogical studies, the completion of which results in the acquisition of competences at level 6 or 7 of the Polish Qualification Framework.

Two groups of data were analysed. One group consisted of the statements made by the student teachers, through which they expressed their views on the child's right to freedom of speech in the preschool environment. The second group consisted of the student teachers' statements concerning some situations of respecting and disrespecting children's right to express themselves. Based on the analysis of the statements from the second group of data, practices that are inclusive and exclusionary to the child's voice were reconstructed. They are analysed in this chapter.

The collected empirical material was subjected to a qualitative analysis of the text. A coding strategy that is typical for grounded theory methodology (Charmaz, 2006) was used. The first stage consisted of an initial coding of the respondents' statements line by line. Next, concentrated coding was performed to synthesise and explain larger data segments (Charmaz, 2006). The next stage consisted of focused coding, which allows combining categories with subcategories (Strauss & Corbin, 1998). This type of coding makes it possible to specify the properties and dimensions of the selected categories. The last step was theoretical coding. The use of these codes allows to determine the relationship between the codes built during concentrated coding (Charmaz, 2006). The application of the coding procedure allowed to capture the inclusive and exclusionary practices concerning the child's voice in preschool presented by the respondents.

Distribution of the Child's Voice in Preschool

In preschools, as in other educational institutions, there are mechanisms for the distribution of children's voices which, in many cases, lead to disregarding and excluding unwanted or uncomfortable expressions of their needs by adults (Jones & Welch, 2010; Potter & Whittaker, 2011; Razer et al., 2013). Based on the respondents' statements concerning the preschool reality in this aspect, the perceptions of preschool teachers about children which justify underestimating and disregarding preschoolers' views have been identified. These ideas are based on the assumption that preschoolers are not independent in their thinking, have no life experience or knowledge, and do not have mature views. Thus, preschoolers cannot have opinions which would be significant for the decisions made by adults in matters concerning these children. This finding is consistent with other studies on the significance of pupils' voices (Jones & Welch, 2010; Kilkelly et al., 2005).

Another perception of teachers concerning preschoolers, which was emphasised by the respondents, is perceiving the child's voice as lacking value. Therefore, children's attempts to express their views and their displays of free expression are seen as noise. Freedom of children's expression disturbs the calm and planned course of the class and is therefore undesirable for teachers. Consequently, from the very beginning of the institutional educational process, teachers try to teach children the rules for speaking in class, which impose a framework of control over the frequency and quality of the statements made by preschoolers.

The respondents also mentioned that preschool teachers ignore preschoolers' expression, especially if it is an expression of opposition or resistance. Not paying attention to or disregarding the displays of disagreement closes the path to discussion and is a practice that maintains and reproduces the discourse that dominates preschools or school.

Such an approach to preschoolers' views allows the use of different practices to exclude their voices from the educational discourse. Based on the analysis of the respondents' statements, the following exclusionary practices were identified: blocking the child's voice (including silencing, delaying, hampering), disregarding the child's voice (including not listening, ignoring, belittling), and not informing the children about their rights (Table 13.1).

Table 13.1 Exclusionary practices of the child's voice – examples of the respondents' statements

Exclusionary practice of the child's voice	Examples of statements
Blocking the child's voice	During my practice, when a pupil wanted to say something, I often heard the teachers say, for example: "Not now", "Later", "Be quiet", "Pay attention to the lesson", "I will not listen to it now", "Go to your break" (SUG10). In preschool, I met with the fact that children could not show their observations and were quickly "extinguished", which demotivated them very much (SUG11).
Disregarding the child's voice	One may often encounter teachers ignoring the needs expressed by children in preschool: (…) Parents do not listen to their kids, either. The children speak, the parents nod and nothing else happens (SUG25). Often in preschool, you can encounter teachers' ignorance of the needs that children are signalling (SAP26).
Not informing the children about their rights	Adults, unfortunately, do not inform children about them [children's rights]. They do not respect them and do not take them seriously (…) (SUG31).

Each of the exclusionary practices is an element of the silence training, which aims at silencing and subjugating the natural expressions of children. This leads to forced silence and, as Bligh (2011) points out, it should be considered the child's right, not an obligation, to choose to be silent. The right to silence derives from the right to freely express oneself. However, the normalisation of children's forced silence in educational institutions makes it the norm for the child to be quiet, obedient and passive. This practice strengthens the hegemony of the adult voice which claims the exclusive right to create the prevailing discourse in preschool. While there may be several reasons for using the practices that exclude the child's voice from the everyday preschool discourse by teachers, previous research in the Polish context determined the following ones: it is a convenient solution for teachers, they gain the approval and respect of other adults (superiors, colleagues, parents), they meet the expectations of their pupils' parents, they have insufficient knowledge about children's rights (Babicka-Wirkus & Groenwald, 2018).

Based on the respondents' statements, the practices of including children's voices were also distinguished. These activities are based on respecting the voice of each child and treating it seriously. These practices include: active listening to children, treating their statements as a source of information about their lives, and indicating socially established limits and possible consequences of actions (Table 13.2).

The first inclusive practice concerning children's voice is active listening, which is based not so much on hearing as on listening to children and communicating honestly and openly with them (McLamon, 2008; MacNaughton et al., 2003). Active listening is about enabling children to participate, and putting their ideas and solutions into practice. Active listening is important for the child's sense of agency (Ribaeus & Skånfors, 2019). In the literature on the importance of the child's voice, studies on the process of consulting pupils play an important role (McCluskey et al., 2013; McIntyre et al., 2005; Rodgers, 2018; Rudduck, 2007) since they emphasise

Table 13.2 Inclusive practices concerning the child's voice – examples of the respondents' statements

Inclusive practices of children's voice	Examples of statements
Active listening to children	Generally, at work (…), I always try to listen to children who want to tell me about something. I believe that allowing children to speak and learning to listen to them are important features in a teacher's work (SUG39). Always try to listen to what a child has to say (SAP18).
Treating their statements as a source of information about their lives	By allowing children to express themselves we get to know them and therefore it becomes possible to prepare better classes designed for the pupils, their interests and preferences (SUG51).
Indicating socially established limits and possible consequences of actions	Children have the right to decide, and adults are there to show them the boundaries that exist in the normal world (SUG28). Each child should freely express their opinion and it is not stupid. Adults may only help children and make them aware of the consequences (SUG29).

the importance of this practice in strengthening the position of the child in educational institutions as an active creator of change.

Another inclusive practice concerning children's voices is treating the expression of preschoolers as a source of knowledge about them and their life. McLaren (1999) emphasises this aspect, pointing out that children have their history and biography, which they express through various everyday acts. Therefore, teachers should be more attentive and take the child's silence seriously because sometimes more information is conveyed through silence than through words.

Respect for the child's right to free expression of thoughts, views and opinions in preschool is also of great importance for the proper socialization of young children. Through self-expression, preschoolers learn about the existing norms and rules. They are familiar with the rules of social acceptance and learn to interpret and break them. At the same time, by expressing themselves, they learn to deal with social consequences (Howe & Cowell, 2010; James & James, 2012; Perry-Hazan, 2015), which leads to the development of responsibility for their actions.

Discussion

The distinguished inclusive and exclusionary practices concerning the child's voice in preschool are elements of the process of the distribution of voices in this educational space. The mechanism of the distribution of the sensible, described by Rancière (2004), establishes what is visible, audible, and possible, and what is invisible, inaudible, and impossible. The distribution of the sensible has an inclusive and exclusionary sense. At the same time, it defines what is common and shared, and what is not.

Rancière (1999) stresses that distributing the sensible is the order of those who are visible and have a meaningful voice. They decide who is allowed to create social discourse, and who is not. This practice, which is also typical of early childhood education institutions, amounts to recognising some voices (views, opinions of teachers) as based on *logos*, and others (children attending preschool) as 'clattering' – not worthy of attention because they stem from an animal desire to express pleasure or pain.[3] Therefore, there is no point in having discussions with those who do not speak, but who only yammer, making meaningless noise. They represent the *demos* (people), deprived of the right to decide about the shape of reality.

In the space of preschool life, *demos* refers to preschoolers, who usually do not have the right to decide what happens in their preschool, or this right is somehow limited. Sometimes they are given a substitute (illusion, delusion) for participation but it often amounts to some minor aspects of life in the institution, such as the

[3] At this point, Rancière refers to Aristotle, who assumed that man, as the only living creature, had the ability to speak. Voice, on the one hand, is an animal trait and is used to communicate pleasant or unpleasant states. Speech, on the other hand, is a more complex tool and is used to define what is useful and harmful or what is just and unjust. See Aristotle (1996).

appearance of thematic newspapers, or topics of games, which take place outside the strict control of their teachers (Simó Gil et al., 2017). Teachers' actions, which are about disregarding or pretending to listen to children, are examples of excluding children from the preschool issues that are important to them (Jones & Welch, 2010). Underestimating the views of children reveals the pretence that, according to the myths created by these institutions, it is to contribute to the full development of young people. Another consequence of such practices is silencing children. This is a dangerous mechanism which leads to the effective exclusion of children, then young people, and then adults from active participation in social life. Individuals who are effectively discouraged from an early age to use their voice (Giroux, 2001) do not see the need to oppose it if necessary.

Listening to the child's voice changes the child's status in relation to their teacher. This leads to the equality of intelligence between the teacher and the pupil (Rancière, 1991). In such a situation, the role of the teacher is to require the pupil to make an effort and to verify whether this effort has been made. As Biesta (2011, p. 35) stresses, "the one who is the subject of education is summoned to *study* and thus, in the most literal sense, has become a *pupil*". Therefore, it is about a certain process of studying, learning about reality, which is characteristic not only to adults but also to children. Rancière, however, notices the problematic nature of studying and indicates that pupils will "study the explanations of others" (1991, p. 59) and not follow their own reasoning. According to Rancière (1999), the key to the real development of individuals is the use of their voice, since in the act of speaking the individuals do not transmit knowledge, but create it. Therefore, it is essential for the empowerment of children in preschool, and at every stage of their education, to have a real voice. What is more, it goes beyond the traditionally imposed types of relationship between the pupil and the teacher in which the pupil is seen as a passive consumer and the teacher — as an active knowledge provider (Jones & Welch, 2010).

Conclusions

The issue of inclusive and exclusionary practice concerning children's voice depends, to a large extent, on the approach of adults (teachers) to this matter. This is a difficult issue because it requires adults to renounce their privileged position (Babicka-Wirkus, 2019; Jerome, 2012). Respect for the child's right to express their opinion is crucial for the individual and social development of young people and for overcoming barriers blocking their equal participation in social life (especially those attributes that place them in an unprivileged position, for example, race, gender, disability). Only by speaking out actively can one break stereotypes and prejudices and initiate new ways of thinking. Marshall (2006, p. 1) states that "change happens, when those who don't usually speak are heard by those who don't usually listen". Acknowledging the child's voice is crucial for the development of their subjectivity and for the changes in preschools and schools, which are constantly criticised, but are not subject to deeper changes. Therefore, it is crucial to pay attention to the educational process and the views of student teachers on the rights of the child. Preparing students of pedagogy to implement education based on the rights of the child in their future work in educational institutions will contribute to the implementation of Article 29 of UNCRC and the creation of a human rights culture in preschools and schools (Brantefors et al., 2019).

References

Aristotle. (1996). *Politics. Books I and II* (T. J. Sanders, Trans.). Oxford, UK: Oxford University Press.

Babicka-Wirkus, A. (2018). Democracy and children's right to self- expression in lower secondary school. *Voces de la Educación, número especial*, 61–74. https://hal.archives-ouvertes.fr/hal-02523862/document

Babicka-Wirkus, A. (2019). Children's rights and human rights as a key condition for the education of transformative teachers. In M. Kowalczuk-Walędziak et al. (Eds.), *Rethinking teacher education for the 21st century. Trends, challenges and new directions* (pp. 239–252). Verlag Barbara Budrich.

Babicka-Wirkus, A., & Groenwald, M. (2018). Głos dziecka w przedszkolu – między swobodą wypowiedzi a milczeniem [Child's voice in kindergarten – Between freedom of speech and silence]. *Problemy wczesnej edukacji, 1*(40), 95–104.

Biesta, G. (2011). Lerner, student, speaker: Why it matters how we call those we teach. In M. Simons & J. Masschelein (Eds.), *Rancière, public education and the taming of democracy* (pp. 31–42). Wiley-Blackwell.

Bligh, C. (2011). Rights in early years settings and a young child's right to silence. In P. Jones & G. Walker (Eds.), *Children's rights in practice* (pp. 95–108). Sage.

Brantefors, L., Tellgren, B., & Thelander, N. (2019). Human rights education as democratic education. The teaching traditions of children's human rights in Swedish early childhood education and school. *The International Journal of Children's Rights, 27*(4), 694–718. https://doi.org/10.1163/15718182-02704007

Charmaz, K. (2006). *Constructing grounded theory. A practical guide through qualitative analysis*. Sage.

Creswell, J. W., & Creswell, J. D. (2017). *Research design. Qualitative, quantitative and mixed methods approaches* (5th ed.). Sage.

Fielding, M. (2004). Transformative approaches to student voice: Theoretical underpinnings, recalcitrant realities. *British Educational Research Journal, 30*(2), 295–311. https://doi.org/10.1080/0141192042000195236

Friedman, V., Razer, M., & Sykes, I. (2004). Towards a theory of inclusive practice: An action science approach. *Action Research, 2*(2), 167–189. https://doi.org/10.1177/1476750304043729

Giroux, H. A. (2001). *Theory and resistance in education: Towards a pedagogy for the oppression*. Bergin & Garvey.

Harris, P., & Manatakis, H. (2013). *Children's voices. A principled framework for children and young people's participation as valued citizens and learners*. Government of South Australia. https://www.education.sa.gov.au/sites/default/files/childrens-voices-framework.pdf?acsf_files_redirect; https://www.decd.sa.gov.au/sites/g/files/net691/f/childrens-voices-framework.pdf. Accessed 11 Aug 2017.

Howe, B. R., & Cowell, K. (2010). Miseducation children about their right. *Education, Citizenship and Social Justice, 5*(2), 91–102. https://doi.org/10.1177/1746197910370724

James, A., & James, A. (2012). *Key concepts in childhood studies* (2nd ed.). Sage.

Jerome, L. (2012). Children's rights and teachers' responsibilities. A case study of developing a rights respecting initial teacher education programme. In R. C. Mitchell & S. A. Moore (Eds.), *Policies, participation & power relations* (pp. 101–117). Sense Publishers.
Jones, P., & Welch, S. (2010). *Rethinking children's rights. Attitudes in contemporary society*. Continuum.
Kilkelly, U., Kilpatrick, R., Lundy, L., Moore, L., Scraton, P., Davey, C., Dwyer, C., & McAlister, S. (2005). *Children's rights in Northern Ireland*. NICCY and Queens' University of Belfast.
Lansdown, G. (2011). *Every child's right to be heard. A resource guide on the UN Committee on the Rights of the child general comment no.12*. UNICEF. The Save the Children Foundation. https://www.unicef.org/french/adolescence/files/Every_Childs_Right_to_be_Heard.pdf. Accessed 25 Feb 2019.
Lewis, A. (2010). Silence in the context of 'child voice'. *Children & Society, 24*(1), 14–23. https://doi.org/10.1111/j.1099-0860.2008.00200.x
Lundy, L. (2007). "Voice" is not enough: Conceptualizing article 12 of the United Nations Convention on the Rights of the Child. *British Educational Research Journal, 33*(6), 927–942. https://doi.org/10.1080/01411920701657033
MacNaughton, G., Smith, K., & Lawrence, H. (2003). *Hearing young children's voices. ACT children's strategy: Consulting with children birth to eight years of age*. Parkville, Australia, Centre for Equity and Innovation in Early Childhood, Faculty of Education, The University of Melbourne, https://pdfs.semanticscholar.org/f339/e6fa99aa3c57e446a7df58deaa16431d5a18.pdf. Accessed 20 Oct 2017.
Marshall, K. (2006). Children's voices – Early years. In Learning and Teaching Scotland (Ed.), *Let's talk about listening to children: Towards a shared understanding for early years education in Scotland perspective series, 2* (pp. 1–8). Learning and Teaching Scotland.
Masschelein, J., & Simons, M. (2011). The hatred of public schooling: The school as the mark of democracy. In M. Simons & J. Masschelein (Eds.), *Rancière, public education and the taming of democracy* (pp. 31–42). Wiley-Blackwell.
McCluskey, G., Brown, J., Munn, P., Lloyd, G., Hamilton, L., Sharp, S., & Macleod, G. (2013). "Take more time to actually listen": Students' reflections on participation and negotiation in school. *British Educational Research Journal, 39*(2), 287–301. https://doi.org/10.1080/01411926.2012.659720
McIntyre, D., Pedder, D., & Rudduck, J. (2005). Pupil voice: Comfortable and uncomfortable learnings for teachers. *Research Papers in Education, 20*(2), 149–168. https://doi.org/10.1080/02671520500077970
McLamon, J. (2008). *Listening as a way of life – Supporting parents and carers to listen: A guide for practitioners*. National Children's Bureau/DCSF.
McLaren, P. (1999). *Schooling as a ritual performance. Toward political economy of educational symbols and gestures* (3rd ed.). Rowman & Littlefield Publishers, Inc.
Messiou, K., & Ainscow, M. (2015). Responding to learner diversity: Student views as a catalyst for powerful teacher development? *Teaching and Teacher Education, 51*, 246–255. https://doi.org/10.1016/j.tate.2015.07.002
Myck-Wayne, J., & Pierson, M. R. (2019). Inclusive practice for all: Child perspectives. In V. Margrain & A. Löfdahl Hultman (Eds.), *Challenging democracy in early childhood education, international perspectives on early childhood education and development, 28* (pp. 197–211). Springer Nature.
Osler, A., & Starkey, H. (2010). *Teachers and human rights education*. Institute of Education Press.
Perry-Hazan, L. (2015). Freedom of speech in schools and the right to participation: When the first amendment encounters the convention on the rights of the child. *Brigham Young University Education and Law Journal, 2*, 421–452.
Potter, C., & Whittaker, C. (2011). What does the 'voice of the child' mean for children with complex learning and communication impairments? In P. Jones & G. Walker (Eds.), *Children's rights in practice* (pp. 82–94). Sage.

Rancière, J. (1991). *The ignorant schoolmaster. Five lessons in intellectual emancipation* (K. Ross, Trans.). Stanford, CA: Stanford University Press.
Rancière, J. (1999). *Dis-agreement: Politics and philosophy* (K. Ross, Trans.). Minneapolis & St Paul, MN: University of Minnesota.
Rancière, J. (2004). *The politics of aesthetics: The distribution of the sensible* (G. Rockhill, Trans.). New York: Continuum.
Razer, M., Friedman, V. J., & Warshofsky, B. (2013). Schools as agents of social exclusion and inclusion. *International Journal of Inclusive Education, 17*(11), 1152–1170. https://doi.org/10.1080/13603116.2012.742145
Ribaeus, K., & Skånfors, L. (2019). Preschool children as democratic subjects: Agents of democracy. In V. Margrain & A. Löfdahl Hultman (Eds.), *Challenging democracy in early childhood education, international perspectives on early childhood education and development,28* (pp. 233–245). Springer Nature.
Rodgers, C. (2018). Descriptive feedback: Student voice in K-5 classrooms. *Australian Educational Review, 45*(4), 87–102. https://doi.org/10.1007/s13384-018-0263-1
Rudduck, J. (2007). Student voice, student engagement, and school reform. In D. Thiessen & A. Cook-Sather (Eds.), *International handbook of student experience in elementary and secondary school* (pp. 587–610). Springer.
Sargeant, J., & Gillett-Swan, J. K. (2019). Voice-inclusive practice (VIP): A charter for authentic student engagement. *The International Journal of Children's Rights, 27*(1), 122–139. https://doi.org/10.1163/15718182-02701002
Simó Gil, N., Parareda Pallarès, A., & Tellado, I. (2017). Learning democracy in schools: Experiences towards an active citizenship education. *Social Studies: Theory and Practice, 3*(2), 63–79.
Strauss, A., & Corbin, J. (1998). *Basic of qualitative research: Grounded theory procedures and techniques* (2nd ed.). Sage.
United Nations. (1989). *Convention on the rights of the child.* Retrieved June 21, 2018, from: https://www.ohchr.org/en/professionalinterest/pages/crc.aspx
United Nations. (2001). *Committee on the Rights of the Child, General Comment no. 1. The Aims of Education (CRC/GC/2001/1).* United Nations.
United Nations. (2009). *Committee on the Rights of the Child, General Comment no. 12, The right of the child to be heard (CRC/C/GC/12).* United Nations.
Warzecha, B. (2002). Teaching and learning at the limit institutional and social processes of disintegration with the school age young people in Hamburg. *British Journal for Learning Support, 17*(2), 16–21.

Chapter 14
How to Recognise and Support Participation in Schools: Critical Considerations

Tomi Kiilakoski and Reetta Niemi

Abstract Right to be heard is one of the four guiding principles of the Convention on the Rights of the Child. Building schools that are child-friendly in the fullest sense of the term requires promoting participatory school culture. In schools, participation is both a method and a goal. There is a need to promote participation methods that actively seek the opinions of the child, and also to find ways of listening to these opinions carefully. In this chapter, concrete, practical steps for recognising participation, and difficulties in doing so are analysed. Pitfalls in evaluating and recognising participation as a lived experience in classrooms and how children and teachers can work together to create a participatory working environment are considered. Using the theory of practice architectures, we analyse how creating participatory spaces requires changing the way we talk, think, do and relate to others. Using the methodology of pedagogical action research, we show what happens when an individual teacher wants to examine and develop their classroom practices together with pupils.

Keywords Participation · Practice architectures · Finland · Classrooms · Teachers

T. Kiilakoski (✉)
Leading Senior Researcher, Finnish Youth Research Network, Helsinki, Finland
e-mail: tomi.kiilakoski@youthresearch.fi

R. Niemi
Lecturer, Viikki Teacher Training School, University of Helsinki, Helsinki, Finland

Research Associate, South Africa Research Chair: Learning Language Science and Mathematics in the Primary School, University of Johannesburg, Johannesburg, South Africa
e-mail: reetta.niemi@helsinki.fi

J. Gillett-Swan, N. Thelander (eds.), *Children's Rights from International Educational Perspectives*, Transdisciplinary Perspectives in Educational Research 2, https://doi.org/10.1007/978-3-030-80861-7_14

Introduction

Finland has enjoyed considerable success in PISA[1] studies. Its educational model is said to be a paradigmatic example of a well-built educational system based on egalitarian principles (Sahlberg, 2011). However, the perspective of children as rights holders instead of duty bearers in school has not been adopted automatically. It is estimated that children's rights are not taken into account in the way schooling is organised (Hakalehto, 2015), and that there is a lack of information, theories and practices on how to better integrate children's rights into education.

Finland is not alone in this. The ways the building blocks of school cultures or practice architectures of education (Kemmis et al., 2014; Kemmis & Edwards-Groves, 2018) are organised are based on different principles than respecting the rights of the child. It is commonplace to argue that the principle of pedagogical authority is more common than the relatively recent emphasis on children's rights. This notion is highlighted by the Committee on the Rights of the Child, stating:

> Children do not lose their human rights by virtue of passing through the school gates. Thus, for example, education must be provided in a way that respects the inherent dignity of the child and enables the child to express his or her views freely in accordance with article 12 (1) and to participate in school life (United Nations, 2001, §8).

Educational institutions have a long history. They have been formed to contribute to the socialisation process in which the new generations learn how to take part in the economy, civil society and politics. Educational policies have been more interested in thinking about how children may become part of the existing order, rather than how children may learn how to change that order and how to express their views on all the matters affecting them. The Committee on the Rights of the Child strongly emphasises that schools are not isolated islands, and that they too must honour participation rights. The aim of education is to build schools that are child-friendly in the fullest sense of the term. This requires, among other things, promoting participatory school culture (United Nations, 2001, §8). The committee's critique of education emphasises that schools need to rethink and renew their practices to build a participatory atmosphere.

Respecting the views of the child is one of the general principles of the United Nations Convention on the Rights of the Child (UNCRC) (United Nations, 1989). As such, they should be taken into consideration in all of the activities affecting the child that are organised by public powers. The provisions of the UNCRC are interconnected. General principles such as the right to express views and have them taken into account, have weight in education and fall broadly within the 'participatory' provisions of the Convention. Participation is also connected to other goals of the treaty: "child participation is a tool to stimulate the full development of the personality and the evolving capacities of the child" (United Nations, 2009, §79). There are of course other aspects to be considered to ensure the full realisation of

[1] Programme for International Student Assessment (PISA).

this right and finding the proper balance between different provisions is required. Historically, participation has not been emphasised in schools. Therefore, it is not surprising that the Committee on the Rights of the Child has taken a strong stance on promoting participation when discussing education.

Participation is one of the principles school work should be based on. It is one of the principles that should govern schooling, and it has implications for teaching methods as well. This is not the end of the story, though. Besides being a method, participation is a goal as well, since "[t]he overall objective of education is to maximise the child's ability and opportunity to participate fully and responsibly in a free society" (United Nations, 2001, §12). According to UNICEF's *Handbook of Children's Rights* (UNICEF Finland, 2011), this involves promoting health education, global education and anti-racism, but it also involves a democratic component. Social responsibility and active participation in the democratic processes should be taught in schools (UNICEF Finland, 2011, p. 325).

Participation is required on many levels in education. Turning this into practice is not an easy task, especially given the fact that schools are traditionally based on adults' power instead of participatory, dialogical culture (Kiilakoski, 2017). Learning from rights-based approaches is a multi-faceted enterprise, since "a rights-based construct of participation requires that children's views are not only sought actively but are also listened to and taken seriously. What is also significant is the way in which these views are sought and how children's autonomy is balanced with support from adults in forming and expressing their views" (Emerson & Lloyd, 2017, p. 123). To achieve this in schools, methods are needed that actively seek the opinions of the child, and also find ways of listening to these opinions carefully. Studying the effectiveness and quality of different methods for recognising and promoting participation in schools is relevant for evaluating how well educational institutions are able to fulfil their role as supporters and nurturers of a child's growth as both a person and a citizen. In this article, concrete, practical steps for recognising participation are analysed, and difficulties in doing so are also examined. Both of these projects involve difficulties that highlight how the professional role of teachers and practice architectures of schooling influence the ways things can be done. By doing this, we suggest that promoting participation requires analysing activities and also learning from mistakes. The following questions are examined;

1. What pitfalls are there in evaluating and recognising participation as a lived experience in classrooms and the wider school community?
2. How can children and teachers work together to create a participatory working environment?

The remainder of the chapter elaborates on key concepts, practice architectures and participation. Then we describe how understanding participation, doing things in a participatory manner and changing the power relations inside the classroom happened simultaneously in our study.[2]

Practice Architectures of Schools

According to critics, rights-based approaches are new in education, and require changing the current practices (Hakalehto, 2015). Seeing children as rights holders instead of learners, pupils, or clients will likely create pressures to renew the current pedagogical principles and activities. The need for renewal applies to the work of individual teachers and the school culture as a whole.

To further analyse how schools can respond to the increasing demand to promote children's rights, a theoretical perspective on school practices is needed. We will draw on the theory of practice architectures developed by educational philosopher Stephen Kemmis and his colleagues (Kemmis et al., 2014). According to this perspective, all of the practices are socially shared, they require co-operation, they have a history that influences but does not determine the present and they are based on a project that ultimately has an ethical core. Members of the practice are affected and to some extent shaped by the way these practices are organised (Kemmis & Edwards-Groves, 2018). The practices are connected to wider settings (the practice of education), but they always have a local dimension as well. In the context of schools, the "living practice of teaching — like all the practices — only happens in some site, at some time, and it is enmeshed with the local and particular practice architectures of that site" (Kemmis et al., 2014, p. 125). To understand how certain practices might be developed, it is necessary to look at events in a certain site, with certain children, in a school culture that may or may not support participation.

According to the theory of practice architectures, there are three categories of preconditions for practices. These preconditions make the project of practices possible. There are cultural-discursive arrangements of the site (sayings) that make language and specialist discourses of the site possible. These arrangements affect how pupils and teachers talk in the classroom, but also how teachers talk about students, children's rights and the overall aims of schooling. Secondly, there are material-economic arrangements. Schooling is always related to school buildings, the way classrooms are shaped and how schools are located in the local community. Different doings are possible because there is some sort of organisation of physical space, there are material possibilities and resources are allocated. Thirdly, there are social-political arrangements that affect how the issues of power and solidarity are shaped in certain practices. This brings about different relatings between teachers and students, between the school and the wider community and between teachers and parents (Kemmis & Edwards-Groves, 2018).

[2] Our chapter is a joint effort written by a youth researcher who also has a role in developing policy (Author 1) and a teacher-researcher (Author 2) who has a long history in analysing school practice.

These three aspects — sayings, doings and relatings — are intertwined, and they affect each other dynamically. Different configurations are brought about because in every practice, these aspects "hang together" (Kemmis & Edwards-Groves, 2018, p. 121) in a certain manner. For example, some schools may concentrate on sports, whereas others may be inclined to develop friendships and peer relations.

The theory of practice architectures pays attention to local realities and wider cultural resources that affect the practice of teaching. When a rights-based approach is developed in schools, the current practice architectures shape how the promotion of human rights can actually be done. The theory is also a reminder that reforming practices is affected by all three sets of arrangements. Therefore, changing only the way human rights are talked about is likely not enough, since other arrangements, such as how children's rights are respected and enforced in the daily realities of schooling and how the adult community in schools relates to children, also frame the way practices actually work. In the latter part of the chapter, we analyse how these dimensions may be developed simultaneously. Before that, we briefly introduce the way we understand participation.

Participation

Participation is an important concept, especially in Finland, where the term 'hearing' is usually synonymous with participation. Participation is a hot topic in most of the child services, including social work, education, youth work, urban planning and health services. Despite the frequent use of the concept, there is no shared understanding of what participation actually is. In this regard, it has lot of similarities to other vague but powerful political concepts, such as 'sustainable development'. Participation has been used for different political purposes, and the concept has been described as being blurry (Kaukko, 2015, p. 42).

Because of the vague nature of participation, it is necessary to define the concept. Based on our earlier research, we understand participation as having three necessary but insufficient conditions. Firstly, participation requires having a recognised and legitimate role in the community. The recognition needs to be both formal and informal. If children are not sure of their role, they can oppose it or rebel, but it may be hard to find a constructive role (although refusing to act is in some cases a necessary act of participation). Secondly, there needs to be action. If children have a role in schools – for example, as members of the student council – but the structure does not encourage any action, there is no participation. Thirdly, action has to feel meaningful for the participants, and there has to be a feeling of participation (Kiilakoski et al., 2012). As is evident, we view participation as a relation between an individual and a larger entity, such as a peer group, class, school, community, town, society or ecosystem. If all three conditions have been realised, participation is considered a process instead of a formal structure or a singular event.

We hold that participation needs to have a political component (being able to decide and act) and a social component (being a member of a group, a feeling of

Table 14.1 Practice architectures of participation

Practices found in schools	Conditions of participation Recognised role	Action	Feeling of participation
Sayings	It is clearly spelt out that pupils have a right to contribute.	Pupils' ideas are taken seriously, and they are further developed dialogically.	The action is verbalised afterwards.
Doings	Pupils are supported and encouraged to take initiative.	Pupils can do things based on their ideas either on their own or with adults.	Pupils have room to remember and share what happened and how it felt.
Relatings	Power is shared.	There is social cohesion that supports the action.	There is social cognition and mutual dependence after having worked together.

belonging). This dual-sided nature of citizenship and solidarity is, we feel, expressed by Article 29 of the Convention of the Rights of the Child (United Nations, 1989), which states that education should be directed towards "the preparation of the child for responsible life in a free society, in the spirit of understanding, peace, tolerance, equality of sexes, and friendship among all peoples, ethnic, national and religious groups and persons of indigenous origin".

If schools are to promote participation, the practice architectures need to support the promotion of participation in sayings, doings and relatings. Our position is summarised in Table 14.1 above. We do not wish to imply that the following actions should be carried out in all cases, but we wish to point out the ideal state of affairs based on our understanding.

Understanding the Practice

The data for our empirical cases was collected at Viikki Teacher Training School, Helsinki, Finland. A total of 21 pupils (11 girls and 10 boys) and one teacher participated in the first substudy (Case 1). The data collection for this case took place in autumn 2016. At the time of the research, the pupils were in the second grade (approximately 8 years old). Case 2 represents actions that developed in two separate action research cycles that took place in the same classroom in spring 2018 and autumn 2018. By that time, the number of pupils had grown to 25 (13 girls and 12 boys). The "I" in the practical sections described below is the voice of the teacher-researcher, because she is the only author who has had a connection to the students. She implemented these actions as part of her own research project. The use of the first-person singular is also meant to highlight the deeply individual, situational an even embodied knowledge of the teacher. The "we" in this chapter represents our joint interpretations to analyse participation, which we both feel strongly about. Since we hold that all the schools have unique practice architectures, we want to emphasise that at the end of the day, it is all about particular people working in concrete sites instead of abstract principles.

In this study, pupils' participation is firstly an essential component of our methodological approach. We collected the empirical data by following the principles defined for pedagogical action research, which is a specific form of teacher-research (Niemi, 2019a). The core of the methodology of pedagogical action research is supporting pupils' agency. This methodology, first and foremost, tries to construct ways of capturing pupils' perspectives and change classroom practices based on pupils' views. Our study followed that principle: its' goal was to work with pupils, to see them as co-researchers and to support their sense of agency through data collection. In this study, we created and used various visual methods and interviews as tools to listen to the pupils' perspectives.

I also took ethical considerations carefully into account, as outlined in Niemi (2019a). I asked the pupils' parents for their permission to join the study. The pupils were aware of the data collection by the time it took place. They were also aware of their right not to join in the data collection without any consequences. The data collection process was implemented during an ordinary school day with the devices the school provided to us; it did not cause the pupils any extra work, and it was connected to the goals set in the curriculum (Finnish National Board of Education [FNBE], 2014) by improving pupils' transversal competences. This chapter was also presented to the pupils' parents during the parents' evening, and the parents have given their approval of this chapter.

In this study pupils' participation is also a pedagogical approach. In the classroom, the school year is divided into four multidisciplinary learning modules, and the contents of the modules are derived from the school curriculum [1] that is based on the national core curriculum for basic education (FNBE, 2014). The data from the first substudy was based on a cross-curriculum learning project called "From a seed to a product". The project lasted for 50 lessons that took place over 5 weeks. In the project, pupils investigated corn and other plants cultivated in gardens and fields in Finland. At the end of the project, the class created two narratives called "From a seed to a product". The first narrative was a shared visual narrative that included art and handcrafts from the wheat's route from fields to stores. The second narrative was an individually written narrative about the plant the pupil had investigated (also see Niemi et al., 2018).

The second substudy was based on the multidisciplinary module called "Europe" which lasted for the whole school year. When this data collection took place, the pupils were searching for information about Europe's climate, and they used that information in their own research and work. Music and social studies created another multidisciplinary module. In that module, the pupils first searched for information about children's rights and got to know the United Nations Convention on the Rights of the Child. Afterwards, they composed songs and wrote lyrics. During the data collection, the Finnish language was used in both modules (also see Niemi, 2019b).

CASE 1: Stairs May Lead Astray

The literature contains a number of guides and models to support promotion of participation (e.g., Hart, 1992; Treseder, 1997; Shier, 2001; Reddy & Ratna, 2002; Lundy, 2007; Landsdown, 2010). It is also claimed that researchers should find key indicators to evaluate the evidence of the cultural climate regarding young people's right to be heard and taken seriously, and to measure the extent, quality and impact of the actual participation in which pupils are engaged (Landsdown, 2010).

One of the most influential models has been Roger A. Hart's (1992) ladder of participation, in which he presents an eight-step model that begins with nonparticipation: (1) manipulation, (2) decoration and (3) tokenism. The model ends with degrees of participation: (4) assigned but informed; (5) consulted and informed; (6) adult-initiated, shared decisions with children; (7) child-initiated and directed; and (8) child-initiated, shared decisions with adults.

I thought that by simplifying Hart's (1992) model and by using photographs, I could reach my pupils' perspectives on participation and measure the quality of the teaching methods they were engaged in in order to develop my teaching and increase those practices that the pupils considered to be participatory. I elaborated Hart's model into a five-step model as follows, moving from children as objects to children as decision-makers:

1. I had no influence on my work. Adults made all the decisions.
2. Adults asked for my opinion, but it was not taken into account.
3. My role was to help adults in the learning project.
4. I worked with the adults first, but later on, I was able to take the lead on the project, and the adults helped me.
5. I was able to make all the decisions. The adults only helped me.

At the end of the project, I made a nine-slide PowerPoint presentation. Those slides contained pictures I had taken from different practices of the project. The practices on the slides were as follows: 1. investigative learning practices, 2. taking a trip to a garden and picking a plant, 3. planting peas and investigating living conditions of plants, 4. searching for knowledge on the internet, 5. writing a narrative, 6. joining feedback discussions, 7. doing notebook tasks, 8. creating a visual narrative and 9. baking sweet buns. When looking at those pictures, I discussed with the pupils what was happening in each picture and what other practices related to the project belong to the category (also see Niemi et al., 2018).

After that, I gave my pupils printed handouts of the slides. I asked the pupils to cut out the pictures from the handouts and place them on the rungs. What happened then was something I was not prepared for. The pupils were not sure what to do. One pupil even said: "Teacher, this is too difficult". I explained the stairs again and again. We also made a deal that they could choose how many pictures they wanted to use from the handout pictures. When I finally got the stairs back, most of the pupils had used two pictures. The first one was placed on the fifth stair, and the second one was placed on the first stair.

I realised that I had failed in data collection, and the only thing I was able to do with that data was to reflect on what had gone wrong and why. The ladders led nowhere. This was due to the fact that the existing practice architectures had been counter-productive in analysing participation. Firstly, the language used in this task was created by me. The pupils were not part of the process of creating the language related to the task. The language was too detached from the lives of the children. This related to both dimension of sayings (abstract language) and relatings (vocabulary was decided by an adult, not together through sharing power).

I also realised that participation is a far more complicated issue than only focusing on the question, "did you have an influence on your own learning?" Like any other practice, there are three elements behind it: sayings, doings and relatings. The discourse to describe participation was taken from classic research instead of being based on the lived realities of the site. The 'sayings' dimension of participation was not suitable for the class. The doings required evaluating the experiences based on this action. The power issues (relatings) were more based on the traditional pedagogical authority, and the teacher decided what to do. The traditional practice architectures shaped the way the topic of participation was approached. The conclusion from this should not be that the task of evaluating participation is too difficult for the children. On the contrary, new types of thinking and doing and relating were required from the teacher.

In the data collection, I had also used another method, diamond ranking (Clark, 2012), in examining my pupils' meaningful experiences (Niemi et al., 2018). When the pupils had had the opportunity to talk freely from their experiences, they also brought up topics related to participation. That provided me with a new direction to examine my pupils' experiences of participation.

CASE 2: Digital Visual Artefacts

In my studies, I have elaborated on the idea of doing diamond ranking[3] suitable to digital devices (Niemi et al., 2015; Niemi & Kiilakoski, 2019). This created more freedom for students. The second round of data collection started by discussing our previous experiences with diamond ranking and the use of iPads in conducting it. Then, I discussed with the pupils which application they would prefer to use. According to the pupils' suggestions, I wrote the names of the applications on the chalk board, and the pupils were allowed to use those or other applications they found through the iPad. The only limitation was to keep on expressing the most positive experiences, the neutral experiences and the experiences that needed

[3] The original diamond ranking involves a subset of nine photographs. The participants, working in pairs or threes, cut out these pictures and stick them onto a piece of paper in a diamond shape, ranking them by position so that the preferred picture is at the top and the most disliked is at the bottom. The participants also annotate the diamond with comments and explanations for the ranking (Clark, 2012).

improvement. The pupils were also supposed to give me advice on how to improve these practices. I also hoped they could use an application that would make it possible for them to interview themselves, but that was not necessary (also see Niemi, 2019b).

The purpose of the self-interview was that pupils would record the reasons for their choices. Doing ordinary interviews during the school day is difficult or even impossible for teachers, because teachers cannot leave the classroom alone in order to interview pupils on lessons. New digital devices and applications give pupils the opportunity to interview themselves, and the teacher can then listen to these interviews after lessons. Also, another purpose of the self-interviews was to reduce the power relation that a teacher always has with pupils (also see Niemi, 2019b).

The pupils ended up using three applications for expressing their experiences: Book Creator (n = 20), iMovie (n = 3) and PowerPoint (n = 2). It took 90 min to finish the books, but due to self-interviewing and the lack of quiet space, it took an additional 45 min (one lesson) to finish the self-interviews. However, all data were collected as part of a normal school day, and all the activities were something that could fulfil the goals of the curriculum (also see Niemi, 2019b). Traditional practice architectures such as length of the class still shaped the outline of the activity, but the results were different.

Pupils described experiences that related to social and political aspects of participation when they were able to talk freely from their experiences. Through various kinds of group work, pupils had chances to face a social field where they were recognised, and they interacted with the social emotions of the field. The pupils' most positive experiences related to the social dimension of participation, to situations in which they had felt a sense of relatedness to each other, free communication and a sense of being competent in the eyes of others. When speaking freely from their learning experiences, the pupils also expressed experiences that related to the political dimension of participation (see, e.g., Thomas, 2007). They spoke about situations in which they had been able to have an impact, influence the study group, participate in decision-making and take responsibility. The pupils' experiences with political participation related to two main aspects: a sense of autonomy and taking responsibility.

Both in Niemi and Kiilakoski (2019) and in this study, the pupils' experiences (sayings) were used to improve classroom practices. In Niemi and Kiilakoski (2019), each pupil's experiences (sayings) were discussed with me. In those discussions, each pupil reflected on how the practices that had caused negative experiences could be improved and turned into new practices (doings) or new roles in a classroom community (relatings). For this data, I listened to pupils' self-interviews (sayings) at home, and brought up to the classroom discussion issues that had caused the most negative experiences in the data. I promised to change my practices (doings), and in doing so, I added drama lessons to my teaching. The practices evolved with the process.

The pupils themselves played a role in increasing the desired topics such as modern dance in physical education lessons. The lesson on modern dance, which took place in winter 2019, was taught by two pupils. What happened after that was that there were many pupils who asked if they could also plan a lesson for physical education based on their own hobbies.

Case 2 represents a method that gives teachers a tool to recognise the participation which uses language and methods which are accessible to the children. It also gave pupils a possibility to have an impact on how they wanted to join data gathering. They had a right to refuse to join, they had a right to choose an application they felt was the best, and they had a right to use the amount of pictures they wanted. What should be noted is that the method itself is not only about using digital tools, as its success is based on common practices. There have been systematic efforts to learn participation skills in the classroom throughout their school career. The pedagogical use of new devices is based on the existing culture of working together. Compared to the first example, the practice architectures of teaching were more suitable to actually help the children to express their views and to have an impact. As is evident, the sayings have evolved – not only the ways students were able to describe their experiences, but also the way teacher reacted. The relatings have evolved, and now the students have more power. This all manifests itself in the doing dimensions and the creation of a more democratic and shared pedagogical space.

Conclusion

Promoting participation in schools is identified as one of the major challenges schools have to face. It is one of the necessary elements in creating education which is child-centred, child-friendly and empowering (United Nations, 2001, §2). In our chapter, we have articulated how profound importance the existing practice architectures play in renewing the practices. The successes of efforts to change the current ways of doing things and talking about them are partly due to the way practice has been seen before. Without connection to the practice architectures, the change does not happen, and if it happens, it will live a nasty, short and brutish life.

Every child should have an opportunity to participate. In Finland the national core curriculum demands this, so pondering about the desirability of participation is, to put it bluntly, a waste of time. Based on our conception of participation we understand the current challenge of promoting participation as follows:

- Recognise role of the children: Requires giving agency to children in choosing the vocabulary to analyse participation and securing the emotionally safe environment so that children are able to express their opinions. Both formal and informal support is needed.
- Action: Requires doing something meaningful together. Working in a class environment necessarily involves working with other students. This in turn requires making sure that both social and political dimensions of participation are present.
- Feeling of participation: Requires asking children if they felt they were able to participate. Evaluation is needed.

Sometimes people lament that the promotion of participation undermines pedagogical authority since children have the potential power to alter the processes planned by teachers. We feel that the answer to this concern can be based on the theory of practice architectures. If the action is rooted in the practice architectures, it is not about a drastic change. Instead of revolution, there is a reinterpretation of some features of practice architectures in the dimensions of sayings, doings and relatings. At the heart of education is the commitment to promoting the good of each individual. Due to this, promoting a participatory and more democratic school culture is not a drastic change in the basic project of education. Securing participation rights is respecting the good of the individuals and is also a step towards building more democratic societies. Our experiences show how the activities require a mutual learning process and changing the practice architectures based on the mutual understanding.

Describing our mistakes even briefly points out that promoting participation is likely to require rethinking the practices, recognising the difficulties and locating them in the existing ways of doing things. We hope to have shown that despite our emphasis on the need to change the existing practices there are many elements in the practice architectures of schooling that also support participation. Some of these elements are already there, some are embryonic. There is an evolving professional discussion on how to promote participation, there are scientific studies on Finnish schools, methodologies are being developed, and the conception of teachers as enablers of learning instead of traditional authorities all make promoting participation easier. Al though the practice architectures are developing on many level, but there is still lot to be done.

In this chapter, we have used pedagogical action research as our methodology. We have shown how it works when an individual teacher wants to examine and develop their classroom practices together with pupils. We have also shown how an individual teacher can learn from their failures. Since the existing practice architectures do not support child participation fully, reflecting on the failures and successes is needed to create participatory spaces and methods.

In terms of participation, it is not, however, enough that pupils' participation is only seen through research initiatives or other one-time-programs. Participation has to be an integral part of everyday life in classrooms. Ways of evaluating and recognising participation need to be developed, and they have to be integrated to the practice architectures of the school. If the methodology is used only as tool to get a tick to a box to show that pupils' participation is taken care of, the methodology may turn to tokenism.

The methodology presented is of course far from perfect. This methodology also only focuses on individual teacher and one classroom. It leaves the rest of the school out of the study. The whole-school approaches require that the school community has the opportunity to learn together and has a safe space to talk about how practice architectures should be developed. This points to the holistic nature of participation: in order to promote participation, one needs to build practice architectures that respect the participation of children and adults alike. We believe that the methods that we presented in the second case of our study are something that can be transferred to other contexts, and that these methods can be integrated into the practice architectures which support the development of the whole school.

[1] Since August 2016, each pupil must be provided with the opportunity to join at least one multidisciplinary learning module per school year. At the same time, the teacher has to ensure that the requirements of the subject-based curriculum are met (FNBE, 2014).

References

Clark, J. (2012). Using diamond ranking as visual cues to engage young people in the research process. *Qualitative Research Journal, 12*(2), 222–237.

Emerson, L., & Lloyd, K. (2017). Measuring children's experience of their right to participate in school and community: A rights-based approach. *Children and Society, 31*, 120–133.

Finnish National Board of Education. (2014). *Perusopetuksen opetussuunnitelman perusteet 2014*. Retrieved 31.3.2021 from https://www.oph.fi/sites/default/files/documents/perusopetuksen_opetussuunnitelman_perusteet_2014.pdf

Hakalehto, S. (2015). Johdatus lapsen oikeuksiin koulussa. In S. Hakalehto (Ed.), *Lapsen oikeudet koulussa* (pp. 50–87). Kauppakamari.

Hart, R.A. (1992). *Children's participation, from tokenism to citizenship.* : UNICEF. Retrieved from http://www.unicef-irc.org/publications/pdf/childrens_participation.pdf

Kaukko, M. (2015). *Participation in and beyond liminalities: Action research with unaccompanied asylum-seeking girls*. University of Oulu.

Kemmis, S., & Edwards-Groves, C. (2018). *Understanding education*. Springer.

Kemmis, S., WIlkinson, J., Edwards-Groves, C., Hardy, I., Grootenboer, P., & Bristol, L. (2014). *Changing practices, changing education*. Springer.

Kiilakoski, T. (2017). "Niillähän se on se viimenen sana" – nuoret osallisuudestaan yläkoulussa. In A. Toom, M. Rautiainen, & J. Tähtinen (Eds.), *Toiveet ja todellisuus. Kasvatus osallisuutta ja oppimista rakentamassa* (pp. 253–282). Finnish Educational Research Association.

Kiilakoski, T., Gretschel, A., & Nivala, E. (2012). Osallisuus, kansalaisuus ja hyvinvointi. In A. Gretschel & T. Kiilakoski (Eds.), *Demokratiaoppitunti. Lasten ja nuorten kunta 2000-luvun alussa, Publications 118* (pp. 11–19). Finnish Youth Research Network/Youth Research Society.

Landsdown, G. (2010). The realisation of children's participation rights: Critical reflections. In B. Percey-Smith & N. Thomas (Eds.), *A handbook of children and young people's participation. Perspectives from theory and practice* (pp. 11–23). Routledge.

Lundy, L. (2007). "Voice" is not enough: Conceptualising Article 12 of the United Nations Convention on the Rights of the Child. *British Educational Research Journal, 33*(6), 927–942.

Niemi, R. (2019a). Five approaches to pedagogical action research. *Educational Action Research, 27*(5), 651–666.

Niemi, R. (2019b). A teacher performing action research: Capturing pupils' perspectives of didactic relations. *Estonian Journal of Educational Research [Eesti Haridusteaduste Ajakiri], 7*(2), 58–75. https://doi.org/10.12697/eha.2019.7.2.03b

Niemi, R., & Kiilakoski, T. (2019). "I learned to cooperate with my friends and there were no quarrels": Pupils' experiences of participation in a multidisciplinary learning module. *Scandinavian Journal of Educational Research, 64*, 984. Advance online publication. https://doi.org/10.1080/00313831ublic.2019.1639817

Niemi, R., Kumpulainen, K., & Lipponen, L. (2015). Pupils as active participants: Diamond ranking as a tool to investigate pupils' experiences of classroom practices. *European Educational Research Journal 14*(2), 138–150.

Niemi, R., Kumpulainen, K., & Lipponen, L. (2018). The use of diamond ranking and peer interviews to capture pupils' perspectives. *Improving Schools, 21*(3), 240–254.
Reddy, N., & Ratna, K. (2002). *A journey in children's participation.* : The Concerned for Working Children. Retrieved from https://resourcecentre.savethechildren.net/sites/default/files/documents/2625.pdf
Sahlberg, P. (2011). *Finnish lessons. What can the world learn from educational change in Finland?* Teachers College Press.
Shier, H. (2001). Pathways to participation: Openings, opportunities and obligations. A new model for enhancing children's participation in decision-making, in line with Article 12.1 of the United Nations Convention of the Right of the Child. *Children and Society, 15*, 107–117.
Thomas, N. (2007). Towards a theory of children's participation. *International Journal of Children's Rights, 15*(3), 199–218.
Treseder, P. (1997). *Empowering children and young people: Training manual.* Save the Children and Children's Rights Office.
UNICEF Finland. (2011). *Lapsen oikeuksien sopimuksen käsikirja* [Handbook on the Convention on the Rights of the Child].
United Nations. (1989). *United Nations Convention on Rights of the Child.* UN general assembly resolution.
United Nations. (2001). *General comment no 1. Article 29(1): General aims of education.* Committee on the Rights of the Child. United Nations.
United Nations. (2009). *General comment no 12. The right of the child to be heard.* United Nations.

Chapter 15
Children's Human Rights and Intercultural Education: Curricular Prescriptions and Teachers' Practices in Switzerland

Zoe Moody

Abstract As previously noted in its Concluding observations on Switzerland's periodic reports, the United Nations Committee on the Rights of the Child has raised concerns, in 2015, about the fact that human rights education is not carried out systematically in all cantons. On the ground, implementation of Article 29 – more specifically developing respect for human rights, preparing the child for a life in a free society and fostering a spirit of understanding, peace, tolerance and equality between people – depends very much on teachers' goodwill and training. Based on two studies carried out in Switzerland this chapter will focus on two requirements of Article 29: educating children about rights and about intercultural relations. First, a critique of Article 29 and how it articulates CHRE and intercultural education will be provided. Then, we will underline how curricular or local prescriptions impact teachers' involvement in children's rights and intercultural education. Third, we will highlight the limited benefits of ready-to-use teaching material and the ambivalence of teachers towards this kind of tools. Finally, teachers' lack of training on those issues and associated consequences will be addressed.

Keywords Children's human rights education · Intercultural education · Convention on the rights of the child · Curricular prescriptions · Teacher practice

---

Z. Moody (✉)
Centre for Children's Rights Studies, University of Geneva, and Valais University of Teacher Education, St-Maurice, Switzerland
e-mail: zoe.moody@unige.ch

J. Gillett-Swan, N. Thelander (eds.), *Children's Rights from International Educational Perspectives*, Transdisciplinary Perspectives in Educational Research 2, https://doi.org/10.1007/978-3-030-80861-7_15

Introduction

Since the adoption of the *United Nations Convention on the Rights of the Child* (UNCRC) in 1989, issues related to children's rights have gained increased attention in various areas, such as education. Among the obligations that flow from the Convention is the obligation for signatory States to grant children with sufficient information about their rights, through appropriate and active means, and to promote human rights, fundamental freedoms, equality, tolerance and cultural diversity (United Nations, 1989, Articles 29 and 42). These requirements are readily understood as a legal basis for Children's Human Rights Education (hereafter CRHE), which is defined – in line with the broadly accepted definition of Human Rights Education – as teaching children *about* (knowledge), *through* (respect of) and *for* (ability to take action for) their rights.

As previously noted in its concluding observations on Switzerland's periodic reports, in 2015 again, the United Nations Committee on the Rights of the Child raised concerns about the fact that CHRE is not carried out systematically in all cantons.[1] Neither children nor professionals working with children are taught about children's human rights in an organised and generalised manner. Furthermore, we observe on the ground that the implementation of Article 29 – be it the promotion of human rights and fundamental freedoms or more broadly the values underpinning a human rights culture (equality, tolerance and cultural diversity) – depends very much on teachers' goodwill and training.

Based on two studies carried out in Switzerland (French and German speaking regions) on children's human rights and intercultural education, this chapter will focus on two requirements of Article 29 in multicultural contexts: educating children about rights and about intercultural relations. The aim is threefold: (a) provide a critical analysis of Article 29 and related international documents, highlighting their potential and limits; (b) define how much the Swiss curricular or local prescriptions are in line with the international framework and how they impact teachers' involvement in children's rights and intercultural education; (c) highlight some barriers on the ground (ready-to-use teaching material, lack of training) impacting the implementation of Article 29 and broader principles of CHRE and intercultural education. Data from the two studies will be used to illustrate the practical dimensions of this analysis.

Article 29: A Meeting Point Between Children's Human Rights and Intercultural Education

In the UNCRC, Article 29 describes the aims of education. Various complementary and sometimes conflicting aims are set forth, opening both areas of uncertainty and interesting prospective dimensions. This section aims to provide a critique of Article

[1] The 26 cantons of Switzerland refer to the administrative subdivisions of the Swiss Confederacy.

29, notably the declarationist, uncritical and more or less limited approach it proposes, while also considering it as a fertile meeting point between children's human rights education and intercultural education.

The Aims of Education

It is recognised that the right to benefit from rights-informed educational programs or rights-infused learning environments is rooted in the Universal Declaration of Human Rights ([UDHR], 1948), which states that:

> Education shall be directed to the full development of the human personality and to the strengthening of respect for human rights and fundamental freedoms. It shall promote understanding, tolerance and friendship among all nations, racial or religious groups, and shall further the activities of the United Nations for the maintenance of peace. (Article 26, §2).

The international community laid with this article the foundation stone of a tradition of human rights education (HRE), soon completed by an array of documents that reiterate the right to enjoy education on human rights: the *International Covenant on Economic, Social and Cultural Rights* (1966), the Declaration on *Human Rights Education*, launching a *Decade* on the topic (United Nations General Assembly [UNGA], 1994), followed by a *World Programme on Human Rights Education* (UNGA, 2004) and the adoption by the General Assembly of the *United Nations Declaration on Human Rights Education and Training*, in 2011. Article 29 of the UNCRC is however considered by some as the "most relevant to school-based HRE, since it is directed at children learning about human rights" (Gerber, 2017, p. 180).

From the outset, HRE was closely related to the "full development of the human personality" on the one hand and to the promotion of "understanding, tolerance and friendship among all nations [...]" on the other (UDHR, 1948, Article 25(2)). The authors of the UNCRC repeated and expanded this logic when drafting the article on the aims of education for children. Indeed, Article 29(1) is divided into five subparagraphs. The first recalls that education should support the development of the child's personality and abilities to their fullest potential (§1a). Then, the "development of respect for human rights and fundamental freedoms" is set as an aim of education (§1b). The following two subparagraphs highlight the respect the child should have for his/her cultural identity, language and religion and for those different from his/her own (§1c), which is very closely linked to the fact that children should be prepared to lead a responsible life in the spirit of understanding, peace, tolerance, equality of sexes, and friendship among all peoples (§1d). Finally, learning to respect the natural environment is set forth (§1e).

The qualitative dimensions of education as defined in Article 29 highlight the educative values the international community agreed upon. As stated by the United Nations Committee on the Rights of the Child in its first General Comment on the aims of education:

> This agreement overcomes the boundaries of religion, nation and culture built across many parts of the world [... by recognising] the need for a balanced approach to education and one which succeeds in reconciling diverse values through dialogue and respect for difference. Moreover, children are capable of playing a unique role in bridging many of the differences that have historically separated groups of people from one another. (United Nations, 2001, §4)

Considered by some as a means to "fill in some of the gaps left by the general language of Article 29" (Gerber, 2017, p. 181), this UN General Comment shows how essential the role of children is, in the eyes of the international community, for peace building and international cooperation and understanding. Perceived as neutral individuals and uncorrupted minds, children are seen as the future creators and actors of a dignified world, from which hatred, conflict and violence could be eradicated (see Moody, 2016). The prerequisite of this idealistic conception of childhood and the future of mankind requires giving children sufficient knowledge about human rights, alterity, intercultural relations and sustainable development as well as passing on the underpinning values. Education becomes the means of promoting a "universal" and shared social project, embodied by the future generation.

Article 29 and CHRE

Article 29 provides a rather "declarationist" approach of education as defined by Keet (2012), aiming to develop children's knowledge and "respect" for human rights, cultures and their natural environment. Some describe this as the promotion of "good behaviour" – or pupil obedience (Trivers & Starkey, 2012) – rather than CHRE. Indeed, expecting children to know and respect a global social project such as human rights or the peaceful coexistence of various cultures does not provide any information about how they may be educated towards developing a critical stance or competencies in order to become actors of the evolution of such ideas.

The UN Committee on the Rights of the Child (United Nations, 2001), in its General Comment related to Article 29, indicates that it:

> Not only adds to the right to education ... a qualitative dimension which reflects the rights and inherent dignity of the child; it also insists upon the need for education to be child-centred, child-friendly and empowering, and it highlights the need for educational processes to be based upon the very principles it enunciates. (§2)

By so doing, the UN Committee points to the commonly agreed fact that CHRE comprises both *contents* and *processes* (Brantefors & Quennerstedt, 2016; Gerber, 2017; Thelander, 2016) and should therefore be undertaken as a global approach, including education *about*, *through* and *for* rights (Phillips, 2016; Struthers, 2015). Education *about* rights comprises acquiring knowledge and understanding of rights, norms and principles as well as the mechanisms that protect them. Learning and teaching *through* processes that respect the rights of all is considered a prerequisite to develop skills for active citizenship. Finally, education *for* rights leads to the empowerment of the individual, fostering the ability to take action for or to speak up against rights violations.

Although this definition is widely adopted and appears as such in most international documents (e.g., the latest *United Nations Declaration on Human Rights Education and Training* 2011), it is noteworthy that it remains under discussion amongst HRE scholars, who highlight that there are many definitions prevailing. Most of these definitions are complementary but remain subtly diverse in their formulation of goals and principles (Flowers, 2004; Gerber, 2017). More specifically, it is argued:

> The institutionalisation and centralisation for the HRE discourse [by the United Nations and its agencies] has gradually eroded diverse ways of knowing and interpreting human rights by regulating the production, distribution and consumption of the HRE discourse as a means of social control. (Coysh, 2017, p. 174; see also Keet, 2017)

Moreover, the concept of empowerment – or more broadly the emancipatory project of HRE – can be said to be rather unstable in its theoretical foundations and pedagogical implementation.

On pedagogical level, a fertile framework for theorising this kind of empowerment process – claiming for the respect of their own rights and actively defending others' rights – is being developed. This framework lies at the intersection between Freire's pedagogy of the oppressed (2007/1970) and his notion of critical consciousness – leading to an in-depth understanding of social contradictions and the power of taking action against the oppressive elements in one's life (see notably Bajaj, 2017; Nazzari et al., 2005; Simpson 2017). Tibbitts (2005 p. 109) argues that Freire's proposition of emancipatory transformative learning is "the direct link between personal and social transformation, as well as the notion of critical reflection as a redistribution of power." This relates to some of the dimensions UNCRC State Members' educational systems need to guarantee: developing the child's personality and talents, while instilling a culture of human rights and leading the child to become an actor of its evolutions.

Bajaj (2017), for her part, links Freire's notion of critical consciousness to that of empowerment. She argues that it is the pathway towards social and individual transformation, through groups of individuals analysing conditions of inequality and taking action to overcome them. This relates to the philosophical tradition of cosmopolitanism "that posits a shared human community and a global notion of citizenship and belonging" (Bajaj, 2017, p. 7). This undoubtably supports the link drafted in Article 29(1) between teaching children about their rights (§1b) and getting prepared for a life in a free and globalised world (§1d), while learning about the various cultural systems coexisting worldwide and how to support this coexistence (§1c).

Values, Cultural Diversity and Intercultural Dialogue

The philosophical standpoint underpinning the notion of a shared humanity and linked responsibilities as a basis for a culture of human rights appears in Article 29. UNCRC Member States' education systems need to foster children's respect for their own cultural identity, language and values, those of the country in which they live or from which they may originate, and for different civilizations while developing a spirit of tolerance, equality and friendship among all peoples. Pedagogical implementation of philosophical ideals can however be complex.

In 2001, the UN Committee on the Rights of the Child agreed that difficulties may arise in this kind of exercise. It recognised that some values expressed in Article 29 "might be thought to be in conflict with one another in certain situations" (§4). More specifically, it suggested the efforts to promote understanding and friendship among peoples, "might not always be automatically compatible with policies designed, […] to develop respect for the child's own cultural identity" (§4). By so doing, the Committee acknowledged the diversity of realities worldwide and the fact that the unity of humankind is not a given everywhere (see Eberhard, 2009). It however gave a rather simple way out, recommending, as mentioned above, "a balanced approach to education" in order to "reconciling diverse values through dialogue and respect for difference" (§4).

It is known that focusing on differences is problematic to consider diversity and to enter an intercultural dialogue. Described as the "heterogeneity paradigm" (Sliwka, 2010), to highlight differences puts to the fore what separates people – often in a simplistic manner – while overlooking cultural similarities and potential meeting points. It means that alterity or otherness is not linked with one's self. This fosters distance between cultures instead of exchange, and therefore denies the complexity of interculturality. The "diversity paradigm" (Sliwka, 2010) posits that differences have to be acknowledged and then interlinked in order to co-create a new framework of reference and possibly enter an intercultural dialogue, in which interculturality can be contextualised (Eberhard, 2009).

The "balance" the UN Committee calls for cannot be simply supported by the acceptance of otherness. Rather it requires the articulation of *enculturation* and *acculturation* processes, or preferably *intercultural dialogue*. Enculturation describes the process through which the child assimilates the language, norms and traditions of his or her group and acts accordingly, with increased consciousness over the years. This process is closely related to education, which supports it to a certain extent. If enculturation is a means to stabilise culture, acculturation conversely describes the phenomena resulting from direct contact between groups and different cultures, leading to subsequent changes in the cultural patterns of one or other group (Herskovits, 1967). These changes will often have varied impact on the groups depending on whether they represent a dominant culture or not, which is probably in contradiction with the values of the UN Charter. Education therefore strives towards more intercultural approaches, "an education able to negotiate between cultures rather than to show that there is more than one culture" (Coulby,

2006, p. 247; see also Akkari, 2009). In intercultural education the contact between cultures is not the ultimate goal but a means to enter intercultural dialogue through which one's relation to the other shall be redefined (Abdallah-Pretceille & Porcher, 1999).

Philosophically, this intercultural dialogue can be the place for an open discussion on "the good life" of which human rights may be a possible expression (Eberhard, 2011). This leads us to conceptually support the general aims set forth in Article 29. Preparing the child for responsible life in a free society can be achieved as a whole, in coherence with the norms and values underpinning his or her own culture(s), including that of human rights and those required for a peaceful intercultural coexistence. However, the difficult task of fostering critical thinking and aiming towards genuine transformative learning remains, in order to imagine educational systems within which the child's identity and personal values can be affiliated and anchored, whilst favouring individual empowerment.

Implementing Article 29 in Swiss Multicultural Contexts

This section builds upon the results of two studies – one quantitative (surveys n = 278) and one qualitative (interviews, observations) – carried out on teachers practices related to CHRE and intercultural education in the two main linguistic regions of Switzerland (French and German speaking regions). Based on these empirical observations, the aim is twofold: first to underline how Article 29 and the complexity of its requirements are translated, if at all, in Swiss curricular or regional prescriptions. Second, the way teachers get involved in CHRE and intercultural education in multicultural contexts will be described. The limited benefits of ready-to-use teaching material and teachers' ambivalence towards such tools will be highlighted by so doing. The lack of professional training on those issues will also be underlined.

Curricular Prescriptions

In 2007, cantonal governments agreed to harmonise compulsory schooling in Switzerland, which was and remains under the competence of the cantonal authorities. This led to the adoption of the *Harmonisation of Compulsory Education* (HarmoS) *Agreement*. This framework document does not explicitly refer to human rights or CHRE nor does it specify that learning environments should be rights-based. It does however mention respect for the diversity of cultures in Switzerland (Article 2(1, 2)) and that all pupils should acquire cultural identity and a sense of responsibility towards others (Article 3(1, 3)). More specifically, cantons are required to support the organisation of courses for migrant children in their language and culture of origin (art. 4(4)). Based on the *HarmoS Agreement*, three curricula for primary and lower-secondary schools were developed. We will here focus on the "Plan d'études romand", introduced between 2011 and 2014 in the French-speaking cantons, and the "Lehrplan 21", which German-speaking and multilingual cantons have started to implement since 2015.[2]

Although there is no specific entry for CHRE within the Plan d'études romand (PER), learning about rights is one aim of *Citizenship education*. This broad approach of education is conceived as complementary to *Education for sustainable development* and operationalised through the subject matter *Citizenship* and a cross-curricular domain *Living together and exercising democracy*. Beyond the fact it should aim to "prepare students to participate actively in democratic life by exercising their rights and responsibilities in society" (CIIP, 2010, Introduction Générale), it is argued that encouraging children to get involved as citizens in their schools primarily provides opportunities to highlight "the need to agree on rules of life and to respect the laws" as well as "the resultant protection and security" (CIIP, 2010, Commentaires généraux pour la Formation Générale). In respect to cultures, knowledge about the dominant Swiss cultures is provided in the languages subject matters and one transversal goal aims to foster "recognition of otherness and respect" (CIIP, 2010, Formation Générale 25).

In its introduction, Lehrplan 21 refers to democracy, politics and fundamental rights. It states that based on fundamental rights, values such as democracy, gender equality, non-discrimination and social justice inform the educational process. It however contains no reference to a rights-based approach and what it would mean for schools. In the core-curriculum, *Political education* and the transversal idea of *Sustainable development* can be linked to CHRE: the subject *Politics, democracy and human rights* needs to be addressed. Pupils should know about the development and meaning of human rights and be able to identify patterns of discrimination; they are also supposed to tackle issues of power and law, and to discuss values, norms, and conflicts (D-EDK, 2014, p. 33). However, the curriculum does not specify how this kind of education should be undertaken, it merely defines some general principles, such as orientation towards the future and participatory learning. Regarding culture, *Cultural identity and intercultural understanding* is another topic to be addressed under the *Sustainable development* heading (D-EDK, 2014, pp. 38–39). The Lehrplan 21 thus promotes both an understanding for Swiss cultures and understanding of other cultures.

Although Swiss curricula are not very prescriptive in respect to developing CHRE and intercultural education, Swiss NGOs (e.g., education21, International Institute for the Rights of the Child, Graines de Paix) consider these mentions – linked to the international prescriptions Switzerland has ratified – sufficient grounds for their promotion activities in the field. They produce pedagogical material to provide all school-level teachers with the necessary tools to equip learners with knowledge on human rights and intercultural, as well as specific cognitive and

[2] For reasons of feasibility, our studies did not include the Italian-speaking canton and its "Piano di studio". For a comparative curricular analysis of the three curricula see Rinaldi et al. (2020).

socio-emotional skills and behavioural capacities. This process is generally supervised by quality assessment specialists. It often includes collaboration with teachers from the field on the one hand for testing the material and researchers on the other for external evaluation. Our studies (Broyon & Moody, 2015; Broyon et al., 2017) took place in this specific context. In addition to assessing the pedagogical quality of the material and its potential impact, we studied the pedagogical means teachers are provided with and the way they handle and implement them. Moreover, we analysed sets of practices in relation to a specific context, that is the school climate, regulations and socio-cultural environment.

Teachers' Practices

In respect to teachers' practices, the first interesting finding comes from the answers 210 Francophone teachers and 68 Germanophone teachers gave to our survey about a specific form of Children's rights teaching material (Broyon & Moody, 2015). At the time only the French curriculum was implemented and references to rights as an object of teaching and learning were absent or not generalised in the German curricula. It was therefore instructive to note that the need to teach about rights had an impact how important Francophone teachers considered children's rights in school, in classroom management and in their teaching: 10% more Francophone teachers (FT) than Germanophone teachers (GT) answered it was very or quite important. This is also reflected in how often FT teach lessons on children's rights and/or human rights. As shown in Fig. 15.1, almost 50% of FT said they taught such subjects four times a year or more whereas, two thirds of GT said that they did not do so more than twice a year, and 53% only once a year. These answers show how impacting curricular prescriptions can be in respect to developing CHRE.

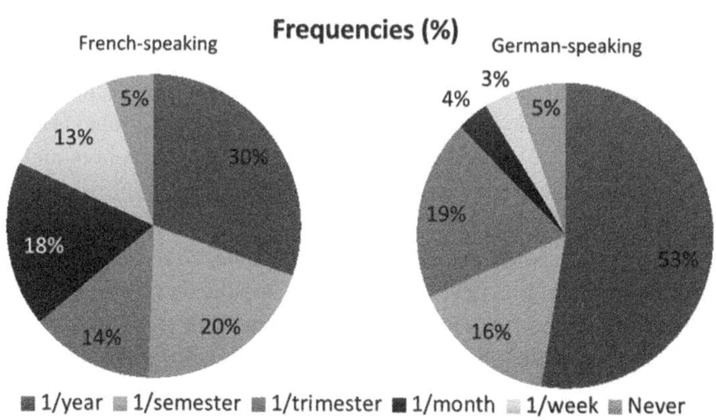

Fig. 15.1 How often teachers provide lessons on children or human rights (by linguistic region)

Another interesting finding is that the ready-to-use material – pedagogical activities provided for the 20th of November and distinguished for each teaching cycle (4–8, 8–12, and 12–15 years old) – does not seem to correspond to their needs. Although the surveyed teachers say they use it (50–60% announce a biannual use) and appreciate the links with topical issues and the place for innovation it gives (e.g., inclusion of media in the classroom), they indicate that the educational sheet format does not allow easy teaching differentiation based on the children's age, special needs, or language. This is all the more striking that children with special needs are very concerned by the topic. More specifically, we notice a strong focus on developing knowledge *about* rights and little use of CHRE or teaching to develop values and competencies (CHRE *for* and *through* rights). When comprehensive approaches occur, they are generally related to effective classroom management aims or to problems or conflicts solving. CHRE is therefore not conducted in a systematic and more worryingly integrated way but rather as an occasional activity to celebrate the UNCRC or to deal with individual or social issues.

Our second study reveals some similar issues while also giving directions for improving the quality of CHRE and intercultural education in Switzerland. This research was carried out in a very multicultural school and in the context of a school project. Ready-to-use material to address children's rights and cultural diversity – in this case two teaching manuals comprising 40 activities for 4–6- and 6–8-year-olds – was given to teachers who were required to teach the whole manual during the school year; they provided more or less 30 lessons. Interviews conducted with the teachers show that teaching about rights and cultural diversity is very impact-driven in their eyes. Having spent many hours addressing the topics, teachers do drift away from strict knowledge building. However, they mainly focus on skill transfer within the classroom or in the schoolyard, as reflected in the positive appreciation of a teacher interviewee: "*They [the children] understand the rules and use them*". Interestingly, children do not place as great emphasis on whether the "*technics work*" (child interviewee): most of them recall non-formal learning activities and pay much more attention to incoherence between what is taught and the attitudes of adults.

Although teachers are very interested in controlling the impact the activities have, it is clear that most of them (training, experience and age controlled) are ill-equipped to assess the development of psycho-social competencies or develop cross-curricular (inter- or transdisciplinary) teaching (see also Brantefors & Quennerstedt, 2016). Both the interviews carried out with teachers and with children show that various psycho-social competencies (emotional, social and cognitive) are developed throughout such teaching. Teachers agree that children verbalise better their feelings, show more empathy, "*speak rather than react*". However, they do not think that their pupils develop many psycho-social competencies. More surprisingly, facing children who adopt the same viewpoint as their friends, teachers interpret it as lack of critical thinking, when it actually appears to be the first stages of a decentration process (essential to enter intercultural dialogue).

The last point to be highlighted is the difficult differentiation within this kind of teaching. Apparently, teachers scarcely adjust the material, although many children in their classes spoke little to no French. It appears as though CHRE and intercultural education could be provided to a unified group, with no didactical adaptation. This points towards a lack of proficiency in respect to the objects taught and how they relate to each other. The most striking aspect of this is the fact that the manuals used in our second study provide a booklet for children to take back home, in order involve the parents in the project. None of the interviewed teachers let the children bring it to their parents: one teacher argues that it depends on the interest of parents and that it could lead to "*increase differences between children*". Another fears "*loyalty conflicts*" induced between what she understands as culturally based values.

Conclusion

In the UNCRC, Article 29 describes the aims of education and ensuing responsibilities for Member States. Although it is understood by some as the most appropriate international document in respect to CHRE, we have underlined the declarationist and knowledge-focussed approaches it proposes. We have also highlighted that the aims of education, as defined in the UNCRC, do not strive towards fostering critical thinking and develop competencies that may enable children to enter a more transformative or even transgressive stance in the 'responsible life' in a cosmopolitan society. Finally, the limited educational value of acknowledging the copresence of various cultures has been shown, arguing that ultimately the goal should rather be to enter an intercultural dialogue, most importantly around human rights.

Interestingly, an analysis of curricular prescriptions and teachers' practices in Switzerland highlight that these shortcomings are also translated there. Curricula provide practitioners with knowledge-based and narrow aims in respect to children's rights and intercultural education. They barely enter methodological considerations. They do not either address which conditions are needed for rights-infused and culturally-responsive teaching and learning, and even less for global and meaningful activities/projects to learn how to act as a right holder and an intercultural mediator. Finally, ready-to-use material, despite the fact it is appreciated by teachers, maintains the focus on teaching about rights and different cultures. It does not support any global or cross-curricular approach to strive towards the complex goals that Article 29 opens to. Even more problematic, this lack of support leads to exclusive practices through undifferentiated teaching. Therefore, all children do not have access to the activities proposed.

Rights and intercultural teaching and learning cannot rely solely on a 'balanced' and child-friendly approach as suggested in the UN General Comments notably. Rather, curricula as well as initial and continuous teacher training should prepare and support practitioners to propose ambitious and articulated opportunities to their pupils, through which they can understand relevant content and concepts and learn to tackle skilfully the tensions underpinning relations between humans, groups of humans, their rights locally and globally, and build a common future. This is a requirement to allow children's enactment of rights and intercultural dialogue in and through education. These are the minimal conditions to implement Article 29, as a meaningful framework for children's human rights and intercultural education, and progressively move beyond.

References

Abdallah-Pretceille, M., & Porcher, L. (1999). *Diagonales de la communication interculturelle*. Anthropos.

Akkari, A. (2009). *Introduction aux approches interculturelles en éducation*. Université de Genève, Carnets des sciences de l'éducation.

Bajaj, M. (2017). *Human rights education: Theory, research and praxis*. University of Pennsylvania Press.

Brantefors, L., & Quennerstedt, A. (2016). Teaching and learning children's human rights: A research synthesis. *Cogent Education*, 3. https://doi.org/10.1080/2331186X.2016.1247610

Broyon, M.-A., & Moody, Z. (2015, July). *Évaluation externe du projet de fiches pédagogique é21 sur les droits de l'enfant: Rapport final*. University of Teacher Education Valais.

Broyon, M.-A., Moody, Z., & Namani, L. (2017, November). *Évaluation externe de l'impact de l'utilisation systématique de la collection Grandir en Paix dans un établissement scolaire: Rapport final*. University of Teacher Education Valais.

Conférence intercantonale de l'instruction publique de la Suisse romande et du Tessin [CIIP]. (2010). *Plan d'études romand*. https://www.plandetudes.ch/

Coulby, D. (2006). Intercultural education: Theory and practice. *Intercultural Education, 17*(3), 245–257.

Coysh, J. (2017). *Human rights education and the politics of knowledge*. Taylor & Francis.

Deutschschweizer Erziehungsdirektoren-Konferenz [D-EDK]. (2014). *Lehrplan 21*. BKZ Geschäftsstelle.

Eberhard, C. (2009). Au-delà d'une anthropologie des droits de l'homme: Les horizons du dialogue interculturel et du royaume de Shambhala? *Revue interdisciplinaire d'études juridiques, 63*(2), 155–200. https://doi.org/10.3917/riej.063.0155

Eberhard, C. (2011). *Droits de l'homme et dialogue interculturel*. Éditions Connaissances et Savoirs.

Flowers, N. (2004). How to define HRE? A complex answer to a simple question. In V. B. Georgi & M. Seberich (Eds.), *International perspectives in human rights education* (pp. 105–127). Bertelsmann Foundation.

Freire, P. (2007/1970). *Pedagogy of the oppressed*. Continuum.

Gerber, P. (2017). Good practice in human rights education in schools. In A. Sjöborg & H.-G. Ziebertz (Eds.), *Religion, education and human rights: Theoretical and empirical perspectives* (pp. 179–203). Springer international.

Herskovits, J. (1967). *Les bases de l'anthropologie culturelle*. Payot.

International Covenant on Economic, Social and Cultural Rights. (1966). Resolution 2200A (XXI).

Keet, A. (2012). Discourse, betrayal, critique. The renewal of human rights education. In C. Roux (Ed.), *Safe spaces: Human rights education in diverse contexts* (pp. 7–28). Sense Publishers.

Keet, A. (2017). Does human rights education exist? *International Journal of Human Rights Education, 1*(1), 1–18. Retrieved from http://repository.usfca.edu/ijhre/vol1/iss1/6

Moody, Z. (2016). *Les droits de l'enfant: genèse, institutionnalisation et diffusion (1924–1989)*. Editions Alphil.

Nazzari, V., McAdams, P., & Roy, D. (2005). Using transformative learning as a model for human rights education: A case study of the Canadian human rights Foundation's international human rights training program. *Intercultural Education, 16*(2), 171–186.

Phillips, L. G. (2016). Educating children and young people on the UNCRC: Actions, avoidance and awakenings. In J. Gillett-Swan & V. Coppock (Eds.), *Children's rights, educational research and the UNCRC: Past, present and future* (pp. 39–60). Symposium Books.

Rinaldi, S., Moody, Z. & Darbellay, F. (2020). Children's Human Rights Education in Swiss Curricula An Intercultural Perspective into Educational Concepts. *Swiss Journal of Educational Research, 42* (1), 64–83.

Sliwka, A. (2010). From homogeneity to diversity in German education. In *OECD, effective teacher education for diversity: Strategies and challenges* (pp. 205–217). OECD.

Simpson, G. (2017). "From the normative to the transformative": Defining and promoting justice and human rights as part of violent conflict prevention and peacebuilding. *Journal of Human Rights Practice, 9*(3), 379–400. https://doi.org/10.1093/jhuman/hux030

Struthers, A. E. C. (2015). Human rights education: Educating about, through and for human rights. *The International Journal of Human Rights, 19*(1), 53–73.

Tibbitts, F. (2005). Transformative learning and human rights education: Taking a closer look. *Intercultural Education, 16*(2), 107–113.

Trivers, H., & Starkey, H. (2012). The politics of critical citizenship education. In R. C. Mitchell & S. A. Moore (Eds.), *Politics, participation & power relations* (pp. 137–151). Sense Publishers.

Thelander, N. (2016). Human rights education: Teaching children's human rights – A matter of why, what and how. In J. Gillett-Swan & V. Coppock (Eds.), *Children's rights, educational research and the UNCRC: Past, present and future* (pp. 61–79). Symposium Books.

United Nations Committee on the Rights of the Child [CRC]. (2001). *General Comment No. 1: Article 29(1) The aims of education*. CRC/GC/2001/1.

United Nations. (1989). *United Nations convention on the rights of the child* [UNCRC]. (1989, 20 Nov.). Resolution 44/25.

United Nations. (1948). *United Nations declaration on human rights* [UNDHR]. (1948, 10 Dec.). Resolution 217A.

United Nations. (2011). *United Nations declaration on human rights education and training.* (2011, 19 Dec.). Resolution 66/137.

United Nations General Assembly [UNGA]. (1994, December 23). *Decade for human rights education*. Resolution 49/184.

United Nations General Assembly [UNGA]. (2004, December 10). *World programme for human rights education.* U.N. Doc. A/59/113.

Chapter 16
Countering Scepticism and Mistrust Towards Children's Rights Within Education: Fulfilling Article 29 in Mexico Through Teachers' Training on Human Rights

Gabriela Martinez Sainz

Abstract According to Article 29 of the Convention on the Rights of the Child (UNCRC), one of the key aims of education is the development of respect for human rights. Such aim derives into two concrete obligations. One, education must foster children's knowledge of human rights; two, it must provide opportunities for children to experience human rights in their school as an integral part of their learning processes. Despite the importance of these obligations, at the local level, their fulfilment within schools and classrooms is far from a reality. In contexts with increasing levels of violence and rights abuses such as Mexico, there is a widespread scepticism towards rights and misconceptions that have permeated into the educational system. Many schools and teachers are sceptics about human rights in general and children's rights in particular. This chapter discusses the strategies used to deal with teachers' criticisms towards rights and foster their commitment to children's rights in their professional practice. The analysis identifies the main tensions these rights – and the notion of children as rights-holders– pose to teachers to better understand how countering mistrust and scepticism is key for the fulfilment of the aims of education established in Article 29 of the UNCRC.

Keywords Children's rights education · Professional practice · Critical education · Child-centred education · Human rights training

G. Martinez Sainz (✉)
University College Dublin, Dublin, Ireland
e-mail: gabriela.martinezsainz@ucd.ie

J. Gillett-Swan, N. Thelander (eds.), *Children's Rights from International Educational Perspectives*, Transdisciplinary Perspectives in Educational Research 2, https://doi.org/10.1007/978-3-030-80861-7_16

Introduction

According to Article 29 of the Convention on the Rights of the Child (UNCRC), one of the key aims of education is the development of respect for human rights and fundamental freedoms. Such aim derives into two concrete obligations. On one hand, education has the responsibility to foster children's knowledge of human rights; on the other, it must provide opportunities for children to experience human rights in their school as an integral part of their learning processes. As stated in the General Comment of the UNCRC (GC1), the established aims translate into a specific type of education that is not only child-centred and child-friendly but that is underpinned by the principles of rights, that empowers children and strengthens their capacity to fully enjoy and exercise their rights (United Nations, 2001). For the fulfilment of the aim of education, the derived obligations as well as the implementation of the type of education implied within schools and classrooms, the role of teachers is instrumental. Teachers can adapt the content of human rights to children's comprehension levels, needs and interests (Bell, 1999; Jerome et al., 2015) but also to do it in a contextually relevant manner (Bajaj et al., 2016; Fritzsche, 2004; Tibbitts, 2017) that gives them the opportunity to learn through experiencing their own rights (Lundy & Martínez Sainz, 2018) within and beyond schools.

However, at the local level, a widespread scepticism towards human rights among teachers hinders not only the fulfilment of the obligations related to human rights but also the type of education advanced by the UNCRC. Such scepticism and mistrust towards rights are particularly common in contexts with increasing levels of violence and rights abuses, where rights are often seem as naïve and abstract ideals rather than enforceable instruments or guidelines for action (Cassidy et al., 2013; Struthers, 2016). This is the case of Mexico, in which many schools and teachers are sceptics about human rights in general, and children's rights in particular, dismissing their relevance or value within formal education. Thus, countering such mistrust and scepticism is key for the fulfilment of Article 29 of the UNCRC in the country. In this chapter, I discuss the strategies and preferred practices of human rights training programs directed to teachers in Mexico analysing how the pedagogical strategies of human rights educators responsible for teacher education programs focus specifically on dealing with teachers' criticisms towards rights and foster their commitment to children's rights in their professional practice. The analysis of these strategies makes it possible to identify the main tensions these rights –and the notion of children as rights holders– pose to teachers to then understand how these tensions become obstacles for achieving the aims of education established in Article 29. The data upon which this chapter draws is part of a larger project examining the intersection of knowledge, reflection and teaching practices in Human Rights Education and other relevant findings of the project have been reported elsewhere (Martínez Sainz, 2018a, b, c).

The Aims of Education and Human Eights

The aims of education are explicitly defined in the CRC as an attempt to emphasise not only the right to education but also the right to a "specific quality of education", one that "reflects the rights and inherent dignity of the child" by being "child-centred, child-friendly and empowering" (United Nations, 2001).

> Human rights education should provide information on the content of human rights treaties. But children should also learn about human rights by seeing human rights standards implemented in practice, whether at home, in school, or within the community. Human rights education should be a comprehensive, life-long process and start with the reflection of human rights values in the daily life and experiences of children. (United Nations, 2001, §15)

The two obligations that derived from the aims of education are the corner stone of Human Rights Education, as an acknowledgement that education must foster respect for human rights among children through the development of knowledge, skills, attitudes and behaviours. HRE has then a threefold approach to fulfil these obligations: education *about*, *for*, and *through* human rights (United Nations, 2011). The first perspective is a theoretical one – education *about* human rights– that encompasses "providing knowledge and understanding of human rights norms and principles, the values that underpin them and the mechanisms for their protection" (United Nations, 2012, p. 3). The second perspective is a practical one –education *for* human rights– that focuses on "empowering persons to enjoy and exercise their rights and to respect and uphold the rights of others" (United Nations, 2012, p. 3). Finally a perspective related to the environment where HRE takes place – education *through* human rights or human rights in education– concerned with the respect of educators and learners' rights throughout the educational process (curricula, materials, methods and training), and how this process should reflect human rights values and principles with the participation of teachers, learners and civil society.

Teachers' Role Securing Rights and the Aims of Education

Teachers have a determinant role to advance the three different perspectives of HRE and fulfil the 'aims of education' in relation to rights. They are responsible of disseminating relevant and meaningful information about rights in the lessons, of creating environments in which human rights are practised and lived in, and ultimately, of incorporating children's rights as an integral part of their learning processes. Teachers are instrumental actors in the fulfilment of the aims established for children's rights in the UNCRC and can be decisive advocates within schools and classrooms. Nevertheless, there are several ways in which children's rights are commonly breached in schools (Lundy & Martínez Sainz, 2018) which raises the question about teachers' attitudes towards rights and whether these can be barriers rather than enablers for the aims of education as established in the UNCRC.

Previous research suggests that teachers attitudes towards rights vary according to grades in which they teach as well as their levels of experience, becoming more positive among those working in lower levels and with less years of teaching (Pirsl et al., 2005). While there is evidence that support that HRE can change teachers' attitudes (Messina & Jacott, 2013) and help to increase their degree of appreciation towards rights (Gündoğdu, 2010) there is little information of how exactly HRE can counteract negative attitudes such as mistrust or scepticism among teachers. Such evidence results essential due to the demonstrated role of teachers' motivations and attitudes for the teaching, learning and overall implementation of children's rights (Brantefors & Quennerstedt, 2016; Jerome, 2016).

Children Rights and Education in Mexico

I selected Mexico as a "critical case" (Flyvbjerg, 2006) for this study due to the paradoxical situation in relation to children's rights. There is a significant progress in the legal framework to protect children's rights and fully incorporate them into the education system. In 2011 a Constitutional reform on human rights recognised all international treaties that Mexico has signed and ratified as legally enforceable instruments in domestic courts and tribunals (SEGOB, 2011) including the UNCRC and the Optional Protocol to the Convention on the Rights of the Child. The reform had deep implications for education and children's rights. For instance, the Constitution explicitly mentions now that the education provided by the State should develop the respect for human rights in line with the goals of education established in Article 29 of the UNCRC. It also reinforced the direct obligation of civil servants –including teachers working in the public education sector– to promote, protect and guarantee children's rights and are responsible for the prevention, investigation, sanction and reparation of human rights violations and abuses (SEGOB, 2011; United Nations, 2013). Furthermore, as a result of the constitutional basic education in the country –from Pre-School, Primary, and Secondary levels– has to integrate children's rights into the curriculum and promote a rights-based approach for teaching across all subjects and levels (SCJN, UN and CDHDF, 2013; SEGOB, 2011).

Despite the progressive legal framework, the number of violations and abuses towards children has systematically increased in the last decades. There are more than 40 million children in Mexico, which represents around 35% of the total population of the country. Half of these children live in poverty with at least one of their social rights being neglected or denied (CONEVAL and UNICEF, 2012). Indigenous children and adolescents are the most disadvantaged and suffer the lowest level of fulfilment of their basic rights in the country (UNICEF, 2018). The increasing levels of violence pose a security risk for children affecting negatively their right to education (Jarillo et al., 2016). And children are one of the most affected group of internal forced displacement due to violence in the country (CMDPDH, 2018). The contrast between the legal and material conditions to protect and promote children's rights make it difficult to classify Mexico either as a "human rights respecting society" or a "human rights violating society." The Mexican case proves that the heaven-hell binary distinctions often found in human rights literature is far from straight-forward (Okafor & Agbakwa, 2001). It is within this paradoxical situation and the tension between the legal provisions (heaven) and material conditions (hell) of children's rights in Mexico, in which human rights educators work.

Research Design and Methods of Data Collection

The findings presented in this chapter are the result of a qualitative case study of 15 human rights educators working in three different institutions in Mexico, including public and non-governmental organisations. The data of this case study was collected for a period of 6 months using a multi-method approach to data collection that not only allowed the incorporation of different sources of data but also the triangulation of the findings and the analytical categories identified (Yin, 2011). All the methods of data collection were open-ended. The first one, individual semi-structured interviews, examined educators' professional trajectories and teaching experience. The second method, a think-aloud task, presented each practitioner with a list of statements related to human rights to which they had to agree or disagree and elaborate on their reasons to do so. This method of data collection looked into their meaning-making processes about rights. The third method of data collection were participant observations of the training activities which allowed to analyse educators' practices and strategies in action. Finally, document analysis made it possible to collect data from the programs design, handbooks and teaching materials. Extracts form the data used in findings of this chapter indicate the method from which the data was collected. A multi-level (case, cross-case and across cases analysis) and hybrid approach to data analysis (including inductive and deductive coding) was conducted using qualitative data analysis (QDA) software to develop a contextually relevant and data-driven framework in which each educator was considered an individual idiographic case.

Findings

Scepticism and Mistrust Towards Rights

All educators (15/15),[1] regardless of their mastery of the subject or years of experience teaching human rights, claimed that widespread scepticism and general mistrust towards rights was one of the main challenges in their professional practice.

[1] Indicates the number of educators to which each statement is referring to out of the total cases

They all (15/15) agreed that the most recurrent misconception used to express such scepticism is that "human rights only defend criminals" which emphasises the general mistrust towards the value, legal implications or social benefits of human rights. One of the educators even argued that the most difficult aspect of learning to teach human rights is related to the skills needed rather than the content of the subject itself. He believed he had to develop persuasive skills to convince individuals and organisations about the importance and significance of human rights, which was not a simple task. As he explained, as a result of the scepticism and mistrust towards rights, his work consisted mostly of convincing individuals to change their personal and professional practices, as well as promoting institutional reform:

> In many of the cases there is still a lot of ignorance, but I believe that there is a lot of scepticism [about human rights]. I mean people do not believe that this [rights-based] system will solve anything or that is any different from the previous one, that it can resolve part of the problems. Then what I need to do is to keep on encouraging people to truly believe in these issues, to believe that there is an opportunity [to change things]. Is not that [human rights] are a panacea, nor that they will resolve all our problems, but they give us new alternatives (Educator #3, SSI[2])

In the particular case of teachers, educators working with schools (11/15), argued that such scepticism and mistrust towards rights were often related to power structures in the classroom and the implications concerning discipline that recognises children as right-holders can have. As one of the educators explained, training programs with teachers are difficult because they are more concerned about discipline rather than rights, thus they tend to be suspicious about the idea of empowering children to exercise their rights:

> Teachers and civil servants are very difficult. – [Interviewer] Shouldn't they be on the same side [as you promoting human rights]? –Yes and no. Yes, they should be but [in reality] is not like that, because instead, they consider human rights as a limitation of their work. '[From a human rights perspective] I cannot ground them, I cannot control them', because the only forms of control teachers know are rooted in violence [not in human rights]. (Educator #13, SSI)

According to her and other educators (9/15), for many teachers in Mexico, human rights are a limitation to traditional approaches to classroom management and promoting these rights in the classroom can lead to a lack of respect towards authorities and poor discipline. Often the scepticism is associated with a challenge towards teachers' expertise, particularly those with a considerable number of years in the profession.

> [Children's rights] is a topic that makes them [teachers] uncomfortable and bothers them a lot, because it is not about their rights but the rights of their students. I talk about rights…, human rights, regardless of your age but [teachers' reactions] are: 'What are you going to tell us? You want to teach me how to teach if I've doing these for 22 or 35 years?' They look down at you… (Educator #2, SSI)

[2]Abbreviations for the sources of the data: SSI = Semi-structured interview, TAT = Think-aloud task, OB = Observation.

Thus, educators have to confront teachers' misconceptions and clarify the role of human rights in the classroom before implementing any pedagogical strategies. One of the basic misconceptions they tackle is the "meritocratic" understanding of human rights. As one of the educators working with teachers exemplified:

> This is what is called a 'toxic' idea, the belief that you have to earn your rights. This is a discourse that is commonly directed to children... This discourse is usually used by teachers or parents, when they try to emphasise that children do have rights but they also have responsibilities, and they try to make it look as if these rights are a consequence of..., 'you only have rights as a consequence of fulfilling your responsibilities' when in reality is not like that. (Educator #12. TAT)

Many educators (7/15) acknowledged there could be several reasons for teachers to be sceptic about human and children's rights. Educators explained that reflecting on the interactions they had with teachers –and with other groups that also receive HRE training– helps them to understand better the reasons underpinning their scepticism and decide how to tackle them. Whereas some educators (8/15) focused on providing safe space for people to express freely their doubts and concerns about rights; others (6/15) emphasised the practical benefits of rights as tools capable of helping them in their professional practice and decision-making. The wide array of actions and pedagogical strategies educators implemented in teacher education programs pursued specifically two broad goals: the first one, dealing with teachers' criticisms towards rights and, the second, foster their commitment to children's rights in their professional practice.

Dealing with Criticisms

Most educators (8/15) considered persuasion as a key pedagogical strategy to teach human rights in Mexico. As one of them explained, persuading people attending the training programs –in this case teachers– about the importance of human rights is determinant not only for their work but for the actual enforcement of rights themselves:

> From my perspective how good or bad you are [as an educator]... you have to convince [learners]. Most of the time from this convincing will depend on how efficient and how effective they are in defending the values [underpinning human rights], so they can see them as their own [values]. Because at the end of the day, human rights cannot defend themselves [...] someone has to assume them as their own and has to defend them. (Educator #5, SSI)

Even though persuasion seems to be necessary, several of them (7/15) acknowledged that this strategy posed a significant challenge. As educators explained, there is a balance between convincing people of the importance of human rights but also being critical about their shortcomings and limitations. Without a critical stance, there is a risk of antagonising teachers, of coming across as insensitive towards their concerns and only reinforcing misconceptions or negative assumptions rather than fostering a change of attitudes. At the same time, their critical approach should not undermine the importance and value of children's rights.

One way in which educators attempted to achieve this balance while persuading teachers was by distinguishing between the normative nature of rights and the reality of their practice. As some of the educators argued, that the aspirational nature of rights can serve as a motivation as well as guidelines for their practice:

> Even though we know that in reality is not like that, [in reality human rights are not universal], they are an aspiration. An ethical and legal imperative that motivates so human rights through the members of the society can move forward towards that direction. (Educator #3, TAT)
>
> [Through human rights] we can build a society, a healthy, free, plural society. A balanced and horizontal society in which we all have the same opportunities. And it is something really utopic [...] but what utopias are for if it is not to keep us walking towards them. (Educator #14, TAT)

By making this distinction, educators could acknowledge the reality of human rights in Mexico making the point that shortcomings in their implementation are not a reason to reject them. On the contrary, by accepting that there is a gap between the ideal human rights pose and their actual implementation and practice, educators can emphasise the importance of working for their protection without ignoring the criticisms teachers may have. Another way in which educators attempted to persuade teachers was through the distinction between individual and systemic challenges for the implementation of rights. For instance, one of the educators constantly pointed out that the implementation of human rights in schools was inoperable due to the lack of minimal conditions for these rights to be respected regardless of the efforts of teachers:

> Well, you realise that human rights... they sound really nice in theory but in practice, there is no such thing. In practice, the minimal conditions for a culture of legality and respect towards human rights do not exist [in schools], there is a lack of respect amongst them [the students] and their schoolmates. (Educator #8, SSI)

For him, the structural limitations for the respect and promotion of human rights are evident in everyday situations and almost impossible to overcome. Without such minimal conditions, the whole project of human rights can be seen as a utopian endeavour that can lead teachers to challenge the notion of human rights itself. Another pedagogical strategy several educators (7/15) employed to address misconceptions among learners and their criticisms towards rights was the deconstruction of concepts. For instance, Educator #5 argued that deconstructing concepts was necessary to explain in an accessible way the abstract and complex content of human rights. He used this pedagogical strategy most of the time as it helps him to set a common ground with learners. Establishing common ground and language was also a concern for some of the other educators (8/14), as the following observation notes show:

> She is explaining to participants that the main objective is to provide educators and practitioners with a space to share, discuss and learn from each others' best practices for teaching human rights. To do so, she says is important to establish common definitions and homogenise terms. Even though she is providing her institution's official definition she is making

> sure to emphasise in her explanation that human rights extend beyond the legal framework and are a way of living and treating others respecting their human dignity. For her presentation of the definition of human rights, she is presenting extracts of legal instruments, like the Constitution and UDHR, and other official documents on Peace Education. After she finished her explanation she asked participants to share their own definitions and views, so they could all clarify the underpinning values of human rights. (Educator #6, OB)

Establishing common ground and language for discussion not only allow for a more productive dialogue when addressing criticism towards rights but can foster engagement among teachers. As one of them explained, such engagement is instrumental to change learners' "mind-set and attitudes" (Educator #8). Many of the educators (10/15) agreed that the aim was not only to convince learners about the importance and significance of human rights but to foster their commitment towards them that incites them to act in such a way that respects and promotes these rights.

Fostering Commitment

For educators deciding what strategies to implement to fosters learners' commitment towards human rights was extremely difficult. All of them (15/15) agreed that such commitment was the educational goal for the programs they delivered, although differed on the underpinning reasoning for it. For some of them (5/15) individual commitment was a learning outcome, a manifestation of capacity building and skills development; whereas for others (6/15) such commitment was the starting point for the development of further competencies to promote and protect rights. Regardless of their reasoning though, most (12/15) educators focused on two key strategies to achieve this goal: cultivating empathy and modelling good teaching practices.

There were multiple ways in which educators cultivated empathy among teachers, however, the most recurrent strategies included role-playing, storytelling and real-life scenarios. Many educators (11/15) implemented some sort of role-playing, in which they asked learners to either switch positions or consider the challenges others might have to address a wide variety of issues from discrimination, harassment, non-violence in the classroom and conflict resolution. "Putting in someone else's shoes" was a common reference among educators when they discussed role-playing as a pedagogical strategy and its advantages. As one of the educators explained:

> But if I can develop skills in hand with emotions... [...] I raise a problem so they can translate them into their daily life. For example, if we talk about stereotypes, about prejudices, [I ask them] "How was your first day at work? How did other people see you? How did you feel? What stereotypes did you have to handle?" ... I use absolutely plain language, and that makes people [feel safe and] say "Oh, here we can talk!" [...] the goal is to sensitize them, so they put themselves in each other's shoes. (Educator #4, SSI)

With similar objectives in mind, other educators (6/15) used fictional stories in a variety of formats to cultivate empathy among learners, including picture books and comics, videos or documentaries. As one of the educators argued, cultivating empathy through these activities not only raise awareness of rights abuses and violations but to encourage teachers to commit towards their protection and promotion.

> It is important that they are able to see themselves as equal, […] to empathise with other's suffering, […] to respect each other, to discuss and share, and teach each other what we know (Educator #2, SSI)

Her teaching strategies are designed to allow teachers to experience an environment of respect and promotion of human rights during the programs. Her goal was that her teaching strategies will help participants to experience a sense of empowerment to stand up for their own rights, but also to become empathic about the rights of the other. Similarly to her, several educators (6/15) advocated for modelling good teaching practices as a key strategy to foster a commitment towards rights as it shows teacher how to translate rights into practice.

> This session is a workshop for teenagers of a secondary public school, there are X students and two teachers in the group. The students sit informally in the space designated for 'circle time' arranged as a small hill with artificial grass simulating a park, while teachers grab two chairs and sit behind them. Once everyone is in their places Educators#11 explains how this space works and the format of the session. She starts by making clear that everyone has the right to share their opinion and be heard so respect is vital so they can listen and be listened to. From the start, there are no prearranged rules they have to follow but instead, she and Educators#12 would like to establish with them agreements on how to behave and conduct during the workshop. At the beginning students were reluctant to participate or talk about the agreements of conduct, so both teachers stood up from their chairs and start to talk proposing to use the same rules that apply in their classrooms. Educators#11 stopped them and, although gently, firmly explained that the current space was not a classroom and reminded them that students were in charge of proposing and selecting the agreements. So, instead of overruling their ideas by imposing the classroom rules, teachers should encourage them to speak and express their ideas by giving students the space and time they needed. After a couple of minutes in silence, students started to talk and gave some suggestions for the agreements. (Educators #11 and #12, OB)

For these educators, deciding the agreements that will guide the workshop is an essential introductory strategy, and it is particularly helpful to demonstrate teachers how to a respectful and collaborative class management approach can work, and at the same time, give learners an example of how human rights are relevant for them in common tasks.

When all the previous strategies were not enough to address the scepticism and mistrust among teachers, several educators (7/15) relied on a legal analysis of children's rights and the protection framework in Mexico to make clear their responsibility. As one of them explained, when teaching human rights it is important not only explain what rights children are entitled to but also to emphasise the personal and social commitments the full enjoyment that these rights demand from them.

> … It is complicated to put [human rights] into practice. It is complicated because most people consider human rights as someone else's responsibility not their own. If the State is the one that has to secure your rights, then the State is the responsible, right? But they are overlooking the other part… where do you left your commitment [towards these rights]? (Educator #9, SSI)

By emphasising the role individuals play in the protection of rights, educators like her are not dismissing the role of the State in guaranteeing human rights but fostering a sense of co-responsibility. Thus, by teaching a co-responsible view towards rights, these educators encourage individuals to have a commitment in the protection and used the current legal framework of the country to make their case:

> [To teachers] you might need to follow an instruction from the Ministry of Education or your own institution but you and me, we all have a higher mandate and that is the Convention of the Rights of the Child. All adults are responsible for children enjoying their rights, it is an obligation for all of us. (Educator #13, SSI)

For most educators (9/15) teaching about co-responsibility became paramount after the Constitutional reform on human rights. When working with teachers and education personnel for example, many educators (9/15) used legal instruments such as Mexican Constitution and the Convention of the Rights of the Child to explain why they are duty-bound by law to protect children's rights. However, for most of them (7/9) the legal aspect needed to be reinforced by appealing to teachers' moral responsibilities, thus the objective of many of the strategies educators implemented was to remind teachers they role in securing children's rights.

Discussion and Conclusion

The findings of the study show the preferred strategies educators in Mexico implement to address the widespread scepticism and mistrust towards rights among teachers. These strategies demonstrate an instructional scaffolding in which educators first address teachers' misconceptions and then the focus on their negative attitudes so they can finally work on fostering commitment and putting rights into practice. Such scaffolding is consistent with suggestions in previous research about the importance of embedding children's rights into teachers' pedagogies not only concerning their practices but also their values (Devine & McGillicuddy, 2016). According to practitioners' experiences and reflections, a general lack of knowledge about rights and how these work are the main root of teachers' misconceptions and inaccurate interpretations, which inevitably lead to scepticism and mistrust. Such lack of knowledge further confirms previous research on the limited knowledge teachers have on human rights and the importance of incorporating human and children's rights into teacher education (Decara, 2014; Jerome et al., 2015; Messina & Jacott, 2013; Struthers, 2016; Waldron et al., 2011). It is also possible that the violence of the country informs and in some instances reinforces teachers' misconceptions, as similar findings can be found in other contexts that had experience high levels of violence (Zembylas et al., 2015).

The analysis of the preferred strategies human rights educators implement to deal with criticisms towards rights and to foster teachers' commitment to children's rights, serve to identify two main tensions rights pose to teachers. The first tension is related to power, as revealed through teachers' concerns about discipline, classroom management and respect towards adults over children's empowerment and participation. The second one is related to child agency as teachers' focus on responsibilities and their reluctance to recognise children's as actual and legal rights-holders show. These tensions resonate to concerns and challenges raised by teachers in relation to rights in other contexts (Cassidy et al., 2013; Kuran, 2014; Struthers, 2016). The identified tensions are underpinned by an adult-centric perspective, that fails to recognise children's agency (González Coto, 2012), that is, children as active autonomous agent capable of making decisions about their rights. The implicit adult-centrism and the identified tensions, if left unaddressed, will act as obstacles for the realisation of the aims of education in schools as classrooms, at least as established in the Article 29 of the UNCRC (United Nations, 2001).

The type of education and established aims by the UNCRC demand from teachers pedagogical practices that are child-centred that teaches children about their rights, that empowers them to exercise their rights while protecting the rights of others, and that are conducted in an environment in which children's rights are fully respected. Considering the evidence of the determinant role of teachers' inclinations, motivations and attitudes for the teaching, learning and overall implementation of children's rights (Brantefors & Quennerstedt, 2016; Decara, 2014; Jerome, 2016), is important that HRE not only recognises but fully address teachers' mistrust and scepticism towards rights. Although persuasion has been considered an intrinsic element to teaching in order to engage learners (Smith, 2003), the findings of this cross-case analysis confirm its key role in HRE as suggested previously by (Al-daraweesh, 2013). This requires through an un-learning process in which misconceptions, assumptions and inaccurate interpretations of rights are challenged and used as catalyst for a critical HRE (Bajaj et al., 2016; Martínez Sainz, 2018c; Zembylas & Keet, 2019) that recognises the shortcomings of rights and the long way to go before these are fully exercised. A re-learning process must follow, in which teachers can work through the difficulties or challenges to teach about, for and through children's rights; which will bring their experiences at the centre of HRE facilitating an hermeneutical perspective in which teachers as learners gain awareness about their own stances and interpretations of rights (Al-Daraweesh & Snauwaert, 2013). The proposed un-learning and re-learning processes recognise the role teachers can have as agents of change in relation to children's rights and for the realisation of the aims of education; however, these require the creation of safe spaces (Roux, 2012), not only in teacher education programs but also in the communities of practice in which teachers are involved.

References

Al-daraweesh, F. (2013). Human rights and human rights education: Beyond the conventional approach. *In Factis Pax. Journal of Peace Education and Social Justice, 7*(1), 38–58.

Al-Daraweesh, F., & Snauwaert, D. T. (2013). Toward a hermeneutical theory of international human rights education. *Educational Theory, 63*(4), 389–412. https://doi.org/10.1111/edth.12030

Bajaj, M., Cislaghi, B., & Mackie, G. (Eds.). (2016). *Advancing transformative human rights education. Appendix D to the report of the Global Citizenship Commission*. Open Book Publishers.

Bell, C. (1999). *Teaching human rights: Teaching and learning manual*. National Centre for Legal Education, University of Warwick.

Brantefors, L., & Quennerstedt, A. (2016). Teaching and learning children's human rights: A research synthesis. *Cogent Education, 3*(1), 1–18. https://doi.org/10.1080/2331186X.2016.1247610

Cassidy, C., Brunner, R., & Webster, E. (2013). Teaching human rights? 'All hell will break loose!'. *Education, Citizenship and Social Justice, 9*(1), 19–33. https://doi.org/10.1177/1746197913475768

CMDPDH. (2018). *Episodios de desplazamiento forzado interno en México*, 86. Comision Mexicanade Defensa y Promesion de los Derechos Humanas, Episodos, Mexico.

CONEVAL & UNICEF. (2012). *Pobreza y derechos sociales de niñas, niños y adolescentes en México, 2008–2010*. CONEVAL.

Decara, C. (2014). *Mapping of human rights education in Danish schools*. Danish Institute for Human Rights.

Devine, D., & McGillicuddy, D. (2016). Positioning pedagogy – A matter of children's rights. *Oxford Review of Education, 42*(4), 424–443. https://doi.org/10.1080/03054985.2016.1197111

Flyvbjerg, B. (2006). Five misunderstandings about case-study research. *Qualitative Inquiry, 12*(2), 219–245. https://doi.org/10.1177/1077800405284363

Fritzsche, K. P. (2004). What human rights education is all about – 15 theses. In V. B. Georgi & M. Seberich (Eds.), *International perspectives in human rights education* (pp. 162–167). Betelsmann Foundation.

González Coto, M. (2012). La agencia de la niña y el niño en la condición pre-ciudadana. *Actualidades Investigativas En Educación, 12*(2), 1–19.

Gündoğdu, K. (2010). The effect of constructivist instruction on perspective teachers' attitudes toward human rights education. *Electronic Journal of Research in Educational Psychology, 8*(1), 333–352.

Jarillo, B., Magaloni, B., Franco, E., & Robles, G. (2016). How the Mexican drug war affects kids and schools? Evidence on effects and mechanisms. *International Journal of Educational Development*. https://doi.org/10.1016/j.ijedudev.2016.05.008

Jerome, L. (2016). Interpreting children's rights education (CRE): Three perspectives and three roles for teachers. *Citizenship, Social and Economic Education, 15*(2), 143–156. https://doi.org/10.1177/2047173416683425

Jerome, L., Emerson, L., Lundy, L., & Orr, K. (2015). *Teaching and learning about child rights: A study of implementation in 26 countries*. UNICEF.

Kuran, K. (2014). Teacher perspectives on civic and human rights education. *Educational Research Review, 9*(10), 302–311. https://doi.org/10.5897/ERR2013.1707

Lundy, L., & Martínez Sainz, G. (2018). The role of law and legal knowledge for a transformative human rights education: Addressing violations of children's rights in formal education. *Human Rights Education Review, 1*(2), 04–24. https://doi.org/10.7577/hrer.2560

Martínez Sainz, G. (2018a). Building professional agency in human rights education: Translating policy into practice. *International Journal of Human Rights Education, 2*(1), 1–30.

Martínez Sainz, G. (2018b). Human rights education and training programs in Mexico: A cross-case analysis of practitioners' professional knowledge and practices. *Mexican Law Review, XI*(1), 103–130. https://doi.org/10.22201/iij.24485306e.2018.1.12513

Martínez Sainz, G. (2018c). The challenges of teaching children their rights in a violent context. In G. Martínez Sainz & S. Ilie (Eds.), *International perspectives on practice and research into children's rights* (pp. 83–110). Centro de Estudios en Derechos Humanos.

Messina, C., & Jacott, L. (2013). An exploratory study of human rights knowledge: A sample of kindergarten and elementary school pre-service teachers in Spain. *Human Rights Review, 14*(3), 213–230. https://doi.org/10.1007/s12142-013-0267-1

Okafor, O. C., & Agbakwa, S. C. (2001). Re-imagining international human rights education in our time: Beyond three constitutive orthodoxies. *Leiden Journal of International Law, 14*(3), 563–590.

Pirsl, E., Marusic-Stimac, O., & Pokrajac, A. (2005). Attitudes of students and teachers towards civic education and human rights. *Metodički Obzori, 2*(2), 19–34.

Roux, C. (Ed.). (2012). *Safe spaces. Human rights education in diverse contexts*. Sense Publishers.

SCJN, UN, CDHDF. (2013). *Reforma DH. Metodología para la enseñanza de la reforma constitucional en derechos humanos*. Retrieved from http://www.reformadh.org.mx/

SEGOB. (2011). *Reforma constitucional en materia de derechos humanos*. Diario Oficial de la Federación.

Smith, R. (2003). Unfinished business: Education without necessity. *Teaching in Higher Education, 8*(4), 477–491. https://doi.org/10.1080/1356251032000117571

Struthers, A. E. C. (2016). Human rights: A topic too controversial for mainstream education? *Human Rights Law Review, 16*(1), 131–162. https://doi.org/10.1093/hrlr/ngv040

Tibbitts, F. (2017). Evolution of human rights education models. In M. Bajaj (Ed.), *Human rights education: Theory, research, praxis*. University of Pennsylvania Press.

UN [United Nations]. (2001). *General Comment No. 1 on Article 29 (1) of the Convention on the Rights of the Child*. United Nations. https://doi.org/10.3126/jnps.v29i1.1601

UN [United Nations]. (2011). *Draft United Nations declaration on human rights education and training, education*. United Nations.

UN [United Nations]. (2012). *World programme for human rights education. Second phase*. United Nations.

UN [United Nations]. (2013). *Informe sobre la situación de derechos humanos en México: actualización 2012 y balance 2013*. United Nations.

UNICEF. (2018). *Informe Anual México 2018*. UNICEF.

Waldron, F., Kavanagh, A., Kavanagh, R., Maunsell, C., Oberman, R., OReilly, M., Pike, S., Prunty, A., & Ruane, B. (2011). *Teachers, human rights and human rights education*. The Centre for Human Rights and Citizenship Education.

Yin, R. K. (2011). *Qualitative research from tart to finish*. The Guildford Press.

Zembylas, M., & Keet, A. (2019). *Critical human rights education. Advancing social-justice-oriented educational praxes*. Springer.

Zembylas, M., Charalambous, P., Lesta, S., & Charalambous, C. (2015). Primary school teachers' understandings of human rights and human rights education (HRE) in Cyprus: An exploratory study. *Human Rights Review, 16*(2), 161–182. https://doi.org/10.1007/s12142-014-0331-5

Chapter 17
Perspectivising Children's Rights and Education in Research: Analysing the Teaching and Learning of Children's Rights on the Basis of Human Rights Education (HRE) Theory

Lotta Brantefors and Nina Thelander

Abstract In research about children's rights and education diverse theoretical perspectives related to various theoretical traditions and academic disciplines are used. This multi- disciplinary research field seems sometimes to be too dispersed with a lack of a main collective theory and with an overly strong focus on the Convention. In this chapter, the question of theory, specifically the use of Human Rights Education (HRE) theory as a basis for analyses of children's rights education, is examined. Theoretical models and concepts of HRE are discussed and how they can strengthen and perspectivise research about teaching and learning children's rights. The HRE theory examples are mainly from two recently published books: Bajaj 2017, *Human rights education, theory, research, praxis* and Zembylas and Keet 2018, *Critical human rights, citizenship and democracy education*. In the chapter we also present examples of HRE with illustrations from our recent study – a Swedish large-scale, three-year project about the teaching and learning of children's rights in early childhood education and school. The main findings are that HRE theories could help to analyse experiences and contribute to a collective platform for research on children's rights education. The theories will make it easier to perspectivise the education proposed in Article 29 in the Convention and to see the plurality in HRE as well as in children's rights and education.

Keywords Children's rights · Education · Teaching & learning · Human rights education · (Human rights education) theory

---

L. Brantefors (✉)
Department of Education, Uppsala University, Uppsala, Sweden
e-mail: lotta.brantefors@edu.uu.se

N. Thelander
Faculty of Humanities and Social Sciences, Karlstad University, Karlstad, Sweden
e-mail: nina.thelander@kau.se

J. Gillett-Swan, N. Thelander (eds.), *Children's Rights from International Educational Perspectives*, Transdisciplinary Perspectives in Educational Research 2, https://doi.org/10.1007/978-3-030-80861-7_17

Introduction

The Convention on the Rights of the Child states the right *to* education through Article 28, and the child's rights *in* and *through* education comprising the 'aims of education' through Article 29 (United Nations, 1989). The aims have then been further developed in General Comment No.1: The Aims of Education (Article 29) (United Nations, 2001). There are five subparagraphs of aims: "the holistic development of the full potential of the child (29 (1) (a)), including development of respect for human rights (29 (1) (b)), an enhanced sense of identity and affiliation (29 (1) (c)), and his or her socialization and interaction with others (29 (1) (d)) and with the environment (29 (1) (e))" (United Nations, 2001).

However, these general statements are not always translated the same way in children's rights education and they depend on different circumstances. International research shows that teaching and learning is performed differently in different contexts concerning these matters (Brantefors & Quennerstedt, 2016). It is also clear that the theories used in the analyses perspectivise what is researched (Brantefors & Thelander, 2017). Depending on the "spectacles" used, different "stories" will be told. In this chapter the question of theory will be discussed, specifically Human Rights Education (HRE) theory (e.g., Bajaj, 2017) as a possible basis for analyses of children's rights education. In the chapter, we also discuss how the choice of theory will have an impact on what we find in an analysis of how Article 29 is carried out in practice. For example, if a critical theory is used for the analysis, the question of who benefits in the described situation will be particularly in focus.

If we look back on the research situation concerning children's rights and education, we find that it has attracted a great deal of attention over the years among educational researchers from different countries and various academic disciplines using different theoretical approaches (Quennerstedt, 2011). As a research field, children's rights in education is characterised by being multi-disciplined, but most studies are anchored in the UN Convention of the Rights of the Child (United Nations, 1989). Through long-term implementation work, a dominant international consensus on children's rights, based on the Convention, has been developed. Critical voices, however, point out that the Convention in many cases has turned into a norm that is not questioned and problematised sufficiently. Instead, it is viewed as a standard-setting instrument, also among many researchers. Such an approach could risk only reproducing knowledge, if it does not take into account for example different contexts and various theoretical perspectives (Reynaert et al., 2009).

Freeman (2018) reminds us of the importance of considering children's rights, as well as the Convention, as a dynamic process linked to societal changes and developments. He also emphasises the importance for researchers of critically questioning and discussing children's rights. Moreover, he also stresses that when the Convention was launched, "it was taken for granted that the Convention was all we needed to know about children's rights" (Freeman, 2018, p. 2). Today, children's rights in education is a well-established research field (Freeman, 2018). Despite the fact that different theories and theoretical perspectives have been discussed, few researchers have pointed out that research about children's human rights in education could be criticised for a lack of theorising (Quennerstedt & Quennerstedt, 2014). The theoretical perspectives used are diverse and related to various theoretical traditions and academic disciplines. There is for example no main theory/theories similar to that of Human Rights Education theory (e.g., Bajaj, 2017). Another problem here could also be that when publishing in established journals of human rights education, research about teaching and learning children's rights without any links to HRE might be questioned and considered lacking.

Together, the challenges mentioned above – the dispersed research field, the lack of a main theory, and the problem of publishing – have prompted us to take a closer look at the theories of HRE. The aim in the chapter is to discuss how theoretical models and concepts of HRE can strengthen and perspectivise research about teaching and learning children's rights.

In the following sections, three examples of HRE theories will be presented together with illustrations from our present research – a Swedish large-scale, three-year project about the teaching and learning of children's rights in early childhood education and school (Quennerstedt et al., 2014, 2019; Brantefors et al., 2019), theoretically based on European Didaktik (didactics) (e.g., Gundem, 2011; Klafki, 1995; Hudson & Meyer, 2011) and Dewey's educational theories (1916). Before the presentation of the three examples of HRE theory, we will first introduce the concept of Human Rights Education.

Human Rights Education (HRE)

In this brief introduction to human rights education (HRE), we present three meanings of HRE. When HRE is mentioned, what is usually meant is (i) the definition given in the World programme for HRE (United Nations, 2006) about what such an education should include: Human rights education should include the three elements knowledge and skills, values and attitudes, and capacity for action to be considered complete (United Nations, 2006). (ii) The second meaning of HRE refers to human rights education as a research area in formal and informal education, such as for example in NGOs (cf. Bajaj, 2017). (iii) The last and third meaning of HRE refers to the theories of human rights education and comprises different models and systematised knowledge used in research. In the present chapter, it is the third meaning of human rights education – the theories of HRE – that is at stake. In the next section, we discuss three examples of HRE theory that we have found particularly useful in research on children's rights and education, mainly from two recently published books: Bajaj, 2017, *Human rights education, theory, research, praxis*, and Zembylas & Keet, 2018, *Critical human rights, citizenship and democracy education*. First, the liberal and critical tradition of HRE is introduced. In the next section, ideological approaches to HRE are presented. And in the third section, the contextual situation/location of HRE is discussed.

Three Examples of HRE Theory

The Liberal and Critical Tradition of HRE

HRE theory is not only one theoretical tradition; it consists of several theoretical traditions. The theory can be more or less critical and transformative (cf. critical theories in education, critical pedagogy, cf. Freire [1996]) or more or less liberal. Most theories in human rights education derive from a European liberal tradition based on the individual's right to life, freedom and equity. However, these (Western) groundings have been criticised for only serving Western powers and people. When taking human rights for granted and not questioning the foundations or the power structures, we mostly act in the liberal tradition. Zembylas (in Bajaj, 2017) summarises the criticism against the liberal tradition as follows:

> Human rights, over the years, have become essentialised and universal norms often expressed in juridical terms, whereas their history indicates that human rights are a Western concept grounded in liberal views, serving the interest of Western powers [e.g., Mutua 2002] acting in neo-colonial terms [Baxi 2007; Spivak 2004]; human rights are vague, abstract, and more symbolic than substantive [Ignatieff 2001; Rorty 1998]; and human rights are used to impose and legitimate political hegemony, even when they do not always intend to address the causes of social grievance and suffering [Brown 2004], (Zembylas, 2017, p. 48).

From a critical perspective, the liberal tradition is viewed as being symbolic, legitimising values of power and domination, and lacking substantial meaning. In other words, in a liberal tradition human rights as an emancipative idea seem to be taken for granted. Critical educators therefore emphasise the need to be critically aware of the values and patterns of power and domination, otherwise there is a risk that these values will be legitimised in education (Cranston & Janzen, 2017).

A major critique against a strategy in the liberal tradition is that of the "declarationist" strategy, which indicates the lack of discussion in a liberal tradition of the emancipatory possibilities embedded in the idea of human rights. Bajaj (2017) states that "[r]ecent critiques [Keet 2007] have noted that the overly 'declarationist' strategy of HRE, which anchors itself in normative standards, limits its emancipatory potential since it fails to consider broader debates in the field of human rights" (p. 7). Also Zembylas (2017) emphasises this critique against the declarationist strategy: "[T]he rhetoric of human rights often remains at a metaphysical or rationalist level or ends up being an empty and abstract moral ideology" (in Bajaj, 2017, p. 47). The problem is that neglecting considerations of power and domination in education can mask inequalities for children and young people in having their rights fulfilled. With a declarationist strategy, education is mostly performed in a "comfort zone" (cf. McLaren, 2015) where questions about inequalities, power and domination are missing. Education performed in a "comfort zone" is polite to all pupils, but is more or less lacking a discussion about social structures and social injustice. Bajaj (2017) points out that "creating sympathy for and solidarity with others, without [challenging social structures is] leading up to 'empty sentimentality'" (p. 7). With "comfort zone education", the potential of human rights could be lost and the result will be fewer possibilities for social change.

The most common strategy in HRE seems to be the declarationist strategy which usually neglects the emancipative potential of education. This is also what the results of the children's rights teaching and learning project show (Brantefors, 2019; Brantefors et al., 2019; Quennerstedt et al., 2019). During a period of 3 months, none of the teachers nor the pupils raised any critical questions related to power, domination or social structures. All education has been carried out with a declarationist strategy and in a comfort zone of politeness and kindness. To raise and discuss more critical questions and perspectives related to power did not seem to be relevant. Therefore we also agree with critical educators that a more critical human rights education could "move the field forward closer to its emancipatory promise" (Bajaj, 2017, p. 7). This means that in educational research (and of course also in the teaching and learning of rights), questions of power and domination need to be asked.

Ideological Approaches to HRE

Another important tool for analyses of human rights education are theoretical categorisations of different approaches to HRE. Bajaj (2017) suggests three ideological approaches to HRE: HRE for Global Citizenship, HRE for Coexistence, and HRE for Transformative Action. (i) HRE for Global Citizenship fosters membership of in an international community by teaching about human rights and skills related to universal values and standards. (ii) HRE for Coexistence focuses on the interpersonal and inter-groups aspect of human rights where education about human rights is regarded as a way of coping with ethnic or civil strife. (iii) HRE for Transformative Action usually involves learners who are economically or politically marginalised. Here, HRE is informed by the ideas of Paolo Freire, where the aim is to cultivate the pupils' critical consciousness and teach them how they can socially change their situations. The third category is sometimes also fused with the philosophical tradition of cosmopolitanism described by several researchers (Bajaj, 2017). The approaches are all examples of systematised experience of HRE and are based on international educational research. They are possible models to compare with when analysing different approaches to human rights education and each approach has a different aim and a different reason why human rights should be taught. This means that teaching about rights is not a unilateral phenomenon but there are different approaches to and different motives for teaching human rights around the world.

Another theoretical categorisation that is similar to the approaches outlined above and that also distinguishes between different human rights education approaches comprise *the five rights curriculum emphases* that are the results of empirical analyses of the teaching and learning of rights (Brantefors & Thelander, 2017; Brantefors et al., 2019). The emphases are based on a curriculum theoretical perspective and the concept of curriculum emphasis (cf. Roberts, 1982). This concept is used to distinguish between different educational approaches concerning the content, the aim, and the processes in rights education, and helps to show the plurality of educational intentions when for example comparing different teaching and learning situations.

The five rights curriculum emphases that are similar to the three approaches described above are the following: participation emphasis, empowerment emphasis, awareness emphasis, rights respecting emphasis, and democratic emphasis. In relation to participation emphasis, the principal aim in the teaching of human rights is participation and to prepare for participatory democratic citizenship. The older the children, the more their views, voices and experiences should be included in decision-making. This emphasis is similar to the second HRE approach of coexistence and HRE for global existence. In relation to empowerment emphasis, the principal aim is to empower children to be actively engaged with others. For school-age children, social action is more critical and emancipative and includes reaching out to society at large. The empowerment emphasis is similar to the third approach of HRE for transformative action. In relation to rights awareness emphasis, the principal aim is to create an awareness of rights. This emphasis stresses knowledge about human rights and it is thought that knowing about human rights will help children to protect and enjoy rights and develop a society with a human rights culture. This emphasis resembles the second approach of HRE for global citizenship. The principal aim of the fourth rights respecting emphasis is to develop good social relations and good behaviour. Instead of rules, human rights and rights-based relations are in focus. The idea here is that respecting human rights helps children to learn responsibility for others. Finally, in relation to the fifth democratic curriculum emphasis, the overall aim is to educate children to be democrats. The last two emphases are not similar to any of the HRE approaches.

Interestingly enough, it is possible to discriminate between more than three approaches when using the curriculum emphases concept. Another point of interest here is the fifth emphasis – the democratic emphasis. This emphasis is recognised in a Scandinavian context – Sweden (Brantefors et al., 2019) and Norway (Osler & Solhaug, 2018) – showing a conflation of human rights and democratic education: "In everyday discourse, the terms "human rights" and "democracy" are often conflated, and the emphasis is generally on democratic *practices* in schools' (Osler & Solhaug, 2018, p. 278). This example leads us to the third example of HRE theory.

Location

The question of location and contextual differences is discussed in detail in HRE theory and is related to the political situation and the nation in focus. Different traditions and approaches are distinguished based on location and HRE can no longer be characterised as a singularly understood practice, but rather reflects where such programs are located. Bajaj (2011) stresses that HRE is affiliated with different constituencies in different nations, exemplifying with a description of the current situation by Felisa Tibbitts:

> HRE in post-conflict or post-colonial countries tends to be associated with the rule of law and authorities trying to establish their legitimacy. Among groups that experience a high amount of discrimination, and within countries that are highly repressive and undemocratic, HRE tends to be focused on popular empowerment and resistance in relation to these issues. HRE in countries that are democratic but struggling with development can be oriented towards the infusion of human rights principles within sustainable development. In countries that enjoy strong democratic and economic development, HRE is often focused on issues of discrimination, for example in relation to migrants, minorities, or women (Tibbitts in Bajaj, 2011, p. 486).

This citation shows how different contexts make for different human rights education and that the proposed HRE is also part of the solution of a national/regional problem. The last statement, suggesting that in countries enjoying strong democratic and economic development the focus is often on issues of discrimination in relation to migrants, minorities and women, could well be illustrated through the example of Sweden. Comparing with the results of the Swedish project in compulsory school Year 5 (children aged 10–11 years old) and Year 8 (young people aged 14–15 years old), there are several connections to what Bajaj explains. The findings in our project show that the teachers mix human rights and democratic rights and the main value they discuss is equal value and the struggle against discrimination (Brantefors et al., 2019). The results of the project show a focus on democracy, discrimination, migration, and the question of inequality. HRE is not an isolated area of education in this case, but part of the teaching and learning of fundamental and democratic values (cf The Education Act, Sverige [Sweden] 2016). In the beginning of the project, we had no theories that could explain the contextual differences, but after studying the theories of location we have become more aware of the global differences. This statement may seem simple, but the obvious fact is that different locations make for different human rights education. Arranging human rights education in South Africa, for example, is different from doing so in Bosnia or Turkey (cf. Brantefors & Quennerstedt, 2016). When we compare the educational aims, content, and processes over the world, we find that the aims of education differ and there is a plurality of meanings of human rights education. Some instances of human rights education aim for teaching participation, while other instances focus on rights consciousness (Brantefors & Quennerstedt, 2016; Brantefors & Thelander, 2017). This means that not only the aims are different, but also the content and the processes differ in relation to the aims. These differences in human rights education are also mirrored in the theories of HRE, as has been presented above.

Discussion and Conclusions

In this chapter we have presented three examples of HRE theory that we think could contribute to analyses of children's rights and education. The most important challenge we faced is the lack of a collective theory for analyses of children's rights and education. Regarding this lack, we are sure that the HRE theories could help us analyse our experiences and contribute to a collective platform for our research on children's rights education. We are also sure that the theories will make it easier to perspectivise the education proposed in Article 29 in the Convention (United Nations, 1989, 2001) and to see the plurality in HRE as well as in children's rights and education. As we have shown in the chapter, there are several tools for analysing these matters and depending on the research question there are different choices to make in the analyses. Mapping the different traditions of children's rights education globally for example is a challenging task, but through using the available theories we could develop the theory further and create a collective platform for our experiences and further research. Using critical theories could also help us analyse structural problems of power, which could make researchers and teachers aware of the limitations (or the benefits) of their education. With a critical perspective, the question of teaching in the comfort zone could be the first question to be asked about the education that is analysed. Here our research (Quennerstedt et al., 2019) indicates that most children's rights education is performed in the comfort zone, where discussions of difficult problems are usually lacking.

We have three main suggestions about children's rights education research that we think could be valuable to discuss:

- Theory: The first and most important question to be asked when analysing children's rights education is what is a theory? We need to clarify what is a theory and what is not a theory. Are for example the legal documents about rights also theories about rights? We would argue they are not. The criticism proposed by Reynaert et al. (2009) a decade ago prevails in many situations. Using the documents for analyses of empirical data, asking if the analysed situation or for example the curriculum is consistent with the documents or not, is of course a possibility. However, that is not necessarily a theoretical analysis, but an analysis of the implementation of content in the legal treaties. We suggest that the use of theory should be based on the definition of theory as systematised experience.
- Plurality of meanings: We need to be aware of the plurality of meanings (the different traditions) and the plurality of educational options. From research, we can learn about these different traditions and how they are performed. It is important to challenge perspectives that are taken for granted and to problematise our own perspectives and starting points in research. One example of a theory that could become useful in that kind of analysis is the above mentioned educational theory of Didaktik (didactics) (e.g., Hudson & Meyer, 2011).
- A comparative (global) perspective: Finally, due to the different contexts at the global level, it is obvious that HRE and children's rights education are not the same globally and that there are different ways of doing HRE or children's rights education and also different theories. We suggest that as a researcher you have to be aware of the different traditions of human rights or children's rights education performed worldwide and compare your own research to other perspectives.

To conclude, the present chapter has been created as an answer to the question of what is included in what sometimes seems to be a research field that is too dispersed and places too much focus on the Convention (United Nations, 1989). Here we have discussed some possible theoretical options that might be of value in further displaying the plurality of the field.

References

Bajaj, M. (2011). Human rights education: Ideology, location, and approaches. *Human Rights Quarterly, 33*, 481–508. https://doi.org/10.1353/hrq.2011.0019

Bajaj, M. (Ed.). (2017). *Human rights education: Theory, research, praxis*. University of Pennsylvania Press.

Brantefors, L. (2019). 'They don't have as good a life as us': A didactic study of the content of human rights education with eleven-year-old pupils in two Swedish classrooms. *Human Rights Education Review, 2*(1), 47–69. https://doi.org/10.7577/hrer.2832

Brantefors, L., & Quennerstedt, A. (2016). Teaching and learning children's human rights. A research synthesis. *Cogent Education, 3*(1), 1–18.

Brantefors, L., & Thelander, N. (2017). Teaching and learning traditions in children's human rights: Curriculum emphases in theory and practice. *International Journal of Children's Rights, 25*, 456–471. https://doi.org/10.1163/15718182-02502009

Brantefors, L., Tellgren, B., & Thelander, N. (2019). Human rights education as democratic education. The teaching traditions of human rights in Swedish early childhood education and school. *International Journal of Children's rights, 27*(2019), 694–718.

Cranston, J., & Janzen, M. D. (2017). A critical approach to teaching about, through, and for human rights. *The Canadian Journal for the Scholarship of Teaching and Learning, 8*(3), 1–17.

Dewey, J. (1916). *Democracy and education*. Free Press.

Freire, P. (1996). *Pedagogy of the oppressed* (Rev ed.). Continuum.

Freeman, M. (Ed.). (2018). *Children's rights: New issues, new themes, new perspectives*. Brill.

Gundem, B. B. (2011). *Europeisk didaktikk: Tenkning og viten* [European didactics: Imagination and knowing]. Universitetsforl.

Hudson, B., & Meyer, M. A. (Eds.). (2011). *Beyond fragmentation: Didactics, learning and teaching in Europe*. Budrich, Barbara.

Klafki, W. (1995). Didactic analysis as the core of preparation of instruction. *Journal of Curriculum Studies, 27*, 13–30.

McLaren, P. (2015). *Pedagogy of insurrection: From resurrection to revolution*. Peter Lang.

Osler, A., & Solhaug, T. (2018). Children's human rights and diversity in schools: Framing and measuring. *Research in Comparative and International Education, 13*(2), 276–298. https://doi.org/10.1177/1745499918777289

Quennerstedt, A. (2011). The construction of children's rights in education – A research synthesis. *International Journal of Children's Rights, 19*, 1–18.

Quennerstedt, A., & Quennerstedt, M. (2014). Researching children's rights in education: Sociology of childhood encountering educational theory. *British Journal of Sociology of Education, 35*(1), 115–132.

Quennerstedt, A., Tellberg, B., Brantefors, L., & Thelander, N. (2014). *Education as a greenhouse for children's and young people's human rights*. Vetenskapsrådet [The Swedish Research Council].

Quennerstedt, A., Tellberg, B., Brantefors, L., & Thelander, N. (2019) *Teaching children's human rights in early childhood education and school: Educational aims, content and processes*. Rapporter i pedagogik. Örebro University.

Reynaert, D., Bouverne-De Bie, M., & Vandevelde, S. (2009). A review of children's rights literature since the adoption of the United Nations convention on the rights of the child. *Childhood, 16*(4), 518–534.

Roberts, D. (1982). Developing the concept of "curriculum emphases" in science education. *Science Education, 62*(2), 243–260.

Sverige [Sweden]. (2016). *Skollagen (2010:800) [The Education Act]: med lagen om införande av skollagen (2010:801). 7*. [uppdaterade] uppl. Wolters Kluwer.

UN; United Nations. (1989). *Convention on the rights of the child. General Assembly, resolution 44/25*, 20 Nov. 1989. U.N. Doc. A/RES/44/25. Retrieved 04.10.2019 from https://www.ohchr.org/en/professionalinterest/pages/crc.aspx

UN; United Nations, the Committee on the Rights of the Child. (2001). *General comment no. 1 on the aims of education,* crc/gc/2001/1. https://www.ohchr.org/EN/Issues/Education/Training/Compilation/Pages/a)GeneralCommentNo1TheAimsofEducation(article29)(2001).aspx. Accessed 19 Feb 2019.

UN, UNESCO, Office of the United Nations High Commissioner for Human Rights. (2006). Plan of action. World programme for human rights education. First phase. .

Zembylas, M. (2017). Emotions, critical pedagogy, and human rights education. In M. Bajaj (Ed.), *Human rights education: Theory, research, praxis*. University of Pennsylvania Press.

Zembylas, M., & Keet, A. (Eds.). (2018). *Critical human rights, citizenship, and democracy education: Entanglements and regenerations*. Bloomsbury Academic.

Chapter 18
Child Rights Knowledge and Children's Education Rights

Jenna Gillett-Swan and Nina Thelander

Abstract Education related rights are more complex than they appear on the surface. As such, the pursuit of their realisation highlights a number of wicked problems that may offer more questions than answers. The wicked problems in children's rights and education critically considered in this chapter are positioned in terms of: (1) the varied interpretations and translations of the Convention in educational practice, (2) where rights knowledge and rights competencies sit in discussions about the 'aims of education', and (3) the (in)divisibility of rights articles in pursuit of furthering rights knowledge and rights competence. These themes are considered to reflect the cross-cutting "bigger picture" implications of the volume for future research and practice, in addition to those emphasised in each individual contribution.

Keywords Child rights · Rights knowledge · Education rights · Rights competence · Article 29 · Rights education · Human Rights Education (HRE)

Introduction

Education related rights are more complex than they appear on the surface. As such, the pursuit of their realisation highlights a number of wicked problems that may offer more questions than answers. The wicked problems in children's rights and education critically considered in this chapter are positioned in terms of: (1) the

J. Gillett-Swan (✉)
Faculty of Creative Industries, Education, and Social Justice, Queensland University of Technology, Brisbane, Australia
e-mail: jenna.gillettswan@qut.edu.au

N. Thelander
Faculty of Humanities and Social Sciences, Karlstad University, Karlstad, Sweden
e-mail: nina.thelander@kau.se

J. Gillett-Swan, N. Thelander (eds.), *Children's Rights from International Educational Perspectives*, Transdisciplinary Perspectives in Educational Research 2, https://doi.org/10.1007/978-3-030-80861-7_18

varied interpretations and translations of the Convention in educational practice, (2) where rights knowledge and rights competencies sit in discussions about the 'aims of education', and (3) the (in)divisibility of rights articles in pursuit of furthering rights knowledge and rights competence. These themes are considered to reflect the cross-cutting "bigger picture" implications of the volume for future research and practice, in addition to those emphasised in each individual contribution.

As evidenced throughout the range of international contexts showcased in this volume, two things become very clear. First, using the 'aims of education' as a reference point from which to explore different facets of children's rights in education offers considerable insight towards a holistic understanding of children's education related rights beyond provision alone. In doing so, the volume's aim to extend and broaden the ways children's education-related rights are considered has been achieved. Second, the volume also reflects how some of the issues researchers have been grappling with for a number of years—such as participation—need to remain in focus for child rights researchers as there is still a lot more work that needs to be done. This is the crux of what underlies the issues presented as fundamentally wicked problems. That, despite some of these issues attracting considerable attention within and outside the field, the widespread acceptance and implementation of children's rights in education across contexts remain variable.

This concluding chapter extends and builds on the insights presented in the preceding chapters by framing the discussion in terms of the broader cross-cutting themes emerging across the volume as a whole. The chapter begins by revisiting the conceptualisation of educational rights issues as wicked problems before connecting the concept of rights translation to the imperative for a certain level of basic child rights knowledge, and describes some of the means by which this can be achieved such as through HRE. The chapter concludes by suggesting a way forward in extending the onus for children's educational rights realisation to be recognised as being beyond the responsibility of those in schools alone, and acknowledging schools as an important site for rights. Through unpacking each of these themes, the chapter offers new insights for making progress towards combatting some of the challenges to full educational rights realisation for *all* children across a multiplicity of contexts.

Revisiting Education Rights Issues as Wicked Problems

The complexity and interconnectedness of wicked problems offers a lens from which issues within the field of children's rights and education may be understood. As well as being difficult to define and solve, wicked problems can (and often do) evolve beyond how they are initially conceived and considered. However, there is also a moral dimension to wicked problems (Wexler, 2009) that may be particularly pertinent when rights are in play. As, when it comes to children's rights, *everyone* has the obligation to protect, respect, and fulfil them. In education practice, these obligations may be less often considered or even known, which is an observation also reflected through a number of contributions to this volume and unpacked further below. In this way, discussion of wicked problems relating to children's rights and education may need to extend beyond problem identification and complexity to one of advocacy, responsibility, and professional accountability. This extension may include emphasising the imperative and professional obligation to know the Convention and associated responsibilities, and consider how these texts are interpreted and translated within and across educational contexts.

Rights Translation

The diversity of experiences, entry points, and discussions raised throughout this volume highlight that, even when the same Article is used as the reference point from which each contribution is based, no two contexts, experiences, or foci are the same—regardless of national context. Even across all this diversity, the full remit of Article 29 is difficult to capture, as the content of the Article itself is wide ranging and has its own complexities. This complexity is also reflected through the actions of States Parties themselves whose monitoring reports to the Committee reflect variable priorities in relation to their commitment to children's rights and education. For example, **I'Anson's** contribution builds on this idea through teasing out the complexity of Article 29 both in terms of its manifestation of educational values and principles, and problematising the wide-ranging implications of the general nature of the aims and values of education through the Convention and General Comments. **Wyness** also draws attention to the tensions and contradictions in the Convention where provision articles are to be decided by adults, yet at the same time, participation principles imply that children's views should also be taken into account. He suggests a broader model of participation may offer a partial solution. **Martinez Sainz** contributes to this discussion by focusing on localised application and tackling apparent tensions between protection and participation mandates in school-based practices when the empowerment of children within education is (mis) perceived as a risk to a teacher's power. Such misperceptions become an obstacle to achieving children's rights in education when discipline and control are prioritised over recognising children as rights-holders. The identification of these and other tensions across local and general applications are therefore highlighted as wicked problems in themselves. However, these and other issues identified and discussed throughout the volume also point to the importance of ensuring translations and interpretations of rights into practice are based on accurate knowledge, thus emphasising the importance of Article 42 in rights translation processes.

Collectively, the volume reflects the necessity of knowing the Convention, at the level of each Article and as a whole, as well as the dynamic process of the general comments and the role they play in interpreting the Convention. This acknowledgement has also provided a way to continue and extend the critical questions that have been raised throughout the volume. Such questions include the extent to which children's rights are actually known in the wider community—not only *in* education, but also beyond those who have a direct obligation or personal or professional interest to know, including among children's families and caregivers. The interconnectedness and indivisibility of rights fortify the necessity to understand the Convention as a whole, as well as in its constituent parts. The Vienna Declaration (1993) further affirms the indivisibility, interrelatedness, and interdependency of all rights, in that rights should have equal emphasis with one another, and are often interconnected in enabling their provision. In seeking to understand more about how different national and international contexts interact with the nuances of rights affordances in education, it becomes clear that (lack of) wider rights knowledge is, and can be, a significant barrier to implementation. Therefore, the importance of each individual having rights knowledge becomes even clearer when viewing rights implementation through the language of translation (I'Anson et al., 2017; Robinson et al., 2020).

Despite knowledge and understanding being a somewhat obvious precondition to ensuring actions respect and protect the rights of oneself and others, it is somewhat perplexing how widely *un*known the substance and substantive content *within* the Convention on the Rights of the Child actually is (af Ursin & Haanpää, 2018; Alderson, 1999; Howe & Covell, 2010, 2020; Dunhill, 2018; Lundy et al., 2013; Quennerstedt, 2016; Quennerstedt et al., 2019). The variability in knowledge and understanding of the Convention, and level of comprehension of the related responsibilities of duty bearers, is concerning in contexts such as education, where children and adults interact with one another on a daily basis. Where this knowledge gap becomes particularly problematic is in how each translation of the Convention may be increasingly diluted: from the text itself and how it is interpreted and implemented in practice, through to the substantive content, meaning, and intent of each Article individually and as an interconnected whole. If duty bearers (adults) and rights holders (children) are obtaining their understanding and knowledge of children's rights through avenues that have already been diluted, then understandings of the scope and breadth of children's rights affordances also become narrowed. This is, of course, if they are even actively accessing rights knowledge at all. The more the message is translated in different ways and in different forms, the greater risk there is that the original message will have a different meaning or emphasise an aspect with particular relevance for those relaying the rights knowledge to the other party. Even so, the Convention holds a number of different sorts of rights. Therefore, it is important to have the whole picture when considering the educational implications for children's education related rights.

From Rights Incompetent to Rights Competent

Despite the requirement for the Convention to be made known to adults and children alike through Article 42, there remains conflation, misunderstanding, and general misinterpretation about what children's rights are and what they entail. Some of this confusion may be due in part to variable opportunities for acquiring accurate rights knowledge, or through their own experiences where something may be attributed as (or considered to be) a right, when it is not actually a right at all. An example of this is child wellbeing and child rights that are "routinely 'twinned' even though they are distinctive paradigms with different histories, rationales and indeed substance" (Lundy, 2019, p. 598). Lundy (2020) further problematises an increasing tendency towards rights inflation and rights dilution as a wicked problem increasingly observed in rights discourse and the field of child rights more broadly. This tendency places the discipline at risk of reputational damage built on misinterpretations and conflation of rights. The breadth of what rights really entail and what are included as rights can be eye-opening for those who come into rights education with a superficial, impartial, or inadequate understanding of what rights are (or are not). Accurate rights knowledge is not only important, it is also the minimum standard required to ensure educational practices are rights-respecting, rights-based, and grounded upon a true understanding of what rights are. For example, **O'Brien** and **Winter and de Bruin** highlight how the lack of knowledge of rights treaties and associated obligations by school staff may be contributing to why and how possible rights violations against children are occurring in schools every day. Implications of depth and sufficiency of rights knowledge within schools is therefore both a gap and a wicked problem for the field. **Moody** furthers this critique in questioning the sufficiency of educational policy documents in addressing children's rights. She highlights that children's rights in education are not met when children's rights to education *about* rights are not fully addressed. This critique includes the issue that teachers are not trained to teach human rights. If teachers are not trained to teach human rights then the quality, adequacy, and accuracy of *what* and *how* they teach rights comes into question. This lack of training in itself may also lead to rights issues such as those discussed by O'Brien, and Winter and de Bruin. **Biffi and Monta's** analysis of commonalities between the capability approach and children's rights offers further insight as, "the possibility to enact one's own rights relies, initially, on helping children to learn how they can enact their rights in the *here and now*" *(emphasis in original)*. In turn, this requires that children are educated about their rights, which means educators also need to be educated about children's rights.

The obligations of States' Parties "*to make the principles and provisions of the Convention widely known, by appropriate and active means, to adults and children alike*" are stipulated through Article 42 and fall at the beginning of Part II of the Convention (United Nations, 1989, *emphasis added*). However, given this second part of the Convention focuses on reporting procedures and implementation, the framing of Article 42 as a measure of implementation rather than a right in itself, may therefore weaken its potential and application in practice. If Article 42 is fronted as a full right, like those in Part I of the Convention are, then it becomes one of the most important tools for fulfilling human rights education (Kilkelly, 2019). Todres (2020) similarly "asserts that a significant factor in the failure to achieve widespread acceptance of children's rights is the insufficient attention given to implementation of article 42", which is "simultaneously one of the most important and most overlooked provisions" (p. 112) of the treaty. A deeper understanding of how widespread knowledge and acceptance of children's rights are requires further interrogation. Could it also be that there is widespread unconscious incompetence regarding children's rights where people are simply not aware of what they do not know? As such, one may not realise that their knowledge is partial or that children have their own set of rights and are entitled to special provisions to ensure their realisation. There may then be an assumption that child rights knowledge is there, but with a lack of criticality in determining *how* the knowledge gets there, *what* knowledge is imparted, and the accuracy of the information obtained. For example, how is education about child rights incorporated within initial teacher education training? Is it based on developing knowledge of the full Convention or only specific articles, principles, or parts therein? How extensive are the teacher professional development opportunities offered that focus on child rights training and awareness, and the resulting professional, practical and legal obligations that may change over time in relation to evolving national legislation, educational policy, and curricula?

If child rights knowledge is communicated predominantly through translations of the original Convention text, such as simplified or child-friendly versions, interpretations of the Convention may be increasingly diluted by the time they reach practice and professional accountability imperatives (Hanson & Lundy, 2017; I'Anson et al., 2017; Lundy, 2019). In some cases, the interpretations may even be inaccurate, incomplete or both inaccurate *and* incomplete. It may be then from these partial understandings that subsequent practice is derived. It is not just the presence or existence of rights knowledge that is important, but also understanding how rights are performed in practice. This is the concept of *doing* rights (Lundy & Brown, 2020; Quennerstedt et al., 2019). However, if the doing of rights is based on insufficient or partial understandings of rights, the basic knowledge of rights and knowledge imparted and practiced as a result becomes muddied. For example, interpretation based on translations of the original Convention text into other versions—simple, child friendly, other languages is an example of rights becoming 'lost in translation'. The implications of such translations may not be sufficiently problematised. The issue of knowledge of the content of the convention and dynamic processes and practices to enact the convention lead us to consider the implications of Article 42 further.

Connecting Rights Knowledge to the Aims of Education

Rights knowledge and awareness become even more crucial to ensure rights are: (a) not diluted further; (b) accurate in how they are understood; and (c) fulfilling Article 42 to make the Convention known to children and adults. However, Article 42 shares a similar position to the 'aims of education' in Article 29 in the comparatively scant academic attention towards it (Quennerstedt et al., 2019; Todres, 2020). The teaching and learning about rights is just one part of the implementation of

Article 29 (United Nations, 2001). However, the deficiency in specific attention towards making the Convention known is distinct from the expanse of research on Human Rights Education [HRE].

HRE is defined in the World Program for Human Rights Education (United Nations, 2006) and the more recent Declaration on Human Rights Education and Training (United Nations, 2011), as education *about, through,* and *for* human rights with three different aspects to be considered: (i) knowledge and skills about rights; (ii) understanding values and attitudes within human rights; and (iii) developing capacity for acting for human rights. The overall aim of HRE is to reduce violations against human rights (Tibbits, 2017). In the educational context, Tibbits (2017) describes HRE as involving: (i) values and awareness focusing on facts about human rights and are most common in schools; (ii) accountability—professionals learning about children's rights; and (iii) transformation—the learners take action to promote and protect human rights for social change. However, while the Convention (and child rights generally) are a *part* of HRE, they are still worthy of unique attention in their own right. For example, as **Brantefors and Thelander** argue, HRE theories could also be an instrument for studying teaching and learning within and across various contexts from the "same" point of view, offering a lens from which the practices and processes of teaching and learning about children's rights can be viewed.

When viewing the UDHR (United Nations, 1948) as the overarching human rights framework from which all other rights treaties (Covenants, Conventions, and Declarations) are derived, the Convention on the Rights of the Child can be viewed as an elaboration on what is required to ensure children are provided the rights to which they are entitled. As such, additional knowledge and understanding of the specific provisions enshrined in the Convention are also required. Howe and Covell (2020) further argue, there are at least three main reasons why education about children's rights is so important and needs to be taken into special account on their own—as distinct from HRE. First, children's human rights education is a matter of duty outlined in Article 42. Second, it is part of the implementation process of children's rights. Third, when educating children about their rights they will also bring their knowledge and experiences of rights into adulthood. This emphasises the importance of children's rights education having bearing on the present, while also important in preparation for their futures.

Children's human rights education (whether positioned as children's rights or children's human rights) *has* to be viewed as a dynamic process, and an essential starting point in formal educational contexts from which children and young people's rights knowledge can be developed, while also being regarded as a part of the broader human rights agenda. Wider acknowledgement and recognition of the role of Article 42 is required not just for knowing about children's rights, but also to recognise the responsibilities of duty bearers—particularly in educational contexts.

Supporting Children's (Human) Rights Education *in* Education

When children begin their human rights education during their early years of development, they develop the foundations for rights knowledge and awareness, whether they have subsequent experiences from a rights-based environment or not. When it comes to human rights, what children learn and experience in school is also carried on into adulthood. For example, through **Curl and Cook-Sather's,** and **Spina et al.'s** contributions, these effects are considered in terms of how increased accountability discourse in education limits the scope and ability for children's education to support children in developing to their fullest potential as described in Article 29. The focus on quantification of student capacity and what is (or is not) valued in education, therefore places further limits on the realisation of children's rights—particularly those who may not 'tick the boxes' of what is (or is not) considered to have educational value. Similarly, **Starnawski et al.'s** critique of the role of policy and educational institutional practices offers further insight into multi-layered and multi-levelled systemic influences that can both enable and hinder rights realisation in education contexts even beyond educational accountability mandates.

Conceptualisations of children's position within education—who speaks, who is heard, and who decides whose perspective is worth listening to—are issues raised in **Ceballos et al.'s** contribution. The establishment of conditions conducive to inclusive participatory practices that may be variably afforded in current practice is therefore emphasised. **Babika-Wirkus** also argues for the importance of valuing young children's voices as a key aspect in enabling their participation and contrasts the differential value placed on some voices over others. In particular, how teachers' voices are highly valued and listened to in comparison to the children's voices that were considered "chatter". Ultimately, as **Kiilakoski and Niemi** describe, participatory educational spaces require changes in the way adults talk, think, and relate to others. They argue that enabling participation within education provides a way to change power relations and that changing the way human rights are talked about is likely not enough, as the extent of rights practices occurring within schools also influences the way rights may be understood and practiced outside of school.

Schools and early childhood settings are important sites for rights; this is where rights-respecting approaches must be modelled and embedded into the fabric of school culture. Rights respecting education has a positive impact on children's knowledge awareness of rights, not only for themselves but also strongly connected to knowing how they can respect and protect the rights of others (Howe & Covell, 2020). What should also be recognised in discussions about children's rights, is that they also refer to provisions and responsibilities for at least three sets of actors: the child/rights holder, the parent/caregiver/guardian, and the States party/their representatives. In educational contexts, it is not uncommon for the interests and perspectives of these three parties to collide or come into tension with one another. To ensure the affordance of rights *for* children, surely knowledge of, and about rights is necessary. Without knowledge of one's own and others' rights, it is difficult to claim your rights, or indeed know when rights have been breached either by/for yourself and/or others. Article 42 is "crucial to the implementation of the convention since it requires the duty-bearers to build the capacity of the rights-holders (children) to claim their rights" (Lundy, 2012, p. 405). As Kosher and Ben-Arieh (2017, p. 257) also describe, "Children knowing about their rights increases the likelihood that children will assert and advocate for rights in various contexts", and:

> Without knowledge of their rights, children may be unaware that harmful treatment they experience is a violation of their rights for which there are, or should be, remedies. They are also far less likely to be able to advocate for and realize their rights, if they are unaware of them. Children might also be less cognizant of when their own actions infringe on the rights of others. Similarly, without knowledge of children's rights, adults will be unclear as to when their actions violate the rights of children or, alternatively, what steps they can take to help children realize their rights. (Todres, 2020, p. 112)

When considering tensions surrounding rights, there are two points in particular to note here. First, the possible tensions in reconciling different—and possibly divergent—perspectives of the actors involved. Second, possible tensions of rights themselves that may conflict with the rights of another (or multiple others). For example, when the provision of one's right to education is called into question, restricted, or removed in response to challenging, disruptive, and/or violent behaviour. It is not as clear cut as weighing the rights of one against the rights of others as a purely quantitative exercise (Gillett-Swan & Lundy, 2021). By contrast, the ripple effects of a fully rights-respecting classroom environment can also have a positive impact on teachers' work satisfaction which can then also influence classroom climate in a positive way (Howe & Covell, 2020). Children and young people's educational experiences of inequality **(Lúcio and Antunes)** and exclusion **(Häbig et al.)** provide further insight into how actions, attitudes, beliefs, and practices of school staff can perpetuate school cultures that inhibit rather than enable the realisation of children's rights. The role of education in fostering equality and inclusion similarly feeds into wider discussions in educational research on social (in)justices and overcoming the wicked problems associated with student experiences of inequality, discrimination, and/or marginalisation. The way children's rights are actively promoted (or ignored) in educational contexts matters. Education about children's human rights is fundamental to supporting children's personal, physical and social development, and can contribute to making a difference for each individual child as well as society. Focusing on educating children as well as educating teachers and other actors on all levels aids in supporting the realisation of Article 42, while also fostering a human rights-respecting society for all people.

Where to from Here?

Duty bearers—including teachers—have a vital role to play in the assurance, affordance, and education on, for, about, and through rights. The importance of teachers and what is happening in the classroom and at the school level should not be underestimated (Howe & Covell, 2020; Quennerstedt & Moody, 2020). In addition, "the concept of children's rights education as a building block towards" implementation, and ultimately "incorporation" of the Convention, "in addition to being a measure of Convention implementation in its own right, is clearly worthy of greater analysis" (Kilkelly, 2019, p. 331). Ultimately, the disconnect between rights knowledge and rights action becomes more evident when examining rights implementation in education from a practice lens. The obligation for rights to be known through Article 42 provisions, makes claims of lack of awareness or understanding about children's rights an insufficient claim or justification for placing limits on children's rights. Yet, in relation to children's *education* rights, the emphasis tends towards being on the more commonly known aspects of children's right *to* education, which are reflected more often than demonstrations of understanding and awareness of education's aims. Indeed, the prioritisation of Article 29 over Article 42 is problematised by Todres (2020, p. 131), as even though these articles support one another, "Article 29 might be better understood, at least in some respects, as a component of Article 42."

The Committee on the Rights of the Child provides guidance on actions to support the realisation of Article 42, which includes incorporating children's rights in education as well as education about rights for all those working with and for children (United Nations, 2003). For example, if children's rights are integrated as a core subject within the school curriculum, or treated as one, the why (aim), the what (content), the how (methods), and the when (progression and sequencing) are all tightly related to context, and each together form essential preconditions to effective rights Didaktik[1] (Brantefors & Thelander, 2017). This is also an expectation of the Committee who "expects to see the Convention reflected in professional training curricula, codes of conduct, and educational curricula at all levels," and stipulates that "training should be 'systematic and ongoing', including training and retraining" (United Nations, 2003, §53). In doing so, children's status as rights-holders is emphasised and better respected (Lundy et al., 2013).

Before this training can be truly effective, there needs to be greater accountability for those reticent to fulfil their obligations to, and for children's rights. Todres (2020, p. 114) is rightly critical of the Committee's response to inadequate enactment of Article 42 by States Parties as, "[i]n both its general guidance and specific assessments of states parties' progress under the CRC, the Committee has addressed Article 42 in largely superficial terms." Kilkelly (2019, p. 324) argues that there is some evidence to suggest that "States Parties who have adopted some or all measures of implementation are likely to be those in which conditions consistent with respect for children's rights exist". But how can these conditions be created, even at the microlevel, if (or when) those with the responsibility for ensuring rights progress are reticent to do so?

[1] The concept Didaktik is based on the European tradition (mostly non anglo-saxian) and framework of theory and praxis of teaching and learning

Todres (2020, p. 116) contends that, for an article so crucial to children's rights awareness for professionals, the Committee treats it as a "marginal issue". Indeed, "especially key to the success of any strategy to implement the Convention is training and awareness raising strategies that find their expression in article 42" (Kilkelly, 2019, p. 330). Referring to General Comment 5 on the General Measures of Implementation, Todres problematises the Committee's somewhat cursory focus on Article 42, as, while the Committee recognises "that without full implementation of Article 42, 'it is most unlikely that the rights set out in the Convention will be realized for many children'...the Committee's mapping of Article 42's requirements provides limited guidance to states as to how to effectively ensure children's rights are *widely known*" (Todres, 2020, p. 114, emphasis in original).

However, Lundy (2012, p. 394) argues that the "worth of a rights framework lies in the way in which its *values* are internalised and replicated by signatory states" (*emphasis added*). A deeper exploration of the aims of education therefore supports and enables a greater understanding of the values underpinning children's education rights. Therefore, the importance of the Convention also lies in the manner and degree to which its values are made known to children, so that they can assert and implement their rights, and to adults who work with and for children, so that they can be aware of and satisfy their legal responsibilities towards children and young people. Perhaps the key to successful implementation ultimately lies in "creating a culture of support for children's rights among civil society, the public and the media" (Kilkelly, 2019, p. 333). In this way, perhaps it is time for these conversations to extend beyond the academic fields of children's rights in education and more into the public sphere.

Conclusion

The historical tendency for education rights to be predominantly associated with being a right *to* education—such as via Article 28—is limiting and may undermine a human rights framework that emphasises the interconnectedness and indivisibility of rights (Vienna Declaration, 1993). In this way, the focus on Article 29 as the basis for the education rights related discussions occurring throughout the volume, offers a particular contribution and helps to extend knowledge within education rights research about how these rights may be recognised in practice. Second, the volume also highlighted the complexity inherent within understanding education rights, that there is much more to interpreting *each* Article than may first be apparent. That an entire volume unpacking Article 29 across different educational jurisdictions and international contexts can be experienced and understood in so many different ways further highlights this point. Why this plurality and multiplicity of diverse experience particularly relevant is in (a) supporting and furthering the education rights discourse within the field and outside of the field, and (b) in problematising the variations and interpretations of the Convention text that risk becoming misappropriated and conflated into variations of what rights are. While abridged versions can be a useful and accessible entry-point to teaching and learning about children's rights, they should not be the only source nor the basis from which rights knowledge is obtained.

Education is a fundamental human right. Education also plays a vital role in the affordance of children's rights through its content, provision, aims, and substance. It must be recognised that children have a right to know about their rights and doing so, supports the dual aims of both Articles 29 and 42 (*making the Convention known*) (Todres, 2020). This chapter situated the discussion of the 'aims of education' within the rights knowledge imperatives for education contexts by focusing on Article 42 and its implications. The importance of knowing the content of the Convention was positioned not only as an obligation of implementation but also as essential to ensure the realisation of all of the other articles in the Convention, including children's education rights.

As an edited collection, this volume contributes to providing a diverse international snapshot of educational perspectives on affordances and realisations of children's rights in education through the aims of education as a reference point. In doing so, it contributes to child rights implementation imperatives of making the Convention known through focusing on and unpacking some of the complexity of the aims of education. The issues that concern the contributors to the volume are all matters that are not unique to the specific context from which they provide their examples. Instead, these contributions offer a snapshot of the work that occupies the concerns, focus, and questions of practice and provision in rights-based educational research.

While this concluding chapter focused on the education context specifically, it is important to recognise there are also others who may not have a direct interest in the day-to-day decisions relating to children's rights or have a direct stake in children's education related rights imperatives. However, these people still have an important role to play in terms of the power to make things happen through their own rights knowledge, awareness, and understanding. Societal perceptions and attitudes can be a powerful driver for change. The power of "the people"—regardless of their direct personal stake in affording children's education rights in practice, may be a way forward in shifting the way that children's education rights are more widely realised within and beyond school and education communities.

However, without a wider understanding of *all* rights, there is also a greater risk of societal rights illiteracy and rights ignorance built upon partial understandings of rights. There needs to be greater attention towards children's rights knowledge in education, and particularly how, where, when, and to what end, duty bearers (adults) and rights holders (children) are provided the necessary opportunity and information to fulfil the obligations and affordances enshrined in the Convention. This needs to go beyond the field of educational rights research alone. Making the Convention known could fall within the broader field of HRE/CRE, but it also goes beyond this. Understanding the 'aims of education' requires a much broader entry point from which the intricacies and conversations about Article 29 (and children's education rights generally) must extend beyond a focus on rights in isolation. However, there is a tension in that there is so much involved in each right individually (and Article 29 is no exception), that broadening too quickly risks superficial or inadequate understanding and grasp of what is actually required and involved in respecting, protecting, and fulfilling each right. In this way, there is a place in educational rights research for both the focus on specific articles *as well as* in the way *all rights* fit together as an interconnected whole. The field must also move beyond a predominantly western contextual focus. There is a need for greater concentration towards how to extend knowledge and understanding of children's rights and education in research and practice in contexts less represented in the existing discourse (Quennerstedt & Moody, 2020). A broader and deeper knowledge of children's rights and its connection to education is needed. Doing so will contribute to ensuring that children's rights are better afforded across diverse, global educational contexts. Coming back to the focus of the volume, this needs to be a greater priority in education. The challenge now is making it a reality.

References

af Ursin, P., & Haanpää, L. (2018). A comparative study on children's rights awareness in 16 countries. *Child Indicators Research, 11*, 1425–1443.

Alderson, P. (1999). Civil rights in schools: The implications for youth policy. *Youth and Policy, 64*, 56–72.

Brantefors, L., & Thelander, N. (2017). Teaching and learning traditions in children's human rights: Curriculum emphases in theory and practice. *The International Journal of Children's Rights, 25*(2), 456–471.

Dunhill, A. (2018). Does teaching children about human rights, encourage them to practice, protect and promote the rights of others? *Education 3–13, 46*(1), 16–26.

Gillett-Swan, J. K., & Lundy, L. (2021). Children, classrooms and challenging behaviour: Do the rights of the many outweigh the rights of the few? *Oxford Review of Education*. https://doi.org/10.1080/03054985.2021.1924653

Hanson, K., & Lundy, L. (2017). Does exactly what it says on the tin?: A critical analysis and alternative conceptualisation of the so-called 'General Principles' of the Convention on the Rights of the Child. *The International Journal of Children's Rights, 25*(2), 285–306.

Howe, R. B., & Covell, K. (2010). Miseducating children about their rights. *Education, Citizenship and Social Justice, 5*(2), 91–102.

Howe, R. B., & Covell, K. (2020). Human rights education. In J. Todres & S. M. King (Eds.), *The Oxford handbook of children's rights law* (pp. 699–717). Oxford University Press.

I'Anson, J., Quennerstedt, A., & Robinson, C. (2017). The international economy of children's rights: Issues in translation. *The International Journal of Children's Rights, 25*(1), 50–67.

Kilkelly, U. (2019). The UN Convention on the rights of the child: Incremental and transformative approaches to legal implementation. *The International Journal of Human Rights, 23*(3), 323–337.

Kosher, H., & Ben-Arieh, A. (2017). What children think about their rights and their well-being: A cross-national comparison. *American Journal of Orthopsychiatry, 87*(3), 256–273.

Lundy, L. (2012). Children's rights and educational policy in Europe: The implementation of the United Nations Convention on the Rights of the Child. *Oxford Review of Education, 38*(4), 393–411.

Lundy, L. (2019). A lexicon for research on international children's rights in troubled times. *The International Journal of Children's Rights, 27*, 595–601.

Lundy, L. (2020). *Rights inflation and rights dilution*. "Wicked Problems in Children's Rights in Education" Webinar. Recording available via European Educational Research Association accessed 25.08.2020.

Lundy, L., & Brown, A. (2020). Revisiting the three 'R's in order to realize children's educational rights: Relationships, resources, and redress. In J. Todres & S. M. King (Eds.), *The Oxford handbook of children's rights law* (pp. 387–404). Oxford University Press.

Lundy, L., Kilkelly, U., & Byrne, B. (2013). Incorporation of the United Nations Convention on the Rights of the Child: A comparative review. *The International Journal of Children's Rights, 21*, 442–463.

Quennerstedt, A. (2016). Children's human rights at school—As formulated by children. *The International Journal of Children's Rights, 24*(3), 657–677.

Quennerstedt, A., & Moody, Z. (2020). Educational children's rights research 1989-2019: Achievements, gaps and future prospects. *The International Journal of Children's Rights, 28*, 183–208.

Quennerstedt, A., Tellgren, B., Brantefors, L., & Thelander, N. (2019). Teaching children's human rights in early childhood education and school: Educational aims, content and processes. *Reports in Education 21*, Örebro University, Sweden.

Robinson, C., Quennerstedt, A., & I'Anson, J. (2020). The translation of articles from the United Nations Convention on the Rights of the Child into educational legislation: the narrowing of Article 12 as a consequence of translation. *The Curriculum Journal, 31*(3), 517–538.

Tibbitts, F. (2017). Evolution of human rights education models. In M. Bajaj (Ed.), *Human rights education: Theory, research, praxis*. University of Pennsylvania Press.

Todres, J. (2020). Making children's rights widely known. *Minnesota Journal of International Law, 29*(1), 109–150.

United Nations. (1948). *Universal declaration of human rights*. UN General Assembly.

United Nations. (1989). *UN Convention on the Rights of the Child*. United Nations.

United Nations. (2001). *UN Committee on the Rights of the Child, General Comment No. 1 Article 29: The aims of education. CRC/GC/2001/1*. United Nations.

United Nations. (2003). *UN Committee on the Rights of the Child, General Comment No. 5 Implementation, CRC/GC/2003/1*. United Nations.

United Nations. (2006). *World programme for human rights education. First phase*. United Nations.

United Nations. (2011). *UN declaration on human rights education and training*. UN General Assembly.

Vienna Declaration. (1993). *Vienna declaration and programme of action*. World Conference on Human Rights.

Wexler, M. N. (2009). Exploring the moral dimension of wicked problems. *International Journal of Sociology and Social Policy, 29*(8), 531–542.

Correction to: Participation and Social Exclusion – Are They Mutually Exclusive Phenomena?

Julia Häbig, Enikö Zala-Mezö, Pascale Herzig, and Daniela Müller-Kuhn

Correction to:
Chapter 10 in: J. Gillett-Swan, N. Thelander (eds.),
***Children's Rights from International Educational Perspectives*,**
Transdisciplinary Perspectives in Educational Research 2,
https://doi.org/10.1007/978-3-030-80861-7_10

Chapter 10: Participation and Social Exclusion – Are They Mutually Exclusive Phenomena? was previously published non-open access. It has now been changed to open access under a CC BY 4.0 license and the copyright holder updated to 'The Author(s)'. The book has also been updated with this change.

The updated version of this chapter can be found at
https://doi.org/10.1007/978-3-030-80861-7_10

J. Gillett-Swan, N. Thelander (eds.), *Children's Rights from International Educational Perspectives*, Transdisciplinary Perspectives in Educational Research 2, https://doi.org/10.1007/978-3-030-80861-7_19

The manufacturer's authorised representative in the EU is Springer Nature Customer Service Centre GmbH, Europaplatz 3, 69115 Heidelberg, Germany. If you have any concerns regarding our products, please contact ProductSafety@springernature.com

Printed and bound by CPI Group (UK) Ltd, Croydon, CR0 4YY
30/09/2026
02225290-0009